MULTIMEDIA TECHNOLOGY IV

PROCEEDINGS OF THE 4TH INTERNATIONAL CONFERENCE ON MULTIMEDIA TECHNOLOGY, SYDNEY, AUSTRALIA, 28–30 MARCH 2015

Multimedia Technology IV

Editor

Aly A. Farag
University of Louisville, Louisville, KY, USA

Jian Yang
Tsinghua University, Beijing, China

Feng Jiao
Nanjing University of Information Science and Technology, Nanjing, China

CRC Press
Taylor & Francis Group
Boca Raton London New York Leiden

CRC Press is an imprint of the
Taylor & Francis Group, an **informa** business

A BALKEMA BOOK

CRC Press/Balkema is an imprint of the Taylor & Francis Group, an informa business

© 2015 Taylor & Francis Group, London, UK

Typeset by MPS Limited, Chennai, India
Printed and bound in Great Britain and the USA

Published by: CRC Press/Balkema
                P.O. Box 11320, 2301 EH Leiden, The Netherlands
                e-mail: Pub.NL@taylorandfrancis.com
                www.crcpress.com – www.taylorandfrancis.com

ISBN: 978-1-138-02794-7 (Hardback)
ISBN: 978-1-315-68698-1 (eBook PDF)

Multimedia Technology IV – Farag, Yang & Jiao (Eds)
© 2015 Taylor & Francis Group, London, ISBN: 978-1-138-02794-7

Table of contents

Multimedia Technology IV – Farag, Yang & Jiao (Eds)
© 2015 Taylor & Francis Group, London, ISBN: 978-1-138-02794-7

Preface

On behalf of the 4th International Conference on Multimedia Technology (ICMT 2015), it is my great pleasure to welcome you to the conference, which is held from March 28th to 29th, 2015 in Sydney, Australia.

This event is organized by GRSS Chapter of IEEE Nanjing Section, China, sponsored by University of Louisville, Tsinghua University and Nanjing Yun-Hong-Cheng conference service LTD. It also gets technical support of many scholars from more than fifty universities. I want to thank them for their hard work in paper reviewing. Their great support is very important for this event.

This international conference has attracted hundreds of academies, scientists, engineers, postgraduates and other professionals. We like to provide a high-level international forum for researchers and engineers to present and discuss recent advances, new techniques and applications in the field of Multimedia Technology.

We collect the excellent papers in this proceeding, which mainly discuss the hot topics on image/signal processing, video/audio processing, multimedia data communication/transmission, useful multimedia tools, etc.

I would like to take this opportunity to express my special thanks to production manager Lukas Goosen and Leon Bijnsdorp from CRC Press for their great support in publishing the proceedings.

Thanks,
Prof. Aly A. Farag
General Chair of ICMT 2015

Organizing Committee

General Chair

Prof. Aly A. Farag, *Professor of University of Louisville, USA*

Technical Program Committee Chair

Prof. Jian Yang, *Tsinghua University, China*

Publication Chair

PhD. Jiao Feng, *Nanjing University of Information Science & Technology, China*

Technical Program Committee

Wei Xu, *Jilin Agricultural Science and Technology College, China*
V.P.S. Naidu, *National Aerospace Laboratories, India*
Rajkumar Kannan, *Bishop Heber College, India*
Aniruddha Bhattacharjya, *Amrita Vishwa VidyaPeetham University, India*
Mu-Song Chen, *Da-Yeh University, Taiwan, China*
Shashikant Patil, *SVKM'S Nmims University, India*
Charles Z. Liew (Session Chair), *Smart Sys Research Group, USA*
Hemant Kumar Mehta, *Devi Ahilya University, India*
Xiaofei Zhang, *Nanjing University of aeronautics & astronautics, China*
Ganesh Chandra Deka, *Employment & Training, Ministry of Labour & Employment, India*
Lv Teng, *Army Officer Academy, China*
Jijun Lu, *Goldman Sachs, USA*
Min-Shiang Hwang, *Asia University, Taiwan, China*
Kunpeng Zhu, *The Chinese academy of sciences institute of advanced manufacturing technology, China*
Peter Revesz, *University of Nebraska-Lincoln, USA*
Veera Jyothi Badnal, *Chaitanya Bharati Institute of Technology, Hyderabad, India*
Vuda Sreenivasarao, *Bahir Dar University, Ethiopia*
Fernando Ferri, *IRPPS – CNR, Roma*
Abhishek Shukla, *R.D. Engineering College Technical Campus, Ghaziabad*
Hadj Hamma Tadjine, *Aktive Sicherheits & Fahrerassistenz (VI-D), Germany*
Yas Alsultanny, *Arabian Gulf University, Kindom of Bahrain*
Kiran Kumari Patil, *Reva University, India*
Adham Atyabi, *Salford University, UK*
R. Guruprasad, *CSIR-National Aerospace Laboratories, India*
Yong Bian, *Yale University, USA*
Sun-Yuan Hsieh, *National Cheng Kung University, Taiwan, China*
Ion Tutanescu, *University of Pitesti, Romania*
S. Satyanarayana, *KL University, India*
Jose M. Merigo Lindahl, *University of Manchester, UK*
Francesco Zirilli, *Universita di Roma La Sapienza, Italy*
Mainguenaud Michel, *Institut National des Sciences Appliquees, France*
Sotirios G. Ziavras, *New jersey Institute of Technology (NJIT), USA*
Manuel Silva, *Institute of Engineering of the Polytechnic Institute of Porto, Portugal*
Jijun Lu, *Goldman Sachs, USA*
Vassilios Moussas, *Tech. Educ. Inst. (T.E.I.) of Athens, Greece*
Junjie Lu, *Broadcom Corporation, Irvine, CA, USA*
Shuixian Chen (Session Chair), *Institute of Information Engineering, Chinese Academy of Sciences, China*
T. Venkat Narayana Rao (Session Chair), *C.S.E, SNIST, Hyderabad, A.P, India*

Multimedia Technology IV – Farag, Yang & Jiao (Eds)
© 2015 Taylor & Francis Group, London, ISBN: 978-1-138-02794-7

Sponsors & Co-organizers

Organizor: GRSS Chapter of IEEE Nanjing Section

Technical Sponsors:

University of Louisville

Tsinghua University

Nanjing Yun-Hong-Cheng conference service Ltd.

Multimedia Technology IV – Farag, Yang & Jiao (Eds)
© 2015 Taylor & Francis Group, London, ISBN: 978-1-138-02794-7

SDN based load balancing and its performance

Fan Zhang, Jinyao Yan, Bo Liu & Haiyan Ma
School of Information Engineering, Communication University of China, Beijing, China

ABSTRACT: In recent years, with the continuous development of network, we need the network more flexible, and hope our network can be supply-demand equilibrium. With SDN emerged, the industry generally believes that SDN is the future direction of network evolution. Besides, with the continuous development of network, servers have to offer more and more services for the increasing number of visits, the load has a sharp increase. Prove the ability of servers to solve this problem needs a lot of money, and it doesn't works well. Load balancing maybe a better way to solve this problem. The main content of this paper is that we achieve load balancing based on SDN. And then we analyze some main factors which are affecting the response time of web page under load balancing policies of random and round robin by experiment.

Keywords: Load-balancing; SDN; POX-controller; OpenFlow; Performance

1 INTRODUCTION

As the rapid development of the Internet, multimedia servers especially Web servers are facing large number of visits, that cause the load of servers become very heavy. The servers cannot afford so many visits. One way to solve the problem is that we can improve servers' performance. That cost a lot, but the result doesn't seem good. Another way to solve the problem is load balancing [1]. Load balancing has multiple servers to provide those service, these servers share the load pressure and work better than one high-performance server when the load is heavy. So load balancing technology has become a key technology to build high-load Web sites.

There are many policies of load balancing, and different policies are applied to different scenarios. Here are some mainstream load balancing policies [1]: random policy (Randomly assign service requests to servers), the round-robin policy (Assign service requests to servers one by one), the based on response time policy (In this policy, we will get each server's response time periodically. While the service request arrives, we will assign next service request to server which has smallest response time), the based on number of connections policy (the load balancing will get the number of connections, and then assigned next service request to the server which has minimum number of connections), the based on processing capacity policy (The load balancing will monitor each server's processing capacity. The processing capacity depends on the server's CPU model, number of CPU and memory size. Then, we assign next service request to server which has the best processing capacity). In these policies, the last three load balancing policies can reflect the real-time condition of each server.

In traditional network, there are two ways to achieve load balancing: software based load balancing and hardware based load balancing. The software based load balancing means we install additional software on each server to achieve load balancing. It is easy to deploy, flexible, and inexpensive. But the additional software need consume server resources, and that reduce the servers' performance. The hardware based load balancing installed load balancing devices between the server and the external network, use dedicate hardware devices to complete the load balancing. In servers' performance, hardware based load balancing is better than software based load balancing, but a load-balancing device often require significant investment.

Well, SDN can solve this contradiction [2, 3]. We write the load-balancing policies as components into application layer; control layer run these components, and send flow tables to switches; switches forward these data as fast as they can (The Application layer, the control layer and the forwarding layer are three layers of SDN's core technology system, we will talk about them below). There is no need to install additional software on servers, that not only inherit the software based load balancing's advantages, simple configuration, flexible and inexpensive, but also can solve the problem of software based load balancing: the servers' performance.

2 BACKGROUND OF SDN

SDN [4] is the abbreviation of Software Defined Networking, it is a new network architecture based on software. SDN's biggest feature is that it's underlying network infrastructure transparent to upper layer

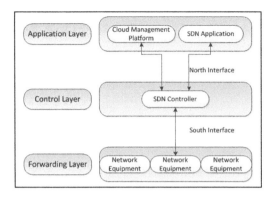

Figure 1. Core technology system of SDN.

applications by having loosely coupled control plane and data plane and supporting centralized network state control.

Since SDN is not very mature so far, different participants has different understanding for SDN, different companies propose different kinds of implementations based on their own superiority. They can be divided into three categories: based on dedicated interface, based on overlay network and based on open protocol. The biggest advantage of the implementation which is based on dedicated interface is that it can rely on the existing network equipment, and we can change a few things to make SDN being used. But there is a risk of network equipment manufacturers and the ability to be locked. The implementation based on overlay network can easily integrate with virtual management, but the practical implementation and application will be affected by the quality of the underlying network. The current major implementation of SDN is based on open protocol. This implementation achieves the separation of control plane and forwarding plane, it also support control globalization, and has the greatest influence of this area.

Figure 1 illustrates SDN's core technology system. SDN's core technology system can be divided into three layers: application layer, control layer and forwarding layer. As the drive of control layer, application layer can load different components to perform different functions; control layer is connected to the forwarding layer through the South Interface, it can control forwarding layer's actions by send flow table to forwarding layer; forwarding layer is composed by high-performance network forwarding devices, these devices don't need to consider kinds of protocols, they only need to forward as fast as they can through the flow table.

SDN switches need to be controlled by remote SDN controller, and these control instructions should be conveyed through South Interface. So the protocol of the South Interface is very important to SDN. The most famous South Interface is OpenFlow [5] protocol. As an open protocol, this protocol has already won the broad support in the industry, and it is also the standard of SDN now [6]. Next, we will simulate network

topology, and in this topology, the South Interface connected the controller and switch is based on OpenFlow protocol.

3 IMPLEMENTATION

In traditional network, load balancing is often achieved through load-balancing devices. But in SDN, we achieve load balancing by using the controller choice servers.

There are many controllers in SDN, here we choice the POX controller. The POX controller [7] is evolved by the NOX controller [8], which is written by both Python computer language and C++ computer language. It is the NOX controller rewrite by Python computer language. Because of the Python's simpler, understandable and good scalability, POX can run on multiple platforms, and it also has been more rapid development and wide application [9].

POX controller not only has many built application components, but also can we write our own components [10] to achieve various functions. In order to achieve load balancing, we need to write a load balancing component at first. Here is the main idea to write load balancing module. In the beginning, we create a virtual IP address for the server cluster, and this IP address represents the IP address of the server cluster. Clients will not know the IP address of each server, they just know this virtual IP if they want services. When clients visit this virtual IP address, the controller will choice one server by our load balancing policy, and rewrite destination address of the request packets as the server's address. Then controller will send this request to the server. After the reply packets come into controller, controller will rewrite the packet address again. The source address is reduced to the virtual IP address, and then controller send reply packet back to client. After these steps all above, the load balancing process is completed. Then, the controller will write these forwarding actions into flow table, and send flow table to switches. Switches will forward packets all by flow table in order to have a high efficiency operation [11]. In order to guarantee the accuracy of the load balancing, the flow table will be cleared automatically after the connection from client to server is broken.

The method is simple to achieve random policy. We can store all available servers in a list, when the client visit comes, controller will choice one server for the request in the list through Random Function in Python.

We need to create another list if we want to achieve round-robin policy. This list is named alternate server list, in the beginning, we put all available servers into this list. When one server is selected, we remove this server from the alternate server list; when the alternate server list is empty, all available servers will be put into this list again to achieve round-robin policy.

We use Mininet [12] to simulate the experimental environment. Mininet is a Network Simulator consists of some virtual end-hosts, switches, routers. It uses the lightweight virtualization technology, making the

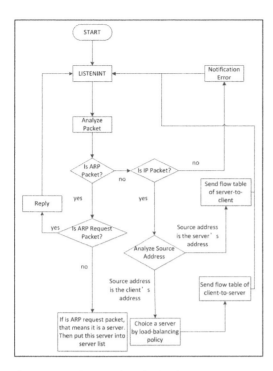

Figure 2. Detail chart of Load-balancing component.

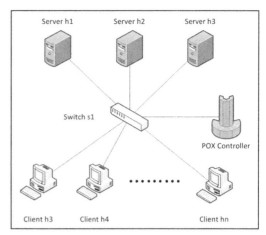

Figure 3. Network topology.

Table 1. Change policy.

	Server Number	Client Number	Time Interval	Policy
1	3	12	0.1 s	Random
2	3	12	0.1 s	Round-robin

Table 2. Change time-interval.

	Server Number	Client Number	Time Interval	Policy
1	3	12	0.1 s	Round-robin
2	3	12	0.2 s	Round-robin
3	3	12	0.3 s	Round-robin
4	3	12	0.4 s	Round-robin
5	3	12	0.5 s	Round-robin
6	3	12	1 s	Round-robin

Table 3. Change both client-number and time-interval.

	Server Number	Client Number	Time Interval	Policy
1	3	12/6/1	0.1 s	Round-robin
2	3	12/6/1	0.2 s	Round-robin
3	3	12/6/1	0.3 s	Round-robin
4	3	12/6/1	0.4 s	Round-robin
5	3	12/6/1	0.5 s	Round-robin
6	3	12/6/1	1 s	Round-robin

system more like the real network. We can create a network topology which can support SDN easily.

4 SYSTEM PERFORMANCE EVALUATION

4.1 Experimental design

In order to test and verify our SDN based load balancing, and analyze the main factors that affect the response time of web page under load balancing, we design three experiments. In these experiments, we will observe the effect of different load-balancing policies and the efficiency of the servers by compare the HTTP response time [13] when clients visit servers. We simulate the network topology by Mininet. The Figure 3 shows us the topology of the experimental network. We put three servers into our topology, and in order to keep the network environment remains the same, the number of servers won't be changed. These three servers' name is h1 to h3. But we will change the number of clients for different experiments to find the effect of different number of clients.

In the first experiment, we use Mininet create the same number of servers and clients. In the case of a fixed request time interval, we change the load balancing policy to compare HTTP response time between random and round-robin policy. Here are experimental conditions of the first experiment in Table 1.

In the second experiment, we just change the request time interval and observe changes of HTTP response time under different request time interval, all policies in this experiment are set to round-robin. Table 2

shows us the experimental conditions of the second experiment.

In the third experiment, we change the number of client, and we also use the round robin policy here. The third experiment's conditions are in Table 3.

3

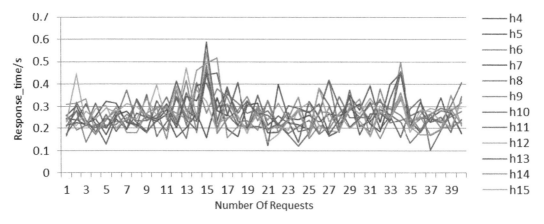

Figure 4.   Random policy result.

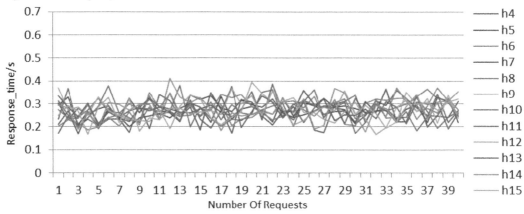

Figure 5.   Round-robin policy result.

4.2 Results

Figure 4 illustrates the result of HTTP response time by using random policy in the first experiment. In this Figure, h4 to h15 are 12 servers' names. Figure 5 illustrates the result of HTTP response time by using the round-robin policy in the first experiment.

Compare Figure 4 with Figure 5, we can find: Under random policy, HTTP response time is in the range 0.15 to 0.4 s. Sometimes the majority of the clients' response time is particularly big, while others are small (Just like the 15th request and 34th request). That means under random policy, most of the clients are exactly randomly assigned to the same server and lead to this server has a heavy load, so the HTTP response time of these clients are longer than usual. But other clients are provided services by servers that have small load, so their HTTP response time is shorter. Under round-robin policy, HTTP response time is in the range 0.2 to 0.35 s. It is more stable than random policy, and will never appear the crowding phenomenon.

Figure 6 shows us the HTTP response time in different request time interval.

In Figure 6, we can find that when request time interval is in the range 0.1 to 0.4 s, HTTP response time decreased rapidly. After request time interval is

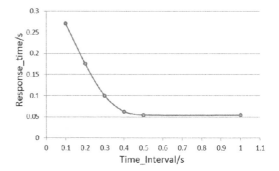

Figure 6.   Different request time interval results.

greater than 0.4 s, HTTP response time did not change significantly. That is because servers need time to handle requests, when time interval is smaller than 0.4 s, servers cannot completely handle the request before the next comes, so the next request need to wait. That really has a big effect to HTTP response time. After request time interval is greater than 0.4 s, servers have enough time to handle the previous request, so the request time interval will no longer affect the HTTP response time.

4

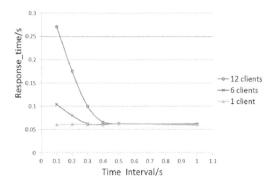

Figure 7. Different client-number results.

When we put the second experiment and the third experiment together, we can see the result clearly in Figure 7.

The result shows that when the request time interval is equal to 0.1 s, the HTTP response time of 12 clients is significantly bigger than 6 clients and 1 client. As time interval becomes bigger, the servers have enough time to handle requests. HTTP response time will no longer be affect by the number of clients.

5 CONCLUSION

In this paper, we abandon the way which achieves load balancing by dedicate hardware devices in traditional network, and use the SDN controller's powerful global control to achieve load balancing. It is one of the SDN's features: centralized control. We also can change load balancing policies through load different load balancing component, that's the flexibility of SDN. In the last three experiments, we test and verify the two load balancing policies that we have achieved, and find that random policy may have the congestion problem; then by qualitative analysis and comparison, we point out that in the same context, how do the client number and the request time interval influenced the HTTP response time.

Now, because of SDN is not mature yet, the performance of SDN based load-balancing in this paper isn't better than the traditional network load-balancing. But with the development of SDN, we believe that SDN based load balancing will be popular and the performance will be better.

REFERENCES

[1] Jindal A, Lim S B, Radia S, et al. Load balancing in a network environment: U.S. Patent 6,327,622 [P]. 2001-12-4.
[2] Wang R, Butnariu D, Rexford J. OpenFlow-based server load balancing gone wild [J]. 2011.
[3] Koerner M, Kao O. Multiple service load-balancing with OpenFlow [C]//High Performance Switching and Routing (HPSR), 2012 IEEE 13th International Conference on. IEEE, 2012: 210–214.
[4] Lei baohua, Wang feng, Wang xi and Wang heyu, "Deciphering SDN: Core Techniques and Practical Guide," Beijing: Publishing House of Electronics Industry, 2013, pp. 2–18.
[5] T. O. Consortium, "Openflow switch specification/ version 1.1.0," February 2011, http://www.openflo-w.org/wp/documents/.
[6] McKeown N, Anderson T, Balakrishnan H, et al. OpenFlow: enabling innovation in campus networks [J]. ACM SIGCOMM Computer Communication Review, 2008, 38(2). 69–74. http://www.noxrcpo.org, POX Controller.
[7] Gude N, Koponen T, Pettit J, et al. NOX: towards an operating system for networks [J]. ACM SIGCOMM Computer Communication Review, 2008, 38(3): 105–110.
[8] Fernandez M. Evaluating OpenFlow controller paradigms [C]//ICN 2013, The Twelfth International Conference on Networks. 2013: 151–157. http://openflow.stanford.edu/display/ONL/POX Wiki, POX Wiki.
[9] Uppal H, Brandon D. OpenFlow based load balancing [J]. University of Washington. CSE561: Networking. Project Report, Spring, 2010. http://mininet.org, Mininet.
[10] Handigol N, Seetharaman S, Flajslik M, et al. Plug-n-Serve: Load-balancing web traffic using OpenFlow [J]. ACM SIGCOMM Demo, 2009.

Multimedia Technology IV – Farag, Yang & Jiao (Eds)
© *2015 Taylor & Francis Group, London, ISBN: 978-1-138-02794-7*

A SAMP reconstruction algorithm based on Haar wavelet tree

Jiandong Yang, Xiuyun Li & Dengyin Zhang
Key Lab of Broadband Wireless Communication and Sensor Network Technology,
Nanjing University of Posts and Telecommunication, Ministry of Education,
Nanjing, China

ABSTRACT: Due to the long computing time and lower accuracy of compressed sensing reconstruction algorithm, this paper proposes a SAMP reconstruction algorithm based on Haar wavelet tree. The algorithm combines the SAMP reconstruction algorithm and structure characteristics of wavelet tree, according to the characteristics of wavelet tree to select the son atoms which have a directly relationship with the father atom. At the same time, the algorithm use addition threshold and deletion threshold to control the number of selected atoms. Simulation results show that the efficiency of the algorithm is improved by 28.5% and 38.7% compared with SAMP algorithm at the sparsity of 1000 and 2000 respectively, and the probability of successful reconstruction is improved by nearly 13.2% on average.

Keywords: Image processing; compressed sensing; Haar wavelet tree; reconstruction algorithm

1 INTRODUCTION

After nearly ten years of development, compressed sensing theory has been widely used in image processing, audio and video compression, wireless communication network etc. Compressed sensing's principle is that the original signal is sparse or in some kind of transform domain is sparse, then it can be from a high-dimensional space projected onto a low-dimensional space through a measurement matrix, by solving an optimization problem, the original signal can be reconstructed from the amount of projection with a high probability. However, in the real world most of the data are not sparse, therefore we need to select reasonable sparse matrix to transform the original data to a sparse domain.

At present, more and more scholars use wavelet as sparse matrix for compressed sensing to improve the efficiency of compressed sensing. An adaptive compressed sensing algorithm has been proposed in [1], which made a two-dimensional image into low frequency part and high frequency part through wavelet transform. Since the high frequency part is of sparsity, only the high frequency part was compressed, then the low frequency part and the reconstructed high frequency part were used to reconstruct the original image. The improved algorithm [2] used SAMP (Sparsity Adaptive Matching Pursuit) to reconstruct the high frequency part in the reconstruction process, which can reconstruct the original image under unknown sparsity.

Wavelet transform and compressed sensing can not only are combined in the transformation stage, but also can be combined in the reconstruction stage. Considering that the sparse coefficients satisfy regularity of wavelet tree, effective atoms are selected by the characteristics of wavelet tree at images reconstruction stage. Combined with the iterative threshold algorithm, the algorithm can achieve higher efficiency of reconstruction [3]. During the process of reconstruction, the algorithm reconstructed sparse coefficients according to their characteristics of connectivity tree [4], which improved the reconstruction efficiency and reduced the number of iterations, thus having a good compressed sensing performance. Using wavelet transform to deal with the raw data at the stage of sparse representation, the relationship of the atoms as well as atoms with measured values in sensing matrix was explored based on the characteristics of wavelet coefficients' tree structure in the reconstruction stage, and reconstructed sparse coefficients by combining with orthogonal matching pursuit algorithm (OMP) [5], which can reduce the number of iterations and improve the quality of the reconstruction.

This paper presents a reconstruction algorithm based on the wavelet tree, which combines SAMP algorithm and wavelet tree structure characteristics. When choosing the effective atoms, the algorithm selects the atoms which have a directly parent-child relationship based on the characteristics of wavelet tree. Meanwhile, the algorithm controls the number of selected atoms by deletion threshold and addition threshold. This algorithm can not only reduce the calculation time, but also improve the accuracy of the reconstruction.

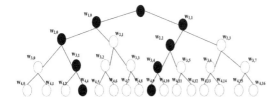

Figure 1. The structure of wavelet coefficients.

2 SAMP RECONSTRUCTION ALGORITHM BASED ON HAAR WAVELET TREE

2.1 Compression process

The basic method of compression is to use wavelet to decompose the performance data, and then uses compressed sensing to sparse and observe the wavelet coefficients. The compression process of performance data are as follows.

1) M attributes of performance data $X_1, X_2, \ldots, X_M$ are decomposed into K-level, each performance data is decomposed into low-frequency component V and high-frequency component W. The vast majority of the low-frequency component have a large value (useful value), does not have the sparsity, thus the low-frequency component cannot compression. The length of high-frequency component is $N_2 = N - 2^{L-K}$, the i-th attribute of performance data is expressed as $X_i = V_i + W_i$, here $W_i = [w_{i,1}, w_{i,2}, \ldots, w_{i,N}]$.
2) Because the high frequency coefficient is sparse, it can be expressed as $W = \psi W$. Sparse matrix ψ is a $N_2 \times N_2$ unit matrix.
3) We use gauss random matrix as the measurement matrix, $\Phi \in R^{M \times N}, M \ll N, \varphi = [\varphi_1, \varphi_2, \ldots, \varphi_M]^T$, $\varphi_i = [\theta_{i,1}, \theta_{i,2}, \ldots, \theta_{i,N}]^T$. By using M row vectors of the matrix to project the high frequency coefficient W and calculate the inner product of W and φ_i ($i = 1, 2, \ldots, M$) to obtain observations $Y = [y_1, y_2, \ldots, y_M]^T$, here $Y = \phi W = \phi \psi W = \Theta w$, Θ is the perception matrix.
4) Transmission of the low-frequency component and the observation of high-frequency component.

2.2 Sparse coefficient analysis

The original data X (sample length $N = 2^L$) after L layer of Haar wavelet transform, its sparse coefficients can be expressed as:

$$X = \upsilon_0 \gamma + \sum_{i=0}^{L-1} \sum_{j=0}^{L-i} w_{i,j} \psi_{i,j} \qquad (1)$$

Wavelet basis contains extended function γ and wavelet function $\psi_{i,j}$, υ_0 is the expansion coefficient, $w_{i,j}$ is the wavelet coefficient, where i and j are the wavelet function's scale and offset. Wavelet coefficient has a tree structure [2].

The sparse coefficients can be composed of connected tree model, black nodes represent the large value of sparse coefficients (the value has an important role for the reconstruction), white nodes represent the small value of sparse coefficients. Black nodes can be formed a connected tree with a root node. If any of the coefficients $w_{i,j}$ are belong to the large set of values, then its parent node must belong to the large value collection.

2.3 Reconstruction algorithm

The algorithm proposed in this paper combines Haar wavelet tree and SAMP algorithm. When choosing the effective atoms, this algorithm selects the atoms which have a directly parent-child relationship based on the characteristics of wavelet tree. If the wavelet coefficients monotonically decrease along the root, we can quickly find the accurate estimated value through the wavelet tree. If it is not, when choosing a wavelet coefficients away from the root, its parent node will be selected, and the parent node may be has a small value. This will cause that the selected atoms have a big error. This paper introduces the addition threshold μ_1 and deletion threshold μ_2 to control the number of selected atoms at each iteration, where μ_1 is used to prevent useless atoms selected and μ_2 is used to delete the already selected atoms. The steps of the algorithm are as follows:

Input: sensing matrix Θ, measure vector Y, step length S.

Output: the approximate value of high-frequency coefficients W'.

Step 1: Initialization phase

1) Initialize the residual $r_0 = Y$. Here α_i is the i-th column vectors of the sensing matrix Θ, and Λ is the column index set of sensing matrix, $\Lambda = [1, 2, \ldots, N]$. Set the addition threshold μ_1 and deletion threshold μ_2 according to the experience. Initialize stage $= 1$.
2) Candidate set $C_0 = []$; Pre-collection set $s_0 = []$.

Step 2: Choose effective atom phase

1) Select subscript set of the effective atoms of P-th iteration $s_p = \{\max(1, R_n) : R_n || \langle r_{p-1}, \alpha_{Rn} \rangle \geq \mu_1 \max_{i \in \Lambda} \langle r_{p-1}, \alpha_i \rangle|, \Lambda = \Lambda / \Lambda_{p-1}\}$
2) According to the twice relationship between father nodes' index value and the son nodes' index value of Haar wavelet tree, we select the corresponding wavelet tree of every R_n elements, and store the index value of all families in the candidate set C_p, $C_p = F_{p-1} \cup S_p$.
3) Calculate the reconstructed high-frequency coefficients by candidate set C_p, $w'_{Cp} = (\Theta_{Cp}^H \Theta_{Cp})^{-1} \Theta_{Cp}^H Y$.
4) By using the deletion threshold μ_2 to cut the candidate set C_p, put the useless index value to Γ_R, $\Gamma_R = \{\max(1, C_j) : C_j || W'_{C_j}|_{C_j \in C_p} \leq \mu_2 \max_{C_j \in C_p} |W'_{C_j}|\}$
5) $C = C_P / \Gamma_R$; $r = Y - \Theta_C \Theta_C^* Y$,
6) If meet the stop condition of iteration, then stop iterating. If don't meet the stop condition and the

8

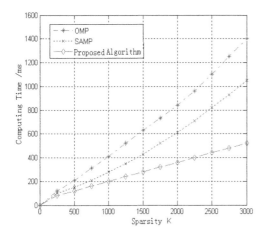

Figure 2.   Comparison of running time.

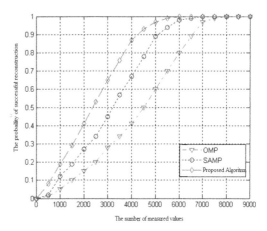

Figure 3.   Comparison of the probability of successful reconstruction.

K-th residual modulus is greater than the last residual modulus, then update stage = stage + 1 and I = stage × s. Otherwise update $C_k = C$, $r_k = r$, $P = P + 1$.

Step 3: Output $w^* = \Theta_C^* Y$

The reconstructed high-frequency coefficients are not the original performance data. Based on the reconstruction of the high-frequency coefficients, the original performance data can be obtained through the inverse wavelet transform of low-frequency coefficients and the reconstructed high-frequency coefficients.

3   EXPERIMENTAL RESULTS AND ANALYSIS

For convenience of analysis, we select a random CNU device as the experiment subject. Collecting performance data of the device; continuous acquisition is 24 hours, and acquisition cycle is 5 s. The total number of data collected is 17280, and the sampling number is $N = 2^{14} = 16424$. For more data can be compressed, multi wavelet transform should be undertake. Here we set 4-th level wavelet decomposition, and set addition threshold $\mu_1 = 0.5$ and deletion threshold $\mu_2 = 0.5$ based on the experience in [3]. In order to reflect the performance of SAMP reconstruction algorithm based on the Haar wavelet tree, we made a comparison with the SAMP algorithm [7] and OMP algorithm [8].

3.1   Comparison of computing time

Here we set sparsity K is unknown, observation value is set to a constant value M = 4000. The simulation results shown as Figure 2, the running time of three kind of algorithm will increase with sparsity K increasing. In the same sparsity, the running time of OMP algorithm is the longest, followed by SMAP algorithm and proposes algorithm. Only one atom is chosen to update the effective atoms set at each iteration by the OMP algorithm, resulting in a longer time for

reconstruction. SAMP algorithm reconstruct coefficients with fixed step size, its running time is shorter than OMP algorithm. The algorithm proposed in this paper can select multiple valid atoms at each iteration, thus it greatly reduces the running time.

3.2   Comparison of the probability of successful reconstruction

We set sparsity K is unknown, and the number of measured value is variable. The simulation results shown as Figure 3, ① With the increase of the number of measured values, the probability of successful reconstruction of three algorithms increase gradually. When the number of measured value reaches a certain level, there is a 100% probability of the reconstruction. ② In a small number of measured value and the same case, the algorithm proposes in this paper has the highest probability of reconstruction, followed by SMAP algorithm and OMP algorithm. The OMP algorithm will have a lower accuracy of the reconstruction when the sparsity is unknown. The algorithm proposes in this paper improves the efficiency of selected atoms at each iteration and increases the probability of successful reconstruction by taking full advantage of the sparse coefficients which have the characteristics of tree structure.

3.3   Comparison of the accuracy of the reconstruction

The accuracy of reconstruction shown as Figure 4. The reconstructed high-frequency coefficient is very close to the original one by using the algorithm proposes in this paper, followed by SMAP algorithm. However, the reconstructed high-frequency coefficient of the OMP algorithm has a large difference with the original one. Especially a lot of useful values are not accurately reconstructed. The results show that our algorithm has a higher accuracy of reconstruction.

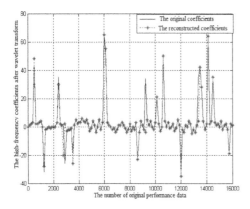

a. The proposed algorithm in this paper

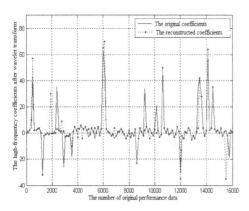

b. SAMP algorithm

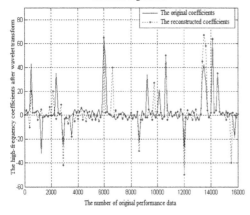

c. OMP algorithm

Figure 4. Comparing the reconstructed high-frequency coefficients with the original.

4 CONCLUSIONS

Combined with the SAMP algorithm and wavelet tree structure characteristics, this paper proposes a SAMP algorithm base on the Haar wavelet tree. When choosing the effective atoms, the algorithm selects the atoms which have directly parent-child relationship based on the characteristics of wavelet tree. Meanwhile, the algorithm use deletion threshold and addition threshold to control the number of elected atoms. Experimental results show that, this algorithm can not only reduce the calculation time, but also improve the accuracy of the reconstruction.

ACKNOWLEDGEMENTS

This research work is supported by the National Natural Science Foundations of P.R. China (NSFC) under Grant (61071093), National 863 Program (2010AA701202), Sweden-Asian International Cooperation Project (348-2008-6212), Jiangsu Province Major Technology Support Program (BE2012849), Jiangsu Province IOT application demonstration project (SJ212025), Jiangsu Province industry-university-research prospective joint research project (BY2014014), Jiangsu Province practice innovation plan (CXZZ13-0476), and SRF for ROCS, SEM (NJ209002).

REFERENCES

[1] Yigang Cen, Xiaofang Chen, Lihui Cen, et al. Compressed sensing based on the single layer wavelet transform for image processing [J]. Journal of communications, 2010, 32(8): 52–55.

[2] Guoqing Liu, Jing Lin. Adaptive compressed sensing based on the single layer wavelet transform for image processing [J]. Journal of Hefei University of Technology, 2012, 35(1): 141–145.

[3] Qiusheng Lian, Ying Xiao. Image compressed sensing algorithm based on wavelet tree structure and iterative shrinkage [J]. Journal of Electronics & Information Technology, 2011, 33(4): 967–971.

[4] Needell D., Tropp J.A. CoSaMP: iterative signal recovery from in-complete and inaccurate samples [J]. Applied and Computational Harmonic Analysis, 2008, 26(3): 301–321.

[5] Fangfei Wang. A study on tree-based backtracking orthogonal matching pursuit for sparse signal recvery [C]. Beijing Jiaotong University, 2012.6

[6] Baraniuk R G, Gevher V, Duarte M F, et al. Model-based compressive sensing [J]. IEEE Trans on Information Theory, 2010, 56(4): 1982–2001.

[7] Do T T, Lu Gan, Nam N, Tran T D. Sparsity adaptive matching pursuit algorithm for practical compressed sensing [C]. In 42nd Asilomar Conference on Signal, Systems and Computers. Pacific Grove, USA: IEEE Press, 2008: 581–587.

[8] Simon H. Adaptive Filter Theory [M]. 4th. USA: Person Education, Inc, 2002: 96–100.

[9] Donoho D L. Compressed sensing [J]. IEEE Transactions on Information Theory, 2006, 52(4): 1289–1306.

[10] Candes E, Romberg J, Tao T. Robust uncertainty principles:exact signal reconstruction from highly incomplete frequency information [J]. IEEE Transactions on Information Theory 2006, 52(4): 489–509.

Multimedia Technology IV – Farag, Yang & Jiao (Eds)
© 2015 Taylor & Francis Group, London, ISBN: 978-1-138-02794-7

The effects of receiver concentrators on received power in indoor visible light communications

Yuhan Liu, Yunfeng Peng & Yumin Liu
School of Computer and Communication Engineering, University of Science and Technology Beijing, Beijing, China

ABSTRACT: The channel performance of indoor visible light communications (VLC) utilizing LEDs is invested. Through numerical simulation, we find that there exists an optimal FOV for receiver concentrators at which the received power achieves its highest.

Keywords: visible light communications; power; concentrator

1 INTRODUCTION

The channel is the most important part impacting performance of visible light communication (VLC). VLC channel analysis can help to deeply understand indoor VLC and to design VLC systems with satisfactory performances.

The influence of interference and reflection is discussed based on numerical analyses in [1], which considers both line-of-sight and diffuse. A new algorism including wavelength-dependent white LED characteristics and spectral reflectance of indoor reflectors is present in [2]. Since the LED lights provide both illumination and communication, the utilization ratio of power for communication is very low. One way to improve the power utilization is to add a concentrator in the VLC channel [3]. However, to our best knowledge, little attention has been given to evaluate the power utilization efficiency in this system.

In this work, we extend the algorithm of [4] to compute the received power. Through numerical simulation, we find that there exists an optimal FOV for receiver concentrators at which the received power achieves its highest.

2 MODELS

In this paper, we model the VLC environment as an empty rectangular house, without any other interference sources, such as background light. LED source, ideal channel (with or without a concentrator), and ideal receiver are assumed.

2.1 Channel model

LED light sources without commercial beam shaping components can usually be modeled as a Lambert light source having uni-axial symmetry radiation intensity [2]:

$$R(\phi) = \frac{(m+1)}{2\pi} P_t \cos^m(\phi) \tag{1}$$

Here, $m = -\frac{\ln 2}{\ln(\cos(\phi_{1/2}))}$ is the mode number of the radiation lobe, and $\phi_{1/2}$ is half of the view angle of the LED. ϕ represents the angle of the LED irradiance and P_t is the emitted power.

We use the algorithm proposed in [4] to divide the channel into three parts, the transmitter to reflective elements, reflective elements to reflective elements, and reflective elements to the receiver. In this paper, we only consider the light-of-sight (LOS) for simplicity. Then we can express the gain of the LOS as:

$$H_{TR} = \begin{bmatrix} g_{T_iR_1} & \cdots & g_{T_iR_r} \\ \vdots & \ddots & \vdots \\ g_{T_iR_1} & \cdots & g_{T_iR_r} \end{bmatrix} \tag{2}$$

Here, $g_{T_iR_j}$ is the LOS gain from the i_{th} transmitter to the j_{th} receiver. And $g_{T_iR_j}$ can be expressed as:

$$g_{T_iR_j} = \frac{(m_s+1)A_{R_j}}{2\pi R_{T_iR_j}^2} \cos^{m_s}\left(\phi_{T_iR_j}\right)\cos\left(\psi_{T_iR_j}\right)u(FOV_{R_j} - \psi_{T_iR_j}) \tag{3}$$

A_{R_j} is the receiving area of jth receiver and $R_{T_iR_j}$ is the distance between the ith transmitter and the jth receiver. FOV is the field of view of the jth receiver. Besides, the angles of irradiance and incidence are presented by jth and $\psi_{T_iR_j}$ respectively. We can get the received power by equation

$$P_r = H_{TR}P_t \tag{4}$$

2.2 Concentrators

In order to ensure the routine lighting, LED sources are usually sparsely placed on the ceiling, so that the power utilization is very low for communication. We can see from (1) that the received power is proportional to the effective light-collection area, so that increasing the effective area of the receiver can improve the power. One way to increase the effective receiving area of the receiver is to add a concentrator in front of receiver. Typically, non-imaging concentrator is usually chosen for such purpose [3].

The effective light-collection area for LOS without a concentrator is

$$A(\psi) = \begin{cases} A\cos\psi, & 0 \leq \psi \leq \dfrac{\pi}{2} \\ 0, & \psi \geq \dfrac{\pi}{2} \end{cases} \quad (5)$$

where A is the physical area of the receiver and ψ is the incidence angle to the receiver. When a non-imaging concentrator is added in the channel, the effective light-collection area for LOS becomes [3]

$$A_1(\psi) = \begin{cases} A\cos\psi g(\psi), & 0 \leq \psi \leq \psi_c \\ 0, & \psi \geq \psi_c \end{cases} \quad (6)$$

where $g(\psi)$ is the gain of the concentrator, and it is a function of FOV and its own internal refractive index n[3]:

$$g(\psi) = \begin{cases} \dfrac{n^2}{\sin^2\psi_c}, & 0 \leq \psi \leq \psi_c \\ 0, & \psi \geq \psi_c \end{cases} \quad (7)$$

where ψ_c indicates FOV. Since the FOV of the concentrator is within $\frac{\pi}{2}$, we can conclude that the gain of the concentrator is proportional to the refractive index, but will reduce as the FOV increasing. We usually use a hemispherical concentrator, which has $\psi_c \approx \frac{\pi}{2}$ [3]. Therefore, the received power of the LOS for this scenario is

$$P_r = H_{TR} P_t \cdot g \quad (8)$$

In this work, we define the ratio of power utilization as light power received by the receiver to that of LED transmitter $r = \frac{P_t}{P_r}$.

3 SIMULATION AND RESULTS

We assume that the house is a totally dark of 5 m × 5 m × 3 m rectangular without any optical noise or shadows. The LED lights are on the ceiling with 3 m over the floor and are arranged as Fig. 1.

And we just consider the LOS received power. The parameters used in the simulation are showed in Table 1.

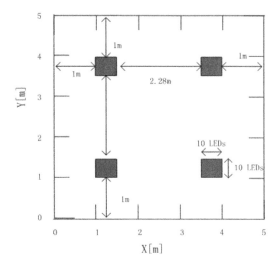

Figure 1. The arrangement of the LED lights

Table 1. Simulation parameters.

Name	Value
Room size	5*5*3
WLED array num	4
WLED num in each array	10*10
WLED space in each array	4 cm
WLED half view angle	54 deg
WLED height	3 m
WLED emitted power	174 mW
Receiver surface height	0 m
Receiver physical area	1 cm²
Receiver FOV	20~40 deg
Concentrator refraction index	1.2~1.8

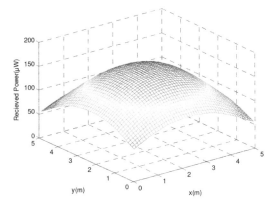

Figure 2. Received power distribution without a concentrator.

Fig. 2 and Fig. 3 shows received power distribution on the floor without and with a concentrator respectively. We can see that the power from the sources is distributed to each point of the floor. The received power for case of concentrator is ranging from 200 uw

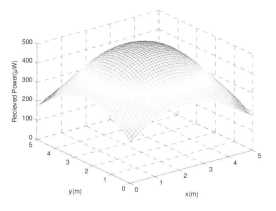

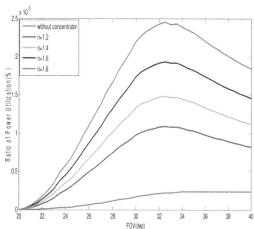

Figure 3. Received power distribution with a concentrator $n = 1.8$.

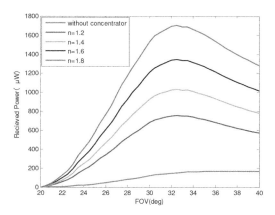

Figure 4. Received power.

Figure 5. Ratio of power utilization.

we find that adding a concentrator in the channel of the VLC can increase the power utilization by ten times. Besides, we also find that there exits an optimal FOV at which we can make full of the concentrator to achieve the highest received power.

ACKNOWLEDGMENT

This work is supported by the National Natural Science Foundation of China (61471253), National Major Projects (2015ZX03001013), and Open Research Program of State Key Laboratory of Advanced Optical Communication Systems and Networks Shanghai Jiao Tong University (2013GZKF031311).

to 400 uw, however, that for case of without concentrator is ranging from 50 uw to 100 uw. The optimal receiver place is the central part of the floor for both cases.

Fig. 4 shows the received power of LOS with and without a concentrator. We can see that there exists an optimal FOV, at which the power reaches the peak. When we continue increase FOV, the power will decrease. Fig. 5 shows the ratio of received power utilization. We can see that the maximum of the power utilization without a concentrator is just 0.000235%. And the maximum of the power utilization with a concentrator can reach 0.0011%, 0.0015%, 0.0020%, and 0.0024%.

4 CONCLUSION

The power receiving efficiency for VLC system is investigated and analyzed. By numerical simulation,

REFERENCES

[1] Komine T, Nakagawa M. Fundamental analysis for visible-light communication system using LED lights [J]. Consumer Electronics, IEEE Transactions on, 2004, 50(1): 100–107.
[2] Lee K, Park H, Barry J R. Indoor channel characteristics for visible light communications [J]. Communications Letters, IEEE, 2011, 15(2): 217–219.
[3] Kahn J M, Barry J R. Wireless infrared communications [J]. Proceedings of the IEEE, 1997, 85(2): 265–298.
[4] Jupeng Ding. Visible light communication indoor channel modeling & performance optimization [D]. Beijing University of Posts and Telecommunicaions, 2013.

Multimedia Technology IV – Farag, Yang & Jiao (Eds)
© 2015 Taylor & Francis Group, London, ISBN: 978-1-138-02794-7

Cognitive approaches for physical impairment-aware routing and wavelength assignment in dynamic optical networks

Shuang Wang, Zonglong Chen, Yumin Liu & Yunfeng Peng
School of Computer and Communication Engineering, University of Science and Technology Beijing, USTB Beijing, China

Hao Zhang
Institute of Microelectronics, Chinese Academy of Sciences, CAS, Beijing, China

ABSTRACT: A Cognitive Impairment-Aware Routing and Wavelength Assignment (C-IARWA) is proposed on retrieving solutions from the Knowledge Base (KB), to increase computational efficiency, which outperforms the traditional IARWA both in computational efficiency and blocking ratio.

Keywords: Physical impairments; cognitive model; impairment-aware routing and wavelength assignment (IARWA); knowledge base (KB)

1 INTRODUCTION

Next generation optical networks are evolving from opaque to translucent and eventually to transparent networks. And the wavelength-routed optical network (WRON) is most likely to become the next generation optical network [1]. In WRONs, signals travel directly through all-optical nodes, and physical impairments accumulate along the lightpath, which would decrease the quality of transmission (QoT) of the optical signal. If the QoT measured by Optical Signal Noise Ratio (OSNR) drops to the value lower than the predefined threshold, the lightpath cannot be established, so that the impairment aware routing and wavelength assignment algorithm (IARWA) is used to treat the physical impairments as important limitations [2, 3].

In our previous work, we proposed a cognitive routing and wavelength assignment (CRWA) algorithm architecture assuming an ideal network without considering transmission impairments. The CRWA is not only depending on general knowledge of the RWA problem, but also on the similar previous solutions stored in a knowledge base (KB) [4]. Furthermore, the KB can be improved by introducing new cases.

Although CRWA showed a better performance compared with conventional RWA, we also need to consider the impact of these physical layer impairments to achieve a high quality lightpath. Therefore, in this work, we improve the CRWA to a cognitive impairments aware RWA (C-IARWA) concentrating on the ASE noise and the homo-wavelength crosstalk and some other insert losses in cognitive approaches.

2 C-IARWA MODEL

In this section, we first describe the OSNR model about physical impairment briefly, including the ASE noise, the crosstalk and some insert losses, and then, we describe the main process of the C-IARWA.

2.1 OSNR model

When the optical signal propagates along the lightpath, it will be affected by various impairments. We consider the change of the OSNR along the lightpath as the effect of physical impairments, and then, calculate the OSNR at the destination node, compared it with the threshold $OSNR_{QoT}$ to judge whether the light path can be established.

A Wavelength Routing Node (WRN) is composed by many components, such as tap, optical amplifier, cross connect switch (XCS), receiver and transmitter. Fig. 1 shows a representative WRN [5]. The XCS inside the WRN contains multiplexers, demultiplexers and a Wavelength Routing Switch (WRS), which is responsible for routing the signals.

For present work, we consider the OSNR model as the standard of the lightpath, which is given by:

$$OSNR = P_{sig} / P_{noise} = P_{sig} / (P_{xt} + P_{ase}). \quad (1)$$

In (1), the P_{sig} is the power of the optical signal, and the P_{noise} is the power of the noise accumulated along the lightpath. Furthermore, the received power of both

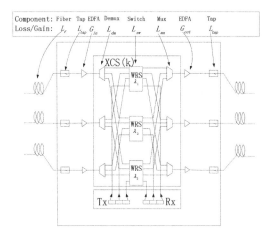

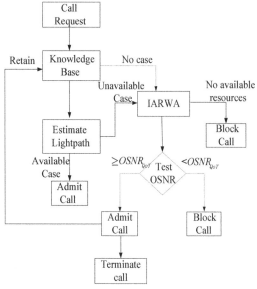

Figure 1. The architecture of the WRN and the parameters.

will get losses and gains at intermediate nodes along the lightpath. For example, to establish a lightpath on wavelength ω_i between source and destination node, the output power of the signal (P_{sig}), crosstalk (P_{xt}), and ASE noise (P_{ase}) on wavelength ω_i at the kth node were defined as the following equations [5]:

$$P_{sig}(k, \omega_i) = \frac{G_{in}(k, \omega_i)G_{out}(k, \omega_i)}{L_f(k-1,k) L_{dm}(k) L_{ns}(k) L_{sw}^2(k) L_{tap}^2} P_{sig}(k-1, \omega_i). \quad (2)$$

In (3), P_{xt} is signal power propagating in same wavelength ω_i of the ith fiber link shared the switch with other signal at the kth node, n is total number of the fiber links attached to this node, and ε is the switch crosstalk ratio:

$$P_{xt}(k, \omega_i) = \frac{G_{in}(k, \omega_i)G_{out}(k, \omega_i)}{L_f(k-1,k) L_{dm}(k) L_{nx}(k) L_{sw}^2(k) L_{tap}^2} P_{xt}(k-1, \omega_i)$$
$$+ \sum_{i=1}^{n} \varepsilon P_{sw}(k, \omega_i). \quad (3)$$

The N_{ase} is the ASE noise, which is expressed as [5]:

$$N_{ase} = 2n_{sp}(G-1) h v_i B_0. \quad (4)$$

In (4), n_{sp} is the spontaneous emission factor for EDFA, G is the gain of optical amplifier, h is the Planck constant, v_i is the optical frequency of ω_i, and B_0 is the bandwidth of optical filter. Furthermore, the ASE noise spread along the lightpath and get gains and losses. So we use (5) as the expression of the P_{ase} [5]:

$$P_{ase}(k, \omega_i) = \frac{G_{in}(k, \omega_i)G_{out}(k, \omega_i)}{L_f(k-1,k) L_{dm}(k) L_{ns}(k) L_{sw}^2(k) L_{tap}^2} P_{ase}(k-1, \omega_i)$$
$$+ \frac{G_{in}(k, \omega_i)}{L_f(k-1,k) L_{dm}(k) L_{ns}(k) L_{sw}(k) L_{tap}^2} N_{aseout}(k-1, \omega_i) \quad (5)$$
$$+ \frac{1}{L_{dm}(k) L_{sw}(k)} N_{aseout}(k-1, \omega_i).$$

Having arrived at the destination node, the optical signal power and the noise power should be calculated, which are used to evaluate the OSNR.

Figure 2. The process of the C-IARWA algorithm.

2.2 C-IARWA algorithm

In the proposed C-IARWA, the KB consists of lots of previous solutions about the impairments aware IARWA, and the parameters (e.g. source node, destination node, and the quality of the lightpath) of these cases are important information to establish a lightpath. The process of the C-IARWA algorithm is shown as Fig. 2.

When a new request arrives, important information such as the end node and the required quality of the signal will be collected firstly, and then the most similar cases having been solved previously will be retrieved from the KB. Afterwards, the estimator will check the availability of related route and wavelength resources. If the route and the wavelength resources are available, the call request will be admitted and the lightpath will be established. Furthermore, if there is no similar case stored in the KB or the resource of the case retrieved from the KB is unavailable, we use traditional IARWA to calculate a new solution to satisfy the request. After the establishment of the lightpath, the request and the solution are retained in the KB as a new case. If there is no route or no wavelengths are free along the chosen route, the call request is blocked.

3 SIMULATION AND RESULTS

3.1 Simulation environments

In this section, we conducted a set of simulations to proving the C-IARWA algorithm by comparing with the IARWA algorithm. In Table 1, we present parameters used. And the topology of the NSFNET network with 14 nodes and 21 links has been used (Fig. 3).

Table 1. Parameters in simulation.

Parameter	Value
Wavelength spacing	50 GHz
Optical bandwidth (B_0)	70 GHz
Signal power per channel	0 dB
Input/Output of EDFA gain (G_{in}/G_{out})	12 dB/6 dB
ASE factor (n_{sp})	1.5
Multiplexer/Demultiplexer loss (L_{nx}/L_{dm})	4 dB
Tap loss (L_{tap})	1 dB
Fiber loss (L_f)	0.2 dB/km
Switch loss (L_{sw})	4 dB
Switch crosstalk ratio (ε)	25 dB

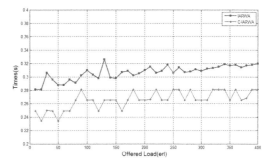

Figure 5. The average computation time.

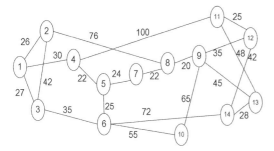

Figure 3. NSFNET with 14 nodes and 21 links.

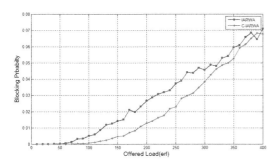

Figure 4. The blocking probability.

Each node of the network stores 16 wavelengths. Signals travel in the 10 Gbps optical system, and other parameters are in the Table 1.

Requests are generated between the node pairs of source and destination following the Poisson distribution and the holding time of every call is generated following the exponential distribution.

3.2 Results

Fig. 4 shows the blocking probability for various offered load about the two algorithms. As the offered load increases, the blocking probability also will be raised, what's more, the blocking probability of the C-IARWA is lower than the IARWA, for example, when the offered load is around 250 erl, the blocking probability of the C-IARWA is lower than IARWA about 1%. This is because, the C-IARWA not only depend on general IRWA algorithm, but also on the similar previous solutions stored in the KB, while the traditional impairments aware algorithm just rely on the calculation results of IARWA.

Fig. 5 shows the average computing time for different offered load. It's an important performance to indicate the setup time of the available path. From the curve, we can learn that the average computing time of the C-IARWA is 16% lower than the IARWA. The mainly reason is that the C-IARWA algorithm solves these problems based on previous cases stored in the KB.

4 CONCLUSION

We introduced the physical impairments into the CRWA algorithm to be a new algorithm, i.e., C-IARWA, which can solve IARWA problems based on previous knowledge in dynamic optical networks. According to the result, the blocking probability of the C-IARWA is lower than the IARWA at 1%, when the offered load is around 250erl. And also the computational efficiency is improved about 16% compared with traditional IARWA algorithms.

ACKNOWLEDGMENT

This work is supported by the National Natural Science Foundation of China (61471253), National Major Projects (2015ZX03001013), and the Open Research Program of State Key Laboratory of Advanced Optical Communication Systems and Networks Shanghai Jiao Tong University (2013GZKF031311).

REFERENCES

[1] J. Berthold, A. A. M. Saleh, L. Blair, and J. M. Simmons, "Optical networking: past, present, and future," J. Lightwave Technol., vol. 26, no. 9, pp. 1104–1118, May 2008.
[2] Guo W., Zhang J., Gao G., et al. An effective routing strategy through impairment-aware RWA in transparent optical network. Asia Communications and Photonics

Conference and Exhibition (ACP), 2009 Asia. IEEE, 2009, 2009: 1–7.

[3] Azodolmolky S., Pointurier Y., Angelou M., et al. A novel impairment aware RWA algorithm with consideration of QoT estimation inaccuracy [J]. Journal of Optical Communications and Networking, 2011, 3(4): 290–299.

[4] Zonglong Chen, Shuang Wang, Hao Zhang, Yumin Liu, Yunfeng Peng. "Cognitive Routing and Wavelength Assignment Algorithm for Dynamic Optical Networks," International Conference on Optical Internet (COIN), 2014, unpublished.

[5] B. Ramamurthy, D. Datta, H. Feng, J. P. Heritage, B. Mukherjee, Impact of Transmission Impairments on the Teletraffic Performance of Wavelength-routed Optical Networks, IEEE/OSA Journal of Lightwave Technology, vol. 17, no. 10, pp. 1713–1723, Oct. 1999.

Multimedia Technology IV – Farag, Yang & Jiao (Eds)
© 2015 Taylor & Francis Group, London, ISBN: 978-1-138-02794-7

A study of setting a proper burial depth for submarine cables

Yingjian Wang & Miao Zha
Naval University of Engineering, Wuhan, China

Feng Yuan
91497army Ningbo, China

ABSTRACT: As the development of international telecommunication, the submarine cable is widely used. Burying the submarine cable is an effective protection, but it lacks a method to inform people on how deep a suitable dig should be. To solve this problem, the article analyzed factors threatening the safety of the submarine cable, balancing the influences of both the penetration depth and the probability of the target event on the burial depth. We put forward a method by working out a deep evaluation matrix, the burial depth is then evaluated by plotting the penetration depth and the damage probability in the matrix.

Keywords: burial depth; submarine cable; target event; security level; acceptance criteria

1 THE PRESENT SITUATION OF SUBMARINE CABLE PROTECTION

Protecting the submarine cable by burying it became popular in the early 1980s. The burial depth standard was set at 0.6 m, not considering the seabed sediment properties and various other possible environmental disasters. In recent years, the general engineering burial depth has been increased to 1.0–1.5 m, the fishery activity area is 3.0 m, and the busy shipping area reached 5.0–10.0 m. Although the high burial depth is safer, it brings many difficulties to offshore constructions. It needs more advanced equipment, takes more time, and would greatly increase the cost. What is more, burying the cable too deeply would increase the difficulties for the submarine cable maintenance and repairs, leading to a waste of cost and time. Therefore, analyzing the influencing factors of submarine cable burial depth, making a comprehensive consideration of various influencing factors'. Based on those we determine a reasonable burial depth. This not only ensures the safety of the submarine cable system, but also reduces the construction problems, and be is economical.

2 FACTORS THAT AFFECT THE SETTING OF THE BURIAL DEPTH

The factors influencing the determination of the submarine cable burial depth can be divided into four aspects: the submarine cable's own ability to resist damage, the environment conditions of the bottom of the sea, external threats, and the security level of submarine cable need to reach.

2.1 *Resisting ability of submarine cable itself*

The submarine cable is armoured to different types for different environmental conditions; its ability to resist damage ranges from weak to strong. Choosing the right type for some extreme environments can help us to reduce the burial depth, such as America's AT&T SL100 submarine cable series. The single armoured cable is designed for anchor damage resistance. Owing to its special structural design, it can work normally without being deeply buried.

2.2 *Sediment conditions*

Under different seabed sediments, anchors' penetrating depths are different. The same burial depth, its protection also have differences. The seafloor soil structure is complex, and in order to facilitate it, it is usually divided into two major categories, clay and sand. Both have different physical and mechanical properties. The clayey soil grain is exquisite and sticky, the soil particles interact with soil water significantly, and with the increasing of water content, the changes of state are solid, semi-solid, plastic state, and flow dynamic plasticity. The clayey soil strength comes mainly from cohesion and friction. Sand particles are rough, and loose; their tightness is usually measured by relative density (RD). The sand soil strength comes mainly s from the friction of the rough soil particles' surface, which is influenced by the surface roughness, density, particle shape, and the grading. The soil shear strength is one of the important parameters of the soil mechanics. It refers to the resistance of the soil shear failure limit ability. Table 1 shows the engineering of the soil shear strength parameters of grading.

Table 1. Classification of soil shear strenth.

Sediment classification	Strength/density description	Strength Su/kPa	Typical bottom description
I	Very soft/Very loose	<10	Very loose muddy sand or very soft silt clay, often rich in organic matter
II	Soft/Loose	10–20	Muddy sand or loose soft silt clay, containing some organic matter
III	Tight/Dense	20–45	More dense muddy sand or compacted clayey silt, and silt clay
IV	Hard/Dense	45–150	Muddy sand or hard compacted clayey silt, and silt clay
V	Tough/Very close	150–300	Muddy sand or very hard very dense silt clay, or sandy clay
VI	Weathering bedrock	>300	Weathering bedrock

Table 2. Fishing anchor penetrating depth.

Anchor type	Hard bottom, clay or rock shear strength is greater than 72 kPa	The seabed between hard and soft, shear strength between 18–72 kPa sand, and gravel clay	Soft bottom, the shear strength between 2–18 kPa silt, silt, and soft clay
Net fishing boat anchor	<0.5	2.0	>2.0
Hydrodynamic hunting boat anchor	<0.4	0.6	1–3
Trawl fishing boat anchor	<0.4	0.5	>0.5

The softer the bottom sediment condition is, the deeper the external object impact (such as anchor) can penetrate. To protect the submarine cable, we need to choose a deeper burial depth than the external objects can penetrate. For the same burial depth, the harder the bottom sea oil is, the higher the security level that the submarine cable can reach.

2.3 The external environment threats to submarine cables

External environmental threats to the submarine cable are the main factors influencing the submarine cable burial depth. The submarine cable external environmental threats include natural, shipping and transportation, fishery and installation factors etc.

Statistical data shows that shipping transportation, fishery and installation construction and other human factors are the main factors causing damage to submarine cables.

Natural factors, such as seismic activity, sediment migration, underwater landslides, exposed rocks and wear, although are small probability events, can change the depth of the buried cable. After a time of seabed sediment movement, some cables may even be exposed on the seabed, which greatly increases the risk of the submarine cable by fishing or anchor damage. Normally, the submarine cable routing avoids the channel, but the shipping anchor damage causing the submarine cable fault is still happening. A ship sails into a forbidden anchor area is for some reasons happening all the time all over the world. With the increased number of fishing vessels, a fishery anchor harming a submarine cable is becoming more and more serious, as anchor hooking causes the submarine cable communication to be frequently interrupted. Fishing methods include nets and purse seines. The penetrating depths of fishing tackles, trawls, and common anchors used by fishing boats are shown in Table 2. Except for the harm done by the shipping and fishing boats, marine engineering installation vessels are also creating problems. These ships equipped with larger and a greater number of anchors can easily damage the cable if it is anchored nearby. The ship anchor holding power capacities of marine constructions of different tonnage are shown in Table 3.

2.4 The security level of submarine cable need to reach

Economic benefit has to be considered in a submarine cable system construction. Of different engineering level and security level, the required burial depth can diverse. The cable's working life and the nature of work will determine the cable system's safety level. Safe level classifications are based on the ability to resist accidental damage. Under normal circumstances, to ensure that the submarine cable is working normally, it is better to set a high safety level. However, the higher security level, the protection measures are more and burial depth are deeper, the cost is too much, some practical operation project does not require such special high level of security, need not buried too deep. Therefore, choosing the right safe level has a great impact on determining the burial depth.

Table 3. Marine construction anchor holding power and penetrating ability.

Tonnage/t	Anchor type	The quality of the anchor/kg	The anchor holding power/kN	Penetration depth/m
<50	Navy anchor, Hall	<50	<3.4	<1.0
50–100	anchor Markov anchor,	50–100	3.4–6.9	<1.5
100–200	ChanFuEr anchor,	100–200	0.69–1.03	<1.5
200–500	Grapnel anchor	200–500	10.3–35.7	<1.5
500–1 000		500–1 000	35.7–70.1	<2
2 500–2 700	Hall anchor (90%),	2 000	139	>2
3 500–7 500	Speke anchor (10%)	3 000	208	>2
8 000–13 500		5 000	348	>2
12 000–16 000		6 000	418	>2
25 000		8 000	557	>2
28 000		9 000	626	>2
35 000		10 000	690	>2

3 SELECT A PEFECT BURIAL DEPTH FOR THE SUBMARINE CABLE

3.1 Principles

Determining the burial depth needs a comprehensive consideration of factors such as reliability, and economy. For instance, designing a dam should be based on the location characteristics;a dam located in a croweded city should be much safer than the one located in remote mountains with few people. The former may have to be designed to resist the worst flooding in 100 years, the latter may just need to be designed to resist the worst flooding in 50 years. This type of design can save on the construction exspenses.

Spending less money in order to to reach better protection is the basic principle to designing a burial depth. Therefore, we can start from the following three aspects; a) the external threat penetration depth, where the burial depth must be deeper than the external threat penetration depth; b) the frequency of an external threat, defending the main threat by using its penetration depth as a defence; c) the security level –, the higher the security level is,the deeper the burial depth needs to be.

3.2 Steps and calculation method

The flow of determining the submarine cable burial depth is shown in Figure 1: a) investigate the laying area, the main work is the investigation of sediment conditions, and statistical target events; b) set a proper security level, according to the required working years and conditions, developing acceptance criteria, rate the penetration and harm frequency level based on the acceptance criteria, then build a deep evaluation matrix; c) find the target event, mark it on the evaluation matrix, and determine the burial depth according to the matrix.

Calculating the penetration of target events is critical. The main parameter is the target volume. There are many factors that can affect the target events' penetration, including target shape, weight, angle of the target in the water and sea bottom sediment types, depth, size

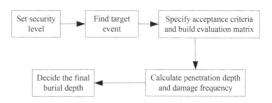

Figure 1. Flow of setting the submarine cable burial depth.

and direction of ocean wave, etc. The target weight, the bottom sediment types and depth are crucial.

Target events' penetration varies according to the bottom sea environment, it mostly depends on the soil shear strength, a large target in general can reach 0.5–1.0 m under a seabed of sand, about 2 m of ooze; muddy is deeper. The target falling into the sea can be described by the following equations [1]:

$$m\dot{v} = -\frac{1}{2}\rho_w c v^2 A_a + mg - mg\frac{\rho_w}{\rho_a} \tag{1}$$

$$s(t) = \int_0^t v \, dt \tag{2}$$

$$\begin{cases} v(t) = a\tanh(bt) \\ s(t) = \frac{a}{b}\left[\ln(e^{2bt}+1) - bt - \ln 2\right] \end{cases} \tag{3}$$

m = mass of the target
ρ_w = density of water
ρ_a = density of target
A_a = projected area of the target in the flow direction
g = gravitation acceleration
c = 1.1 drag-coefficient of the target
v = velocity of dropping
t = dropping time
a, b are experience factors relate to sediment condition
$a = 0.124\,6\sqrt{m/A_a}$, $b = 68.549\,1\sqrt{A_a/m}$

vt can be worked out from Equation 3. Using energy conservation can be used to work out the penetrating depth of target events [1].

$$h = \frac{mv_t^2}{2f} \tag{4}$$

21

Table 4. Damage frequency classification.

Grade	Frequency p
1	$0 \leq p < 10\%$
2	$10\% \leq p < 40\%$
3	$40\% \leq p < 80\%$
4	$80\% \leq p < 90\%$
5	$90\% \leq p < 100\%$

Table 5. Sediment and panetration classification.

	Depth h/m			
Grade	Sand	Mud	Rock	Frequency p
1	$0 \leq h < 1.0$	$0 \leq h < 2.0$	$0 \leq h < 0.3$	p_1
2	$1.0 \leq h < 2.0$	$2.0 \leq h < 3.0$	$0.3 \leq h < 0.6$	p_2
3	$2.0 \leq h < 3.0$	$3.0 \leq h < 4.0$	$0.6 \leq h < 0.9$	p_3
4	$3.0 \leq h < 5.0$	$4.0 \leq h < 8.0$	$0.9 \leq h < 1.2$	p_4
5	≥ 5.0	≥ 8.0	≥ 1.2	p_5

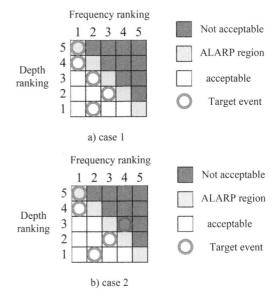

a) case 1

b) case 2

Figure 2. Burial depth evaluation matrix.

$\bar{f}$ = friction of the target penetrating seabed it is related to the sediment shear strength.

When evaluating target event damage probability p, usually according to submarine cable system safety level, respectively statistic frequency for shipping, fisheries and engineering installation, then according to the standard set damage probability level of acceptance. As shown in Table 4, under a certain condition of sediment, classify the target events penetration depths into five grades, then sum up the damage probability of events in the same grade, as shown in Table 5.

Make a matrix according to the target events' penetrating depth and damage probability [4, 5], then the matrix will be divided into different regions on the basis of security level (not accept area, the ALARP area and accept area); mark the target in the matrix, and then according to different situations determine the submarine cable buried depth, as shown in Figure 2. In case 1, if all the target events are in the accept area, the final burial depth H can be described as:

$$H = h_{1\max} p_1 + h_{2\max} p_2 + h_{3\max} p_3 + h_{4\max} p_4 + h_{5\max} p_5 \qquad (5)$$

$h_{i\max}$ = The maximum depth of the target event penetrating in grade i ($i = 1, 2, 3, 4, 5$);

p_i = The sum of all damage probabilities of the target events in grade i ($i = 1, 2, 3, 4, 5$);

In case 2, one target event is in the not accept area, in order to protect the cable, the burial depth must be set to its level.

$$H = h_{n,\max} \qquad (6)$$

$h_{n,\max}$ = The maximum depth of not accept grade n ($n = 1, 2, 3, 4, 5$).

4 CONCLUSION

Using the evaluation matrix, the submarine cable burial depth can be effectively obtained under a certain security level. A different subsea environment needs a different burial depth. This method provides important guidance to submarine cable construction.

REFERENCES

[1] Liu Xiao-hu, Yi Wei. "Risk assessment about anchor damage to submarine cable" The 7th national conference on engineering structure safety. 2009, pp. 268–272.
[2] Zhuang Yuan, Song Shao-qiao. "Study on the depth of submerged pipeline". Journal of Dalian Maritime University, 2013, 39(1), pp. 61–64.
[3] Yang Ke-gui. "Characteristics of Optical Submarine Cables and Related Technology". Electric Wire & Cable, vol. 4, pp. 18–20, 2005.
[4] Det Norske Veritas. Risk assessment of pipeline protection [S]. Recommended practice. No. DNV-RP-F107. 2001.
[5] Allan P.G. "Selecting appropriate cable burial depths" [C] IBC Conference on Submarine Communicaton, pp. 1–13, 1998.
[6] Wang Yu-shuang. "The Application Research of BPI Index in Burial Protection Project of 500 kV Submarine Cable". Science Technology and Engineering, vol. 7, pp. 1474–1483, 2012.
[7] Tan Jian, Li Heng-zhi, Tian Bo. "Discussion on Damage of Accidental Anchoring Operation upon the Submarine Pipelines". Ship & Ocean Engineering, 2008, 37(1), pp. 142–144.

Multimedia Technology IV – Farag, Yang & Jiao (Eds)
© 2015 Taylor & Francis Group, London, ISBN: 978-1-138-02794-7

Electricity information collection system based on 230 MHz-WiMAX network and multi-network fusion technology

Mingming Pan & Shiming Tian
China Electric Power Research Institute, Beijing, China

Xin Jin, Chengcheng Lv & Weidong Wang
Information & Electronics Technology Lab, Beijing University of Posts and Telecommunications, Beijing, China

ABSTRACT: In recent years, with the increasing demand for electricity, it is necessary to build a electricity information collection system with satisfied communication performance. Considering the implementation, reliability, economy of wired and wireless communication, a electricity information collection system based on 230 MHz-WiMAX network and multi-network fusion technology is proposed in this paper. The system combines the characteristics of 230 MHz-WiMAX network and some other wireless network, which chooses the best way wireless communication according to the communication network load, the transmission conditions and other factors, etc. This paper mainly studies the multi-network fusion technology applied in the electricity information collection system.

Keywords: electricity information collection system; 230 MHz-WiMAX network; multi-network fusion technology

1 INTRODUCTION

With the growth of social demand for electricity, existing electricity information collection system can't meet today's technology requirement, because there are many deficiencies, such as single system function, communication collection rate is not high, system functions can't be extended, etc. All of these problems can't meet the diversified development of grid operations [1]. Therefore, in order to adapt to the trend of power grid, construction of a new generation of information collection system, which includes the information collection, analysis and information resource sharing functions, has great significance.

The electricity information collection system is the physical basis of smart grid construction, which includes advanced sensing, communications, automatic control technology [2], can realize data collection, data management, power quality data statistics and analysis functions. Besides, the system is mainly to timely collect electricity information of users, found abnormal electricity, monitor and control electricity load of users. The electricity information collection system consists of master station layer, communication channel layer and collecting devices layer [3].

Master station layer is the core layer of the information collection system, which is a network system combines software and hardware. Its main function is collection instruction delivery, scheduling, electricity information collection, storage, and analysis. Master station layer is mainly composed of database server, disk array, application server, preset communication server, interface server, workstations, firewall and related network equipment. Collecting devices layer is the information source of electricity information collection system, responsible for collection and provide information about the power of the whole system. According to the electricity information collection, collection environment, functions, there is also a variety of the equipment in the collecting devices layer, such as producing electrical energy collection terminal, special transformer electric energy collection terminal, public transformer electric energy collection terminal, concentrator, electric energy meter. Communication channel layer includes two parts, the remote communication and the local communication [4]. Local communication is the process that collection terminals send the electricity information to concentrators. Then the concentrators sending the collected information to the master station layer is called remote communication.

Since the existing communication technologies have many deficiencies, such as the frequency resource of 230 MHz digital radio station communication constraints and the channel utilization is low, installation and operating costs of electricity GPRS collection system are greatly increased and the coverage of these communication networks is not widely enough, etc. Thus, the communication mode of electricity information collection system can't commendably achieve the purpose of electricity information collection. In order to improve the communication performance of electricity information collection system, this paper focuses on the remote communication and propose a 230 MHz-WiMAX network and multi-network fusion technology instead of the existing single communication mode.

The electricity information collection system consists of master station layer, communication channel layer and collecting devices layer. The master station layer can communicate with marketing application and other application modules through specific interfaces. And the communication between the main station and the collecting devices takes the optical fiber private network, 2G/3G/4G public networks and the 230 MHz WiMAX private network as the transmission network.

2 230 MHz-WiMAX NETWORK AND MULTI-NETWORK FUSION TECHNOLOGY

The 230 MHz WiMAX network and multi-network fusion solution is proposed in order to solve the current shortage of grid communication. The structure of communication channel layer is illustrated in Figure 1. Although the three kinds of communication have their own advantages and disadvantages, the solution combines the advantages of a variety of communication methods, selects the appropriate communication network for users and can handover dynamically among these communication networks to ensure the timeliness and reliability of users' information transmission, according to the user's location, communication environment and transmission information.

The multi-network fusion can be a good solution to the frequency resources limitation of 230 MHz band, due to 230 MHz WiMAX private network uses OFDM and OFDMA technologies [5], the communication channel can be divided into several sub-channels and each sub-channel includes several sub-carriers. In addition, 230 MHz WiMAX has large coverage area, high spectrum efficiency, which can effectively improve the transmission rate to guarantee the real-time of the electricity information collection system. And the security of data transmission can also be guaranteed by WiMAX unique security mechanisms. Thus, we can analyze the reason of failures faster and safer in order to resolve the current 230 MHz wireless private network low communication rate, poor real-time performance, fewer access points, low collection failure rate and other issues.

We need to re-deploy 230 MHz WiMAX network, if we want to implement WiMAX network, and it is difficult to achieve seamless coverage, especially the suburbs or in remote mountainous area where users are much less. So we can use 2G/3G/4G wireless public networks for electricity information collection in the area of 230 MHz WiMAX networks can not cover to avoid high cost of deployment. Although the real-time and security are not guaranteed for electricity information transmission, the 2G/3G/4G networks are already deployed by mobile operators. Therefore, the public network has greater advantages in the initial system deployment that power sector just need to rent the network instead of spending on construction costs.

Due to the openness of the wireless environment, information security during transmission can't be guaranteed. Besides, wireless network is susceptible

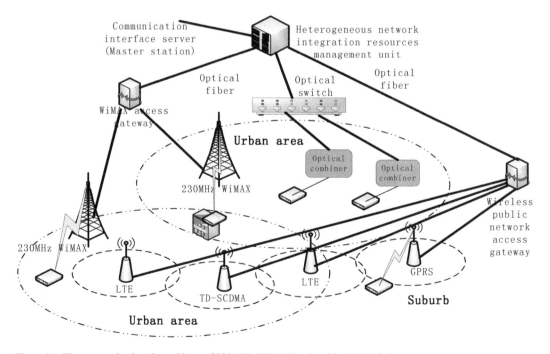

Figure 1.　The communication channel layer of 230 MHz WiMAX and multi-network fusion.

to interference of the external environment, which leads to the signal transmission quality decline, the reduction of transmission efficiency, the real-time of transmission can't be guaranteed. Thus, we also fuse optical fiber private network, because of its high transmission rate, less affected by outside interference, small transmission delay and high reliability [6]. And the optical fiber needs to cooperate to use with 230 MHz WiMAX and 2G/3G/4G networks so that they will give full play to their strengths.

In addition, the solution introduces a heterogeneous network integration resource management unit. The management unit integrates the resources of these three communication networks and communicates with the server of master station. In order to guarantee real-time and reliability of the system during the electricity information measurement process, the management unit should select the appropriate transmission network for the users, according to the communication network load, the transmission conditions and other factors, etc.

3 SIMULATION AND ANALYSIS

To illustrate how the proposed electricity information collection system based on multi-network fusion solution for selecting communication network, we take the time delay as major factor to analyze communication network performance through simulation in this section.

We can get the time delay of 230 MHz WiMAX, LTE and GPRS, according to the number of message per minute, protocol overhead, bandwidth requirements, the requirement of transmission rate of different electricity users and the transmission rate of these three communication networks. The simulation result is shown in Figure 2. As can be seen from the figure, when the total number of users is different and the proportion of each type of user is same, LTE and WiMAX are far superior to GPRS on the delay characteristics.

So electricity information collection system should give priority to the use of LTE and 230 MHz-wimax when electricity information collection has high real-time demand.

Under the same conditions, select LTE and 230 MHz WiMAX, and the network of multi-network fusion for comparison. The result is shown in Figure 3. The time delay of multi-network fusion is smaller when the number of users is less than 2500. And its delay is just as same as 230 MHz WiMAX when the number of users is more.

And when the total number of users is same, change the proportion of each type of user. The delay simulation result is as shown in Figure 4 and Figure 5. When the number of users is relatively small (the number is less than 2000). LTE performs better in terms of time delay, compared with 230 MHz WiMAX. But 230 MHz WiMAX is better than LTE with the increase in the number of users. Thus, Wireless private network is better in guaranteeing the real-time of transmission than public network. So the multi-network fusion solution can take advantage of each network to make the system performance better.

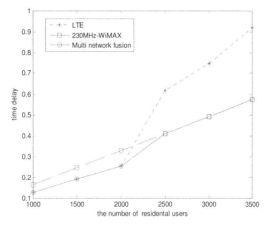

Figure 3. Time delay of multi-network fusion.

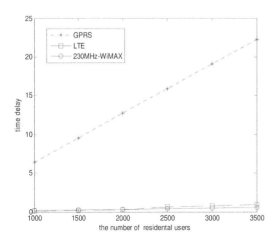

Figure 2. Time delay of three communication networks.

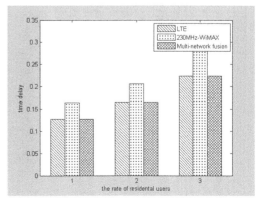

Figure 4. Time delay of the total number of users is 1210.

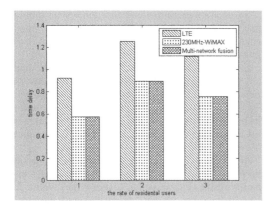

Figure 5.   Time delay of the total number of users is 4235.

4 CONCLUSIONS

In this paper, we presented the structure of electricity information collection system, the deficiencies that the communication channel layer has, and then proposed a new electricity information collection system based on 230 MHz WiMAX and multi-network fusion technology. This new system selects the appropriate transmission network for the users to guarantee real-time and reliability of information transmission, according to the communication conditions and some other factors. The results of simulation show the multi-network fusion solution can make the system to achieve the best performance through choosing the appropriate network. Electricity information collection system based on 230 MHz-WiMAX network and multi-network fusion technology will be the mainstream of future electricity information collection system.

ACKNOWLEDGMENT

The authors would like express their gratitude to the National State 863 project with NO. 2011AA05A116 and Science and technology project of State Grid Corporation of China, the project "Research on intelligent electric technology based on improving power marketing management service level".

REFERENCES

[1] Wei XV, Bin Wang, Yuanjian Jiang, Power Line Carrier Communication Technology and its Applications in Electric Energy Data Acquisition System [J]. Electrical Measurement & Instrumentation. 2010. 47(7A):44–46.
[2] Zhang Wen-liang, Liu Zhuang-zhi, Wang Ming-jun, Yang Xu-sheng, Research Status and Development Trend of Smart Grid [J]. Power System Technology. 2009(13).
[3] Hu Jiangyi, Zhu Enguo, Du Xingang, Du Shuwe, Application Status and Development Trend of Power Consumption Information Collection System [J]. Automation of Electric Power Systems. 2014(2).
[4] Jingbo Li, Xiaozhong Liu, Comparision of Three Local Communication Modes Used By Low-Voltage Power Consumption Information Collection System [J]. Telecommunications for Electric Power System. 2010. 31(214):61–65.
[5] Zhu Rong, Key Technology and Network Structure of WiMAX [J]. Information Security and Communications Privacy. 2010(1).
[6] Cao Maohong, Liu Li, Current Status and Development Trends of Optical Fiber Communication Technology [J]. OME Information. 2007(3).

Multimedia Technology IV – Farag, Yang & Jiao (Eds)
© 2015 Taylor & Francis Group, London, ISBN: 978-1-138-02794-7

Design and implementation of safety monitoring system for underground

Liu Yang, Wei Liang, Li Peng, Li-Wang Zhu, Xin Qian & Yu-Feng Liu
School of Computer Science and Engineering, Hunan University of Science and Technology, Xiangtan, China

ABSTRACT: Analyzing the traditional ventilation environment in mine, the paper puts forward a underground mine gas Monitoring intelligent system. First of all, it introduces the overall design ideas of the hardware and software of the system. Secondly, in the view of the improvement of system's performance, it gives a detailed introduction to amplifier circuit, protection circuit and nonlinear correction circuit of Gas sensor. Thirdly, it designs the underlying software of gas ventilation monitoring intelligent system. Lastly, it analyzes and compares the stability of system in simulation experiment platform. The experimental results show that the system is feasible in the case of practical environment. This system can not only ensure the minimum power consumption of mine ventilation system, but also has higher stability and anti-jamming on the demand for methane gas ventilation.

Keywords: Component, Intelligent ventilation, Network partition, Gas detection, Methane

1 INTRODUCTION

In the process of mine production, predicting and preventing the danger caused by mine gas outburst have been a major research topic which raises great concern in the main coal-producing countries. Statistics [1] show that: gas explosion, coal spontaneous combustion as well as fire disaster, roof fall, water hazard and electrical transport accident are the five chief disasters in coal mines. Among these, the gas explosion does most harm to the production of coal mine enterprises. It not only causes great casualties, but also destroys the production and safety facilities under the mine and disrupts production. Furthermore, it even lead the secondary hazards like coal-dust explosion, fire in mine, roof fall etc. Thus, it may aggravate disaster and make it hard for production to recover in short time. Over 95% of the coal mine in China are gas mine, therefore, we must strengthen the monitoring of gas in order to solve the problem of gas explosion. Through using the gas monitoring device or system, we can achieve the real-time monitoring for mine gas in all regions, which makes outside world able to obtain the information of the subsurface mine in time and make accurate but timely judgments on the production; When the concentration exceeds the limit and pose a threat to the safety of mine, relative departments can take effective measures to it in time, as a consequence, they avoid and reduce the gas accidents, ensure the normal production and assure the safety of miner as well [2–3].

At present, scholars in and abroad have done a lot of research on the ventilation intelligent monitoring system, Tian [4] analyzed it from two aspects—the safety reliability and economic rationality, and put forward the influence of the form of ventilation network on airflow stability. Meanwhile he has done some research about the effect of the fan operation on the stability of airflow, and given us a comprehensive evaluation to the mine ventilation system optimization schemes. Zhao [5] considered it from three aspects—technical feasibility, economic and safety consideration, and proposed a scheme to evaluate the ventilation system optimization and transformation comprehensively from the following aspects: the wind pressure, the wind amount, the ratio of air volume supply/demand, the ventilation way, the ventilator's input power and the fan's running stability etc. Wang [6] optimized the main ventilator to reduce threats caused by harmful gases. And he developed a set of test program and auxiliary equipment of ventilation control to control the main fan anti and the speed adjustment. The basic idea to ensure safety is to synchronize the supply air rate to dilute the gas content according to the gas concentration. Currently, although many methods [7] has been used to conduct the research on safe concentration, there still hasn't stable ventilation intelligence monitoring system.

In order to solve the problems of gas concentration monitoring above, firstly, the paper proposes a new ventilation intelligence monitoring system; secondly, it introduces elaborately the main circuit module function of the ventilation intelligence monitoring system; finally, it experiments and analyzed the stability of the ventilation intelligence system based on the site environmental simulation.

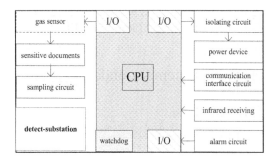

Figure 1. Block diagram of intelligent gas sensor (IGS).

2 DESIGN OF INTELLIGENT GAS VENTILATION SYSTEM

2.1 The hardware structure of system

Design of intelligent gas ventilation system includes hardware and software design two parts, the general principle is multi-functional, low consumption, easy to install, debug and maintain. The gas ventilation system mainly includes the analog collection, display of measurement results, uploaded to station and alarm, power control and output functions etc, and it usually designed at single-chip microcomputer. The single-chip would collect the heating analog bridge; after operation and processing, record and display gas concentration; then compare to the EEPROM setting, start sound and light alarm if more than the limit; output the signal through the isolation circuit; it can communicate with station digitally to upload; the monitoring results and receive the alarm signal; the adjustment and calibration of sensor completed in the infrared remote control which ensured the convenient and reliable operation. Block diagram of intelligent gas sensors shown in Figure 1.

According to the function requirements of the intelligent gas sensor (IGS), combined with the overall architecture of system and communication interface standard, considering the need to record the date and time of the gas concentration transfinite alarm, add a real-time clock circuit, due to detect the gas concentration area generally need to control the temperature, so add a temperature sensor, like gas concentration, the temperate can be displayed on the LED, then upload data to station through the RS-485 interface. Intelligent power supply of the gas sensor can be used alone mine flame-proof type and the Ann power box, it can be used for mine contains explosive gas environment, but also has the function of backup battery power supply, the output of the specifications of the power supply for 12 volts DC.

2.2 The circuit design of intelligent gas sensor

Intelligent gas sensor hardware circuit mainly includes the microprocessor, the gas signal collection circuit, infrared remote control receiving, RS – 485 communication interface circuit, display circuit, sound and light alarm, real-time clock (RTC) and temperature sensor

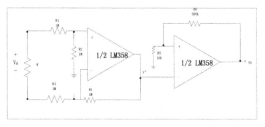

Figure 2. Schematic diagram of amplification circuit which using LM358.

circuit. Among them, the RS – 485 communication interface circuit is the same as substation board, display and sound/light alarm circuit designed with some conventional devices, like digital tube, LED light and buzzer etc.

(1) The design of the signal amplifying circuit

In the concentration of 0–4% in environment, due to the output voltage of gas detection circuit is very small (mV), amplifying circuit must be used for the small voltage signal to ensure the effective identification to MCU. Based on the considerations of cost and the low voltage power supply, this design choose the op-amp LM358 manufactured in MOTOROLA. Because the two independent, high gain, internally frequency compensated dual operational amplifier consisted in LM358 is very suitable for the single power supply whose voltage range is very wide to use. The using range includes: sensor signal amplifier, audio amplifiers, dc gain module, as well as all the other available conventional operational amplifier of the single power supply or batteries. The principle of gas sensor signal amplifier circuit which used LM358 design as shown in Figure 2.

The function of the first-level LM358 circuit is converting differential voltage V_R to ground voltage V', the conversion relations as follows:

$$V_{Out1}=R_{22}/R_{21}\times(V_{IN1+}-V_{IN1-})=V_{IN1+}-V_{IN1-} \tag{1}$$

Secondary LM358 circuit's function is to amplify the ground voltage V' for the V_0 to output, the conversion relations as follows:

$$V_0=(1+R_6/R_5)\times V' \tag{2}$$

In order to provide MJC4 the heating voltage of 2.8 V, we decided to choose ON Semiconductor integrated three-terminal voltage regulator integrated circuit LM317, which is an easy to use, widely used, and the output voltage is variable.

The output voltage can be calculated with the following formula:

$$V_0=1.25\times(1+R_{12}/R_{10}) \tag{3}$$

Amplifying circuit composed of LM358 two-stage amplifier circuit, according to the above circuit we can known that:

$$V_{Out1}=R_{22}/R_{21}\times(V_{IN1+}-V_{IN1-})=V_{IN1+}-V_{IN1-} \tag{4}$$

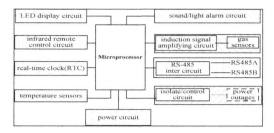

Figure 3. Hardware architecture of IGS.

$$V_{Out2}=(1+R_{26}/R_{25})\times V_{Out1} \qquad (5)$$

$$R_{26}/R_{25}=59 \qquad (6)$$

$$V_{Out2}=(1+59)\times V_{Out1}=60\times(V_{IN1+}-V_{IN1-}) \qquad (7)$$

The amplify circuit whose magnification is 60 times can amplify the output of 0–75 mV of catalytic combustion type gas sensor into 0–4.5 V. which satisfied the needs of the A/D conversion greatly, the output amplified signal will entered into the on STC Microcontroller by single chip microcomputer P16 feets in order to have the A/D conversion.

(2) The design of isolation control interface circuit

The function of gas sensor isolation control interface circuit is to transfer the gas concentration to power instrument. MCU produce the frequency signal (f) through internal timers and the software program, then output by the I/O P20, through the photoelectric coupling 6N137 isolation drive, and then sent to the PWM which communicate with the power instrument. According to the received gas density, the power instrument will give the power or not message to the machine and equipment in the surrounding area. Isolation control interface circuit design as shown in Figure 3. The two power supply (VCC and VDD) of 6N137 is isolated by two power supply separately.

As a result of the frequency range of signal is 200 to 1000, and the range of frequency measurement is 0.00% to 5.00%, the switching relationship between the frequency signal and the concentration of methane are as follows (f corresponding to the frequency value of Methane concentration, p corresponding to the actual concentration of Methane):

$$f = \frac{2000-200}{500}\times p + 200 \qquad (8)$$

3 INTELLIGENT VENTILATION SYSTEM SOFTWARE DESIGN

The template is used to format your paper and style the text. All margins, column widths, line spaces, and text fonts are prescribed; please do not alter them. You may note peculiarities. For example, the head margin in this template measures proportionately more than is customary. This measurement and others are deliberate, using specifications that anticipate your paper

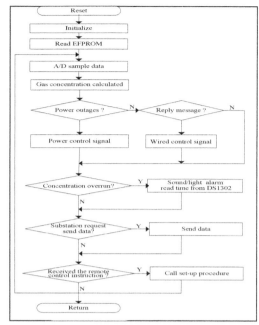

Figure 4. SGS main program flow chart.

as one part of the entire proceedings, and not as an independent document. Please do not revise any of the current designations.

Intelligent gas ventilation software main program mainly complete the gas concentration signal sampling, digital filtering, data calculation of gas concentration, concentration of transmitted to break all signal output, collect data to the monitor, alarm, and perform calibration for remote control and other tasks. Gas ventilation system of the main program process as shown in Figure 4.

4 INTELLIGENT SYSTEM STABILITY ANALYSIS

According to the analysis above, we carried on some related experiment under different temperature and humidity to verify its performance on the system stability and the accuracy of the machine. We choose the concentration 50%, 60% and 80% respectively of standard methane gas sample as a test, the data shown in Table 1, the maximum relative error of the experimental data is 0.4652, the sample gas concentration was 50% maximum concentration value of 0.0462. When the gas concentration is 80%, the concentration of system remains within the scope of CH_4 in 0% to 1%. Therefore, this system has realized the design goals, performance is superior to the design target, test results show that the system performance good strong antijamming capability, good stability, small fluctuations in the data, to satisfy the conditions of methane gas in mine ventilation requirements.

Table 1. The test results of stability.

T (°)	potency	CH₄ standard	measure	absolute-error	differ-potency	relative-error
5	50%	0.6	0.5931	0.0256	0.0462	0.0781
		1.5	1.9843	0.0688	0.0469	0.0458
		3.0	3.8654	0.2569	0.0367	0.0665
15	60%	0.6	0.4987	0.0259	0.0843	0.0231
		1.5	3.6951	0.0274	0.0943	0.4652
		3.0	4.8856	0.3641	0.0423	0.0234
20	80%	0.6	6.3967	0.0138	0.0157	0.0458
		1.5	5.7667	0.0125	0.0254	0.0144
		3.0	8.5612	0.3321	0.0243	0.0897

5 CONCLUSION

In this paper, we introduced an overall design scheme of intelligent monitor control system for gas ventilation which has high stability. Then, we narrated the principle of the design of gas monitoring system hardware principle and software design process and the realization of the measurement correction algorithm, and gave the corresponding design results respectively; Finally, we gave the system some tests under the condition of different temperature and humidity on the system stability and accuracy of machine, and the results show that the system based on network partition structure has good anti-interference ability, at the same time, the system has good stability, can meet the conditions of methane gas in mine ventilation requirements.

ACKNOWLEDGMENT

This work is supported by the National Nature Science Foundation of Hunan province (Grant11JJ9014, 13JJ3091, 14JJ3062), A Project Supported by Scientific Research Fund of Hunan Provincial Education Department (14A047), A general project of science plan of Hunan province (2013FJ4046). A Project Supported by Scientific Research Fund of Hunan Provincial Education Department (ZZ4008).

REFERENCES

[1] Hu Qiant-ing and Zou Yin-hui. 2007. "New technology of outburst danger prediction by gas content," *Journal of China Coal Society*, 32(3): 276–280.
[2] Fu Jian-hu and Cheng Yuan-ping. 2007. "Situation of Coal and Gas Outburst in China and Control Countermeasures," *Journal of Mining & Safety Engineering*, 50–95.
[3] Huang Guang-qiu, Liu Hong-dong and Ma Liang. 2007. "Computer Simulation on Methane Gas Emitting and Overspreading and Congregating in Underground Coal Mine," *Journal of System Simulation*, 32(3): 276–280.
[4] Tian Shui-cheng, Wang-Li and Li Hong-xia. 2006. "Application of risk evaluation in coalmine gas hazard based on model of SPA," *Journal of Safety and Environment*, 6(6): 103–106.
[5] Lv Jin-duan, Chen Wen-ge and Hu Jiao. 2007. "Research and Application of NOSA Information Management System for Power Plant. Guangxi Electric Power."
[6] Wang Cong-lu, Li Shu-qing and Wu Chao. 2004. "Theory of Dissipative Structure and Mine Ventilation System. China Safety Science Journal," *J*, 6:11–13.
[7] Bhattacharjee S, Roy P and Ghosh S, et al. 2012. "Wireless sensor network-based fire detection, alarming,monitoring and prevention system for Bord-and-Pillar coal mines," *Journal of Systems and Software*, 85(3): 571–581.

Multimedia Technology IV – Farag, Yang & Jiao (Eds)
© 2015 Taylor & Francis Group, London, ISBN: 978-1-138-02794-7

Reconstruction method of channel taps in OFDM systems based on inverse

Zhitao Li

Key Laboratory of Crustal Dynamics, Institute of Crustal Dynamics, China Earthquake Administration, Beijing, P.R. China

Ke Xiao & LiJing Wang

Information Technology College, North China University of Technology, Beijing, P.R. China

ABSTRACT: In this paper, we will focus on Channel Estimation (CE) in Orthogonal Frequency-Division Multiplexing (OFDM) systems. The time-varying channels are modeled by a Basis Expansion Model (BEM). Due to the property of time varying, the frequency domain channel matrix is no longer diagonal, but approximately banded. We use a pilot-aided algorithm for estimation of rapidly varying wireless channels in OFDM systems. This algorithm performs well when the channels vary on the scale of a single OFDM symbol duration, which occurs in mobile communication scenarios such as WiMAX, WAVE, and DVB-T. We estimate Fourier coefficients of the channel taps by the pilot information and recover the BEM coefficients of the channel taps from the respective Fourier coefficients using a recently developed inverse reconstruction method. We apply different BEM models to the inverse reconstruction methods and compare their performance to find out the best channel estimation scheme in certain conditions.

Keywords: channel estimation; channel tap; OFDM

1   INTRODUCTION

1.1   *Motivation*

OFDM is a multicarrier modulation technique with several advantages, e.g., high spectral efficiency and robustness against multipath propagation and is increasingly used in high-mobility wireless communication systems, such as the mobile WiMAX, WAVE, and DVB-T. OFDM over doubly selective channels are affected by inter carrier interference (ICI), which is caused by Doppler effects and carrier frequency offset. In the case of scalable OFDM, the required bandwidth grows with the number of subcarriers. Increasing the bandwidth means higher sampling frequency, which in turn proportionally increases the number of resolvable discrete multipath. For example, Mobile WiMAX with K subcarriers typically exhibits a discrete path delay of K/8 [1]. Moreover, OFDM is a likely candidate for future aeronautical communication systems, see [2]. Some bases have been used for modeling doubly selective channels. BEM with complex exponential (CE-BEM) [7], [8], which uses a truncated Fourier series, can recover a banded frequency-domain channel matrix. Unfortunately, the CE-BEM resulting doubly selective channels are [10], [11]. BEM with discrete prolate spheroidal sequences (DPSSs) is presented in [4]. Paper [3] and [12] focus on channel estimation in extreme regimes, where the channel taps noticeably fluctuate within a single OFDM symbol

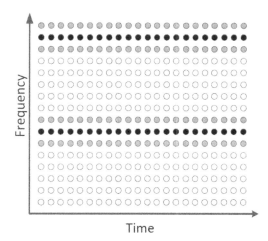

An example of FDKD pilot arrangement with K=16,L=2,D=2; 'O' represents data symbols, 'ⓞ' represents zero pilot symbols, '●' represents non-zero pilot symbols

Figure 1.   FDKD pilot arrangement.

duration. For a channel with L taps, the method presented in [3] requires O(L2) flops and memory to estimate the BEM coefficients. The method of [12] requires only O (L log L) operations and O(L) memory for the same task.

In this paper we use the inverse methods [13] to estimate the DCT-BEM, P-BEM, DPSS-BEM coefficients from the estimated Fourier coefficients and reconstruct the channel taps. The paper is organized as follows. First, we describe our OFDM transmission model, and pilot arrangement which is called FDKD-pilot for doubly selective channel. Also we introduce the method of [12] for estimation of the Fourier coefficients of channel taps. Second, we introduce the inverse methods [13] and apply different types of BEMs to the inverse method including DCT-BEM, P-BEM, DPSS-BEM. We present our simulation results in Section 4 and our conclusion in Section 5.

2   SYSTEM MODEL

2.1   *Transmitter-receiver model*

We consider a baseband single-antenna CP-OFDM system with K the Gibbs phenomenon and is not sufficiently accurate for doubly-selective channels, see [4]. The polynomial BEM (P-BEM) is presented in [9]. Definitive references on pilot-aided transmission in subcarriers. The cyclic prefix is used in every OFDM symbol. The length of cyclic prefix is Lcp. We choose LcpTs exceeds the channels maximum delay to avoid inter symbol interference (ISI). We will deal with one OFDM symbol at a time. Each subcarrier is used to transmit one symbol X[k] (k = 0, ..., K − 1) from a finite symbol constellation e.g. 4QAM. The OFDM modulator uses the inverse discrete Fourier transform (IDFT) of size K to map the frequency-domain symbols X[k] to the time-domain signal x[n]

$$x[n] = \frac{1}{\sqrt{K}} \sum_{k=0}^{K-1} X[k] e^{j2\pi \frac{nk}{K}}, n = -L_{cp}, ..., K-1 \quad (1)$$

The received signal is

$$y[n] = \sum_{l=0}^{L-1} h_l[n] x(n-l) + w[n], n = 0, ..., K-1 \quad (2)$$

CP has been removed in y[n]. w(n) denotes complex additive noise of variance N0, hl[n] is the complex channel tap with the delay l, and L is the maximum discrete-time channel length. Thus, the channels maximum delay is (L − 1)Ts. We make the worst case assumption where L = Lcp. The OFDM demodulator performs a discrete Fourier transform (DFT) of size K to gain the frequency-domain receive signal Y[k],

$$Y[k] = \frac{1}{K} \sum_{n=0}^{K-1} y[n] e^{-j2\pi \frac{nk}{K}} \quad (3)$$

Combining (2) with (3), we get

$$Y[k] = \sum_{l=0}^{L-1} (H_1 * X_1)[k] + W[k] \quad (4)$$

where * denotes the cyclic convolution of length K, and k = 0, ..., K − 1. In this expression, the Y[k], $H_1[k]$, $X_1[k]$, and W[k] respectively denote the DFT of y[n], $h_1[n]$, x[n − l] and w[n]. We can get

$$X_l[k] = e^{-j2\pi \frac{nk}{K}} X[k]$$
$$k = 0, ..., K-1$$
$$l = 0, ..., L-1 \quad (5)$$

And we can also get

$$H_l[k] = \frac{1}{\sqrt{K}} \sum_{n=0}^{K-1} h_l[n] e^{-j2\pi \frac{nk}{K}} \quad (6)$$

are the Fourier coefficients of the channel tap with delay l. We can obtain the channel taps with their D term Fourier series approximately, with a fixed positive integer D as follow

$$h_l[n] = \sum_{d=D^-}^{D^+} H_l[d] e^{j2\pi \frac{dn}{K}} \quad (7)$$

where $D^- = -\lfloor (D-1)/2 \rfloor$, $D^+ = -\lfloor D/2 \rfloor$ ($\lfloor \bullet \rfloor$ denotes the floor operation). We can know, $D^- \leq D^+$, and $D^+ - D^- = D - 1$. We set $H_l[-d] = |H_l[K-d]|$, for a negative index $-d$. $H_l[K-d]$ is defined in (5). Combining (2), (4), (6) and (7), we obtain

$$Y[k] = \sum_{d=D^-}^{D^+} X[k-d] \sum_{l=0}^{L-1} H_l[d] e^{-j2\pi \frac{l(k-d)}{K}} + \tilde{W}[k] \quad (8)$$

where $\tilde{W}[k]$ denotes the additive noise W[k] combined with the approximation error resulting from BEM modeling.

2.2   *Pilot set*

We set that I = K/L is an integer, which can be easily achieved by the choice of L. Typically, K and L are integer powers of 2. We use an FDKD pilot arrangement scheme. In each OFDM symbol, we distribute L pilot groups in one OFDM symbol and the groups are uniformly spaced with size 2D − 1. It is only possible if 2D − 1 ≤ I. The location of the first pilot subcarrier is k_0, $0 \leq k_0 \leq I - (2D - 1)$, and the pilot location is formed as follow

$$k_0 + q + iI \quad (9)$$

where $q = 0, ..., 2D - 2, i = 0, ..., L - 1$. Figure 2 is an example of FDKD arrangement. In each group, all the pilot values are zero except for the central pilot, which is a_0. Under such an arrangement, we can find

$$X[k_0 + D - 1 + iI] = a_0, i = 0, ..., L - 1 \quad (10)$$

which means only L symbols carry non-zero pilots.

By using such pilot scheme, we can protect the central pilot subcarrier from the effect of data and other pilots subcarriers so that we can use the central pilot to estimate the channel response.

2.3 Estimation of Fourier coefficients

An accurate, pilot-aided, FFT-based estimation method for the Fourier coefficients of the channel taps is presented in [12]. At the receiver end, we can estimate the Fourier coefficients from the received signal and the known pilots

$$\hat{H}_l[d] = \frac{1}{a_0\sqrt{K}} e^{j2\pi\frac{l(k_0+D-1)}{K}} \tilde{y}(d-D^-)[l] \tag{11}$$

where

$$\tilde{y}_d[l] = \frac{1}{\sqrt{L}} \tilde{Y}_d e^{-j2\pi\frac{il}{L}} \tag{12}$$

$$= a_0\sqrt{L}H_l[d+D^-]e^{-j2\pi\frac{l(k_0+D-1)}{K}} + \tilde{w}_d[l]$$
$$\tilde{Y}_d[i] = Y[k_0 + D^+ + d + il] \tag{13}$$

Reconstruction of the channel taps from the estimated Fourier coefficients corresponds to the CE-BEM [7]. However, because of the Gibbs phenomenon, the CE-BEM is not accurate for estimation of doubly selective channels.

3 INVERSE RECONSTRUCTION METHOD WITH DIFFERENT BEMS

The inverse reconstruction method [13] is to reconstruct a function as a linear combination of given basis functions from a finite number of Fourier coefficients of this function.

If we have a function f(x) defined on $[-1, 1]$, we consider the first D Fourier coefficients of f(x) are $\hat{f}(d)$

$$\hat{f}(d) = \int_{-1}^{1} e^{-jd\pi x} dx, D^- \le d \le D^+ \tag{14}$$

We approximately reconstruct the function f(x) as a linear combination of fixed $M \le D$ basis functions $\phi_0, \ldots, \phi_{M-1}$

$$f \approx f_M(t) = \sum_{m=0}^{M-1} a_m \phi_m(t) \tag{15}$$

We need to find a_m which minimizes the norm of the difference between the D lowest Fourier coefficients of f and f_M

$$\left(\sum_{D^- \le d \le D^+} \left| \hat{f}(d) - \hat{f}_M(d) \right|^2 \right)^{\frac{1}{2}} \tag{16}$$

where $\hat{f}_M(d)$ is the Kth Fourier coefficient of f_m. The minimization problem in the expression (16) is converted to the following over-determined least squares problem

$$\min_{a \in C^M} \|\mathbf{Pa} - \hat{\mathbf{f}}\| \tag{17}$$

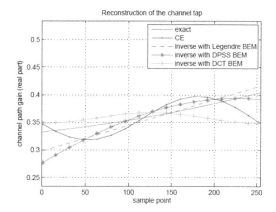

Figure 2. Reconstruction of the channel tap (real part).

where $a = [a_0, \ldots, a_{M-1}]^T, \hat{f} = [\hat{f}(|D^-|), \ldots, \hat{f}(D^+)]^T$, and P is $D \times M$ the matrix whose entries are the respective Fourier coefficients of the basis functions

$$P_{dm} = \hat{\phi}_m(d) \tag{18}$$

$m = 0, \ldots, M - 1, d = D^-, \ldots, D^+$. If P has full rank, then (16) has a unique solution given by

$$\mathbf{a} = \mathbf{P}^+\hat{\mathbf{f}} \tag{19}$$

where P^+ is the MooreCPenrose pseudoinverse of the matrix P.

We note that the inverse reconstruction method can be used to compute BEM coefficients of a function from its Fourier coefficients. This method can be applied to arbitrary BEM if only the basis functions are available. Next we will introduce some basis functions.

3.1 BEM with the Legendre Polynomials

Legendre Polynomials basis functions I

$$p_m[n] = p_m(nT_s)$$
$$p_m(t) = p_m\left(\frac{2t}{KT_s} - 1\right), 0 \le t \le KT \tag{20}$$

we can obtain

$$P_n(x) = \frac{1}{2^n n!} \frac{d^n}{dx^n}\left[(x^2 - 1)^n\right] \tag{21}$$

3.2 BEM with the discrete prolate spheroidal sequences

The discrete prolate spheroidal sequences are optimum waveforms in many communication and signal processing applications because they comprise the most spectral efficient set of orthogonal sequences possible.

Figure 2 shows the quality of the channel taps reconstruction using BEM with different bases, where the

Table 1. Transmission simulation paramerers.

Number of subcarriers (K)	256
Intercarrier spacing (f_s)	10.9 (kHz)
Bandwidth ($B = Kf_s$)	2.8 (MHz)
Sampling time ($T_s = 1/B$)	0.357 (us)
Carrier frequency (f_c)	5.8 (GHz)
Constellation	4QAM

Table 2. Channel simulation parameters.

Max. path delay	11.4 (us)
Max. Doppler shift	21.2%f_s
Average path gain	−2 (dB)
Fading	Rayleigh
Doppler spectrum	Jakes
E_b/N_0	0–30 (dB)

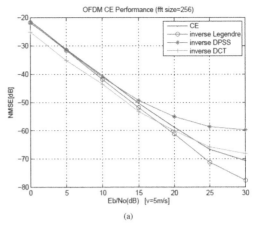

(a)

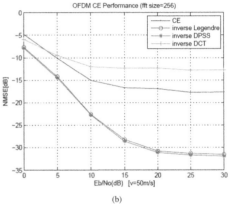

(b)

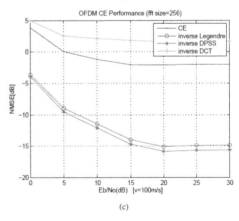

(c)

Figure 3. NMSE versus SNR for fixed receiver velocities.

real part of a typical channel tap is plotted. In Figure 2, we use a three-term Fourier series and a truncated Legendre series, Discrete Cosine series and discrete prolate spheroidal sequences. Although the BEM coefficients are computed from the Fourier coefficients, from Figure 2, we can observe the improvement gained by the BEM reconstruction methods compared to the CE method.

4 COMPUTER SIMULATIONS

4.1 Simulation parameters

We simulate a OFDM system with parameters as Table 1 show. The comb pilots are added according to Section 2.2. The channel we use is Rayleigh fading channel with parameters in Table 2.

4.2 Results of simulation

Figure 3 shows NMSE decreases as the SNR increases for all the methods. From Figure 3(a), where the receiver velocity is 5 m/s and the Doppler shift is low, the performance of these methods are similar especially in low SNR. The inverse method with DCT-BEM performs little better than other ones with low SNR while the inverse method with Legendre-BEM performs best with high SNR.

As the receiver velocity increase to 50 m/s in Figure 3(b), we can obviously observe the worse performance compared to Figure 3(a) which is caused by Doppler frequency shift. From Figure 3(b), we can find the robustness of inverse methods with Legendre-BEM and DPSS-BEM.

While inverse methods with Legendre-BEM and DPSSBEM perform similarly in Figure 3(b) because Legendre sequences is a special case of DPSS, we can find obvious difference between these two in Figure 3(c) where the receiver velocity is 100 m/s and the Doppler frequency shift is very large.

5 CONCLUSION

We firstly estimate the Fourier coefficients of the channel taps by the pilot information and then recover the BEM coefficients of the channel taps from their respective Fourier coefficients using a recently developed inverse reconstruction method. We observe in our numerical simulations that the DCT-BEM works well in conditions where receiver is very low ($v < 20$ m/s,

$f_d < 3.55\% f_s$), Legendre-BEM and DPSS-BEM perform better as receiver velocity increases. DPSS-BEMs superiority is more obvious at higher velocity ($v > 40\,\text{m/s}, f_d > 7.09\% f_s$).

ACKNOWLEDGMENT

This work was supported by Scientific Research Common Program of Beijing Municipal Commission of Education under grant No. 201310009002 and the Funding Project for Academic Human Resources Development in Institutions of Higher Learning Under the Jurisdiction of Beijing Municipality: PHR(IHLB).

REFERENCES

[1] Draft IEEE Standard for Local and Metropolitan Area Networks Part 16: Air Interface for Fixed and Mobile Broadband Wireless Access Systems, IEEE Draft Standard 802.16e/D7, 2005.

[2] E. Haas, "Aeronautical channel modeling," IEEE Trans. Veh. Technol., vol. 51, no. 2, pp. 254–264, Mar. 2002.

[3] Z. Tang, R. C. Cannizzaro, G. Leus, and P. Banelli, "Pilot-assisted timevarying channel estimation for OFDM systems," IEEE Trans. Signal Process., vol. 55, no. 5, pp. 2226–2238, May 2007.

[4] T. Zemen and C. F. Mecklenbrauker, "Time-variant channel estimation using discrete prolate spheroidal sequences," IEEE Trans. Signal Process., vol. 53, no. 9, pp. 3597–3607, Sep. 2005.

[5] Z. Tang and G. Leus, "Pilot schemes for timevarying channel estimation in OFDM systems," in Proc. IEEE Workshop Signal Process. Advances Wireless Commun., June 2007, pp. 1–5.

[6] C. Shin, J. G. Andrews, and E. J. Powers, "An efficient design of doubly selective channel estimation for OFDM systems," IEEE Trans. Wireless Commun., vol. 6, no. 10, pp. 3790–3802, Oct. 2007.

[7] H. A. Cirpan and M. K. Tsatsanis, "Maximum likelihood blind channel estimation in the presence of Doppler shifts," IEEE Trans. Signal Process., vol. 47, no. 6, pp. 1559–1569, June 1999.

[8] M. Guillaud and D. T. M. Slock, "Channel modeling and associated intercarrier interference equalization for OFDM systems with high Doppler spread," in Proc. IEEE Int. Conf. Acoustics, Speech, Signal Process., Apr. 2003, vol. 4, pp. 237–240.

[9] D. K. Borah and B. T. Hart, "Frequency-selective fading channel estimation with a polynomial time-varying channel model," IEEE Trans. Commun., vol. 47, no. 6, pp. 862–873, June 1999.

[10] P. Kannu and P. Schniter, "MSE-optimal training for linear timevarying channels," in Proc. IEEE Int. Conf. Acoustics, Speech, Signal Process., vol. 3, Mar. 2005.

[11] "Design and analysis of MMSE pilot-aided cyclic-prefixed block transmission for doubly selective channels," IEEE Trans. Signal Process., vol. 56, no. 3, pp. 1148–1160, Mar. 2008.

[12] T. Hrycak, S. Das, G. Matz, and H. Feichtinger, "Practical estimation of rapidly varying channels for OFDM systems," IEEE Trans. Commun., vol. 59, no. 11, pp. 3040–3048, 2011.

[13] T. Hrycak, S. Das, G. Matz, "Inverse Methods for Reconstruction of Channel Taps in OFDM Systems," IEEE Trans. Signal Process., vol. 60, no. 5, pp. 2666–2671, 2012.

Multimedia Technology IV – Farag, Yang & Jiao (Eds)
© 2015 Taylor & Francis Group, London, ISBN: 978-1-138-02794-7

A clustering algorithm for data aggregation in spatial-correlated sensor networks

Ri Hong, Zhihuang Su & Hongju Cheng
College of Mathematics and Computer Science, Fuzhou University, Fuzhou, China

ABSTRACT: In this paper, a Data De-noising Clustering (DDC) algorithm for data aggregation is proposed. By considering the noisy data of sensor nodes, the algorithm introduces a Weighted Moving Average (WMA) and improves it, then apply it to data de-nosing. Moreover, we utilize the spatial correlation between nodes to divide nodes into different clusters and present a correlation degree for cluster head selection so that the data of the cluster head have a low distortion on their correlated data while the cluster head is used to represent the cluster and send data to the sink. The experiments result show that the resulting achieved by DDC can provide sensing data with higher accuracy and less energy consumption compared with other algorithms.

Keywords: Sensor networks; clustering; spatial correlation; data aggregation

1   INTRODUCTION

A wireless sensor network is a wireless network consisting of distributed devices using sensor nodes to cooperatively monitor environmental conditions [1]. In recent years, cluster-based approaches for data aggregation have attracted wide attention [2–3], which only the cluster head transmits its data to sink node. In addition, for sensor nodes are usually deployed densely, nodes nearby have similar data. Cheng H et al. in [4] proposed a correlation function of the spatial distance and decay factor for the service-oriented wireless sensor network. Algorithm in [5] proposed a function of the spatial distance between two sensor nodes to depict the spatial correlation between them. Shakya et al. in [6] also presented a spatial correlation model based on the overlapping degree of two nodes' sensing areas. However, it's difficult to pinpoint the locations of sensors nodes and the sensor nodes' sensing areas have no exact relationship with nodes' data. Since sensor networks are generally deployed in harsh environment, the sensor node's data are noisy. Apparently, it's irrational to divide sensor nodes into clusters according to their noise data.

In this paper, we introduce a de-noising algorithm WMA [7] and apply it to data de-noising after improving WMA. Meanwhile, we propose a clustering algorithm to make the nodes in the same cluster have high correlation and the nodes in the different clusters have low correlation. In every cluster, we select a node as the cluster head that has the highest correlation with its cluster members to represent the cluster and send data to the sink node.

The remainder of this paper is organized as follows: Section 2 discusses related works and Section 3 covers the system model. Section 4 presents the DDC clustering algorithm by describing each part of the algorithm in detail, including the construction of clusters, merging clusters, and cluster heads selection. Simulation results and performance evaluation are provided in Section 5. Finally, Section 6 provides conclusions and directions for future work.

2   NETWORK MODEL AND RELATED CONCEPTS

A wireless sensor network consists of a set of static sensor nodes $V = \{s_1, s_2, \ldots, s_n\}$, each node has the same communication radius R. Without loss of generality, node can be represented by i or s_i. Y_i or $Y_{i,t}$ represents the node's noise data at time t, the node's data without noise at time t are expressed by X_i or $X_{i,t}$.

Definition 1: ε-Neighbor Set. The neighbor set of node i is N_i. $N_i = \{j | d\,(i, j) \le R, i \ne j, j \in V\}$, where d (i, j) represents the Euclidean distance between node i and node j. R is the communication radius. For any $j \in N_i$, if $|x_j - x_i| \le \varepsilon$, then j belongs to the ε-Neighbor Set, denoted as $j \in N(i)$.

Definition 2: Independent node. Assume the real data of node i are x_i. For all node $j \in N_i$, if $|x_j - x_i| > \varepsilon$, then the node i is called the independent node, otherwise, i is called the non-independent node.

In our paper, we use the radio model presented in [8]. The energy consumption to transmit a k bit packet to a distance d is calculated by $E_t(k, d) = E^*_{elec}k + E^*_{amp}k^*d^2$ and to receive that packet is calculated by $E_r(k) = E^*_{elec}k$, where E_{elec} is the energy dissipation, E_{amp} is the transmit amplifier.

3 WMA ALGORITHM AND ITS IMPROVEMENT

3.1 Basic knowledge

Assume the raw data of node i at time t is $y_{i,t}$, real data are $x_{i,t}$, then noise $E_{i,t} = y_{i,t} - x_{i,t}$ and $E_{i,t} \sim N(0, \sigma_{i,t}^2)$, where $\sigma_{i,t}^2$ represents the noise variance of node i at time t. $n_{i,t}$ expresses that node i collect $n_{i,t}$ data, which are nearest to t. Given an error range $[-e, +e]$ and $n_{i,t}$, if the average of noise from $n_{i,t}$ sample data, then the confidence $c_{i,t}$ of real data are replaced by $\bar{y}$, where $\bar{y} = \frac{1}{n_{i,t}} \sum_{j=t-n_{i,t}+1}^{t} y_{i,t}$.

3.2 De-noising method

In order to de-noise $y_{i,t}$, WMA method get forecast range $[l_{i,t}, u_{i,t}]$ by Kalman Filter (see [7]). If $y_{i,t}$ located in the forecast range, we assume that $y_{i,t}$ can reach the confidence C and don't need to de-noise, otherwise, we need to improve the confidence of data by local testing and neighbor testing [7]. However, WMA always let local testing and neighboring testing do at the same time while the number of neighbor nodes is more relatively. When the number of neighbor nodes meets the amount of samples required by confidence, Local testing wastes energy actually. So we can measure the amount of neighbor nodes before de-noising, then take different methods according to the number of neighbor nodes: (1) if $n >= n_l$, then select n_l nodes randomly from neighbor nodes and do neighbor testing; (2) if $n < n_l$, then only do local testing. Local testing and neighbor testing are calculated as follows:

1. Local Testing

$$\bar{x}_i^t = \frac{w_{i,t-n} \overline{y_{i,t-n}} + ... + w_{i,t} \overline{y_{i,t}}}{h}, \tag{1}$$

where $h = w_{i,t-n} + \cdots + w_{i,t}$, $w_{i,t} = (w_{max} - 1)c_{i,t}/C + 1$, w_{max} is the default maximum weight.

2. Neighbor Testing

$$\bar{x}_i^t = \frac{\sum_{j \in N_i} b_{j,t} w_{j,t} \overline{y_{j,t}}}{m}, \tag{2}$$

where $m = \sum_{j \in N_i} b_{j,t} w_{j,t}$, $b_{j,t} = \begin{cases} 1 & \text{if } x_{j,t} \in [x_{i,t} - e, x_{i,t} + e] \\ 0 & \text{otherwise} \end{cases}$.

4 DDC CLUSTERING ALGORITHM

We know that the data of sensor nodes are always with noise, while traditional clustering methods often take these raw data into account and will bring deviation. Therefore, the basic idea of the DDC algorithm is that, we use the improved WMA algorithm for data de-noising before clustering, and let non-independent nodes which have high correlation with the nodes in their ε-Neighbor set construct clusters. The DDC algorithm consists of four procedures: Data De-noising (DD) procedure, the Local Cluster Construction (LCC) procedure, Merging Cluster (MC) procedure and Cluster Head Selection (CHS) procedure.

4.1 DD procedure

Owing to the data with noise, we conduct data de-noising for improving the performance of clustering in this procedure. Assume at time t, the raw data of node i are y_i, the data after de-noising are x_i. On the process of data de-noising, for a given confidence C, we calculate the number of nodes, denoted by n_l, according to the section 3, and get forecast range $[l_{i,t}, u_{i,t}]$ by Kalman Filter (see [7]). For each node i, i judges itself whether its raw data locates in the prediction range. If it is, then node i doesn't need to data de-noising. Otherwise, node i need to calculate the amount of the neighbor nodes $|N_i|$, if $|N_i| > n_l$, then select n_l neighbor nodes from N_i to do neighbor testing, otherwise, choose n_l recent historical data of node i for local testing. The following pseudocode is the DD procedure.

Data De-noising Procedure
Input: V, ε, C, Y.
Output: X', ID.

1. Each node judges whether need to de-noise according to the predict area $[l_{i,t}, u_{i,t}]$;
2. For each node i who need to de-noise, calculate $|N_i|$ and n_l on the premise of convince C. If $|N_i| >= n_l$, calculate x_i' by formula (1), else calculate x_i' by formula (2).
3. For each node $i \in V$, calculate its ε-Neighbor set by definition 1. If the ε-Neighbor set of node j is $\varnothing$, then node j is called the independent node and join the set ID.

4.2 LCC procedure

It's noted that non-independent nodes have high correlation with their ε-Neighbor nodes, non-independent nodes can construct local clusters and put their ε-Neighbor nodes in the cluster. Obviously, the larger the number of ε-Neighbor nodes of a sensor node is, the better representative this sensor node is. Therefore, in the each node's range of radius, we take the greedy strategy that give priority to non-independent nodes with more ε-Neighbor nodes to construct local clusters. The details are described in the following.

LCC Procedure
Input: $N(i)$, Non-independent nodes.
Output: ClusterSet = {Cluster$(i)|i \in V$}.

1. ClusterSet = $\varnothing$, for each non-independent node i, sort $\{i\} \cup \{N(i)\}$ by descending the amount of ε-Neighbor nodes;
2. For each non-independent node i;
3. If the node $j \in \{i\} \cup \{N(i)\}$ and all its ε-Neighbor nodes have been received an INDICATOR message, remove node j and goto 3, otherwise j broadcasts an INDICATOR message embedded

with its identity to all its ε-neighbors, then remove j from $\{i\} \cup \{N(i)\}$;

4. If the set $\{i\} \cup \{N(i)\}! = \emptyset$, goto 3, otherwise, goto 2.

5. End For

6. For each $j: j \in V$, if j receives an INDICATOR message from node i then it sends a JOIN message embedded with its identity to i.

7. For each $i: i \in V$, if i receives a JOIN message from node j ($j \in N_i$), it sends back an ACK message to j and Cluster$(i) = $Cluster$(i) \cup \{j\}$.

8. ClusterSet $= \{$Cluster$(i),\ i \in V$ and Independent $(i) = 0\}$.

4.3 MC procedure

In the LCC procedure, we get a series of local clusters, there may exist that some node is in different clusters. So we need to merge some clusters that have same node into one. Obviously, we need to follow the idea that the clusters have high correlation between nodes after merging. If we merge clusters merely, some clusters will contain too many nodes. For two clusters before merging, if the distance between the nodes in two clusters is much far, the nodes' data will have low correlation between the nodes in the cluster after merging, resulting in poor performance. Therefore, we follow two principles: (1) When merging the clusters into one, we should ensure that the max hop count of nodes in the cluster does not exceed a certain threshold m. (2) We prefer a small cluster when merging the clusters into one. The principle 1 guarantees that the correlation between the nodes within the same cluster is not low. The principle 2 ensures the number of nodes in each cluster is uniformity that prevents some clusters from containing too many nodes so as to spatial-correlation between the nodes in the clusters will be weak. The following pseudocode is the DD procedure.

MC Procedure
Input: m, ClusterSet.
Output: Cluster $= \{$Cluster$(i), i \in V\}$, Cluster heads.

1. $Flag = 0$; $N = |V|$
2. While !($Flag$)
3. For each $j: j \in$ Cluster(i), if node j only within the Cluster(i), then N—. If $N = 0$, then goto 6, else goto 3; If node j within the other cluster at the same time, goto 4, if node j within the more than one clusters, calculate the number of clusters denoted as h, then goto 5.
4. If the hop count between nodes in two clusters is less than m, merge two clusters into one, delete two clusters from ClusterSet and join the new cluster into ClusterSet, otherwise, goto 3.
5. Sort the clusters descending by the number of nodes which contain node j. and merge with the Cluster(i) in sequence. When all clusters have been merged, goto 3.
6. End While

4.4 CHS procedure

After the clusters are constructed, we need to select the cluster heads which are s used to represent the cluster. Therefore, whether a node has the highest correlation with other cluster members is a measure of the standard. Here, we give the definition of the correlation degree.

Definition 3: Correlation degree. Assume the data of node i within the cluster k are x_i. Then, the correlation degree between node i and other nodes within the cluster k is defined as $sim(i) = \frac{1}{n}\sum_{j=1, j \in cluster(k)}^{n}(x_j - x_i)^2$, where n is the amount of nodes within the cluster k. By definition, the larger the correlation degree of node i is, the smaller deviations between node i and other nodes are.

4.5 Data collection

When clustering is completed, the cluster heads and independent nodes need to send data to the sink node. In this paper, we use shortest path tree constructed by Dijkstra algorithm for data collection. Sensor nodes only route data except cluster heads and independent nodes.

5 SIMULATION RESULTS

In this section, we verify the actual performance of DDC algorithm through Matlab and compare our DDC algorithm with KCC algorithm [9] and α-LS algorithm [10].

5.1 The default setting of experimental parameters

The default parameters of the experiment are set as follows: the network topology is randomly generated by placing 300 nodes in a fixed region of size $100\,\mathrm{m} \times 100\,\mathrm{m}$. Communication radius r is 20 m, the data threshold ε is set as 0.8, k is set as 3, the energy dissipation E_{elec} is equal to 50 nJ/bit, and the transmit amplifier E_{amp} is equal to 100 pJ/bit/m^2. In this paper, we use the model [11] to produce data. The model use h dummy events $\{I_1, I_2, I_3, \ldots, I_h\}$ whose initial reading are randomly selected from [20, 30] to calculate the raw data of node j by $x_j = \sum_{i=1}^{h}\left(\frac{\sqrt{dist(j, I_i)}}{\sum_{k=1}^{h}\sqrt{dist(j, I_i)}}\right) * I_i$, where $dist(j, I_i)$ is the Euclidean distance between node j and event I_i. The raw data of node j at the time t are calculated by $y_j(t) = x_j(t) + E_{i,t}$.

5.2 Clustering performance index

In this paper, we use the definition of the average relative error proposed by Fei et al. in [12] to measure the representative of the cluster heads within a cluster. That is $\overline{E_g} = \frac{1}{k}\sum_{i=1}^{k}\sum_{j=1}^{n}e_j$, where $e_j = |Y_0 - Y_j|/Y_j$, e_j is the relative error between Y_0 and Y_j, n is the number of nodes with the cluster of j, k is the number of clusters.

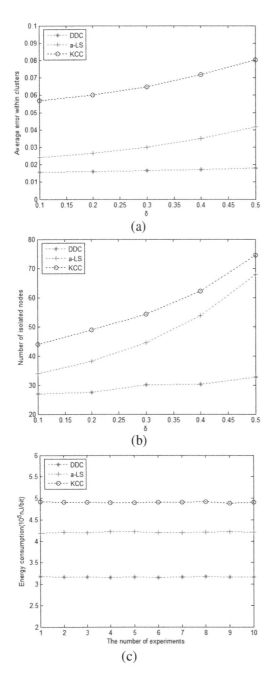

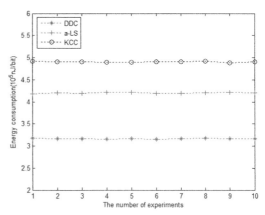

Figure 2. Energy comparison with different methods.

algorithm grow more smoothly than other two algorithms and the value of the average relative error of the DDC method is the smallest among the methods evaluated in our experiment. That is because our algorithm perform data de-noising before clustering, therefore, DDC algorithm is less affected by noise.

Obviously, the number of independent nodes and clusters is also an important indicator of the performance of clusters. As shown in Fig. 1(b) and Fig. 1(c), we can obtain that the sum of the independent nodes and clusters will increase with the addition of δ, but our algorithm grow more flat. That is because the other two algorithms will misclassify part of nodes as independent nodes affected by noise.

5.4 *Comparison of energy*

In this section, we compare the energy consumption of three algorithms. For fairness, we let the other two algorithms collect data by method proposed in section 4. The result as shown in Fig. 2, we can obtain that our algorithm is better than the other two algorithms.

6 CONCLUSION

In this paper, we propose a clustering algorithm for data aggregation based on the noise data. Meanwhile, we utilize the spatial correlation between nodes to divide nodes that have low correlation into different clusters and nodes that have high correlation into the same cluster. Experiments show that the performance of our clustering is better than KCC and α-LS algorithms. We will consider the temporal correlation and energy balance in the future.

ACKNOWLEDGMENT

This work is supported by the National Science Foundation of China under Grand No. 61370210 and the Development Foundation of Educational Committee of Fujian Province under Grand No. 2012JA12027.

Figure 1. Clustering performance for different methods.

5.3 *Performance comparison of clusters*

In this section, we compare the average relative error within the clusters of our algorithm with other algorithms. We consider the impact of the parameter δ on the average relative error of clusters. The value of the parameter δ is set from 0.1 to 0.5. As shown in Fig. 1(a), we can see that, when δ increases, the average error in the clusters of three algorithms increase, but our

REFERENCES

[1] Romer, Kay, and Friedemann Mattern. "The design space of wireless sensor networks." IEEE Wireless Communications, vol. 11, no. 6, pp. 54–61, 2004

[2] Chen H, Mineno H, Obashi Y, et al. "Adaptive data aggregation for clustered wireless sensor networks." Ubiquitous Intelligence and Computing. Springer Berlin Heidelberg, pp. 475–484, 2007

[3] Yoon S, Shahabi C. "The Clustered AGgregation (CAG) technique leveraging spatial and temporal correlations in wireless sensor networks." ACM Transactions on Sensor Networks (TOSN), vol. 3, 2007

[4] Cheng H, Guo R, Su Z, et al. "Service-Oriented Node Scheduling Schemes with Energy Efficiency in Wireless Sensor Networks." International Journal of Distributed Sensor Networks vol. 2014, 2014

[5] Vuran M C, Akan Ö B, Akyildiz I F. "Spatio-temporal correlation: theory and applications for wireless sensor networks." Computer Networks, vol. 45, no. 3, pp. 245–259, 2004

[6] Shakya R K, Singh Y N, Verma N K. "A novel spatial correlation model for wireless sensor network applications" In: Wireless and Optical Communications Networks (WOCN), 2012 Ninth International Conference on. IEEE, pp. 1–6, 2012

[7] Zhuang Y, Chen L, Wang X S, et al. "A weighted moving average-based approach for cleaning sensor data." In: Distributed Computing Systems, 2007. ICDCS'07. 27th International Conference on.IEEE, vol 38, 2007

[8] Heinzelman W.R., Chandrakasan A. and Balakrishnan H. "Energy efficient communication protocol for wireless microsensor networks," in 33rd Annual Hawaii International Conference on System Sciences, USA, 2000

[9] Yuan J, Chen H. The optimized clustering technique based on spatial-correlation in wireless sensor networks. In: Information, Computing and Telecommunication, 2009. YC-ICT'09. IEEE Youth Conference on. IEEE, pp. 411–414, 2009

[10] Ma Y, Guo Y, Tian X, et al. "Distributed clustering-based aggregation algorithm for spatial correlated sensor networks." Sensors Journal, IEEE

[11] Hung C, Peng W, Lee W. "Energy-aware set-covering approaches for approximate data collection in wireless sensor networks." Knowledge and Data Engineering, IEEE vol. 11, pp. 1993–2007, 2012

[12] Yuan F, Zhan Y, Wang Y. "Data Density Correlation Degree Clustering Method for Data Aggregation in WSN." IEEE Sensors Journal, vol. 2013, 2014

Multimedia Technology IV – Farag, Yang & Jiao (Eds)
© *2015 Taylor & Francis Group, London, ISBN: 978-1-138-02794-7*

Intelligent analysis of passenger flow state in integrated transport hub

Ying Hong Li, Zhao Li, Xiaoqing Hao & Hongfang Tian
North China University of Technology, Beijing, China

ABSTRACT: An integrated transport hub undertakes hundreds of thousands of traffic flow every day. In order to meet the need of directing, operation, management and pre-arranged planning, it's important to make a judgment of the running state of passenger flow inside the hub. This paper has proposed a new indicator to judge the running state of passenger flow—passenger flow congestion index. We have set up a linear weighted evaluation model of the state of passenger flow inside the hinge based on the characteristics which are able to reflect the condition of passenger flow, such as density of passenger, passenger flow rate per width, etc. We also got the passenger flow congestion index from this model. Through the simulation and analysis of the state of passenger flow of a actual transport hub, the passenger flow congestion index used in the linear weighted evaluation model proposed in the paper can reflect the actual state of passenger flow and be corresponding with the real condition well. The evaluation criteria of the passenger flow state in the transport hub proposed in the paper is concise and clear, which might also be a valuable reference to the travelers and transport hub managers.

Keywords: traffic engineering; passenger flow congestion index; linear weighted method; running state of passenger flow; integrated transport hub

1 INTRODUCTION

In China, it's one of the main strategies to promote the intelligent transportation level of vigorously developing public transportation. In our country, the transport hub undertakes hundreds of thousands of daily traffic flow, forming the high density of passenger flow, great mobility and numbers of intertwined conflicts. In the confined space, it's quite easy to cause passengers being crowded and stranded, which increases the possibility of stampede accidents. Therefore, it's of particular importance to make an evaluation of the state of passenger flow in the hub to grasp the information of passenger flow timely and accurately, realize real-time information dissemination and dynamic induction, organize warning of large passenger flow accordingly, solve the problem of congestion of passenger flow, and guarantee passengers' safety.

This paper proposed a pedestrian flow congestion index to evaluate the state of pedestrian flow in a traffic hub, and set up a linear weighted evaluation model to obtain the pedestrian flow congestion index based on pedestrian density and flow rate per unit width.

2 PEDESTRIAN FLOW CONGESTION INDEX

Pedestrian flow congestion index proposed in this paper is a relative number that can reflect quantified hub operation status, quantified congestion level and difference in certain time and area, and a relative number that simplifies the complex phenomenon [7].

In essence, it can present the congestion level, trend and rule in a long period of time, and is mainly used to evaluate the operation status of the traffic hub.

Pedestrian operation status in a traffic hub includes 5 kinds of states:

(1) Unimpeded: there's enough space for pedestrians to choose walking speed freely and to provide pedestrians the opportunity to catch up with and surpass others.
(2) Less unimpeded: pedestrians can choose walking speed freely, but are under slight restriction on catching up with and surpassing others, and there will be conflicts when reverse flow and lateral pass exist.
(3) Lightly congested: pedestrians can't choose walking speed freely, and are under restriction on catching up with and surpassing others. There will be significant conflicts when reverse flow and lateral pass happen.
(4) Moderately congested: walking speed and the possibility of catching up with and surpassing others are limited, the speed of forward is low, and it's very difficult to walk reversely and pass laterally.
(5) Severely congested: walking speed is severely restricted, conflict with others is inevitably and frequently. It's almost impossible to walk reversely and pass laterally. Pedestrian flow is uninterrupted and unstable.

Aiming at the above five status, a kind of quantized data–pedestrian flow congestion index range from [0,10] is utilized to describe the current pedestrian flow status in traffic hub, and is divided into 5 degrees, with 0–2, 2–4, 4–6, 6–8, 8–10 corresponding to "unimpeded", "basically unimpeded", "lightly congested", "moderately congested", "severely congested" respectively. Ease of Use.

3 EVALUATION INDEX OF PEDESTRIAN FLOW OPERATION STATUS

Referring "Pedestrian Traffic" which targets China's national conditions, pedestrian density and unit width flow rate these two indexes can comprehensively represent the pedestrian flow rate in front walk, stairs, entrance and exit among masses of index; while for queue area and waiting area, pedestrian density is sufficient to reflect the current pedestrian flow status. This paper has conducted the analysis in detail, modeling, evaluation and simulation, taking flow rate status in stair passageway as example. Methods of analysis and evaluation of flow rate status in other area of the traffic hub are same, which won't be analyzed repeatedly.

Pedestrian density is defined as the average pedestrians per unit area in road or queuing area, and usually expressed as the ratio of pedestrian number to area. Calculation formula is shown as:

$$K = \frac{Q}{L*W} \tag{1}$$

where K represents the pedestrian density, the dimension of which is Pedestrians/m². $L*W$ represents the area of region Y, L is the length of the region, W is the width of the region. Q represents the pedestrian number in region Y.

Flow rate per unit width indicates the average number of passing pedestrians per effective width in pedestrian path. Calculation formula is shown below:

$$P = \frac{Q}{T*W} \tag{2}$$

where P represents the flow rate per unit width, the dimension of which is Pedestrians/m/min. W represents the width of the region. Q represents the number of pedestrians passing through region Y.

In pedestrian simulation module of VISSIM, we setup up different input quantity in different region, and input quantity is increased as the time elapses. The simulation time are 12600 s and the cycle are 180 s, and 630 groups of pedestrian data were collected, namely the pedestrian density and flow rate per unit width.

When pedestrian density is about 2.5, flow rate per unit width reaches the summit. The derived relation between pedestrian density and flow rate per unit width is shown in Fig. 1.

From Fig. 1, we can infer that for a fixed pedestrian density, if is relatively small, then it indicates that the movement of the pedestrian flow is slow, individual pedestrian or external interference have great influence on the pedestrian flow, and the response time to

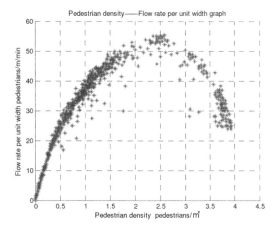

Figure 1. Relation between pedestrian density and pedestrian flow.

deal with interference is short. On the other hand if is relatively large, then it indicates that the movement of the pedestrian flow is smooth, an individual pedestrian has a high consistency with the pedestrian flow, and individual pedestrian or external interference have less influence on the pedestrian flow, but the response time to deal with interference is long, which might lead to stagnation of the pedestrian flow.

Pedestrian density and flow rate per unit width are selected to represent the smooth degree, stability degree and balance degree of distribution.

All the indexes of the pedestrian flow in the traffic hub mainly refer to the "pedestrian traffic" that can reflect the condition of China, and also synthesize the "Transit Capacity and Quality of Service Manual–2nd Ed" which was written by The Transportation Research Board of America. The pedestrian flow congestion index is defined by pedestrian density, flow rate per unit width of stair passageway and threshold of service level of pedestrian path, as shown in table 1.

4 A LINEAR WEIGHTED EVALUATION MODEL OF THE RUNNING STATE OF PASSENGER FLOW

Linear weighted computational model of the passenger flow congestion index:

$$LOS = W_1 X_1 + W_2 X_2 \tag{3}$$

where LOS, W_i and X_i are the passenger flow congestion index, the weight of each index and the dimensionless value of each index respectively.

According to Table 1, the computation of dimensionless value of each index is shown as:

$$X_1 = \begin{cases} 2*(K-K_{Border})/(K_{A\max}-K_{Border}) & (K_{Border} \quad K_{A\max}) \\ 2*(K-K_{A\max})/(K_{B\max}-K_{A\max})+2 & (K_{A\max} \quad K_{B\max}) \\ 2*(K-K_{B\max})/(K_{C\max}-K_{B\max})+4 & (K_{B\max} \quad K_{C\max}) \\ 2*(K-K_{C\max})/(K_{D\max}-K_{C\max})+6 & (K_{C\max} \quad K_{D\max}) \\ 2*(K-K_{D\max})/(K_{E\max}-K_{D\max})+8 & (K_{D\max} \quad K_{E\max}) \end{cases} \tag{4}$$

Table 1. Levels of service for stairways, walkways, queuing and waiting areas.

| Pedestrian flow congestion index | Service level of pedestrian path | | Service level of stair passageway | | Queue and waiting area |
	Pedestrian density Pedestrians/m²	Flow rate per unit width Pedestrians/ m/min	Pedestrian density Pedestrians/m²	Flow rate per unit width Pedestrians/ m/min	Pedestrian density Pedestrians/m²
A (0–2)	≤0.7	≤23	≤0.4	≤33	≤1.11
B (2–4)	0.7–1.1	23–33	0.4–0.7	33–49	1.11–1.43
C (4–6)	1.1–1.4	33–43	0.7–1.1	49–66	1.43–3.33
D (6–8)	1.4–2.5	43–56	1.1–2.0	66–82	3.33–5.00
E (8–10)	>2.5	Variable	>2.0	Variable	>5.00

$$X_2 = \begin{cases} 2*(P-P_{Border})/(P_{A\max}-P_{Border}) & (P_{Border} \quad P_{A\max}) \\ 2*(P-P_{A\max})/(P_{B\max}-P_{A\max})+2 & (P_{A\max} \quad P_{B\max}) \\ 2*(P-P_{B\max})/(P_{C\max}-P_{B\max})+4 & (P_{B\max} \quad P_{C\max}) \\ 2*(P-P_{C\max})/(P_{D\max}-P_{C\max})+6 & (P_{C\max} \quad P_{D\max}) \\ 2*(P_{E\max}-P)/P_{E\max}+8 & (P_{D\max} \quad P_{E\max}) \end{cases} \quad (5)$$

It is essential to determine the weight coefficient of index of linear weighted evaluation method. Subjective weighting methods are based on experience and can be affected by experience easily, which have certain limitations, subjective uncertainty and fuzziness of knowledge. In order to avoid man-made interference to the determination of weight coefficient of index, this paper adopts an objective weighting method—the entropy method, of which the computational steps are shown as below:

1) Establish the sample space matrix and the standard matrix of hierarchical properties

n samples $x_1, x_2, \ldots, x_n$ in evaluation system and evaluation index $u_1, u_2, \ldots, u_n$ in each sample are selected. So the $n \times m$ matrix made up of them can be obtained as:

$$X = \begin{bmatrix} x_{11} & x_{12} & \cdots & x_{1m} \\ x_{21} & x_{22} & \cdots & x_{2m} \\ \vdots & \vdots & & \vdots \\ x_{n1} & x_{n2} & \cdots & x_{nm} \end{bmatrix} \quad (6)$$

2) Normalize matrix

Transform the data of samples into the dimensionless ones and carry out the standardized treatment to the original data. The normalization formula is shown as:

$$r_{ij} = \frac{x_{ij} - \min_j \{x_{ij}\}}{\max_j \{x_{ij}\} - \min_j \{x_{ij}\}} \quad (7)$$

where $\max_j \{x_{ij}\}$ and $\min_j \{x_{ij}\}$ are maximum and minimum of the same index in different samples respectively.

Establish the normalized judgment matrix consists of samples and evaluation indexes, which is shown as below:

$$R = \begin{bmatrix} r_{11} & r_{12} & \cdots & r_{1m} \\ r_{21} & r_{22} & \cdots & r_{2m} \\ \vdots & \vdots & & \vdots \\ r_{n1} & r_{n2} & \cdots & r_{nm} \end{bmatrix} \quad (8)$$

3) Compute entropy of each index

f_{ij} is the proportion of the j_{th} index in the i_{th} sample:

$$f_{ij} = \frac{1+r_{ij}}{\sum_{i=1}^{n}(1+r_{ij})} \quad (9)$$

So the entropy of the j_{th} index is:

$$H_j = -\frac{1}{\ln n}(\sum_{i=1}^{n} f_{ij} \ln f_{ij}) \quad (10)$$

where $i = 1, 2, \ldots, n$; $j = 1, 2, \ldots, m$; H_j is the entropy of the j_{th} index.

4) Compute the entropy weight of each index:

$$W = (\omega_j)_{1 \times m}, \quad \omega_j = \frac{1-H_j}{m - \sum_{j=1}^{m} H_j} \quad (11)$$

Where $\sum_{j=1}^{m} \omega_j = 1$.

5 EVALUATION METHOD AND SIMULATION

This paper utilized the actual collection of pedestrian traffic data and the VISSIM simulating collection of pedestrian traffic data to evaluate the state of passenger flow based on the linear weighted evaluation method.

1) Evaluate the state of passenger flow by simulation based on the actual collection of pedestrian traffic data in the hub.

The state of passengers going downstairs for transferring in Fuxingmen Subway Station in Beijing is as the research subject. And the pedestrian traffic data in every minute is collected by HDV which was installed

45

Table 2. Passenger flow data and linear weighted evaluation results of passenger flow state of Fuxingmen subway station.

| | Passenger flow data | | Result of linear weighted evaluation | | |
Time	Average density	Passenger flow pper width	Passenger flow congestion index	State of passenger flow	Reference of manual
9:21	0.48	15.33	0.00	unimpeded	A
9:24	0.71	22.07	1.91	unimpeded	A
9:27	0.82	24.53	2.50	less unimpeded	B
9:30	0.57	16.93	0.38	unimpeded	A
9:33	0.39	13.40	0.00	unimpeded	A
9:36	0.46	15.20	0.00	unimpeded	A
9:39	0.22	8.33	0.00	unimpeded	A
9:42	0.63	19.33	1.07	unimpeded	A
9:45	0.50	16.93	0.06	unimpeded	A
9:48	0.71	22.40	1.97	unimpeded	A
9:51	0.58	18.40	0.55	unimpeded	A
9:54	0.41	12.73	0.00	unimpeded	A
9:57	0.63	18.27	1.03	unimpeded	A
10:00	0.52	15.53	0.00	unimpeded	A
10:03	0.38	11.40	0.00	unimpeded	A
10:06	0.72	22.40	1.99	unimpeded	A
10:09	0.20	9.07	0.00	unimpeded	A

on the stairs. This experiment is based on the pedestrian traffic data in the 50 minutes between 9:20 a.m. and 10:10 a.m. in January 18th, 2013.

The model in which the density of passenger and passenger flow rate per width in staircase being the inputs and the passenger flow congestion index being the output is built in Simulink/Matlab. The pedestrian traffic data in Fuxingmen Subway Station in Beijing and the evaluation results are shown in Table 2.

Counting the data in staircase from 09:21 to 10:48, there are 16 groups of data in the 48 minutes in pedestrian videos, it is known from the evaluation results of the actual traffic flow data based on the linear weighted algorithm that there are 15 unimpeded states and 1 less unimpeded state of passenger flow over the whole process.

The linear weighted evaluation results of passenger flow state in Fuxingmen subway station in Beijing is shown as Figure 2.

For example, in 09:27–09:30, the density of passenger is 0.82 per/m^2, the passenger flow rate per width is 24.53 per/m/min, and the passenger flow congestion is 2.5 with the congestion level being B (i.e. the state of passenger flow is less unimpeded). Comparing with the video, it can be acquired that the number of passing passengers in the 3 minutes is 368, while the average pedestrian occupancy space is 1.21. Pedestrian's speed can be free to choose, the interaction between passengers is relatively little, overtake other pedestrians at random is restricted, and the state of passenger flow is less clear.

2) Simulation and evaluation of the state of passenger flow based on VISSIM.

Through collecting the pedestrian traffic data generalized by VISSIM (Sampling period is 3 minutes) in

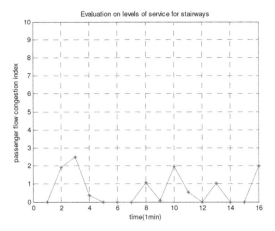

Figure 2. Linear weighted evaluation results of passenger flow state in Fuxingmen subway station.

some area of the station platform of metro line 1 and line 2, the density of passenger and average flow rate per width can be calculated as the inputs. After that, utilizing the linear weighted evaluation model of the running state of passenger flow proposed in this article, the corresponding passenger flow congestion index is acquired through simulation in MATLAB. Due to the limitation of thesis, 40 groups of simulation data are selected at random from a large number of experimental data, which is shown in Table 3 (part of the data).

The linear weighted evaluation results of passenger flow state using VISSIM pedestrian simulation is shown as figure 3.

Table 3. Linear weighted evaluation of passenger flow state using VISSIM pedestrian simulation.

| | Passenger flow data | | Evaluation results | | |
| | | | | | |
Time	Average density	Passenger flow per width	Passenger flow congestion index	State of passenger flow	Reference of manual
20	1.53	47.37	6.29	medium congestion	D
21	1.56	46.11	6.29	medium congestion	D
22	1.60	47.97	6.41	medium congestion	D
23	1.62	46.31	6.39	medium congestion	D
24	1.70	49.86	6.62	medium congestion	D
25	1.93	51.66	7.02	medium congestion	D
26	2.20	53.76	7.49	medium congestion	D
27	2.35	52.99	7.68	medium congestion	D
28	2.42	55.03	7.85	medium congestion	D
29	2.47	54.82	7.92	medium congestion	D
30	2.50	54.23	7.94	medium congestion	D
31	2.56	54.83	8.07	severe congestion	E
32	2.60	53.80	8.12	severe congestion	E
33	2.77	52.48	8.31	severe congestion	E
34	2.84	49.31	8.41	severe congestion	E
35	3.00	50.23	8.57	severe congestion	E

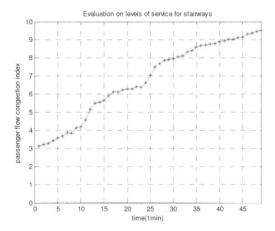

Figure 3. Linear weighted evaluation results of passenger flow state using VISSIM pedestrian simulation.

For the data collected through video in a limited time cannot describe all the states of passenger flow, this article carries out a linear weighted evaluation of the whole passenger flow state using VISSIM. It is to be sure that the input which is the number of passengers per minute should be set to increase successively in VISSIM simulation, which aims to make the simulating data more reasonable and persuasive. It can be seen from the Table 3 that 5 integrated state of passenger flow in staircase were described and evaluated. For instance, during the 23rd 3 minutes, the density of passenger was 1.62 per/m^2, the passenger flow rate per width was 46.31 per/m/min, and the passenger flow congestion was 6.39 with the congestion level being D (i.e. the state of passenger flow was medium congestion). At this time, all pedestrian's speed was limited which was slow, pauses occurred frequently, and the reverse flow caused serious conflicts. It can be seen from the Table 3 that persistent serious congestion had been occurred in staircase since 9:31. At this time pedestrians' speed was limited seriously, the conflicts between them could not be avoided, too many pauses may cause traffic standstill and mass, even some dangerous situation such as stampede. Management should take early warning mechanism in time with evacuation and guide to alleviate the congestion, ensuring the efficient operation of the hub and pedestrians' safety. Other states of passenger flow are not expatiated here which are presented in the table above.

Through the actual collecting data by video and simulating analyses by VISSIM, and evaluating the state of passenger flow using the linear weighted evaluation method, the results go with the evaluation level of "Transport Capacity and Quality of service Manual".

6 CONCLUSION

This article proposes an evaluation index of passenger flow state in hub based on synthetically linear weighted evaluation model, while it simulates and evaluates the passenger flow state by the running state in staircase in railway hub. The passenger congestion index proposed in this article reflects the running state of passenger flow of each service facilities in hub. On a macro level, it can suggest the current state of each facility in hub (congestion or less congestion) simply and directly with making quantitative descriptions about the congestion level. Also, managers and the public can know the congestion level, trend and regularity of running state of passenger flow in each service facility in hub through the passenger flow congestion index. It provides convenience to induce passenger flow whether to travel and selecting the trip mode, which also provides useful reference for hub management and passengers.

ACKNOWLEDGMENT

This paper is supported by "personnel training project of subject construction-national special demand-intelligent control technique for urban roadway (PXM2014-014212-000053)", "The capital city smooth traffic synergy innovation center (PXM2014_014212_000020)".

REFERENCES

Hoffer, R. and D. Dean. 1996. "Geomatics at Colorado State University," presented at the 6th Forest Service Remote Sensing Applications Conference, April 29–May 3, 1996.

Ikegami, R., D. G. Wilson, J. R. Anderson, and G. J. Julien. 1990. "Active Vibration Control Using NiTiNOL and Piezoelectric Ceramics," J. Intell. Matls. Sys. & Struct., 20(2):189–206.

Inman, D.J. 1998. "Smart Structures Solutions to Vibration Problems," in International Conference on Noise and Vibration Engineering, C. W. Jefford, K. L. Reinhart, and L. S. Shield, eds. Amsterdam: Elsevier, pp. 79–83.

Margarit, K. L. and F. Y. Sanford. March 1993. "Basic Technology of Intelligent Systems," Fourth Progress Report, Department of Smart Materials, Virginia Polytechnic Institute and State University, Blacksburg.

Mitsiti, M. 1996. Wavelet Toolbox, For Use with MALAB. The Math Works, Inc., pp. 111–117.

Multimedia Technology IV – Farag, Yang & Jiao (Eds)
© 2015 Taylor & Francis Group, London, ISBN: 978-1-138-02794-7

Industrial insight and core competence of using intelligent logistics system in Taiwan distribution business

Yu-Bing Wang & Ching-Wei Ho
Department of Marketing, Feng Chia University, Seatwen, Taichung, Taiwan

ABSTRACT: This study aimed to determine the factors of concern about adopting an intelligent logistics system into current company core competencies. The biggest challenge of global distribution business demands its logistics professionals never stop developing new skills and enhancing existing ones. This paper investigated the role the RFID system including intelligent solutions in Taiwan distribution business. Since the trend of consumers purchase behaviors is getting more "Online", which includes e-business and the m-business (mobile device business), how an intelligent logistics system can be accepted, implied as the core competencies and adapted by distribution industry are crucial. The growing complexity of logistics which heavily depends on the levels of visibility, responsiveness and accurate shipment and tracking information; for this reason, distribution business today has evolved into a high-technology industry, and the intelligent logistics system can really help. The paper utilized the concept of Taiwan distribution business and to have industrial insight right before develop and design a smart logistics solution. According to the research results, all those hypotheses are positively affecting the RFID usage intention, and finally, managerial implications and opportunities for future research were discussed.

Keywords: Intelligent Logistics system; RFID; Core competencies

1 INTRODUCTION

One RFID consumer survey [1], the RFID Consumer Buzz – Special Report, found that 28 percent of the 7,000 U.S. consumers surveyed were aware of RFID, and that most of them could describe the technology to others [2]. In Taiwan, government departments, the medical and pharmaceutical sectors, and private businesses have followed the RFID trend to take advantage of this new technology to enhance their standard operation processes [3]. These companies are attracted by potential benefits that RFID offers, such as improved supply chain visibility, reduced labor costs, and enhanced process efficiency. This research study investigated the RFID technology adoption and how RFID has been used in Taiwan's logistics industry.

2 FUNDAMENTAL THEORIES

The Intelligent Logistics System-Radio Frequency Identification (RFID) technology is defined as a "wireless data collection technology that uses electronic tags for storing data and recognizing data" [4], and then uses radio waves to automatically identify any objects that have RFID tags. The benefits of adopting an RFID system can be vary. [5] mentioned in Frontline solutions magazine, Michael Dominy, a senior analyst for the Yankee Group, stated "if you

have world-class, leading capabilities in your logistics functions, the amount of benefit you're going to get out of RFID will be very small and incremental". A core competence [16] is a company's competitive advantage or capability within the marketplace. Core competencies typically comprise ability or expertise in a specific area, in this paper is the Taiwan distribution business. Core competencies' criteria according to [16], which allow business to reach a wide range of markets and could make significant contribution to the perceived customer benefits. The distribution business can be a major beneficiary of the RFID system because the intelligent logistics system dramatically enhances supply chain management, inventory management, and labor cost reduction. Chris Murphy, Senior Executive Editor of Information Week Web, said that "Today, without RFID, we don't know what's in the back room and what's in the front of customers' hands" [6]. In addition, a white paper published by the New Times Company pointed out that retailers could expect great inventory savings and labor cost reduction from the adoption of radio frequency identification (RFID) technology. Furthermore, numerous researchers [7], [8] and consulting firms have reported benefits in several areas, including inventory management, human resources management, and stock and shelf management. Based on research theories, the author re-organized Davis theory assists with Ajzen's [9] theory into the framework as the main structure of

Table 1. Constructs and their measurement items.

Construct	Measurement items	Loading	α	CR	AVE
Perceived Usefulness (PU)	I consider that using RFID will raise the efficiency of Operations Management	0.801	0.742	0.795	0.565
	I consider that using RFID will provide more real time information for decision making	0.698			
	I consider that using RFID system will reduce the cost of Operations Management	0.753			
Perceived Ease of Use (PEU)	I consider it is easy to use RFID system	0.793	0.914	0.916	0.732
	I consider it is easy to learn how to use RFID system	0.921			
	I consider instructions for the use of RFID is clear and easy to understand	0.886			
	I consider it is not difficult to integrate RFID into company's current work flow	0.815			
Normative Belief (NB)	I consider the adoption of RFID is coincident with the value and belief of company	0.808	0.917	0.923	0.800
	I consider that using RFID is compatible with Operations Management	0.956			
	I consider that using RFID is in accord with the demand of Operations Management	0.912			
Motivation to Comply (MC)	I consider company's management will support the project of adopting RFID	0.906	0.914	0.917	0.787
	I consider company's management will distribute appropriate resource and budget for the project of adopting RFID	0.872			
	I consider that company's management has already sensed the efficiency that RFID could make	0.883			
Attitude (AT)	I consider our customers can easily buy other similar products or services	0.929	0.925	0.926	0.807
	I consider if we do not adopt RFID, we can easily lose our customers	0.910			
	I consider if we adopt RFID, we will become more competitive in our industry	0.855			
Subjective Norm (SN)	I consider the cost of establishment and maintenance of RFID is too expensive for our company	0.923	0.941	0.942	0.844
	I consider the investment of time and money for training	0.945			

this paper. The structure of this paper aims to utilize the technology acceptance model and theory of planned behavior to examine the criteria of business core competencies. TAM model in this paper evaluates RFID users' perceived benefits in the context of Taiwan distribution business. Furthermore, studies indicated the TPB theory in the context of RFID technology in logistics system is widely used as the core in variety of markets. The author used Davis' [10] technology acceptance concept in combination with Ajzen's theory of planned behavior. She used the two elements affecting the degree of subjective norms-normative belief and motivation to comply, with the TAM's external variables perceived usefulness and perceived ease of use to predict users' attitudes; and combined those variables to construct her research model. By utilizing those variables as the independent variables, this study sought to determine how users accept an implemented technology system by understanding their attitude and behavioral intention toward the technology. Therefore, the study proposes the following assumptions:

H1: The Perceived Usefulness (PU) of RFID system positively affects the Attitude (AT) of RFID adoption in the distribution business in Taiwan.

H2: The Perceived Ease of Use (PEU) for RFID system positively affects the Attitude (AT) of RFID adoption in the distribution business in Taiwan.

H3: The Normative Belief (NB) of RFID system positively affects the Subject Norm (SN) of RFID adoption in the distribution business in Taiwan.

H4: The Motivation to comply (MC) toward using RFID system positively affects the Subjective Norm (SN) of RFID adoption in the distribution business of Taiwan.

H5: The attitude (AT) of using RFID system positively affects the usage intention (UI) of RFID adoption in the distribution business in Taiwan.

H6: The Subjective Norm (SN) of using RFID system positively affects the usage intention (UI) of RFID adoption in the distribution business in Taiwan.

3 RESEARCH METHOD AND STASTICAL RESULT

The research population for this study was the companies list under the distribution-related category from

Table 2. Results of the Hypothesis and the Practical Path.

Hypothesis	Expected Result	Standard Regression coefficient		t-Value
PU->AT	H1	+	0.197	3.454***
PEU->AT	H2	+	0.346	2.764***
NB->SN	H3	+	0.274	2.279***
MC->SN	H4	+	0.308	3.442***
AT->UI	H5	+	0.268	2.711***
SN->UI	H6	+	0.204	4.712***

Fit Index	Threshold	Goodness-of-fit	Source
χ^2/df	<0.3	1.946	[12]
GFI	>0.8	0.832	[13]
AGFI	>0.7	0.782	Chou (2005)
NFI	>0.8	0.877	[15]
CFI	>0.9	0.935	[15]
RMSEA	<0.08	0.076	[12]

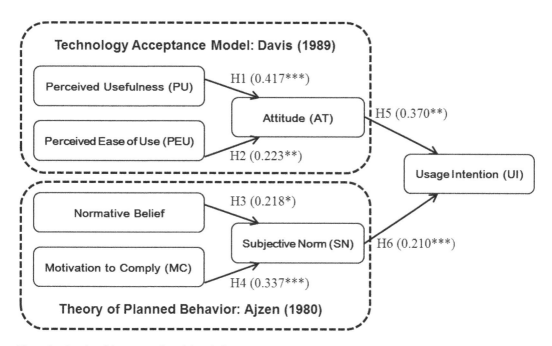

Figure 1. Results of the structural model analysis.

104 Job bank, Taiwan's largest job bank consultant company in June, 2014, and a total of 1913 companies resisted. The author used snowball sampling method within one month period and came out 176 fully completed questionnaires for the data analysis. The Structural equation modeling (SEM) of AMOs had been used to examine the hypotheses and analyze the data. Table 1 shows that the composite reliability (CR) of the latent variable was higher than 0.7, which indicated that all measures had a good reliability [11]. Moreover, the completely standardized factor loadings all reached the level of significance. All the latent variables had a CR above 0.70 and an average variance extracted (AVE) above 0.5.

4 CONCLUSION

Base on the research questions and the findings from the data analysis, the perceived of usefulness, motivation to comply toward adopting RFID system have the most significant predictive power on potential users' attitudes, subjective norm and intentions of adopting RFID system. The results of this study have demonstrated the value and the feasibility of RFID adoption for Taiwan's distribution business. The technology acceptance model (TAM) of [10] in this study also revealed the importance of the attitudes toward RFID adoption and usage intension in terms of potential users' perceptions of attributes of RFID system. The result matched [16]'s core competence concept that provides a significant contribution to the perceived users benefits and subjective norms to access into a wide variety of markets, and proves the evidences of the adoption of intelligent logistics system can been distribution business's competitive advantages. In the context of RFID adoption, from the aspect of the theory of planned behavior (TPB), the normative beliefs in Taiwan' logistics industry toward RFID system adoption were proven to be higher than the perception of motivation to comply toward RFID systems. Furthermore, attitudes toward RFID systems and the subjective norm are also powerful positive impact factors for RFID adoption.

REFERENCES

[1] Chu, Wai Lang, 2006. RFID production to increase 25-fold by 2010, Labtechnologist.com. Retrieved November

[2] Roberti, M. (2005). EPC Reduces Out-of-Stocks at Wal-Mart. *RFID Journal*. Retrieved March 19, 2009, from http://www.rfidjournal.com/article/view/1927/1

[3] Sabbaghi, A., & Vaidyanathan, G. 2008. Effectiveness Supply Chain Management: Strategic values and Challenges. *Journal of Theoretical and Applied Electronic Commerce Research*, 3(2), 71–81.

[4] Expert Barcode & RFID, Inc., 2009 Retrieved July 20, 2010 from http://www.expertbarcode.com/autotech.htm

[5] Kevan, T. 2004. "Calculating RFID's benefits: retailers can expect significant inventory and labor savings, but manufacturers face slim returns. However, the benefits aren't always measured in dollars". *Frontline Solutions*. Retrieved July 23, 2010, from http://findarticles.com/p/articles/mi_m0DIS/is_1_5/ai_112563027/

[6] Murphy, C. 2005. Real-World RFID: Wal-Mart, Gillette, And Others Share What They're Learning. *Information Week Retrieved*. August 08, 2009, from http://www.informationweek.com/news/mobility/RFID/showArticle.jhtml?articl eID=163700955

[7] Lahiri, Sandip. 2006. *RFID Sourcebook*. New Jersey: International Business Machines Press.

[8] Palmer, M. 2004. Principles of Effective RFID Data Management. Enterprise Systems.

[9] Ajzen, I. and M. Fishbein. 1980 Understanding Attitudes and Predicting Social Behavior. Englewood Cliffs, NJ: Prentice-Hall.

[10] Davis, F.D.1989. "Perceived Usefulness, Perceived Ease of Use, and User Acceptance of Information Technology," MIS Quarterly, 13:3, pp. 318–339.

[11] Bagozzi, R. P., and Yi, Y. 1998. "On the Evaluation of Structural Equation Models," *Journal of the Academy of Marketing Science*, 16(1): 76–94.

[12] Hair J.F., Anderson R.E., Tatham R.L., Black, W.C., 1992. Multivariate Data Analysis with Readings, 3rd edn. Macmillan, New York.

[13] Seyal M, Ro T, and Rafal R. Increased sensitivity to ipsilateral cutaneous stimuli following transcranial magnetic stimulation of the parietal lobe. Annals of Neurology, 38: 264–267, 1995.

[14] Chiou H. "Quantitative research and statistical analysis", Wu-Nan Book Inc, 1995.

[15] Bentler, P.M. and Bonnet, D.C. 1980, "Significance Tests and Goodness of Fit in the Analysis of Covariance Structures," Psychological Bulletin, 88(3), 588–606.

[16] Prahalad, C.K. and Hamel, G. (1990) "The core competence of the corporation", Harvard Business Review (v. 68, no. 3) pp. 79.

Multimedia Technology IV – Farag, Yang & Jiao (Eds)
© *2015 Taylor & Francis Group, London, ISBN: 978-1-138-02794-7*

Fast and robust varying affine stitching by proper feature point selection

Ling Rong
*Test Laboratory of Security and Crime Prevention and Information Security Products and Systems
of the Third Institute of the Ministry of Public Security,
The Third Research Institute of Ministry of Public Security, MSTL, Shanghai, China*

Yuli Sun
China Certification Center for Security and Protection, Beijing, China

Ci Wang
East China Normal University, Shanghai, China

ABSTRACT: Image stitching algorithms are often proposed to connect the planar scenes from parallel free camera at the same physical location through parametric transforms. Occlusion inevitably exists and makes the parametric transform abruptly changed, if the cameras are installed on different locations. To solve this problem, smoothly varying affine stitching (SVAS) field has been proposed, but its performance and execution speed may be worse along with the increasing number of feature points. Based on the stability of its cost function, two rules are designed in this paper to do feature point selection, with consideration of their even distribution and similarity. Under the designed criterions, stitching performance is significantly improved.

Keywords: Image stitching algorithms, smoothly varying affine stitching (SVAS), stability

1 INTRODUCTION

Image stitching is to combine some frames into a single seamless scene with a larger view field. It wraps pixels from one coordinate frame to another through certain transform, and does not produce perceptual discontinuity on the non-overlapping image areas. To do stitching, pixels in the overlapping areas must be registered, and then warping field of the pixels in non-overlapping area is estimated from the known registered field.

Traditional registration algorithms initiate features from one frame, and find their corresponding features in the other frame. Transform matrix of every pixel is calculated for precise image stitching. In Harris and CRF algorithms, corner features are used in image registration, which are very sensitive to the noise. Smith et al proposed a simple and robust algorithm named SUSAN (Smallest Uni-value Segment Assimilating Nucleus). Being a local feature, SIFT (Scale-invariant feature transform) algorithm is introduced by Lowe [1]–[3], which is robust against scaling, rotation and shifting. Mikolajczyk [4] tests the performances of different local features and descriptions, and proves that SIFT is the best one. Recently, SURF (Speeded Up Robust Features) is popular in its execution speed, but its precision is still worse than SIFT feature.

Traditional stitching requires the frames captured at the same location and is very sensitive to the disparity.

Referred to optical flow, Liu et al [5] get SIFT features for each pixel, and calculate optical flow based on SIFTs. This algorithm is weak if SIFT feature points are dense and similar. Dornaika et al [6], [7] combine registration with 3D reconstruction, and get some improvements at the cost of heavy computation and memory requirement. Recently, SVASF has been proposed by Lin [8]. It first gets global affine transform by traditional registration algorithm, and then the cost function is designed to calculate the actual offset for each pixel, referred to CPD (Coherent point drift) algorithm.

Registration by SVAS is difficult if SIFTs are dense and share similar feature descriptors. Hereinafter, we sample the feature point in the dense area to improve stitching performance. The computational cost of SVAS is greatly reduced if the unimportant SIFTs are omitted by the proposed scheme. In this paper, we introduce new interpolation scheme for calculating the affine parameter for general pixels from its neighbor SIFT points, and verify its rationality through theoretical analysis.

2 BACKGROUND

Referred with affine over-parameterized optical flow algorithm, Lin et al [10] utilize motion coherence framework [11], [12] to fit in the affine stitching field to form SVASF. The key of SVASF is the cost function construction as

$$E(A) = -\sum_{j=1}^{N} \log\left(\left(\sum_{i=1}^{M} g(t_{oj} - b_i, \sigma_i)\right) + 2\kappa\pi\sigma_i^2\right) + \lambda\psi(A) \quad (1)$$

$$\psi(A) = \left(\min_{\upsilon'(\omega)}\left(\int \frac{\left|\upsilon'(\omega)\right|^2}{g'(\omega)}\right)\right) \quad (2)$$

Regularization term $\psi(A)$ is to refine affine parameter A to make stitching field $\upsilon()$ smoothest, where $g(z,\sigma) = e^{-\frac{\|z\|^2}{2\sigma^2}}$, $g'(\omega)$ and $\upsilon'(\omega)$ are the Fourier Transform of $g()$ and $v()$ respectively. M and N are the feature number in the first and second frames; t_{oj} is a column vector, where the first two entries of t_{oj} are the image coordinates of the SIFT point in the second frame, i.e. target frame, and the remaining entries are SIFT feature descriptors. A is the transform matrix with 6 affine parameters. b_i is the stitched feature point, i.e. feature vector b_{oj} is transformed by affine A. κ and λ are the constants to control the strength of the uniform function and to form single cost function.

Under the constraint (2), EM formulation is employed to get its minimum solution, which is the offset of A as ΔA. As for each pixel, their refined offset $\upsilon(z_{2\times1})$ from the global affine transform A is given as

$$W_{M\times6} = [w_1,...,w_M]^T = G^+\Delta A \quad (3)$$

$$\upsilon(z_{2\times1}) = \sum_{i=1}^{M} w_i g(z - [b_{oi(1)}, b_{oi(2)}], \gamma) \quad (4)$$

$$G(i,j) = g(b_{oi(1:2)} - b_{oj(1:2)}, \gamma) \quad (5)$$

where G is a $M \times M$ symmetric matrix, G^+ is the Moore-Penrose inverse transform of G, and w_i is i-th row of W.

SVASF does not pursue the exactly SIFT feature points matched and its stitching field is not rigid to balance between the feature description differences and the smoothness of the stitching field. For non-SIFT pixel, the affine parameter is interpolated from the known SIFT points under the smoothness constraints of Gaussian function.

SVASF scheme is established on SIFT points, whose coordinates are non-integer. In [8], Lin et al try to use a sparse set of corner features (associated with SIFT descriptor) to reduce the computation. Different from SIFT, corner feature is detected on image resolution, and its coordinates are integers. Their combination will definitely involve additional distortion if these two features are forced to be aligned.

The computational cost of SVASF is exponentially increasing with the number of feature points. An image is taken as an example, which has 671,913 feature points. It requires 58.63 s to do each loop computation by EM algorithm on Intel Core i3-2100 CPU @ 3.10 GHZ, 2.0 GB memory. Furthermore, solution of

(2) is difficult to converge if the feature points are dense and similar, which may be oscillated during EM processing.

3 PROPOSED METHOD

3.1 *Theoretical foundation*

We reiterate SVASF by CPD [9] for simplify as

$$(diag(P \cdot 1)G + \lambda I)W = PX - diag(P \cdot 1)Y_0 \quad (6)$$

where X, Y_0 are the vectors to be matched, P is a matrix related with X and Y_0, 1 is a column vector whose elements are 1s, W is the intermediate value and G is symmetric and positive matrix. λI is the regularization term to avoid $diag(P \cdot 1)G$ being ill-posed. We use the condition number $Cond(A)$ to describe the stability of the equation $Ax = b$, where $x = W$ $A = (diag(P \cdot 1)G + \lambda I)$ and $b = PX - diag(P \cdot 1)Y_0$. If $Cond(A)$ is large, small perturbation on b will introduce large distortion in W estimate. We further observe P, whose element is given as

$$p_{ij} = \frac{e^{-\frac{1}{2}\left\|\frac{b_i - t_j}{\sigma}\right\|^2}}{\sum_{i=1}^{M} e^{-\frac{1}{2}\left\|\frac{b_i - t_j}{\sigma}\right\|^2} + \Delta} \quad (7)$$

where Δ is an regularization term with small value. We define an intermediate matrix $D = diag(P \cdot 1)$, which is a diagonal matrix as

$$D = \begin{pmatrix} \lambda_1 & & 0 \\ & \ddots & \\ 0 & & \lambda_m \end{pmatrix} \quad (8)$$

where $\lambda_i, i \leq M$ is its diagonal elements.

In $diag(P \cdot 1)G$, P measures the similarity of the description vectors in the first and second frames and G reflects the distance of the SIFT feature points. Because P is full rank, λI is integrated into G as

$$G' = G + \lambda'I \quad (9)$$

From the definition of condition number K[13], we get

$$K(DG') = \left\|DG'\right\|\left\|(DG')^{-1}\right\| \quad (10)$$

We further study the relationship of K(DG'), K(D) and K(G') as

$$K(DG') \leq K(D)K(G') \quad (11)$$

Above equation gives the upper bound of K(DG'), i.e. K(D)K(G'), hence that K(DG') can be ameliorated through reducing K(D) and K(G') respectively.

54

3.2 *How to improve stitching performance*

The corresponding feature points will have significantly different description vectors if original and target frames are captured with disparity. The solution accuracy and convergence speed are greatly influenced if these points are involved in calculation. Therefore, we must first delete these points even if they can be exactly matched, which will produce $K(D)$ with large value. In (5), the rows of G will be similar if two feature points are closed in their coordinates. Therefore, the distribution of feature points is desired to be evenly distributed in frames with certain distance. A $M \times N$ matrix $E_{M \times N}$ is introduced to describe the transform matrix from the reference frame and its target frames, and its elements is given as

$$e_{ij} = \left\| z_{reference'(i)} - z_{t \, arg \, et(j)} \right\| \tag{12}$$

where $z_{t \, arg \, et(j)}$ is the j-th feature point coordinate in the target frame, and $z_{reference'(i)}$ is new coordinate of the i-th feature points in the reference frame, wrapped by global affine transform a_{global}. It is heuristic that the feature points in the overlapped areas are easily matched, and their corresponding e_{ij} s are smaller than that on the non-overlapped areas. By setting proper threshold T, we filter out the efficient feature points in the overlapped area, and discard the useless ones, for example in occlusion and non-overlapping areas.

The overlapped area is further divided into some blocks with same dimension, for example $n \times n$, and we find the feature points with the maximum measurement q

$$q = e^{-\frac{c^2}{2}} \times e^{-\frac{l^2}{2}} \tag{13}$$

where c is the Euclid distance of the feature points in the reference frame mapped into the target frame by a_{global}, to its corresponding points in the target frame. l is their feature description difference. Grid processing and maximum q selection can improve $K(G')$ and $K(D)$ respectively, and their efficiency will be demonstrated in the simulation part.

Sparse sampling improves the robustness of (1), but it also increases the nondeterminacy in determining the stitching field for the other pixels. In Gaussian smoothness model, only Euclid distance is considered to determine the affine parameter of pixels by global surface fitting. Registration filed is smooth on objects, rather than on scene. Therefore, content similarity is taken into consideration during stitching field interpolation. Then, Nonlocal means filter is revised as

$$\upsilon(z_{(i)2\times1}) = \sum_{j \in S} \frac{1}{Z(i)} e^{-\frac{\left\| des_{z_{(i)2\times1}} - des_{z_{(j)2\times1}} \right\|^2}{h^2}} e^{-\frac{\left\| z_{(i)2\times1} - z_{(j)2\times1} \right\|^2}{h^2}} \upsilon(z_{(j)2\times1}) \tag{14}$$

$$Z(i) = \sum_{j \in S} e^{-\frac{\left\| des_{z_{(i)2\times1}} - des_{z_{(j)2\times1}} \right\|^2}{h^2}} e^{-\frac{\left\| z_{(i)2\times1} - z_{(j)2\times1} \right\|^2}{h^2}} \tag{15}$$

where $\upsilon(z_{(i)2\times1})$ is the affine parameter to be determined at the coordinator $z_{(i)2\times1}$, $des_{z_{(i)2\times1}}$ is its description vector. It is a 2-dimensional vector with the corresponding pixel's gray and gradient values. S is the nearest 4-points of $z_{(i)2\times1}$, $e^{-\frac{\left\| des_{z_{(i)2\times1}} - des_{z_{(j)2\times1}} \right\|^2}{h^2}}$ reflects the similarity of the processed pixel and the referred feature points, and $e^{-\frac{\left\| z_{(i)2\times1} - z_{(j)2\times1} \right\|^2}{h^2}}$ is their distance similarity.

Affine parameter does not always align with the gird, so that serration will appear around straight-line after wrapping, if integer operation is used. In this paper, we revise nonlocal means filter to interpolate the pixels on grids as

$$newimage(i, j) = \sum_{(m,n) \in S} \frac{1}{Z_{(i,j)}} e^{-\frac{((m-i)^2 + (n-j)^2)}{2\sigma^2}} I_{(m',n')} \tag{16}$$

$$Z_{(i,j)} = \sum_{(m,n) \in S} e^{-\frac{((m-i)^2 + (n-j)^2)}{2\sigma^2}} \tag{17}$$

where (i, j) is the pixel index of the stitching image, (m, n) is the pixel index in its neighbor window S, i.e. $[-1, 1] \times [-1, 1]$ area. The pixel on this location is wrapped from the pixel (m', n') in reference frame by the affine transform, so its value just equals to that in the reference frame as $I_{(m',n')}$.

4 SIMULATION PART

In this part, numerical analysis and some simulations are used to examine the performance of the proposed scheme. In numerical analysis, the upper bound of the condition number is set as the criterion for evaluating the stability of the stitching, and its relationship with feature point selection is studied. As for simulation, we take some couples of frames from the real world, and do stitching to examine the naturalness, speed and robustness of the stitching.

We use SIFT as the feature description, and utilize CPD to construct the cost function (1). During the calculation, parameter σ_t is gradually reduced with iterations until convergence. We begin with $\sigma_t = 1$ and update it as $\sigma_t = \alpha \sigma_t$ until 0.1. The key parameters λ, κ, γ, α are set to 10,0.5,1,0.97 respectively.

In these experiments, we examine subjective quality of the stitching image and its execution speed in implementation. Compared with original SVASF, image quality is enhanced because its solution space is more compact, the acceleration as well as the better convergence come from the less feature points involved in the cost function.

The frames to be stitched in Fig. 1 are captured at different location with larger disparity, and their illuminations are varied, hence that the left side and right side have slightly different brightness. We do not correct this difference for better observing the boundaries of the stitched frames. There is obvious discontinuity

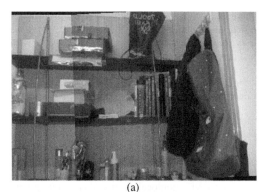

(a)

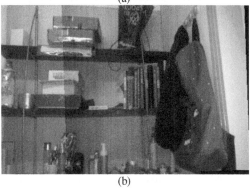

(b)

Figure 1. Stitching result of the couple of images. (a) SVASF; (b) Proposed algorithm.

(a)

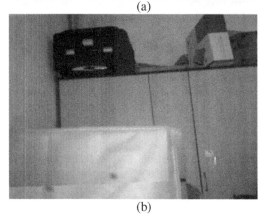

(b)

Figure 2. Stitching result of the first couple of images in Fig. 1, (a) SVASF; (b) proposed algorithm.

in the overlapping area of Fig. 1(a), and deviation of the stitching field reaches 4 pixels in the worst case, such as the second floor of bookshelf. SVASF produces saw-tooth on the straight-line in the overlapping area, which heavily damages the subjective quality of stitching. Compared with SVASF algorithm, the proposed algorithm is significantly better in these areas.

Besides Fig. 1, we further take another example here to prove the robustness of the proposed algorithm, as shown in Fig. 2. The amelioration is still obvious in Fig. 2. The cabinet crack in Fig. 2(b) is more natural than that in Fig. 2(a). There are some stains on things above cabinet in Fig. 2(a), which come from improper registration. However, these things almost disappear in Fig. 2(b).

SIFT description is a vector with 130 bit, so that reducing feature points involved can significantly accelerate the stitching speed. In Tab. 1, we first measure the time consumption of solving (1) for each iteration. Time consumption is reduced from 58.26 s to 0.26 s for No. 1 frame pair, and from 24.90 s to 0.19 s for No.2 frame pair, i.e. about 200 and 120 times acceleration respectively. Speed gain in No. 1 case is better for its much more complicate content and SIFT points involved in stitching.

SVAS and the proposed algorithm approach the desired results by some iteration, and the convergence speed is a very critical measurement to evaluate algorithm complexity. We tabulate the iterations required

Table 1. Comparison of time comsumed per iteration for svas and the proposed algorithm.

Image pair index	Iteration number of SVAS	Iteration number of the proposed algorithm
No. 1 (Fig. 1)	53	17
No. 2 (Fig. 2)	44	13

Table 2. Comparision of convergence rate of svas and the proposed algorithm

Image pair index	Time consumption for one iteration of SVAS	Time consumption for one iteration of the proposed algorithm
No. 1 (Fig. 1)	58.26 s	0.26 s
No. 2 (Fig. 2)	24.90 s	0.19 s

in Tab. 2 for comparison. It is shown that the proposed algorithm only used 1/3 iterations of SVAS in both cases.

Based on the results in Tab. 1 and Tab. 2, it is obvious that the implementation speed is 300 times faster than the SVAS by using the proposed algorithm, but without any subjective quality loss.

5 CONCLUSION

In this paper, we present a method to improve the robustness and implementation speed of the SVAS. Through theoretical and simulation analysis, we prove that redundant feature points go against image stitching, and then give the criterion for feature point filtering. The proposed method gets obvious performance improvement over SVAS. It is especially suitable for hardware implementation for its computational burden is even distributed and easily done on parallel.

REFERENCES

[1] Lowe D. G., "Object Recognition from Local Scale-Invariant Features", IEEE International Conference on Computer Vision, 7(2), 1999, pp. 1150–1157.

[2] Lowe D.G., "Distinctive Image Features from Scale-Invariance Key points", International Journal of Computer Vision, 60(2), 2004, pp. 91–110.

[3] Meltzer J., S. Soatto, M.H. Yang, R. Gupta, "Multiple view feature descriptors from image sequences via kernel Principal component analysis"; Proceedings of the European Conference on Computer Vision, Springer Verlag, 2004, pp. 215–227.

[4] Bay H., T. Tuytelaars, L.V. Gool, "Surf: Speeded up robust features," Computer Vision and Image Understanding, Vol.110(3), Jun 2008, pp. 346–359.

[5] Liu C., "Sift flow: dense correspondence across scenes and its applications," IEEE Transaction on Pattern Analysis and Machine Intelligence, Vol. 33(5), May 2011, pp. 978–994.

[6] Liu F., M. Gleicher, H. Jin, et al., "Content preserving warps for 3d video stabilization," ACM Transactions on Graphics (TOG). ACM, 2009, 28(3): pp. 44.

[7] Chung R., F. Dornaika, "Mosaicking images with parallax," Signal Processing: Image Communication 19.8 (2004): pp. 771–786.

[8] Lin W.Y., S.Y. Liu, Y. Matsushita, et al., "Smoothly varying affine stitching," IEEE Transactions on Computer Vision and Pattern Recognition (CVPR), Jun 2011, pp. 345–352.

[9] Myronenko A., X.B. Song, "Point set registration: Coherent point drift." Pattern Analysis and Machine Intelligence, IEEE Transactions on, Vol 32(12), 2010, pp. 2262–2275.

[10] Lin W.Y., S Liu, Y Matsushita, et al. "Smoothly varying affine stitching", Computer Vision and Pattern Recognition (CVPR), 2011 IEEE Conference on. 2011, pp. 345–352.

[11] Myronenko A., X. Song, and M. Carreira-Perpinan. "Non-rigid point set registration: Coherent point drift," In Advances in Neural Information Processing Systems, 2006, pp. 1009–1016.

[12] Yuille A. L., and N. M. Grywacz, "The motion coherence theory". ICCV, 1988, pp. 344–353.

[13] Petersen K. B., and M. S. Pedersen, "The matrix cookbook", (2006).

[14] DENG S.W., "Image denoising study on Nonlocal-Means Filter", International Conference on Image Analysis and Signal Processing (IASP), 2012, 9–11 Nov, 2012, 1–4.

Multimedia Technology IV – Farag, Yang & Jiao (Eds)
© *2015 Taylor & Francis Group, London, ISBN: 978-1-138-02794-7*

How brand loyalty is affected by online brand community?

Ching-Wei Ho & Yu-Bing Wang
Department of Marketing, Feng Chia University, Taichung, Taiwan

Hsiang-Yuan Chang
IMBA, Feng Chia University, Taichung, Taiwan

ABSTRACT: The study reveals how brand loyalty is affected by the characteristics of online brand community, i.e. the quality of information, relationship and service. A questionnaire survey with consumers was conducted in this research for examining the proposed hypotheses. The results of this study indicated that brand loyalty is affected directly by information quality of online brand community, and brand involvement plays a fully mediating role between the characteristic of relationship quality and brand loyalty.

Keywords: online brand community, brand involvement, brand loyalty

1 INTRODUCTION

Previous studies have shown that information can be exchanged and spread by different forms of media [1]. With the rapid development of information technology and increasingly advanced network function, online community takes the advantage to provide a brilliant platform for people of same interests and concepts to share information and exchange opinions and experiences. About 22.2% of members collected product information from online brand communities; about 72% of members were affected by the information provided in online brand communities and changed purchase decisions [2]. Currently, most related studies focus on the loyalty of online brand communities to brands (or products) and less on the influence of online brand community on brand involvement, and brand loyalty. Therefore, this study will treat the influence of online brand communities on brand involvement and brand loyalty.

2 LITERATURE REVIEWS

Online brand community is a kind of relationship connection combined with virtual community and the knowledge exchange of brand community. In structure, it is composed by the communities which have brand loyalty but are not limited by geographical location [3]. Online brand community was one of major marketing tools in the future [4]. Many enterprises think that online brand communities not only provide a channel for the communication between enterprise and customer, but also can help to collect helpful suggestions from customers [5]. Therefore, online brand community is a kind of customer-oriented structural

social relationship in which a group of people advocate a brand and have interaction and communication through network port [6]. As found from the literatures exploring the successful factors of online platform, most have information quality and service quality factors, for example, [7]. Hoffman & Novak [8] think that long-term customer relationship and development of network communities is also very important, which is the so called relationship quality. These 3 points will be treated as important indexes to measure online brand communities.

Brand involvement originated from [9] and [10] indicated that brand involvement is the approach to attract attention to a specific brand and maintain the interest of customers. By online brand community, a platform to provide information, experience sharing and create particular brand services, enterprises can provide understanding and good impression of brands for customers, and thereby strengthen brand involvement degree. Therefore, the study proposes the following assumptions:

H1: (a) Information quality; (b) Relationship quality; (c) Service quality of online brand community has positive influence on brand involvement.

Furthermore, according to [11] and [12], brand involvement will affect loyalty of enterprise and customer, especially in the situation that customers are in high-risk product consciousness, involvement degree will have great influence on brand loyalty. Therefore, this study can have the following assumptions:

H2: Brand involvement has positive influence on brand loyalty

Besides, online brand community can help to reveal the demand of customers and brand loyalty [4]. [13] found that when community members had more good

Table 1. Constructs and results.

Construct		Loading	α	CR	AVE
Information	IQ1	0.706	0.80	0.86	0.55
Quality (IQ)	IQ2	0.700			
	IQ3	0.731			
	IQ4	0.776			
	IQ5	0.804			
Relationship	RQ1	0.824	0.69	0.83	0.62
Quality (RQ)	RQ2	0.786			
	RQ3	0.749			
Service	SQ1	0.904	0.72	0.87	0.78
Quality (SQ)	SQ2	0.860			
Brand	BI1	0.719	0.82	0.86	0.56
Involvement	BI2	0.719			
(BI)	BI3	0.746			
	BI4	0.706			
	BI5	0.785			
Brand	BL1	0.750	0.83	0.88	0.65
Loyalty	BL2	0.836			
(BL)	BL3	0.793			
	BL4	0.834			

Table 2. Correlation matrix.

	AVE	IQ	RQ	SQ	BI	BL
IQ	0.55	0.741				
RQ	0.62	0.563	0.781			
SQ	0.78	0.457	0.431	0.877		
BI	0.56	0.502	0.446	0.392	0.748	
BL	0.65	0.443	0.401	0.134	0.516	0.804

Note: Diagonals represent the square root of the average variance extracted while the other entries represent the correlations

Discriminant validity is with the standard that the value of each dimension AVE radical sign is greater than correlation coefficients of other dimensions and the correlation coefficient of each dimension must be smaller than 0.85, which was proposed by [19] and [16]. This is to view that the dimension of this study has good discriminant validity (table 2).

impression to the product, brand, companies and other customers in community, they would be more willing to establish long-term and sustainable relationship with company. Therefore, we can conclude that with more comprehensive brand information in the online brand community, closer relationship between members and more satisfying information, customers will have more loyalty to brand. The following assumptions are proposed:

H3: (a) Information quality; (b) Relationship quality; (c) Service quality of online brand community has positive influence on brand loyalty.

3 RESEARCH METHOD AND RESULTS

The data used to test the hypotheses were collected by a structured questionnaire from online brand community members in Taiwan. As the target population in this study was members of online brand communities, the questionnaire was distributed through several posts on Facebook. At the end of the data collection period, 229 questionnaires were collected with 7 missing values. That is, 222 fully completed questionnaires (68.5% male; 31.5% female) were used for the data analysis. This study used partial least squares (PLS) to test the hypotheses and analyze the data.

This study will view the dimension reliability with the standard that Cronbach's value must be bigger than 0.65 proposed by scholar [14]. As for analysis of validity, in the aspect of content validity, this study takes the suggestion of [15] about factor loading with 0.5 as standard. For construct validity, the paper takes the suggestion of [16] about factor loading and Average Variance Extracted (AVE), with 0.5 as standard. Composite Reliability (CR) uses 0.7 as standard [17], [18]. Details are listed in table 1.

4 DISCUSSIONS AND CONCLUSIONS

Among information quality (H1a, $\beta = 0.324$, p < 0.01), relationship quality (H1b, $\beta = 0.166$, p < 0.05) and service quality (H1c, $\beta = 0.165$) in online brand community, only the relation of service quality with brand involvement is not significant. Therefore, we conclude that H1a and H1b are supported. As brand involvement has very significant influence on brand loyalty (H2, $\beta = 0.435$, p < 0.001), we may also conclude that H2 is supported. Besides, through analysis, we may find that (1) the information quality (H3a, $\beta = 0.287$, p < 0.001) of online brand community has significant effect on brand loyalty, indicating that improved information quality may also improve brand loyalty; (2) relationship quality (H3b, $\beta = 0.151$) has no significant effect on brand loyalty; (3) service quality (H3c, $\beta = -0.214$) is significant to brand loyalty but the path value is negative. Therefore, we may conclude that the H3a of this study is valid, and the other two are invalid.

The findings in this study offer important contributions and implications for both marketing academics and practitioners. First, the completeness and realness of information quality is helpful to boost the understanding and interest in a brand. Meanwhile, the quality of relationships with online brand community members has significant influence on the understanding of brand. The better interaction with community members would support the degree of brand involvement. Second, the quality of relationships with online brand community members and the service provided would not have significant influence on brand loyalty, members only care if the information provided by brand community is true and correct. Third, brand involvement has full mediation effect on relationship quality of online brand community and brand loyalty. Therefore, for brand community managers, only keeping the relationships with members is helpless for increasing brand loyalty, to communicate them with brand things in order to boost brand involvement would positively influence the loyalty.

REFERENCES

[1] Kim, J.W., Choi, J., Qualls, W., and Han, K. 2008. "It takes a marketplace community to raise brand commitment: the role of online communities," Journal of Marketing Management, 24(3–4): 409–431.

[2] Kanamori, T. and Kimura, A. 2003. "Net Communities in Brand Marketing," NRI Papers, 63(1): 1–10.

[3] McKnight, D.H., Choudhury, V. and Kacmar, C. 2002. "Developing and Validating Trust Measures for ECommerce: An Integrative Typology," Information Systems Research, 13(3): 334–359.

[4] Casaló, L.V., Flavián, C., and Guinalíu, M. 2008. "Promoting consumer's participation in virtual brand communities: A new paradigm in branding strategy," Journal of Marketing Communications, 14(1): 19–36.

[5] Jang S.C. and Namkung, Y. 2007. "Does food quality really matter in restaurants? Its impact on customer satisfaction and behavioral intentions," Journal of Hospitality & Tourism Research, 31(3): 387–409.

[6] Chiang, I.P. and Chen, S.C. 2012. "Sense of virtual brand community: antecedents and consequences," Electronic Commerce Studies, 10(3): 297–324 (in Chinese).

[7] DeLone, W., and McLean, E. 2003. "The DeLone and McLean model of information systems success: A ten-year update," Journal of Management Information Systems, 19: 9–30.

[8] Hoffman D.L. and Novak T.P. 1996. "Marketing in Hypermedia Computer-mediated Environments: Conceptual Foundations," Journal of Marketing, 60 (July): 50–68.

[9] Mittal, B., and Lee, M.S. 1988. "Separating brand-choice involvement from product involvement via consumer involvement profiles," Advances in Consumer Research, 15(1): 43–49.

[10] Holt, Douglas B. 1995. "How consumers consume: a typology of consumption practices," Journal of consumer research, 22(1):1–16.

[11] Mittal, B., and Lee, M.S. 1989. "A causal model of consumer involvement," Journal of Economic Psychology, 10(3): 363–389.

[12] Knox, S., and Walker, D. 2003. "Empirical developments in the measurement," Strategic marketing, 11(4): 271–286.

[13] McAlexander, J.H, Schouten, J.W, and Koenig, H.F. 2002. "Building brand community," The Journal of Marketing, 66(1): 38–54.

[14] Devellis, R.F. 1991. "Scale development: Theory and applications," Newbury Park, CA: Sage.

[15] Hair, J.F., Anderson, R.E., and Tatham, R.L. 1998. "Multivariate data analysis," 5th edition, Prentice-Hall International, USA.

[16] Fornell, C. and Larcker, D.F. 1981. "Evaluating structural equation models with unobservable variables and measurement error," Journal of Marketing Research 18(1): 39–50.

[17] Nunnally, J.C. and Bernstein, I.H. 1994. "Psychometric theory," New York, NY: MGraw-Hill.

[18] Bagozzi, R.P., and Yi, Y. 1998. "On the Evaluation of Structural Equation Models," Journal of the Academy of Marketing Science, 16(1): 76–94.

[19] Barcly, M.J., and Smith, Jr., C.W. 1995. "The Maturity Structure of Corporate Debt," Journal of Finance, 50(2): 609–631.

Multimedia Technology IV – Farag, Yang & Jiao (Eds)
© 2015 Taylor & Francis Group, London, ISBN: 978-1-138-02794-7

Study on the evaluation of webpage based on eye tracking technology

Tai Yu & Bing Li

Information Management Center, Second Military Medical University, Shanghai, China

ABSTRACT: A typical characteristic of modern society is a wealth of information resources and a wide range of information channels, information has become like air is everywhere and so important that people cannot live without them. And the popularity of the Internet has greatly influenced the way people seek information, the Webpage as an interface presents the digital environment and rich information to users. People seek information through the Internet to carry out a visual search in Webpage, so the availability Webpage for quick, correct location and identification information is vital, have a direct impact on the user experience in Webpage. Eye tracking technology as a tool to explore the cognitive process, the researchers gradually get to more and more applied in webpage usability evaluation. The purpose of this paper is to discuss using eye tracking technology assessment web usability research and the present situation and challenges.

Keywords: Eye Tracking Technology; Webpage Evaluation

1 THE DEFINITION OF EYE TRACKING TECHNOLOGY

Eye tracking is also known as eye-movement, it is considered to be an effective method to study visual information processing. Use special equipment to record the learner's Eye movements (Eye Movement, referred to as "Eye"), it can be used as the basis of analysis of learners' internal mental activity. Research on eye tracking technology has a long history; it has been widely used in many fields. For example, for the study of photo/advertising (Webpage evaluation, design evaluation), dynamic analysis (aerospace, sports, automotive, aircraft driving), product testing (usability testing), scene study (shopping, shop decoration, home furnishing environment etc.) in many fields and human-computer interaction etc.. In addition, eye tracking in the intelligent computer, smart appliances, in areas such as virtual reality and digital games also has a good application prospect.

Eye tracking can be used in measuring point of gaze data that provides information concerning subject's focus of attention. The focus of subject's attention can be used as supportive evidence in studying cognitive processes. Despite the potential usefulness of eye tracking in psychology of programming research, there exists only few instances where eye tracking has actually been used.

2 THE MODE OF EYE TRACKING TECHNOLOGY

In the experimental study of eye movement, the fixation time, fixation frequency, fixation, saccade distance sequence, back to the important parameters, the diameter of the pupil is often viewed as the importance of thinking and mental processing parameters. Therefore, through the observation of participant's real-time eye movement information in the learning process it can be used to analyze and guide the learning basis. Eye movement pattern is generally divided into three kinds: fixation, saccade and pursuit movement. Among them, for a period of time, the relative stability of the eye movement called fixation; rapid eye movement caused the focus point of visual field changes, this behavior is called saccades; eyes slowly and smoothly to track a slow movement of the target, it is called a pursuit movement.

Most commercial eye-tracking systems available today measure point-of-regard by the "corneal-reflection/pupil-centre" method. These kinds of trackers usually consist of a standard desktop computer with an infrared camera mounted beneath (or next to) a display monitor, with image processing software to locate and identify the features of the eye used for tracking. In operation, infrared light from an LED embedded in the infrared camera is first directed into the eye to create strong reflections in target eye features to make them easier to track (infrared light is used to avoid dazzling the user with visible light). The light enters the retina and a large proportion of it is reflected back, making the pupil appear as a bright, well defined disc (known as the "bright pupil" effect). The corneal reflection (or first Purkinje image) is also generated by the infrared light, appearing as a small, but sharp, glint (see Figure 1).

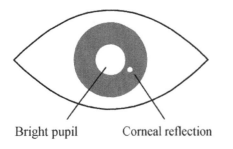

Bright pupil   Corneal reflection

Figure 1. Corneal reflection and bright pupil as seen in the infrared camera image.

3 THE CLASSIFICATION OF EYE TRACKING TECHNOLOGY

At present, the eye tracking system basically can be divided into two categories: Outside-in and Inside-out (Figure 1). Outside – in system through one or more cameras record the subjects of eye movement and through the algorithm of image tracking in the scene gaze, cameras were installed in the front of the subjects, the advantage of this type of system is to put the camera into the display, so basically the subjects cannot see the camera. Inside – out system requires the participants wore a special equipment (such as a helmet or glasses), the images of the eye through the lens reflex into miniature cameras. Miniature cameras recorded the movement of the eye, and through image algorithm to get the actual line of sight.

4 THE INDEX OF EYE TRACKING TECHNOLOGY

The most basic measure of eye tracking study is the fixation and saccade. Fixation is the individual to perceive the details of the formation of the target, the performance of the line of sight to stay in a certain position, is often used to measure point or assign individual attention. After watching the end of a line of sight to move to the next fixation point, moving between two points is watching saccade. Saccade is often used to measure distraction. Generally people believed that the vast majority of information only when watching to get processed; saccades during perception is inhibited, cannot get any information.

In the practical application, the researchers often according to their respective research purpose and the research content, on the basis of the fixation and saccade develop a rich variety of derived indicators. Such as Goldberg believes visits to search the influence of the directivity, to saccade amplitude, scanning path length and the search area density as the search directivity index, the retrospective DE as a symbol of the search difficult; The study by Lorigo et al. found that users in the search results page to view the behavior of each search result as a region of interest, statistics of each region of interest of the number and duration of fixations on impact, so as to explore the user to

Type	Advantages	Disadvantages	Typical products
Outside-in	The price is relatively low. Can be integrated into the computer monitor, basically see the camera.	Subjects moving head cannot be substantially. The visual areas are small. If the camera was found may affect the test result. System is not easy to be calibrated, and often need correction.	Tobii 1750 ASL EVM 504 FaceLAB
Inside-out	Subjects moving head can be substantially. There is no limit to the testable visual areas in theory.	Need to wear in the subjects head, might affect their action or behavior. The price is relatively expensive.	SR Eyelink ASL 501 SMI Iview ISCAN ETL 500

Figure 2. The characteristics of the eye tracking system and typical products.

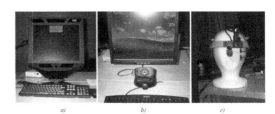

Figure 3. Eye tracking devices, a) Tobii 1750, b) ASL EVM 504, c) ASL 501 head mounted optics.

view and click on the search results page behavior and the influencing factors. Byrne found that when drop-down menu next usability research web pages will look at the time needed for the first shot on target as a measure of plane layout reasonable, the shorter the time represents the target the more likely to be noticed. User interactions with the webpage process is contextualized behavior, so according to different test conditions, researchers have great difference explain to the indicators, even the same indicators in different test conditions may also represent opposite cognitive process. Such as Pool in the study Webpage importance and users in different areas of the level of interest by browsing tasks, with the interest region note video rate as the measurement index, the higher the frequency, the higher the said individual interest in the region. And Golderg found that when research on search directivity using the search task, on the contrary, in this study indicates that the user watched the higher the frequency the more uncertainty in the recognition process. In addition to the fixation point and saccade and their respective derived indicators, pupil diameter, blink rate can also be used as an index of cognitive processing, but because of these two indicators are vulnerable to the influence of other factors such as the brightness of the environment, thus is rarely used in eye tracking study of a webpage.

5 TRADITIONAL USBILITY WEBPAGE EVALUATION METHOD

Availability includes three aspects: the concept of the effectiveness, interaction efficiency and user satisfaction to the product. Put forward of the concept of availability changed people the understanding of the interaction of product, made for the center with the user interface design idea in these years, gradually into the product design and the design concept of developers. The purpose of web usability evaluation is to use various usability research methods to evaluate web usability level. As in the Webpage how to properly present information and navigation design, proper layout browsing environment that enables web users to meet the cognitive processing characteristics and improve web usability.

The interaction between the user and the Webpage through query and browse, this process is directly influenced by the Webpage information architecture. Information architecture as the blueprint of web information content, provide users with a systematic and visualization system. The availability of Webpage usability research is optimized Webpage information architecture, to increase the page accessibility and usability, help users quickly, accurately obtain information and improve the use experience. System usability evaluation method has many, Molich et al. divided these methods into two categories: no user involvement (such as heuristic evaluation, cognitive walkthrough, etc.) and user participation (e.g., usability testing, questionnaires, interviews, etc.), the application of usability testing is the most widely and is considered the most reliable evaluation method. Usability testing by observing the user to use of the product, and measurement performed on the user accuracy and time, to assess whether the product is easy to use. And like other traditional evaluation method, however, usability testing can only be obtained based on the overt behavior data, unable to explore users interact with the products in the process of cognitive processing, most of the time, therefore, cannot explain why the behavior happen. To make up for the deficiency, some researchers will let usability test combined with thinking aloud, and self-reported use, but it brings additional problems, such as ecological validity of the interference test and user self statement has a tendency to rationalize, etc.

In order to solve the above problems, some researchers have begun to gaze tracking technology is applied to the usability evaluation of Webpage. Eye tracking technology based on eye-mind hypothesis, namely the individual is looking at the target designation of him at this time of the most important content of knowledge processing. Using eye tracking technology, researchers can change individual view into visual chart and numerical, from the cognitive level label, navigation and search system etc. elements of information architecture more deeply into Webpage classification. Researchers in the subjects naturally operating state, by recording the eye movement to analyze the operating process of the visual information processing, transfer process includes the spatial position of the screen of interest or attention and attention, it is a beneficial supplement to the traditional test method.

6 THE APPLICATION OF EYE TRACKING TECHNOLOGY IN WEBPAGE EVALUATION F

Eye tracking presents an adaptive approach that can capture the user's current needs and tailor the retrieval accordingly. Applying eye tracking to image retrieval requires that new strategies be devised that can use visual and algorithmic data to obtain natural and rapid retrieval of webpage. Recent work showed that the eye is faster than the mouse as a source of visual input in a target webpage identification task.

Application of eye tracking technology in the study area, overseas has made some achievements. Such as: Goldberg (2002) and Owens (2008), the research on the view of the portal, Granka (2004) for eye movement analysis of the search engine results page, Nielsen (2006) Webpage reading pattern research, and Shrestha (2007) on the web text and picture browsing mode studies, etc. In the above study, Owens website browsing mode study and Nielsen's web reading model research is more typical.

6.1 *The research on website browsing mode*

Portal is the entrance into the Internet, the user contact Internet content and application service, the home page layout is usually two columns or three columns. Goldberg's eye movement study found that browse mode of two columns portal, the subjects is accustomed to progressive rather than a column by column page browsing, the first view is mostly in the upper left corner of the first line of sight, mostly in the first two rows, and the whole process of browsing follow the order from left to right, from top to bottom. Owens extends Goldberg research; he with the help of eye movement instrument to eye movement trajectory of different column website for college students has carried on the comparative study. The experimental results show that the learner browsing the web showing the distribution of the order and attention to certain rules, specific performance:

- The sequence of website browses. The order of the learners to browse the webpage in general is from top to bottom, the first lateral and longitudinal, it shows a "S" type, but there was a difference in the different sections of the Webpage. For two-column pages, the subjects were first scanned in the left column of the first row of the contents, and then browse the right column, the first two rows of the contents of the first visit in the right column and then in the left column, and so on.

- Attention distribution. Experimental results show that the learner's attention is focused on the top of the page, the more looking down the less the number of times. The temporary not shown by the browser window to limit page content is more difficult to come to the attention of the participants.

6.2 *The research on website reading mode*

Nielsen study the website reading mode in the eye movements found that users often use "F" type mode read webpage, its trajectory showing two horizontal stripes and a longitudinal stripe. Users can adopt this model quickly obtain useful information in seconds, so as to improve the reading speed, which is very different from the traditional book reading mode.

"F" type reading mode specific performance: First, the user of the content of the page at the top of the area for horizontal reading, thus constituting a "F" in the first cross; Then, the user's eye moves down slightly, transverse read again, but the line of sight covering area is shorter than the last, this creates a "F" in the second horizontal; Finally, users browse the contents of the page from top to bottom on the left, if the reading is relatively slow in presenting a solid vertical bar graph attention hotspots, such as fast browsing is a discrete point presentation, these bars or scatter formation is "F" last pricked. Of course, the user's reading mode is not entirely always "F" type. For example, sometimes the user will read three times laterally, forming an "E" type; sometimes only a transverse reading, may form

a "L" type. But the overall pattern is roughly similar, which appears as "F" type.

REFERENCES

[1] Brenner, E., & Cornelissen, F. W. 2000. "Separate simultaneous processing of egocentric and relative positions." Vision Research, 40:2557–2563.

[2] Brainard, D. H. 1997. "The Psychophysics Toolbox," Spatial Vision, 10:437–442.

[3] Huk, A. C., Palmer, J., & Shadlen, M. N. 2002. "Temporal integration of visual motion information: Evidence from response times." Journal of Vision, 2(7):228a.

[4] Li, H.-C. O., Brenner, E., Cornelissen, F. W., & Kim, E. S. 2002. "Systematic distortion of perceived 2D shape during smooth pursuit eye movements." Vision Research, 42:2569–2575.

[5] Stampe, D.M. 1993. "Heuristic filtering and reliable calibration methods for video-based pupil-tracking systems." Behavior Research Methods, Instruments, & Computers, 25:137–142.

[6] Ball, L. J., Lucas, E. J., Miles, J. N. V., & Gale, A. G. 2003. "Inspection times and the selection task: What do eye-movements reveal about relevance effects?" Quarterly Journal of Experimental Psychology, 56A: 1053–1077.

[7] Lohse, G. L. 1997. "Consumer eye movement patterns on Yellow Pages advertising." Journal of Advertising, 26:61–73.

[8] Oyekoya O. K., Stentiford F. W. M. 2004. "Exploring Human Eye Behavior Using a Model of Visual Attention". International Conference on Pattern Recognition, April 29–May 2, 2004.

[9] Oyekoya O. K., Stentiford F. W. M. 2005. "A Performance Comparison of Eye Tracking and Mouse Interfaces in a Target Image Identification Task". European Workshop on the Integration of Knowledge Semantics & Digital Media Technology Conference, Nov 30–Dec 1, 2005.

Multimedia Technology IV – Farag, Yang & Jiao (Eds)
© 2015 Taylor & Francis Group, London, ISBN: 978-1-138-02794-7

Application of virtual agent's eye movement by using artificial intelligence

Yingci Zhang

The Computer Science School, Sichuan University of Science & Engineering, Zigong, China

ABSTRACT: From an artificial intelligence perspective, the scanpath concept is identified as the instantiation of a general sequencing principle that permeates the organization of spatial scene knowledge. Methodologies according to the scanpath form a robust basis for smart applications which employed to design and assess a virtual agent's eye movements in gaming environment. In the gaming environment, players expect the protagonist looked life-like as far as possible. To achieve the purpose, a protagonist should have some basic human behaviour such as limbs movement, speaking and eye movement in a virtual world. This paper focuses on the activity of eye movement by discussing about the different aspects of virtual agents. According to the three levels of eye behavior including the core gaze behavior, this paper introduces an experimental simulation to assess virtual agent's eye gaze behavior. By describing the cognitive activities based on different features of the virtual agent briefly, this paper presents an integrated model framework of the agent interaction in the immersed environment. At the end of this paper, we draw a conclusion of some gaze strategies and some simulation results based on the framework and the previous researches. Combining with artificial intelligence (AI), we aim at introducing a substantial idea about eye behavioral science in gaming environment.

Keywords: artificial intelligence (AI); cognitive processes; eye behaviour; gaze behaviour; virtual agent; virtual character

1 INTRODUCTION

Eye movement technology has come a long way. In the last decades, the research of eye movement and it's applications or services have increased manifold by growing open-hardware and open-source communities. And now we can do more complicated tasks beyond simple eye behaviour recording. For example, the eye movement data was used as an input for a robust and dynamic modeling of attentional shifts, including shifts that occur during mental problem solving and in particular with regard to spatial or diagrammatic reasoning problems. It also works in the Virtual Agent community which is closely associated to Virtual Assistants industry. In the gaming environment, players expect the protagonist looked life-like as far as possible. To achieve the purpose, a protagonist should have some basic human behaviour such as limbs movement, speaking and eye movement in a virtual world. The Virtual Agent community is a computer engendered, animated, artificial intelligent (AI) virtual character and has some capacity to improvise its actions. So we can make even better use of the oculomotor system by using advanced, real-time technologies for new tasks.

This paper will introduce the different aspects of virtual agents in the next sub sections. In the part 3, we'll discuss about attention and eye movements control detailed.

2 VIRTUAL AGENT

Essentially, a virtual agent is a computer generated three-dimensional digital representation of human user. It sometimes refers as a computer program [1]. In gaming environment, virtual agent is a three-dimensional graphics with some human characters. That means the virtual agent is concentrated three kinds of advanced skills. First of all, agent should "exhibit life-like qualities". Secondly, agent are able to "follow the directions" which are taken from the external sources (Barbara Hays, 1996). Finally, agents are able to "improvise" many different aspects of behavior [2].

Players always expect the virtual agent could express more human characteristics including speech or even communication, facial expression, limbs movement and eye movement such as eye gaze, steering. However, it's a high difficulty work to design all the behaviour of virtual agent integratedly and then implement autonomous behavior control ability. To simplify the hard work, the scientists put additional concentration into the activity of eye movement esppecially in gaze and steering behaviour.

3 ATTENTIONAL AND EYE MOVEMENTS CONTROL

Eye movement is a cognitive function [3]. In mostly cases, shifts of attentional focus usally cause 'a moving of the mind's eye' [4]. Based on the results of some research to a substantial body and broad psychological, functional anatomical or neural evidence, attentional processes must interact closely with processes in eye movement control. Another reasonable point of view regards the attentional shifts as essentially oculomotor essentially [5]. Thus, the researchers could know the process of underlying shifts of attention from the spatial index provided by a typical scanpath. So the understanding of the cognitive function can be extended to eye movement of virtual agent.

To a protagonist in gaming environment, the eye movement is a cognitive function [3] either. The eye behaviour affects or determines the quality of a protagonist representation. Virtual agent interacts in a nature way with the significant feature of eye behaviour. Either in fighting game or in scene game, it will be more lifely, interesting and expected if some realistic eye control movement on the agent. For instance, we'll analyze the common situation of pursuit and flee in a fighting game in part.

4   ANALYSIS OF EYE MOVEMENT OF VIRTUAL AGENT

We construct a model of eye movement which is composed by gaze behaviour, steering behaviour and idle gaze behaviour.

A virtual agent perform communication and social demonstration by gaze behaviour. In gaming environment, protagonist could express more human characterics when the gaze behaviour is definite and undercontrolled. To obtain this expectant representation need a set of applications of distinct functions such as signaling, attention, adaptable turn-talking [2]. When the gaze is in idle position, we call this kind eye behaviour idle gaze. The performance of a protagonist when he waiting his teammate or taking a walk belongs to the idle gaze behaviour in the gaming environment.

From Reynolds, steering behaviour consists of: seek, pursuit, flee, evasion, offset pursuit, arrival, obstacle avoidance, wander, path following, wall following, containment, flow field following, unaligned collision avoidance, separation, cohesion, alignment, flocking, and leader following [6].

For example, a virtual agent chases a constant subject and the eye movement locks at the subject. In the chasing process, the agent must avoid many barriers. Howerver, the key distinction of pursuit from seek behaviour is that the subject is unfixed. That means the virtual agent would estimate the next position of the unfixed subject. The methodology is: first select a reference point and reexamine each point after a certain period of time [1].

Flee behaviour is another steering character of agent contrary to seek behaviour. The speed is "radially aligned" away from the target and the desired velocity works in the opposite direction [7]. Figure 1 shows steering behaviour of seek and flee. Reynolds gave the equation for steering from Figure 1 is [6]:

$$desired\_velocity = normalize\ (position\ -target) * max\_speed \tag{1}$$

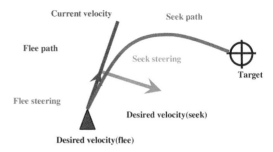

Figure 1.   Steering behavior of seek and flee (Reynolds 1999) [6].

$$steering = desired\_velocity-\ velocity \tag{2}$$

5   APPLICATIONS OF VIRTUAL AGENT'S EYE MOVEMENT IN GAMING ENVIRONMENT

In gaming environment, players interact with computers or any other terminals through virtual agent. Liu et al. proposed a framework for virtual agent behavior modeling [3]. The working flow is shown in Figure 2. The three steps of modeling eye behaviour of protagonist in gaming environment is as follow:

5.1   The first step

The first block of information perception shows us the process of perception and cognize in virtual environment.

- An agent acquires information through synthetic vision when it taking sight. Then the visibility can be accomplished by testing against the virtual human's view frustum [3].
- The process of audition simulation is performed in multiple examining way. Firstly, the agent receives vocal messages and examines them on system. Then the agent estimates how far the current position from the messages' origin.
- Based on the vision information and audition information collected earlier, the agent performs action to limit its focus to confine the object [2].
- Perceptual attention helps agent determine the scale of the focus by both perception processing output and decision making behavior. Then the agent extracts the focal object using intention.
- Memory model helps the agent to remember the perceived objects through sensitivity [8].

5.2   The second step

From Figure 2, decision network and action selection are both used to make behaviour decision. As a matter of fact, decision network complishes it's tasks and then action selection works according to the results of prior work. Figure 3 reveals the hierarchy of decision network which is used to perform agent decision making process. In this part, the response behaviour network choose one network within the excess. Then the chosen

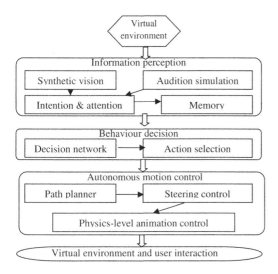

Figure 2. Framework for modeling protagonist eye behaviour.

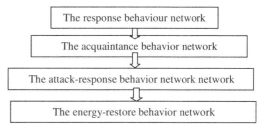

Figure 3. The hierarchy of decision network.

Based on the research, some allpications of virtual agent's eye movement in gaming environment are discussed. A framework is proposed to model eye behaviour of a protagnist because players expect to interact with computers or any other terminals through virtual agent. However, more technologies, model systems and simulation algorithms are expected. By using artificial intelligence, the furture interaction system must be more vivid and realistic for a virtual agent to interact freely with the virtual enviroment.

network is used to handle the analogous behavior network. After that the decision network decides to choose the corresponding action for that particular scene [2].

5.3 *The third step*

There are both static and dynamic objects in virtual gaming environment so that the single search algorithm can't handle this complex and uncertain situation. To implement autonomous motion control, we need define the route of a virtual agent and bring about a target initially. If the objects are dynamic, steering control behavior discussed in the preceding section will help the agent solve the problem. A "sidestep repulsion vector" is used to determine the steering path [2]. The velocity of dodgeing movement of the steering control behaviour is the fastest. As the physical control behaviour determine the physical action, controlling collision detection mechanism would be used to avoid stuck stick on any obstacle [9].

6 CONCLUSION

The part 2 of this paper provides us an overview of a virtual agent in semi-immersive environment. By analyzing and contrasting with attention and eye movement control in the part 3, we draw a conclusion that eye movement is a cognitive function essential. So the eye behaviour affects or determines the quality of a protagnist representation. From some cases we can find out that virtual agent interacts in a nature way with the significant feature of eye behaviour. Especially, gaze behaviour and steering behaviour are two important componants of eye movement model constructed in part 4. Timed automata is used to implement the gaze strategies according to the simulating model.

From Kipp & Gebhard, gaze is a dominant interaction modality with many functions like signaling attention, regulating turn-taking or deictic reference.

REFERENCES

[1] Edward, L., Lourdeaux, D. & Barthes, J, "Cognitive Modeling of Virtual Autonomous Intelligent Agents Integrating Human Factors," Web Intelligence and Intelligent Agent Technologies, WI-IAT '09. IEEE/WIC/ACM International Joint Conferences on, vol. 3, pp. 353–356, 2009.

[2] Avijeet Das, Md Mahmudul Hasan, "Eye Gaze Behavior of Virtual Agent in Gaming Environment by Using Artificial Intelligence," International Conference on Electrical Information and Communication Technology (EICT), pp. 504–511, 2013.

[3] Litao Han, Qiaoli Kong, Bing Liu & Zhiqiang Li, "Building cognitive model of intelligent agent in Virtual Geographical Environment," Computer Science and Automation Engineering (CSAE), 2011 IEEE International Conference on, vol. 3, pp. 660–664, 2011.

[4] Christian Freksa, Sven Bertel, "Eyemovements and smart technology," Computers in Biology and Medicine," vol. 37, pp. 983–988, 2007.

[5] T. Moore, M. Fallah, "Control of eye movements and spatial attention," Proc. Natl. Acad. Sci. USA, vol. 98, pp. 1273–1276, 2001.

[6] Reynolds, C. W., "Steering Behaviors for Autonomous Characters," <http://www.red3d.com/cwr/papers/1999/gdc99steer.pdf>. 2011.

[7] Cafaro, A., Gaito, R. &Vilhjálmsson, H, "Animating Idle Gaze in Public Places," IVA '09 Proceedings of the 9th International Conference on Intelligent Virtual Agents, Springer-Verlag Berlin, Heidelberg, pp. 250–256, 2009.

[8] Grillon, H. & Thalmann, D. "Eye contact as trigger for modification of virtual character behavior," Virtual Rehabilitation, pp. 205.

[9] Steptoe, W., Oyekoya, O., Murgia, A., Wolff, R., Rae, J., Guimaraes, E., Roberts, D. & Steed, A. "Eye Tracking for Avatar Eye Gaze Control During Object-Focused Multiparty Interaction in Immersive Collaborative Virtual Environments," Virtual Reality Conference, VR. IEEE, pp. 83–90, 2009.

Multimedia Technology IV – Farag, Yang & Jiao (Eds)
© *2015 Taylor & Francis Group, London, ISBN: 978-1-138-02794-7*

Improved algorithm of EPZS based on rotary coordinate system and movement similarity

Xi-Jia Song, Yi Lv, Liang Yang & Wei Liu
University of Electronic Science and Technogy of China, Zhongshan Institute, Zhongshan, China

ABSTRACT: In order to reduce the execute time of EPZS (Enhanced Predictive Zonal Search) algorithm on the premise of ensuring the image quality, an accurate judgment of uniformity of motion vectors was made using rotated Cartesian coordinate system in this paper, and different optimize methods were proposed according to the judgment. If the motion vectors were uniformity, parts of redundant search process would be skipped. Otherwise, the median motion vector was substituted by a new one. The experiments verify that the performance of optimized EPZS algorithm is improved obviously. The search time is saved about 28.19%, and the PSNR is raised 0.02 dB on average.

Keywords: H.264/AVC; EPZS; motion estimation; rotary coordinate System; movement similarity

1 INTRODUCTION

Motion estimation (ME) is not only an integral component, but the most time-consuming part of the latest video coding standard of H246/AVC because of its high computation complexity. Experiments show that motion estimation (ME) consumes about 60% (1 reference frames) to 80% (5 reference frames) of the total encoding time when full search method is used. Therefore, fast motion search methods are adopted to realize more efficient video coding [1–3].

Lots of mature arithmetic has been proposed in recent years. For example, Unsymmetrical-Cross Multi-Hexagon-Grid search algorithm (UMHeagonS), simplified UMHeagonS algorithm and Enhanced Predictive Zonal Search algorithm (EPZS), which is focused on in this paper [4–5].

2 A SYNOPSIS OF EPZS

EPZS is a predictive fast motion search algorithm, the main execution steps are as follows:

Step 1: The motion predictor set is divided into four sub-sets, which are denoted as:

$$S = \{S_1, S_2, S_3, S_4\} \tag{1}$$

The four subsets S_1, S_2, S_3, S_4 are as follows:

1) Motion Vector Predictor (MVP), which is the most important predictor, and it is the median value of the adjacent blocks on the left, top, and top-right (or top-left) of the current block.

$$S_1 = \left\{ \vec{MV}_{median} \right\} \tag{2}$$

2) It is composed of collocated block in the previous frame and the spatially adjacent blocks.

$$S_2 = \left\{ \vec{MV}_{t-1}, \vec{MV}_{t,left}, \vec{MV}_{t,up}, \vec{MV}_{t,right\_up}, \vec{MV}_{t,left\_up}, \vec{MV}_{center} \right\} \tag{3}$$

3) S_3 is composed of spatial memory consumption predictors, time-domain predictors and upper layer block predictors.
4) S_4 is made up by window predictors.

Step 2: Check the rate-distortion cost of MVP in accordance with formula (4).

$$J(\vec{m}, \lambda_{MOTION}) = SAD(s, c(\vec{m})) + \lambda_{MOTION} \cdot R(\vec{m} - \vec{p}) \tag{4}$$

The motion search process would be terminated if the cost value satisfied the formula (5)

$$J_{best} \leq J_i \leq TH \tag{5}$$

Here, J_{best} is the best $J(\vec{m}, \lambda_{MOTION})$, and J_i ($i = 1, 2, \ldots, n$) is matching error in different positions, and TH is the termination threshold [6].

Step 3: Search the predictors in S_2, S_3 and S_4 successively and calculate the rate-distortion cost in accordance with formula (4), the location of the one with the smallest cost and the one with the second smallest cost are record.

Step 4: Stop the process of ME if the predictors with the minimum cost meet the termination condition. Otherwise, the search center moves to the location with the minimum rate-distortion cost and continue to next step.

Step 5: Select the extEPZS as search pattern. Utilized this pattern recursively until the center of the pattern has the minimum rate-distortion cost. Then select the small diamond pattern and repeat the search process. This process will be stopped until the vector with minimum rate-distortion cost is the center of small diamond.

Step 6: The search center is moved to the location with the second smallest rate-distortion cost in the step 3 if this location was not checked so far, and another repetitive will be executed. Otherwise, motion estimation process stops.

3   IMPROVED ALGORITHM OF EPZS

There are two shortcomings needed to be improved and optimized in the EPZS execute process described in section 2:

1) A clause in EPZS provides that all of the predictors in subsets S_2, S_3 and S_4 should be checked if EPZS could not meet terminate threshold in the Step 2. But there are too many predictors in subsets S_2, S_3 and S_4. It would consume a large amount of encoding time. Many experiments show that searching predictors in S_4 will not improve the quality of image obviously if the motion vectors of image sequence are uniform, instead, it will increase the encoding time largely. So first of all, we have to decide whether the motion vectors are uniformity or not. If these vectors are uniformity, we skip the searching process of subset S_4. At the same time, the process of searching the location with the second smallest rate-distortion cost can also be omitted. This optimization here can be denoted as OPT1.

2) The initial point which begins EPZS searching process is Motion Vector Predictor (MVP). When the predictors are uniformity, MVP can predict the optimum vector very well and the commutation is really convenient. However, the value of MVP is fixed and can not adaptive change according to the relations of current block and its adjacent blocks. Especially, the value of MVP may deviate from the best vector greatly when the predictors are not uniformity, this will substantially increase the points which needed to check and spend too much encoding time on motion search. So it is necessary to establish a new predictive model of initial searching point, and get a new initial point instead of MVP. This optimization here can be denoted as OPT2.

3.1   *The method of determing the motion vector uniformity*

1) Determine the angle uniformity of motion vectors

Consistency of the vector angle is usually determined in the normal conduct of the Cartesian coordinate system. In the first place, coordinate space is divided into four quadrants, The Quadrant where vector $\vec{V}$ locates in is denoted $Q(\vec{V})$. Then according to the formula (6), we determine the uniformity of vector angle.

$$DQ = \max_{\vec{V}_1 \in V} (Q(\vec{V}_1)) - \min_{\vec{V}_2 \in V} (Q(\vec{V}_2)) \qquad (6)$$

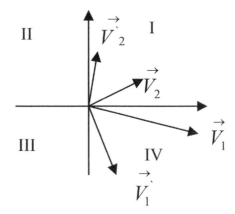

Figure 1.   The general judgment method of angle uniformity.

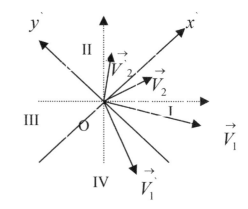

Figure 2.   The improved judgment method of angle uniformity.

Here, DQ is the largest difference between quadrants. It is considered that the angles are uniformity when $DQ = 0$ or $DQ = 1$.

However, this approach has many limitations. As is shown in Fig. 1, the angle consistency of the vector of $\vec{V}_1$ and $\vec{V}_2$ is well, but because of locating in the quadrant IV and the quadrant I respectively, they cannot meet the conditions of $DQ = 0$. If we use $DQ = 1$ to judge the angle uniformity, $\vec{V}_1$ and $\vec{V}_2$ can meet this condition, but $\vec{V}_3$ and $\vec{V}_4$, which are obviously inconsistent in Fig. 1, meet it too. In order to reflect the actual situation better and determine the uniformity of motion vectors accurately, The Cartesian coordinate is counter-clockwise rotated in $\pi/4$ radian, as is shown in Fig. 2, according to the characteristics that the moving objects do much more horizontal and vertical motions than other directions. Then the formula (6) is used again to check the uniformity.

Specific decision process as follows:

Step 1: Choosing predictive vector Set:

$$V = \{\{S_2\}, \{S_3\}\} \qquad (7)$$

It contains all predictive vectors of subset S_1 and S_2.

Step 2: Cartesian coordinate system is counter-clockwise rotated $\pi/4$ radian, divided the original space into four quadrants. The quadrant where vectors $\vec{V}$ located is denoted as: $Q(\vec{V})$.

Step 3: following the formula (6) to check the uniformity of vectors in Set:

$$V = \{\{S_2\},\{S_3\}\} \tag{8}$$

If $DQ = 0$, the moving object has angle uniformity, and vice versa.

2) Determine the uniformity of motion vector amplitude

In order to determine the uniformity of vectors magnitude, we introduce variables DM to represent the vector difference. It consists of the difference value DM_x of the x direction and DM_y of the y direction [7].

Mathematical expression is as followed:

$$DM = DM_x + DM_y \tag{9}$$

$$DM_x = \max_{(V_{1x},V_{1y})\in V}(V_{1x}) - \min_{(V_{2x},V_{2y})\in V}(V_{2x}) \tag{10}$$

$$DM_y = \max_{(V_{1x},V_{1y})\in V}(V_{1y}) - \min_{(V_{2x},V_{2y})\in V}(V_{2y}) \tag{11}$$

If $DM \leq 2$, it is considered that the motion vectors amplitude is uniformity.

3.2 Optimum proposal of initial searching point model

As is known that if a candidate vector is closer to the actual vector, the motion character of its corresponding block is more similar to the current block. The collection of motion vectors can be denoted as follow:

$$V = \left\{\vec{V}_0,\vec{V}_1,\vec{V}_2,\vec{V}_3,\vec{V}_4\right\} \tag{12}$$

Here, $\vec{V}_4$ is the average of the motion vectors of the current blocks and eight neighboring blocks in reference frame.

The predictive vector of initial search point is denoted as $\vec{VP}$, its value can be calculated using following formula:

$$VP_x = \sum_{i=0}^{4} T_i V_{ix} \tag{13}$$

$$VP_y = \sum_{i=0}^{4} T_i V_{iy} \tag{14}$$

Among them, T_i ($i = 0, 1, 2, 3, 4$) is the parameter for each component. The value is depended on the similarity between the i candidate vector, which was got in last motion search, and the actual motion vector. Usually we used the Euclidean distance to describe the similarity of the candidate vector and the actual vector.

$$DIFF_i = \sqrt{(V_{xi}-V_x)^2+(V_{yi}-V_y)^2} \tag{15}$$

In order to simplify operations, used the inequality principle to amplify the $DIFF_i$:

$$\sqrt{(V_{xi}-V_x)^2+(V_{yi}-V_y)^2} \leq |V_{xi}-V_x|+|V_{yi}-V_y| \tag{16}$$

$$DIFF_i = |V_{xi}-V_x|+|V_{yi}-V_y| \tag{17}$$

1) If there are $N(N > 0)$ vectors satisfied:

$$DIFF_i = 0 \tag{18}$$

The T_i is set to $1/N$, and other vectors are set to 0.

2) If none of the vectors satisfy the condition of (18), and there is N ($N > 3$) vectors satisfied the condition:

$$0 < DIFF_i \leq 1 \tag{19}$$

We set the T_i which inside the scope to $1/N$, and others are set to zero.

3) When none of conditions in 1) and 2) are satisfied, parameters of weights T_i can be calculated as follows:

$$L_i = \frac{1}{DIFF_i} \quad (i = 0,1,2,3,4) \tag{20}$$

$$T_i = \frac{L_i}{\sum_{i=0}^{4} L_i} \quad (i = 0,1,2,3,4) \tag{21}$$

4 EXPERIMENTAL RESULTS AND ANALYSIS

This paper selects the four motion sequence as coding objects: Container, Foreman, Bus and Mobile. Sequence is IPPP…, Frame rate: 30 fps, Search range is set to 32, open RDO, adopt Hadamard transform, using CABAC, quantitative parameters QP is set to 28, coding 90 frames. Experimental results are shown in Table 1.

We can get three conclusions from the experimental results:

1) When a single method is used to optimize EPZS algorithm, Either OPT1 or OPT2 can effectively reduce motion search time. Because the OPT1 choose less search points, it can reduce motion estimation time, about 15.90% on average, and SNR declined slightly (about 0.04 dB on average). Because the OPT2 uses the similarity of the motion vectors to select the initial searching point, it can make the algorithm quickly approaching to optimal vector point, and reduce searching time effectively, about 24.36% on average.

Table 1. Experiment results for container sequence.

Sequence algorithm	Container.qcif			
	EPZS	OPT1	OPT2	OPT12
PSNRY (dB)	36.24	36.24	36.28	36.26
Rae (kbit/s)	36.27	36.32	36.27	36.31
ME.T (s)	70.18	64.84	54.83	51.76
ΔPSNRY (dB)	0	0	0.04	0.02
ΔRate (%)	0	0.13	0	0.11
ΔME (%)	0	−14.73	−21.87	−26.25

Table 2. Experiment results for foreman sequence.

Sequence algorithm	Foreman.qcif			
	EPZS	OPT1	OPT2	OPT12
PSNRY (dB)	36.93	36.92	36.96	36.92
Rae (kbit/s)	129.08	129.23	129.12	128.91
ME.T (s)	97.68	82.77	74.45	60.57
ΔPSNRY (dB)	0	−0.01	0.03	−0.01
ΔRate (%)	0	0.12	0.03	−0.13
ΔME (%)	0	−15.26	−23.78	−28.76

Table 3. Experiment results for bus sequence.

Sequence algorithm	Bus.qcif			
	EPZS	OPT1	OPT2	OPT12
PSNRY (dB)	36.59	36.57	36.61	36.61
Rae (kbit/s)	1286.02	1288.08	1288.59	1288.46
ME.T (s)	139.34	116.60	101.36	98.59
ΔPSNRY (dB)	0	−0.02	0.02	0.02
ΔRate (%)	0	0.16	0.20	0.19
ΔME (%)	0	−16.32	−27.26	−29.03

Table 4. Experiment results for mobile sequence.

Sequence algorithm	Mobile.qcif			
	EPZS	OPT1	OPT2	OPT12
PSNRY(dB)	35.52	35.47	35.57	35.56
Rae(kbit/s)	1401.25	1403.49	1402.65	1403.63
ME.T(s)	146.73	121.38	110.72	104.59
ΔPSNRY(dB)	0	−0.05	0.05	0.04
ΔRate(%)	0	0.16	0.10	0.17
ΔME(%)	0	−17.28	−24.54	−28.72

Table 5. Average value of opt12 algorithm.

Algorithm	ΔPSNRY (dB)	ΔRate (%)	ΔME (%)
OPT12	0.02	0.09	−28.19

2) If both OPT1 and OPT2 are adopted in the same time, we can achieve the best results. It can reduce motion searching time about 28.19% on average, SNR can be increased about 0.02 dB on average, and bitrate does not changed acutely.

3) From the result, we also know that more complexity of the sequence, more performance improvement we can get from the optimized algorithm.

5 CONCLUSION

Because of using rotated Cartesian coordinate system, we can get a more accurate judgment of motion vectors uniformity. If the motion vectors are uniformity, parts of redundant process are skipped. Inversely, when the vectors are not uniformity, the median vector can be substituted by a new one which can be obtained from an optimum model. Experiments has shown that the improved method can increase the performance of EPZS availably, in the meantime, it can reduce the motion searching time markedly and does not loss image quality.

ACKNOWLEDGEMENT

The paper is funded by the Science and Technology Planning Project Fund of ZhongShan City, China (2013A3FC0289), funded by Dr Startup project Fund, Zhongshan (413YKQ03), and supported by Team Building Intelligent Systems And Application Research Fund of University of Electronic Science and Technology of China Zhongshan Institute (412YT01), and supported by the teaching reform Fund of University of Electronic Science and Technology of China Zhongshan Institute (JY201418).

REFERENCES

[1] JVT, "Advanced video coding for generic audiovisual services," Recommendation ITU H.264.
[2] Wang Xin-yu, and Zhang Zhao-yang, "A fast motion estimation algorithm applied for H.264/AVC," Journal of Optoelectronics·Laser, vol. 16, pp. 1123–1228, September 2005.
[3] ZhiBo C, and Peng Z, "Yun H, Fast integer pel and fractional pel motion estimation for JVT," Document JVT-F017, JVT 6th Meeting. 2002.
[4] Yi Xiao-quan, and Zhang Jun, Ling Nam, "Improved and Simplified fast motion estimation for JM," Document JVT-P021. Poznan, Poland: JVT 16th Meeting, 2005.
[5] A. Tourapis, "Enhanced predictive zonal search for single and multiple frame motion estimation," Proceedings of Visual Communication and Image Processing, 2002, pp. 1069–1079.
[6] Wei Wei, and Hou Zheng-xin. "A fast motion estimation algorithm with adaptive threshold," Journal of Optoelectronics Laster, vol. 19, pp. 1254–1257, September, 2008.
[7] Duanmu Chun-jiang, and Zhou Dong-hui, "An improved EPZS algorithm for fast block motion estimation", Third International Conference on Education Technology and Training. 2010, pp. 531–534.

Multimedia Technology IV – Farag, Yang & Jiao (Eds)
© 2015 Taylor & Francis Group, London, ISBN: 978-1-138-02794-7

A SaaS-based software modeling for bank intermediary business

Bo Li
Computer Science and Technology Department, Harbin Institute of Technology, Harbin, China
School of Computing, I&D Systems Engineering, Arizona State University, Tempe, USA

Wei-Tek Tsai
School of Computing, I&D Systems Engineering, Arizona State University, Tempe, USA

Haiying Zhou & Decheng Zuo
Computer Science and Technology Department, Harbin Institute of Technology, Harbin, China

ABSTRACT: Software-as-a-Service (SaaS) is a new research orientation for developing software, and has multi-tenancy architecture and customization features, which are very suitable for performance and benchmark test of OLTP transactions. And Bank Intermediary Business (BIB) is the most important business of Bank financial system. This paper focuses on establishing the SaaS-based BIB performance and benchmark architecture and proposes the SaaS-based BIB Database Model (SaaS-BIB-DM), the architecture layer (SaaS-BIB-AL), the data flow view (SaaS-BIB-DF) and the representative transaction model (SaaS-BIB-TM). The database is further extended with the SaaS hybrid two-layer partition methodology and the performance is proved to be better than that in three-tier C/S architecture. And the specific SaaS-based BIB architecture which we proposed is 4-level SaaS-based architecture. Based on the analysis the state-of-art of BIB and SaaS, the paper further investigates future trend of SaaS-based performance testing architecture and benchmark.

Keywords: SaaS; performance; benchmark; testing; modeling; HPFT; OLTP; SOA; MTA; BIB

1 INTRODUCTION

The rapid development in society and economy propose more performance requirements for HPFT (High-Performance Fault-Tolerant) computers in national key industries, which makes the evaluation of HPFT performance and requirements for typical OLTP (On-Line Transaction Processing) applications becoming an important issue for both producers and end users. As SaaS (Software-as-a-service) is arising to be a new research orientation and interesting aspects, the combination research of SaaS and OLTP is necessary. SaaS has the multi-tenancy architecture, specific partition schema that is horizon, vertical or mixed/hybrid database partition schema, and customization. With these features, research on database design/partition, scalability, recovery and continuous testing is becoming more and more important. SaaS is a new approach for developing software, and it is characterized by its multi-tenancy architecture and its ability to provide flexible customization to individual tenant. The most important features of SaaS are MTA (Multi-Tenancy Architecture) and customization, which create many new issues in software and testing fields. SaaS is software that deployed over the Internet and often run on a cloud platform. With SaaS, a software provider licenses an application to customer as a service on demand, through a subscription or a "pay-as-you-go" model [6].

BIB is short for Bank Intermediary Business. BIB is developed as typical On-Line Transaction Processing (OLTP) transactions and provides various services to customers and third partner companies, such as On-Contract business, Trade-Charge agency, Trade-Payment agency, Multi-Trade business etc. BIB system has three actors, which is bank (service provider), third-party Company (multiple service consumers and users) and user (individual service consumer). Research indicates that the business model, database model, transaction/frame model, testing architecture and performance metrics constitute the benchmark and we analyze the BIB in following sections. BIB is one of the most important bank business assets and liability business, such as salary payment agency, water/electric fee charge agency, mobile fee agency etc. BIB has a large amount of data workload and average processing transactions, small transaction response time and high safety requirements [9]. BIB has three participants, which are third party client, client and bank. Bank-driven transactions are the main and key ones for BIB. We analyze the workflow of BIB and propose a new Bank

Intermediary Four-Level Architecture. Layer 1 is the GUI (Graphic User Interface) layer, different tenant (client or third-party client) has different GUI, and user can define its own style GUI panel. Layer 2 is the workflow business process layer, which composed of three- tier of old BIBmodel (Bank Intermediary Business Model) transaction model, third-party client and client will process indirectly by the bank agency software. Layer 3 is the services and composition layer, which composed of various BIB transactions, including 11 BIB transactions, such as New-Contract, Modify-Contract, Cancel-Contract, Trace-Payment, Trade-Charge, Balance-Lookup, Contract-Lookup, Trade-Lookup, Data-Maintain, Trade-Cleanup and Trade-Record Transactions. We will describe these architectures and transactions specific in Section 3. Layer 4 is the database level, we use SaaS hybrid database partition schema here to enhance the performance of database and testing.

This paper is organized as follows. Firstly, the paper introduces the state-of-art of SaaS, BIB and performance testing schemas. Section 2 summarizes the related works. Section 3 proposes a new Bank Intermediary Four-Level Architecture. Section 4 gives the scenario and use case study. Section 5 comes to a conclusion, to provide a scalable framework of BIB based on SaaS.

2 STUDY OF SAAS AND BIB

SaaS is software that deployed over the Internet and/or is deployed to run behind a firewall on a local-area network or personal computer. [2] From software providers' view, SaaS is the software, which licenses the application to customer as a service on demand, through a subscription or a "pay-as-you-go" model and meanwhile has multi-tenant and customization features. Multi-tenant means that the SaaS can be used by multiple users simultaneously but do not interrupt or influence each other. MTA (Multi-tenancy architecture) refers to a principle where a single instance of the software runs on a server, serving multiple client organization or tenants. A realistic SaaS application needs to address multiple issues, such as scalability, database partitioning and consistency, fault-tolerant aspects, security and fairness, parallel processing, isolation, performance and availability simultaneously. From end user's view, SaaS is feeling like using the software individually which is not shared with other tenants.

Recent studies about benchmarks and measurements techniques have been developed to quality and evaluate HPFT system performance, such as TPC-C [10] and TPC-E [11] benchmarks, which are the most significant OLTP benchmark and proposed by TPC council in 90th. TPC-C [10] benchmark simulates an order-entry computing environment where a population of users executes transactions against the TPC-C simple database and TPC-E [11] benchmark models a brokerage firm with customers who generate transactions related to trades, account inquiries,

and market research etc. Although there are many OLTP benchmarks, there is still a lack of benchmarks that is based on actual transactions and using high-performance architectures. The development tendency of BIB (Bank Intermediary Business) in around the world, especially in the difficult economy and financial environment, gives rise to study in the BIB benchmark fields. BIB has large amount of data workload and average processing transactions, small transaction response time and high safety requirements [9]. The most important performance metrics to measure OLTP system is the performance of system, which is discussed in our previous paper [9], [12], such as response time, system utilization, transactions per second. Performance benchmarks must include two major components, a workload which represents the work that the system must perform during the benchmark run time and a set of performance measures that characterizes the performance of the system under benchmark testing. The basis idea is to model the BIB business's architecture, database and transactions in order to establish the real BIB models and propose the suitable BIB benchmark with qualified metrics.

3 A SAAS-BASED BIB ARCHITECTURE AND MODELS

We categorize HPFT computer performance testing methods into three classes, methods based on performance benchmarks such as OLTP TPC serials, methods based on workload testing tools such as HP LoadRunner and Spirent Avalanche and methods based on architecture and workload/workflow analysis, which is studied in this paper. BIBmodel (Bank Intermediary Business Model) is modeled by the key-processing modules of BIB business. In this section, we propose and design the SaaS-based architecture, SaaS-BIB-DM (Database Model), SaaS-BIB-DF (DataFlow) and transactions description.

3.1 A SaaS-based BIB Architecture

Testing comprises activities that validate a system's aspects. New challenges arise at each SaaS testing level and typical SOA (Service-Oriented Architecture) testing is composed of composition testing, integration testing and functional testing. But the most fundamental is the architecture and models. We divide this SaaS-based BIB architecture into four layers, which are layer 1 GUI (different users has different GUI (Graphic User Interface) according to the user-design requirements), layer 2 BIB business process (description of BIB workflow, such as agent-in workflow, agent-out workflow, lookup-workflow etc.), layer 3 Services and Compositions (each BIB services is constructed separately and provides services for the upper layer) and layer 4 database (propose an BIB-DM which is database model of Bank Intermediary Business with the hybrid SaaS partition principles). The specific SaaS-based BIB architecture is showed in figure 1.

Figure 1. A SaaS-based BIB architecture.

3.2 SaaS-BIB-DM (Database Model)

MTA is short for Multi-Tenant Architecture and it is the key feature of SOA (Service-Oriented Architecture). MTA has the following benefits: (1) Accelerate time to value; (2) always on the latest release; (3) you can control your technology adoption; (4) turn the OR into AND; (5) and community collaboration is high; The SaaS-BIB-DM is abbreviation of Software-as-a-Service based Bank Intermediary Business Database Model, which described in the layer 4 of the SaaS-based BIB Architecture. We use the SaaS hybrid database partition schema to enhance the performance of database and testing. We divide the database of BIB into four categories, including Partner Tables (descriptions of third-party company tables), Customer Tables (descriptions of personal account and information tables), Bank Tables (descriptions of bank channel, account, contract and other information tables) and Dimension Tables (descriptions of assistance or accessories). There is three types of data in the SaaS-BIB-DM model, which is metadata, actual data and pivot index. And the database tables' description and the definition of database tables are showed in table 1.

Many partitioning schemes have been studied and we propose a hybrid partition scheme for the SaaS-BIB-DM model, which divide the table into rows and horizontal partitioning the key-value stores.

3.3 SaaS-BIB-WF (Workflow)

The SaaS-BIB-WF is abbreviation of Software-as-a-Service based Bank Intermediary Business Workflow, which described in the layer 2 of the SaaS-based BIB Architecture. The workflow business is composed of three-tier of old BIBmodel's (Bank Intermediary Business Model) actors, including bank, third-party company client and personal client. The workflow is showed in figure 2 and figure 3.

The SaaS-BIB-WF (Workflow) is composed of seven steps and if transform step failed, the workflow will start over from step 1. The workflow starts from the evocation of third-party Company or personal client required the BIB (Bank Intermediary Business) through bank counter or Internet services. Once the bank receives the requirements (processing the agent-transactions), the bank will search the corresponding services and transform to the SaaS-BIB-WF

Table 1. Database tables description.

Category	Description	Table Name	Prefix	Num
Partner Tables	Basic Info of Partner	Partner_Info	PI_	11
	Account of Partner	Partner Account	PA	5
	Salary of Employee	Employee_Salary	ES_	3
Customer Tables	Info of Customers	Customer_Info	CI	10
	Account of Customer	Customer_Account	CA_	9
Bank Tables	Basic Info of Channel	Channel_Info	CH_	3
	Types of Channel	Channer_Type	CT_	3
	Counter Channel Info	Counter_Channel	CH_	3
	ATM Channel Info	ATM Channel	CH_	3
	Call Center Channel	Call_Channel	CH_	3
	Online Bank Channel	Online_Channel	CH_	3
	Product Info Details	Product_Info	PR_	8
	Business Transaction	Business_Info	BI_	8
	Contract Info	Contract	CN_	19
	Teller Permission Info	Teller_Permission	TP_	5
	Bank Agency Info	Agency_Info	AI_	6
	Business Serial Info	Business_Serial	BS	6
	Process Control Info	Process_Control	PC_	6
Dimension Tables	Zip Code Info	Zip_Code	ZC	2
	Product Type Info	Product_Type	PT_	2
	Types of Business	Business_Type	BT_	2

Figure 2. A 3-tier service provider & service consumer & service broker model.

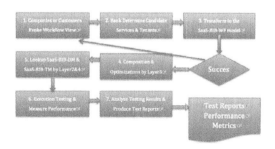

Figure 3. The SaaS-BIB-WF workflow figure.

on-demand form. If the Success judgment is failed, it goes back to step 1. Then step 4 will process them utilizing the layer 3 of SaaS-BIB architecture. Next, the real lookup and process workflow execution and simultaneously record the testing results and generate the results & reports for further analysis.

3.4 SaaS-BIB-TM (Transaction Model)

The SaaS-BIB-TM is abbreviation of Software-as-a-Service based Bank Intermediary Business Transaction Model, which described in the layer 3 of the SaaS-based BIB Architecture. The services and composition layer is composed of various BIB transactions, including 12 BIB transactions, such as New-Contract, Modify-Contract, Cancel-Contract, Trade-Payment, Trade-Charge, Balance-Lookup, Contract-Lookup, Trade-Lookup, Data-Maintenance, Trade-Cleanup, Trade-Record and SaaS-Trace Transactions.

4 BIB TRANSACTION DESCRIPTION AND TEST CASE STUDY

In this section, we first introduce two representative scenarios for Bank Intermediary Business (BIB) to illustrate the nucleus transactions, and each scenario has three participants. And then we explain our designed transactions for configuration and development acquirements.

4.1 BIB transaction description

We consider the most common BIB business, which is Trade-Charge and Trade-Payment. These trade transaction means that the bank is the agency to process financial or account problems for third-party company clients and personal clients.

There are four categories transactions, which have 12 BIB transitions. Contract transactions including three veritable transactions are New-Contract, Modify-Contract and Cancel-Contract. The premise of each transaction is that the third-party company client or personal client has already signed a required contract with the bank tier. These Contract category transactions are the fundamental of every Lookup, or Trade or Trace transactions. The Trade category has two key processing transactions, Trade-Charge and Trade- Payment transaction. The former transaction is applicable for scenario 1 and the latter transaction is applicable for scenario 2 for execution and testing. The Lookup category has three various lookup processing based on different target. Precisely, Balance-Lookup is to inquire the account balance of given customer, Contract-Lookup is to inquire whether the customers or clients have signed these kind of contracts with certificate bank tier, and Trade-Lookup is to inquire the log or trace of requested trade. The Trace category is to record some useful information or documents for execution these transactions or frames. Above all, the SaaS-based BIB benchmark at least has these four metrics: tpsBank (transactions per second of bank business), PCN (Parallel Concurrent Number of users), TRT (Transaction Processing Response Time) and RU (Resource utilization, including memory-RU, disk-RU, CPU-RU and bandwidth-RU), which are described in our previous paper and showed in figure 4.

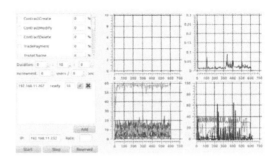

Figure 4. Example of a Saas-based performance testing runtime GUI.

4.2 Test case study

A scenario is a sequence of activities connected by the four operators: sequence, choice, loop and concurrency. Each activity is a data assignment, exchanging an event, doing an action, or executing a sub-scenario. This paper considers about two different scenarios in the future test case study:

(1) Simple scenario 1, the scenario of Trade-Charge Transaction, which is a telephone company, has multiple users who want to pay the mobile phone bills through the bank intermediary business. Then this telephone company will sign a contract with the bank to authorize the bank intermediary business system charging the fees of its mobile users. Instead of go to telephone company to pay the bills each time, users of the telephone company can choose using enormous bank agency to pay the bills which is very convenient since the bank has many bank counter and Internet services are mature and security enough.

(2) Complex or composite scenario 2 is that an international company has to pay salaries each month to its employee and send out the bonus yearly. The international company should sign a contract with the bank intermediary business system to get the service of agency pay salary workflow. According to the contract, it will have a pay salary date and the BIB system will update the balance of the company and the accounts of its employees' simultaneously. This transaction should be done together or done nothing and it is the scenario of Trade-Payment Transaction.

5 CONCLUSION AND FUTURE WORKS

SaaS is characterized by its multi-tenancy architecture and its ability to provide flexible customization to individual tenant, and SaaS is developed in much realistic OLTP business, especially in BIB (Bank Intermediary Business) applied with this new SaaS architecture. We firstly combine the SaaS architecture with a typical OLTP business – BIB. And we propose a SaaS-based BIB architecture, database model, transaction model and workflow model. For case study, we describe two representative scenarios for execution and deployment. These models are the fundamental and essential elements of a representative benchmark.

In conclusion, the complexity of transactions is increasing due to new business offerings, compliance and consolidation, which makes the 4C testing and schema, becomes very important, including Complete & Collaborative Testing, Continuous Validation and Constraint Virtualization. So, for the future study, we will continuous study the 4C of the architecture and BIB business and obtain some useful testing results to fulfill the schema and theory.

ACKNOWLEDGMENT

The authors would like to thank all the colleagues and co-partners who have contributed to the study. The work is supported by the grants from the National High-Tech R & D Plan of China (2009AA01A404), International S & T Cooperation Program of China (No. 2010DFA14400). Also thanks to the visiting scholarship of CSC and thanks to the support of Harbin Institute of Technology, Arizona State University and Tsinghua University.

REFERENCES

[1] Benchmark Characteristics and Benchmark Performance Prediction [C]." 1996 ACM 0734-2071/96/1100-0344. Vol. 14, No. 4, pp. 334–384.

[2] Wei-Tek Tsai, Qihong Shao, Yu Huang, Xiaoying Bai. "Towards a Scalable and Robust Multi-tenancy SaaS [C]." 2010.

[3] Xiaoying Bai, Muyang Li, Bin Chen, Wei-Tek Tsai, Jerry Gao. "Cloud Testing Tools [C]." SOSE2011.

[4] Brian Davis. "iTKO Overview [C]". Interactive TKO, Inc. Jan. 2009.

[5] K. Kanoun, P. Koopman. "Dependability Benchmarking: A Realit or A Dream [C]." IEEE Computer Society. 2008:1.

[6] Wei-Tek Tsai, Yu Huang, Qihong Shao, and Xiaoying Bai. "Data Partitioning and Redundancy Management for Robust Multi-Tenancy SaaS [J]." Int J Software Informatics, Vol. 4, No. 4, December 2010. pp. 437–471.

[7] Wei-Tek Tsai, Qihong Shao, Wu Li. "OIC: Ontology-based Intelligent Customization Framwork for SaaS [C]." 2010.

[8] Wu Li, Yann-Hang Lee, Wei-Tek Tsai. "Service-Oriented smart home applications: composition, code generation, deployment and execution [C]." SOCA 2011.

[9] Bo Li, Haiying Zhou, Decheng Zuo, Zhan Zhang, Peng Zhou and Long Jia. "Performance Modeling and Benchmarking of Bank Intermediary Business on High- Performance Fault-Tolerant Computers [C]." DSN2011. 978-1-4577-0375-1/11 pp. 234-239.

[10] Transaction Processing Performance Council (TPC). TPC-C BENCHMARKTM Standard Specification Version 5.11.2010.

[11] Transaction Processing Performance Council (TPC). TPC-E BENCHMARKTM Standard Specification Version 1.23.0.2010J. Clerk Maxwell, A Treatise on Electricity and Magnetism, 3rd ed., vol. 2. Oxford: Clarendon, 1892, pp. 68–73.

[12] Bo Li, Haiying Zhou, Decheng Zuo. "Workload Performance Characterizaiton and Test Strategy of High-Performance Fault-Tolerant Computers based on BIBbench [J]." ICMEE2011.

[13] Wei-Tek Tsai, Xiaoying Bai & Yu Huang. "Software-as-a-Service (SaaS): Perspectives and Challenges". Science China. May 2012, Vol. 53, No. 1: 1–18.

Multimedia Technology IV – Farag, Yang & Jiao (Eds)
© 2015 Taylor & Francis Group, London, ISBN: 978-1-138-02794-7

Fractional order arc-length term for level set

Shenshen Sun

Department of Computer Technology, Shenyang University, Shenyang, Liaoning, China

ABSTRACT: Generalize CV model of level set from integer order to fractional order, through extending arc-length term to fractional order arc-length term. The Euler-Lagrange equation of fractional order arc-length term is deduced by solving a typical fractional variation problem. And convolution with fractional order mask defined by G-L definition is used to solve numerical approximation of this complicated fractional partial differential equation. Then, following things are found through experiments. Fractional order arc-length term for any an order can be all considered as a curve length-shorten flowing which owns same properties of arc-length term and its convergence iteration times is increased with its order. The segmentation results using fractional CV model with small order are better than the traditional corresponding models. Fractional order arc-length term can be instead of arc-length term and added into other level set models easily.

Keywords: Level set, fractional order partial differential equations, variation method, image segmentation

1 INTRODUCTION

The class of geometric deformation models, also known as level set, has brought tremendous impact to 2D and 3D image segmentation due to its capability of topology preservation and fast shape recovery [1]. Generally, the classical level set framework consists of an implicit data representation of a hyper-surface, a set of partial differential equations (PDE) that govern how the curve moves, so as to minimize a given energy function in order to produce the desired segmentation [2]–[3]. Researchers modified the level set model on the following three aspects: modified data terms, modified regularization terms and improve its computing time.

Existing level set models about data terms can be categorized into two major classes: edge-based models and region-based models. Edge-based models utilize image gradients to identify object boundaries but it has been found to be very sensitive to image noise, such as Geodesic Active Contours (GAC) [4]. Region-based models utilize image feature to identify each region of interest. The popular piecewise constant (PC) models, such as Chan-Vese [5], rely on intensity homogeneity and initial conditions. More advanced techniques attempt to regions using global statistics by known distributions, intensity histogram, texture maps, structure tensors, or shape [6]. More Recently, work for segmenting real images especially medical images has been focused on localizing region-based level set [3] [7]. For example, [8] segment MRI images by an interleaved process of evolution based on a local clustering property and estimation of the bias field. [12] proposed hard and soft additive models to segment a pair of overlapping objects. Multi-phase image segmentation by kernel mapping in Bayesian framework is studied in [16].

For improving the level-set curve evolution speed, the method of only solving PDE around a narrow band in the neighborhood of the zero level set to evolve the curve according to its speed is proposed in [9]. The implicit function is expressed as a continuous B-spline function, and then the minimization of the energy function is directly obtained in terms of the B-spline coefficients through a convolution operation which yields an efficient algorithm [14]. According to phase-field [10], a element switching mechanism between two linked lists realizes curve evolution efficiently [11], [17] describe graphics processor (GPU) based algorithms for solving level set solution to achieve ten times speed improvement.

Regularization terms can be classified into two classes. The one is a term in order to avoid reinitialization. For example, the distance regularization term is defined with a potential function such the derived level set evolution has a unique forward-and-backward diffusion effect, which is able to maintain a signed distance profile near the zero level set [13] and it is expansion of the method [7].

The other is about curvilinear properties, such as area-minimization-based flow, affine shortening flow [17] and length-minimization-based flow. Area minimization based flow is a constant (hyperbolic) term, and length minimization based flow is a curvature (parabolic) term [15]. All of them can make the curve shrink as fast as possible but in a different way. Arbitrary shape initial closed curve will become smooth and converge to round points and then disappear when evolving according to the curvature motion without developing singularities. Length-minimization-based flow is also called as Euclidean geometrical invariability flow which is computed by convolving with a median filter and does not intersect itself during evolution. This phenomena is not like linear geometrical heat flow which is computed by convolving a path-based parametric representation of the curve with a Gaussian function [18].

Level set is a kind of variation PDE model. Recently, a modification of these variation PDE models, which generalizes differential order, has aroused the more and more attentions from some scholars. There are two types of generalization of the differentiations in the vocational PDE models. The one deals with higher-order differentiations, and the other deals with fractional order differentiations [19]. Many definitions of fractional differentiation, a mathematical discipline dealing with the differentiation of arbitrary order, have been proposed and the most popular definitions among them involve: Riemann-Liouville definition, Grunwald-Letnikow definition and Caputo definition [21], [22] deduced the formulation of Euler-Lagrange equations for fractional variational problems by the left and right fractional derivative.

In this paper, we focus on fractional order of level set model, especially aiming our interests at the curvature term. Although many application of such a model can be found, there has been very few, if not none, studies of this problem. The main contributions of the paper are summarized below: 1) Extend the curvature term of Level set model to fractional order term, which is called fractional arc-length minimizing flow. 2) Discuss the relationship between fractional order and closed curve convergence speed driven by fractional arc-length minimizing flow. 3) Some numerical experiments are presented to analyze the improvement due to using fraction order instead of the integer order in Level set model.

This paper is organized as follows: Section 1 introduces prior work on level set and fraction order application in image processing, and describe the proposed fractional order variational level set model in Section 2. A numerical implementation of the proposed model is introduced in Section 3. Experimental results and discussing are presented in Section 4 and the paper is concluded in Section 5.

2 FRACTIONAL ORDER CV MODEL

2.1 Description of the model

Fractional order term of the curve C is considered as a novel regularizing term added into CV model instead of length term of the curve. The curve C is represented implicitly via a Lipschitz function u, by $C = \{(x, y) | u(x, y) = 0\}$. Fractional order term is described as the function u whose derivative of order α has minimal L^2 norm defined as $\int_C |D^\alpha u| dx dy$ (for $\alpha = 1$, $|Du|$ is length, and for $\alpha = 2$, $|D^2 u|$ is curvature), where D^α

denotes the fractional derivative operator defined by $D^\alpha u = (D_x^\alpha u, D_y^\alpha u)$ and $|D^\alpha u| = \sqrt{(D_x^\alpha u)^2 + (D_y^\alpha u)^2}$.

Let us define the evolving curve C in Ω, as the boundary of an open subset ω of Ω (i.e. $\omega \subset \Omega$, and $C = \partial \omega$). In what follows, *inside(C)* denotes the region ω (i.e. $u(x, y) > 0$), and *outside(C)* denotes the region $\Omega \backslash \bar{\omega}$ (i.e. $u(x, y) < 0$). Therefore, we introduce the energy functional $E(c_1, c_2, C)$, defined by

$$
\begin{aligned}
E(c_1, c_2, C) &= \mu \cdot \int_C |D^\alpha(u(x, y))| dx dy \\
&+ \lambda_1 \cdot \int_\omega |u_0(x, y) - c_1|^2 dx dy \\
&+ \lambda_2 \cdot \int_{\Omega \backslash \bar{\omega}} |u_0(x, y) - c_2|^2 dx dy
\end{aligned}
\tag{1}
$$

where $\mu \geq 0$, $\lambda_1, \lambda_2 > 0$ are fixed parameters and u_0 is the original image. In almost all our numerical calculations, we fix $\lambda_1 = \lambda_2 = 1$.

Using the Heaviside function H, and the one-dimensional Dirac measure δ_0, we re-written the energy function $E(c_1, c_2, u)$ as

$$
\begin{aligned}
E(c_1, c_2, u) &= \mu \cdot \int_\Omega |D^\alpha(u(x, y))| dx dy \\
&+ \lambda_1 \cdot \int_\Omega |u_0(x, y) - c_1|^2 H(u(x, y)) dx dy \\
&+ \lambda_2 \cdot \int_\Omega |u_0(x, y) - c_2|^2 (1 - H(u(x, y))) dx dy
\end{aligned}
$$

where c_1 and c_2 are in fact given by

$$
\begin{aligned}
c_1(u) &= average(u_0) in\{u \geq 0\} \\
c_2(u) &= average(u_0) in\{u < 0\}.
\end{aligned}
$$

In order to compute the associated Euler-Lagrange equation for the unknown function u, we consider to use H_ϵ and δ_ϵ as $\epsilon \to 0$ instead of H and δ_0, $\delta_\epsilon = H_\epsilon'$. Let us denote by F_ϵ the associated regularized function, defined by

$$
\begin{aligned}
E_\epsilon(c_1, c_2, u) &= \mu \cdot \int_\Omega |D^\alpha(u(x, y))| dx dy \\
&+ \lambda_1 \cdot \int_\Omega |u_0(x, y) - c_1|^2 H_\epsilon(u(x, y)) dx dy \\
&+ \lambda_2 \cdot \int_\Omega |u_0(x, y) - c_2|^2 (1 - H_\epsilon(u(x, y))) dx dy
\end{aligned}
$$

Keeping c_1 and c_2 fixed, and minimizing F_ϵ with respect to u, we deduce the associated Euler-Lagrange equation for u. First, we should formally compute the fractional order Euler-Lagrange equation for fractional arc-length term as follows. Taking any test function $\eta \in C^\infty(\bar{\Omega})$. Define

$$
\phi(a) = \int_\Omega |D^\alpha u + a D^\alpha \eta| dx dy.
$$

82

We obtain

$$
\begin{aligned}
\phi'(0) &= \frac{d}{da}\int_\Omega |D^\alpha u + aD^\alpha \eta| dxdy \ \big|_{a=0} \\
&= \int_\Omega \frac{1}{|D^\alpha u|}(D_x^\alpha u D_x^\alpha \eta + D_y^\alpha u D_y^\alpha \eta) dxdy \\
&= \int_\Omega ((D_x^\alpha)^*(|D^\alpha u|^{-1} D_x^\alpha u) \\
&+ (D_y^\alpha)^*(|D^\alpha u|^{-1} D_y^\alpha u)) \eta dxdy \\
&= \int_\Omega (({}_x D_b^\alpha)((|D^\alpha u|^{-1} \cdot_a D_x^\alpha u) \\
&+ ({}_y D_b^\alpha)((|D^\alpha u|^{-1} \cdot_a D_y^\alpha u)) \eta dxdy
\end{aligned}
$$

for all $\eta \in C^{\infty(\Omega)}$, where $D_x^{\alpha*}$ is the adjoint of D_x^α and $D_y^{\alpha*}$ is the adjoint of D_y^α. aD_x^α and aD_y^α are the left fractional order derivative, while $({}_x D_b^\alpha)$ and $({}_y D_b^\alpha)$ are the right fractional order derivative.

Parameterizing the descent direction by an artificial time $t \geq 0$, the equation of the fractional order term called fractional order MCM (Mean Curvature Motion)function in $u(t, x, y)$ (with $u(0, x, y) = u_0(x, y)$ defining the initial contour) may be solved through the following gradient descent procedure:

$$
\begin{aligned}
div^\alpha(\frac{D^\alpha u}{|D^\alpha u|})|D^\alpha u| &= |D^\alpha u| * (({}_x D_b^\alpha)((|D^\alpha u|)^{-1} *_a D_x^\alpha u) \\
&+ ({}_y D_b^\alpha)((|D^\alpha u|)^{-1} *_a D_y^\alpha u)) \quad (3)
\end{aligned}
$$

And then, the integral order Euler-Lagrange equation is used to compute other terms and merge them together. So the PDE function of fractional order CV model can be expressed as

$$
\begin{aligned}
\frac{\partial u}{\partial t} &= \mu div^\alpha(\frac{D^\alpha u}{|D^\alpha u|})|D^\alpha u| \\
&+ \delta_\epsilon(u)[-\lambda_1(u_0 - c_1)^2 + \lambda_2(u_0 - c_2)^2] \quad (4)
\end{aligned}
$$

2.2 Relation with the CV Model

Taking $\alpha = 1$, the fractional order CV model described in formula (1) is equal to the CV model. That is because,

$$
\int_C |D^1(u(x, y))| dxdy = \int_C |\nabla u(x, y))| dxdy = Length(C).
$$

At the same way, the result of formula (3), when α is equal to 1, also can be described as the MCM function $div\left(\frac{\nabla u}{|\nabla u|}\right)|\nabla u|$ as state in literature [5].

Taking $\alpha = 2$, symbolic computation is used to solve the update of the function u by formula (3), then obtain

the formula (2). The energy function of the second order term is

$$
\begin{aligned}
E &= \int_\Omega |\nabla^2 u(x, y)| dxdy \\
&= \int_\Omega \sqrt{u_{xx}^2 + u_{yy}^2} dxdy
\end{aligned}
$$

Using Euler-Lagrange equation $\frac{\partial F}{\partial u} = \frac{d}{dxx}\left(\frac{\partial F}{\partial u_{xx}}\right) + \frac{d}{dyy}\left(\frac{\partial F}{\partial u_{yy}}\right)$, where $F = \sqrt{u_{xx}^2 + u_{yy}^2}$, the same result as formula (2) can be obtained by symbolic computation. Above all, it can be seen that integer order CV model (and integer order MCM function) is only special case of fractional order CV model (and fractional order MCM function). Fractional order CV model (and fractional order MCM function) can represent any order differential CV model(and integer order MCM function).

3 EXPERIMENTAL RESULTS

In order to demonstrate the strengths of the proposed fractional order CV model, we performed several experiments. First, compare the convergence iteration times, under different fractional orders, with only fractional order term in the energy function. Next, compare the segmentation results of fractional order CV model with the traditional CV model. Finally, compare fractional order region-scale model with the traditional region-scale fitting model [7] to show that fractional order term can be applied broadly in multifarious level set models.

The experiments of this paper are realized based on [33] software program whose purpose is to evaluate the performance of different level-set based segmentation algorithms in the context of image processing. All codes of the proposed model are implemented using MATLAB language on a computer with AMD E-350 Processor 1.60 GHz CPU, 3G RAM and Windows 7 operating system.

3.1 Relationship between curve convergence iteration times and fractional order

In this subsection, only fractional order term is focused on. That is, minimize the energy function $E(C) = \int_\Omega |D^\alpha u(x, y)| dxdy$.

Under the different fractional order, the convergence evolution procedure results which are driven only by fractional order term is shown in Fig. 2. The

$$
\begin{aligned}
\frac{\partial u}{\partial t} &= \frac{1}{(u_{xx}^2 + u_{yy}^2)^{5\backslash 2}}(u_{yy}^3(-u_{xxy}^2 - 2u_{xxx}u_{xyy} + u_{xxxx}u_{yy}) - u_{xx}^3(u_{xyy}^2 + 2u_{xxyy}u_{yy} + 2u_{xxy}u_{yyy}) \\
&+ u_{xx}^2 u_{yy}(2u_{xxy}^2 + u_{xx}^4 u_{yyyy} + 4u_{xxx}u_{xyy} + u_{xxxx}u_{yy} - 3u_{yyy}^2 + u_{yy}u_{yyyy}) + u_{xx}^4 u_{yyyy} \\
&+ u_{xx}u_{yy}^2(-3u_{xxx}^2 + 2u_{xyy}^2 - 2u_{xxyy}u_{yy} + 4u_{xxy}u_{yyy})) \quad (2)
\end{aligned}
$$

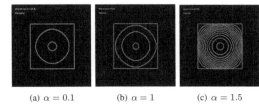

(a) $\alpha = 0.1$ (b) $\alpha = 1$ (c) $\alpha = 1.5$

Figure 1. The initial curve convergence procedure under the different order.

Table 1. Relationship between convergent iteration times and fractional order.

α	0.1	0.2	0.3	0.4	0.5	0.6	0.7
times	125	126	126	127	127	130	135

α	0.8	0.9	1	1.1	1.2	1.3	1.4
times	142	154	175	209	255	328	455

α	1.5	1.6	1.7	1.8	1.9	2
times	674	1094	2000	4408	10988	19723

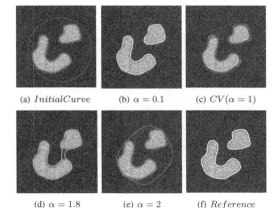

(a) *InitialCurve*   (b) $\alpha = 0.1$ (c) $CV(\alpha = 1)$

(d) $\alpha = 1.8$ (e) $\alpha = 2$ (f) *Reference*

Figure 2. Detection of two different synthetic objects from a noisy image, with various shapes and with an interior contour. $Size = 128 * 128$, $u_0(x,y) = -\sqrt{(x - 70)^2 + (y - 70)^2} + 50$, $\mu = 500$.

initial curve is a square with a hight of 70 pixels and a weight of 70 pixels. Output the current evolutional curve once finishing 50 iteration times, until the curve is disappear.

During evolution iteration processing, the following facts can be observed. Whatever fractional order of the fractional order term is, initial curve all converge during evolutional processing until disappear, which is independent of its shape. In this processing, the curve still remains closed, connected, simple and convex, and at the same time, its center of mass does not move, just as arc-length shorten flow described in [19].

But, their convergence speed or called iteration times is different under different fractional order. The convergence iteration times under different fractional order are shown in Table 1, when a circle with a radius of 50 pixels is looked as the initialize curve.

From Table 1, we can see that the needed iteration times for the initial curve convergence to disappear are related to the fractional order. In general, the less fractional order is, the less the needed iteration times for initial curve convergence to disappear is.

3.2 *Relationship between segmentation correct rate and fractional order*

In this subsection, the fractional order works on segmentation results by fractional order CV model, whose energy function is expressed in formula (1), is researched.

Fig. 2 are all described the obtained different segmentation results under different fractional order by the proposed fractional order CV model. Table 2 provides the corresponding results in terms of Dice coefficient and number of iterations. From Fig. 3– Fig. 7 and Table 2, whatever segmenting synthetic,

real or medical images, it can be concluded that the results obtained by the fractional order CV model under $\alpha = 0.1$ and $\alpha = 1.8$ are much better than the segmentation obtained by the traditional CV model ($\alpha = 1$). Although under $\alpha = 0.1$ and $\alpha = 1.8$ are almost same, the needed iteration times under $\alpha = 1.8$ during segmenting are much longer.

4 CONCLUSION

Fractional CV model is proposed in this paper through deducing fractional arc-length term and putting it into traditional CV model instead of arc-length term. The proposed fractional CV model can be seen as the generalization of the traditional CV model, and at the same time, it can be considered as an important theoretical implication about fractional order in level set research. It can be conclude from experimentation A that any a fractional order of arc-length term all can be viewed as a length-shorten flowing term, and the relationship between fractional order and convergence iteration times is found, that is, the less fractional order is, the less iteration times to be needed and the faster convergent speed is. Fractional arc-length term can be instead of arc-length term and added easily into other level-set models.

ACKNOWLEDGMENT

This paper is founded by The Liaoning Province universities scientific research project (L2014480).

REFERENCES

[1] Jasjit S. Suri, Kecheng Liu, Sameer Singh, Swamy N. Laxminarayan, Xiaolan Zeng and Laura Reden, *Shape*

Recovery Algorithms Using Level Sets in 2-D/3-D Medical Imagery: A State-of-the-Art Review [J], IEEE Trans. Information Technology in Biomedicine. vol. 6, no. 1, pp: 8~28, 2002.

[2] Y.H. Tsai, S. Osher, *Total Variation and Level Set Based Methods in Image Science [D]*, Acta Numer. pp: 1–61, 2005.

[3] Shawn Lankon, and Allen Tannenbaum, *Localizing Region-Based Active Contours [J]*, IEEE Thans. Image Processing. vol. 17, no. 11, pp: 2029–2039, 2008.

[4] V. Caselles, R. Kimmel, and G. Sapiro, *Geodesic active contours [C]*, Int J. Comput. Vis. vol. 22, pp. 61–79, 1997.

[5] Tony F. Chan, Luminita A. Vese, *Active Contours Without Edges [J]*, IEEE Trans. Image Processing. vol. 10, no.2, pp: 266–277, 2001.

[6] D. Cremers, M. Rousson, and R. Deriche, *A review of statisical approaches to level set segmentation: Integrating color, texture, motion and shape [J]*, Int. J. Comput. Vis., vol. 72, no. 2, pp. 195–215, 2007.

[7] Chunming Li, Chiu-Yen Kao, John C. Gore and Zhaohua Ding, *Minimization of Region-Scalable Fitting Energy for Image Segmentation [J]*, IEEE Trans. Image Processing. vol. 17, no. 10, pp. 1940–1949, 2008.

[8] Chunming Li, Rui Huang, Zhaohua Ding, J. Chris Gatenby, Dimitris N. Metaxas and John C. Gore, *A Level Set Method for Image Segmentation in the Presence of Intensity Inhomogeneities With Application to MRI [J]*, IEEE Trans. Image Processing. vol. 20, no. 7, pp. 2007–2016, 2011.

[9] D. Choppp, *Computing Minimal Surfaces via Level Set Curvature Flow [J]*, J. Comput. Phys. vol. 106, pp. 77–91, 1993.

[10] Johan Lie, Marius Lysaker and Xue-Cheng Tai, *A Binary Level Set Model and Some Applications to Mumford-Shah Image Segmentation [J]*, IEEE Trans. Image Processing. vol. 15, no. 5, pp. 1171–1181, 2006.

[11] Yonggang Shi, and William Clem Karl, *A Real-Time Algorithm for the Approximation of Level-Set-Based Curve Evolution [J]*, IEEE Trans. Image Processing. vol. 17, no. 5, pp. 645–655, 2008.

[12] Yan Nei Law, Hwee Kuan Lee, Chaoqiang Liu, and Andy M. Yip, *A Variational Model for Segmentation of Overlapping Objects with Additive Intensity Value [J]*, IEEE Trans. Image Processing. vol. 20, no. 6, pp. 1495–1503, 2011.

[13] Chunming Li, Chenyang Xu, Changfeng Gui and Martin D. Fox, *Distance Regularized Level Set Evolution and Its Application to Image Segmentation [J]*, IEEE Trans. Image Processing. vol. 19, no. 12, pp. 3243–3254, 2010.

[14] Olivier Bernard, Denis Friboulet, Philippe Thevenaz and Michael Unser, *Variational B-Spline Level-Set: A Linear Filter Approach for Fast Deformable Model Evolution [J]*, IEEE Trans. Image Processing. vol. 18, no. 6, pp. 1179–1191, 2009.

[15] Kaleem Siddiqi, Yves Berube Lauzi'ere, Allen Tannenbaum, Member, and Steven W. Zucker, *Area and Length Minimizing Flows for Shape Segmentation [J]*, IEEE trans on Image Processing, vol. 7, no. 3, pp.433–443, 1998.

[16] Mohamed Ben Salah, Amar Mitiche and Ismail Ben Ayed, *Effective Level Set Image Segmentation with a kernel Induced Data Term [J]*, IEEE trans on Image Processing, vol. 19, no. 1, pp. 220–232, 2010.

[17] Aaron E. Lefohn, Joe M. Kniss, Charles D. Hansen and Ross T. Whitaker, *A Streaming Narrow-Band Algorithm Interactive Computation and Visualization of Level Set [J]*, IEEE trans on Visualization and Computer Graphics, vol. 10, no. 4, pp. 422–433, 2004.

[18] Sigurd Angenent, Guillermo Sapiro, and Allen Tannenbaum, *On The Affine Heat Equation for Non-Convex Curves [J]*, Journal of the American Mathematical Society, vol. 11, no. 3, pp. 601–633, 1998.

[19] Farzin Mokhtarian and Alan K. Mackworth, *A Theory of Multiscale, Curvature-Based Shape Representation for Planar Curves [J]*, IEEE trans on Pattern Analysis and Machine Intelligence, vol. 14, no. 8, pp.789–805, 1992.

[20] Y. Zhang, Y.-F. Pu, J.-R. Hu and J.-L. Zhou, *A Class of Fractional-Order Variational Image Inpainting Models [J]*, Applied Mathematics Information Sciences, vol. 6, no. 2, pp. 299–306, 2012.

[21] Mehdi Dalir and Majid Bashour, *Applications of Fractioanl Calculus [J]*. Applied Mathemaitcal Sciences, vol. 4, no. 21, pp. 1021–1032, 2010.

[22] Om P. Agrawal, *Formulation of Euler-Lagrange Equations for Fractional Variational Problems [J]*, J. Math. Appl. no. 272, pp. 368–379, 2002.

Multimedia Technology IV – Farag, Yang & Jiao (Eds)
© *2015 Taylor & Francis Group, London, ISBN: 978-1-138-02794-7*

OMP spectrum sensing algorithm based on differential signal

Weikang Hu, Xiaowei Gu & Xianzheng Kong
School of Telecommunication Engineering, Hangzhou Dianzi University, Hangzhou, China

Zhijin Zhao & Haiquan Wang
State Key Lab of Information Control Technology in Communication System of No. 36 Research Institute, China, Electronic Technology Corporation, Jiaxing, China

ABSTRACT: According to the small variety of received signals in a short timeslot, the OMP spectrum sensing algorithm based on differential signal is proposed. Firstly the algorithm differentiates the previous signal and current signal, and detects its spectrum to acquire the information of channel variation. Secondly the current channel state is exclusive OR of the previous channel state and channel variation. At last, the current occupied spectrum can be obtained by the channel state. Simulation results show that the proposed algorithm can greatly reduce computational complexity and achieve a better performance.

Keywords: spectrum sensing; differential signal; sparsity; support set

1 INTRODUCTION

Wideband spectrum sensing [1] requires several GHz bandwidth sensing. Excessively high sampling frequency and large amount of data are the major challenge for existing hardware devices. Recently, a new sampling theorem has been proposed – Compressive Sensing (CS) [2]. For sparse and compressive signal, the sampling rate based on CS can be lower than Nyquist sampling rate. So it could achieve spectrum recovery and spectrum sensing of wideband signal under low-speed sampling, and decrease the requirement for sample rate considerably.

In [3] CS is firstly applied to wideband spectrum sensing. Signal sparsity is the prior condition of this algorithm. In practice, however, the sparsity is unknown. It is estimated directly by a few observations in the process of sensing [4]. But this algorithm gained the sample information through two stages, which resulted in high computational complexity and low estimation accuracy. A wideband spectrum sensing based on OMP algorithm was proposed in [5], which applied diagonal loading AIC/MDL criteria to estimate the sparsity. The signal sparsity was the ending condition of each iteration of this algorithm, and also the major factor of the computational complexity. All of the above algorithms just focus on how to estimate the sparsity more accurate, while takes no consideration about how to reduce the computational complexity.

According to the small variety of Primary User (PU) signals in a short timeslot, the OMP spectrum sensing algorithm based on differential signal is proposed in this paper. The algorithm utilizes the differential signal

(DS) to detect the spectrum occupancy. The computational complexity can be greatly reduced as the sparsity of sensing signal be lower, meanwhile, the algorithm can achieve a better sensing performance.

The rest of the paper is organized as follows. Section 2 introduces the proposed DS-based approach, and the principle of OMP algorithm is introduced in this section firstly. In Section 3, simulation results of the proposed algorithm and other sensing algorithm are discussed. In Section 4 the conclusions are summarized.

2 PROPOSED DS-BASED APPROACH

Consider that the received signal X is an analog wideband signal, and has the sparse characteristics in frequency domain. The frequency band range is 0 from B_{max}. Each PU signal in received signal is complex Gaussian random process with mean zero, and is independent each other. The whole frequency band is divided into K channels, each channel's bandwidth is B, and they are not allowed to overlap each other. Those channels which are occupied by the PU are called the active channel, and the number of the active channel is p. The active channel set consists of the label of the active channels Π_i, which is denoted as $\Pi = [\Pi_1, \Pi_2, \ldots, \Pi_p]$. The maximum number of active channel is p_{max}. N accesses are applied in compressive sampling, and it is satisfied as $p_{max} < N < K$. The received signal X includes PU signal $\mathbf{S} = [S^{\Pi_1}, S^{\Pi_2}, \ldots, S^{\Pi_p}]$ and noise $\mathbf{W}$. The modulation matrix is denoted as $\mathbf{\Theta}$. Each access samples M datum, which compose the observation sequence

$y_i[k]$. N sets of observation sequence $y_i[k]$ consist of $(qM) \times k$ observation signal matrix $\mathbf{Y}$.

The estimation of signal' spectrum hole is key point in the spectrum sensing, and the reconstruction of signal's PSD can be skipped. So as to access the idle channel for the Secondary User (SU) in time, the reconstruction of spectrum support set is enough. OMP algorithm is a classic compressive sensing algorithm of wideband [6]. OMP is an iterative greedy algorithm that selects at each step the column of matrix $\mathbf{\Theta}$, which is the most matched with the current residuals. This column is then added into the set of selected columns. The algorithm updates the residuals by projecting the observation matrix $\mathbf{Y}$ onto the linear subspace spanned by the columns that have already been selected and then the algorithm iterates. It is shown that when the observation matrix $\mathbf{Y}$ and modulation matrix $\mathbf{\Theta}$ are known, the support set of the signal, that is the active channel set $\mathbf{\Pi}$, can be recovered exactly by the OMP algorithm with high probability.

The spectrum occupation of PU has no big change when the timeslot is short relatively, that is signal sparsity p has no big change. In order to low the computational complexity, the OMP spectrum sensing algorithm based on differential signal is proposed. The active channel set at T and T + 1 time is expressed by Eqn. (1) and (2), respectively, and the PU set of the received signal X at the corresponding time is just given by Eqn. (3) and (4), respectively. The signal set is denoted by Ω.

$$\mathbf{\Pi}^T = [\Pi_1^T, \Pi_2^T, \Pi_i^T, ..., \Pi_p^T] \tag{1}$$

$$\mathbf{\Pi}^{T+1} = [\Pi_1^{T+1}, \Pi_2^{T+1}, \Pi_j^{T+1}, ..., \Pi_q^{T+1}] \tag{2}$$

$$X(\mathrm{T}) = \Omega(S^{\Pi_1^T}, S^{\Pi_2^T}, ..., S^{\Pi_i^T}, ..., S^{\Pi_p^T}) \tag{3}$$

$$X(\mathrm{T}+1) = \Omega(S^{\Pi_1^{T+1}}, S^{\Pi_2^{T+1}}, ..., S^{\Pi_j^{T+1}}, ..., S^{\Pi_q^{T+1}}) \tag{4}$$

The signal sparsity p has no big change when the timeslot is short relatively, and thus the sparsity of differential signal is much smaller than that of the signal $X(\mathrm{T} + 1)$. When PU signal is cosine signal, the spectrum of signal X at T and T + 1 time and the spectrum of differential signal are shown in Fig. 1. From the figure we can see that the simulation result is the same as the above analysis. Therefore utilizing the differential signal to detect the spectrum hole with OMP algorithm in T + 1 time and combining the above result with the T time spectrum information, we can obtain the result of spectrum sensing at T + 1 time to reduce the computation complexity of OMP algorithm.

It is assumed that the spectrum occupation of each PU signal is independent. The process of spectrum sensing is a binary hypothesis test problem for the each channel. If PU exists, the hypothesis is labeled as H_1; otherwise, the hypothesis is labeled as H_0. When H_1 is true, that is the label of channel belongs to the set $\mathbf{\Pi}$, the channel state is recorded as 1; when H_0 is true, that is the label of channel is outside the range of the set $\mathbf{\Pi}$, the channel state is recorded as 0. So the output of the

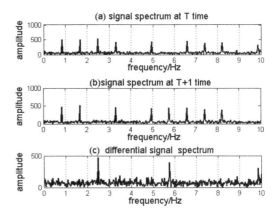

Figure 1.   The signal spectrum.

channel state is 0-1 string, and the channel state set at T time is denoted by $\boldsymbol{\psi}^T$, finally, $\mathbf{\Pi}^T$ can be obtained by $\boldsymbol{\psi}^T$. The changing information of channel state which comes from the differential signal is denoted by $\Delta \boldsymbol{\psi}$. The channel state in sensing process of signal spectrum in Fig. 1 can be expressed as:

$$\begin{array}{ll} \boldsymbol{\psi}^T & 1\ 1\ 1\ 1\ \ 1\ 0\ 1\ 1\ 1\ 1 \\ \underline{\Delta\boldsymbol{\psi} \quad 0\ 0\ 1\ 0\ \ 0\ 1\ 0\ 0\ 0\ 1} & (5) \\ \boldsymbol{\psi}^{T+1} & 1\ 1\ 0\ 1\ 1\ \ 1\ 1\ 1\ 0 \end{array}$$

According to the detection result $\Delta \boldsymbol{\psi}$ of differential signal, the channel state $\boldsymbol{\psi}^{T+1}$ at T + 1 time can be determined by (6), then, the support set $\mathbf{\Pi}^{T+1}$ can be obtained finally.

$$\boldsymbol{\psi}^{T+1} = \mathrm{xor}(\boldsymbol{\psi}^T, \Delta\boldsymbol{\psi}) \tag{6}$$

Therefore steps of this proposed sensing algorithm based on differential signal and OMP (denoted as DS-AIC-OMP or DS-MDL-OMP) can be described as follows

1) Sample the wideband signal X with CS technology at T time, and obtain the observation signal $\mathbf{Y}^{T+1}$;
2) Compute the difference signal as $\Delta\mathbf{Y} = \mathbf{Y}^{T+1} - \mathbf{Y}^T$;
3) Utilize diagonal loading AIC/MDL criteria to estimate the sparsity $\widehat{p}$ of signal $\Delta\mathbf{Y}$;
4) Take $\Delta\mathbf{Y}, \widehat{p}, \mathbf{\Theta}$ as input, estimate the changing information of channel state $\Delta\boldsymbol{\psi}$ with OMP algorithm;
5) Compute the set $\boldsymbol{\psi}^{T+1}$ according to (6), then obtain $\mathbf{\Pi}^{T+1}$;
6) Save the observation signal $\mathbf{Y}^{T+1}$ and the set $\boldsymbol{\psi}^{T+1}$.

When utilizing the OMP algorithm to detect the spectrum hole, the signal sparsity is the ending condition of the each iteration, and also is the major factor of the computational complexity. The detection accuracy depends on the absolute value of the detected signal in the traditional OMP algorithm, and the detection performance is poor when the absolute value is volatile. When the timeslot is short, the sparsity of differential signal is much smaller than that of the original signal, and the computational complexity of the proposed

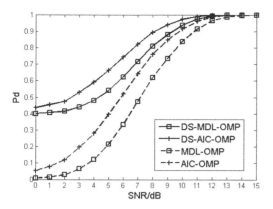

Figure 2. P_d vs SNR: $M = 401$.

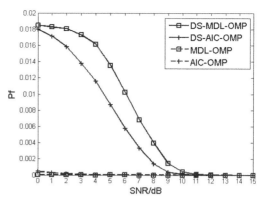

Figure 3. P_f vs SNR: $M = 401$.

algorithm, which uses differential signal to detect the spectrum, could be much lower. The differential signal is irrelevant to the absolute value, so the proposed algorithm could improve the performance further.

3 SIMULATION AND DISCUSSION

The analog wideband received signal $x(t)$ is given by:

$$x(t) = \sum_{i=1}^{p} (s_{\Pi(i)}(t) * h(t)) e^{j2p\Pi(i)Bt} + n(t) \qquad (7)$$

where p is the signal sparsity, the bandwidth of PU which meets the demand $s_{\Pi(i)}(t) \sim N(0, \sigma_s^2)$ is B, that is each PU has the same power. $h(t)$ is the low pass filter. $n(t)$ is a white Gaussian random noise with mean zero and variance σ^2. Signal to Noise Ratio (SNR) is defined as $SNR = \sigma_s^2 / \sigma_n^2$. The bandwidth range is 0 from 360 MHz, and $K = 60$ channels are included, and each bandwidth of channel is 6 MHz. The compression ratio of channel is 50%, that means $N = 30$. The maximum signal sparsity $p_{\max} = 12$. 10000 times Monte-Carlo simulations are conducted to every experiment.

Fig. 2 shows the detection probabilities curves of the proposed sensing algorithm (DS-AIC-OMP/DS-MDL-OMP) and the traditional OMP algorithm (AIC-OMP/MDL-OMP) [5] under $M = 401$ As shown by the figure, the performances of DS-AIC-OMP/DS-MDL-OMP are better than that of AIC-OMP/MDL-OMP. When the SNR ranges from 0 to 7 dB, the detection performance of proposed algorithm is 20%–40% higher than that of traditional OMP algorithm. The disparity of performance reduces gradually as the SNR increases, this is because the OMP algorithm itself has a high detection probability in the case of high SNR.

Fig. 3 shows the false alarm probabilities curves of the DS-AIC-OMP/DS-MDL-OMP and the AIC-OMP/MDL-OMP under $M = 401$. As shown by the figure, the false alarm probability of proposed algorithm is higher than that of the traditional OMP algorithm when the SNR is below 11 dB.

The reason is that the diagonal loading AIC/MDL criteria always makes underestimation in the case

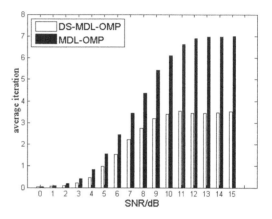

Figure 4. Iterations comparison under MDL criteria.

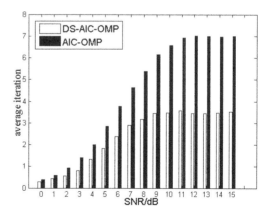

Figure 5. Iterations comparison under AIC criteria.

of low SNR. When the exclusive OR is introduced to the proposed algorithm, the underestimation turns into overestimation which results in high false alarm probability. However, compared with the improvement of detection performance, the cost of false alarm probabilities at the same SNR is acceptable.

Figs. 4 and 5 indicate the iterations comparison of two algorithms under different criteria respectively. As shown by the figures, the diagonal loading AIC/MDL criteria always makes underestimation in the case of low SNR, so the iterations number and detection performance of two algorithms are just a tiny difference. However, in the case of high SNR, two algorithms demonstrate a significant gap in the iterations number as the estimation accuracy of sparsity is improved. When SNR is above 9 dB, the iterations of proposed algorithm are less than 5, while the iterations of traditional OMP algorithm are greater than 6. As a conclusion, the computational complexity of proposed algorithm is less than that of the traditional OMP algorithm.

4 CONCLUSIONS

On the account of traditional OMP algorithm which takes the signal sparsity as the ending condition in the process of iterations, the difference processing is introduced. The signal sparsity has no big change when the timeslot is short relatively. And the sparsity can be reduced by utilizing differential signal to detect the spectrum hole with OMP algorithm, also, the computational complexity could be greatly cut down. Simulation results show that the proposed algorithm can greatly reduce computational complexity under high SNR while achieve a better performance under low SNR.

ACKNOWLEDGMENT

The authors would like to give thanks for the National Natural Science Foundation of China under Grant NO. 60872092.

REFERENCES

[1] Li Li, Bin Qin, Chun-yuan Zhang. "Research on Dynamic Specrum Access Wireless Networks". Computer Engineering, 2007, 33, (22), pp. 124–126. (in Chinese)

[2] Guang-ming Shi, Dan-hua Liu, Da-hua Gao,et al. "Advances in Theory and Application of Compressed Sensing". Acta Electronica Sinica, 2009, 37, (05), pp. 1070–1081. (in Chinese)

[3] Zhi Tian, B. G Georgos. "Compressed Sensing for Wideband Cognitive Radios". IEEE International Conference on Acoustics, Speech and Signal Processing, 2007, pp. 1357–1360.

[4] Yue Wang, Zhi Tian, Chunyan Feng. "Sparsity Order Estimation and its Application in Compressive Spectrum Sensing for Cognitive Radios". IEEE Transactions on Wireless Communications, 2012, 11, (6), pp. 2116–2125.

[5] Zhi-jin Zhao, Peng Zhang, Hai-quan Wang, et al. "Wideband Spectrum Sensing Based on OMP Algorithm" Signal Processing, 2012, 28, (05). pp. 723–728. (in Chinese)

[6] T. Tony Cai, Lie Wang. "Orthogonal Matching Pursuit for Sparse Signal Recovery with Noise", IEEE Transactions on Information Theory, 2011, 57, (07), pp. 4680–4688.

[7] Computational Intelligence in Scheduling (SCIS 07), IEEE Press, Dec. 2007, pp. 57–64, doi:10.1109/SCIS. 2007.357670.

Multimedia Technology IV – Farag, Yang & Jiao (Eds)

A multi-scale extraction for urban road intersection in high-resolution panchromatic imagery

Hongyue Cai, Guoqing Yao & Meng Li
School of Information Engineering, China University of Geosciences (Beijing), Beijing, China

ABSTRACT: Road intersections are import components of a road network and provide useful information for road extraction, image registration, and vehicle navigation, etc. However, there is little research conducted on road intersection extraction. This paper presents a road intersection extraction method with three stages mainly based on the model of road intersection. Homogeneous circular area detection was firstly performed to extract the possible positions where road intersections may exist by multi-scale morphological transform. Then calculated the central position for each candidate road intersection using geometry shape and spectral features. Finally, shape identification was performed using a valley-finding algorithm based on angular texture signature extraction, in order to suppress false positives. The experiments indicate that the proposed method is effective in urban situation and is robust to various interferences.

Keywords: road intersection extraction; high-resolution panchromatic images; multi-scale morphology; angular texture signature; valley-fiding

1 INTRODUCTION

Road data are of major importance in applications such as geographic information system (GIS), cartography, emergency, etc. Dozens of road network extraction methodologies from high-resolution images are proposed in existing literature [1]–[4], many of them rely heavily on road seed points and network topology information. Road intersections can provide useful information such as connectivity, topology and direction, which can be used as a further means to guide road network topology reconstruction [5–6]. Moreover, road intersections have a widely application in image registration, vehicle navigation et al. However, little research has been proposed on road intersection extraction.

Several indirect methods have been exploited [7–8]. Reference [9] use template matching to detect road intersections by statistical and geometry analysis, which is a semi-directly strategy. The drawback of these methods is that road network extraction must be performed in advanced. Fewer works have been proposed to detect road intersection directly. Reference [10] apply a neural network within a given sized window to identify road intersections, which needs seed points for training.

Angular texture signature (AST) which first proposed in [11] is a well-known algorithm designed for road network extraction. Reference [12] and [13] apply AST to extract road network from remote sensing images. AST is also used in finding dominant directions of road in [14] and [15] in order to get the

Figure 1. Model of road intersection.

seed points of road network. Reference [16] and [17] use AST to recognize road intersections effectively. However, both two works are developed for LIDAR or SAR images and are not suitable for high-resolution panchromatic remotely sensed images which without elevation information and with more complicate texture.

In this paper, we present a multi-scale method especially for extracting urban road intersections in high-resolution panchromatic remote sensing imagery, which is an extension of [17].

2 MODEL AND STRATEGY

Road intersection appears in a variety of shapes in high-resolution imagery, but it can be modelled as a homogeneous circular area connected with several road branches, as shown in Fig. 1. We extract road intersections based on this model and the workflow is shown in Fig. 2.

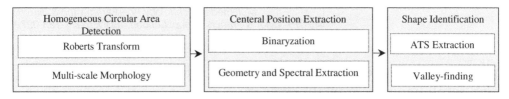

Figure 2. Flow chart of road intersection extraction.

3 HOMOGENEOUS CIRCULAR AREA DETECTION

Homogeneous circular area detection is designed to separate possible road intersections areas from image. Roberts transform is firstly performed to detect homogeneous area followed by multi-scale morphological transform.

3.1 Roberts transform

The gradient of intensity shows the changes in image. We use Roberts transform because it can retain the corner information of rectangle with precision orientation. Let $\phi(\xi, \psi)$ represent the gray value of pixel in image, the Roberts transform is given by:

$$\Gamma[\phi(\xi,\psi)]=| \phi(\xi,\psi)- \phi(\xi+1,\psi+1)|+| \phi(\xi+1,\psi)- \phi(\xi,\psi+1)| \quad (1)$$

After Roberts transform, homogenous areas appear as dark regions as shown in Fig. 3(b).

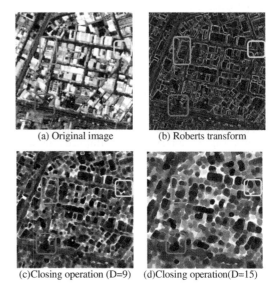

(a) Original image   (b) Roberts transform

(c)Closing operation (D=9)   (d)Closing operation(D=15)

Figure 3. Homogeneous circular area detection.

3.2 Multi-scale Morphology

Closing transform is a basic operation in mathematical morphology which can be used to detect dark objects smaller than structuring element. Here, we chose circularity as the shape of structuring element in order to detect candidate road intersection area and define D as the diameter of circularity. We generally set D greater than the width of road because the width road may increase when approaching the intersection area.

After closing operation, the object with similar shape to structuring element becomes one of the darkest areas in image and the area for each darkest region is about $\Pi \times (D/2)^2$. However, smaller objects are highlighted, while objects larger than structuring element appear as dark region with large area. For example, Fig. 3(c) and Fig. 3(d) are the closing operator result of Fig. 3(b) with the structuring element size of 9 and 15, respectively. The large-scale road intersection in red rectangle appears as darkest areas with similar area to structuring element in Fig. 3(d), whereas not in Fig. 3(c). The small-scale road intersection in yellow rectangle is highlighted in Fig. 3(d), but shows characteristic of road intersection in Fig. 3(c). Therefore, we apply multi-scale morphology closing operation to extract roads intersection with different width.

4 CENTRAL POSITION EXTRACTION

In this step, central position is obtained for further processing by binaryzation, geometry and spectral feature extraction.

Binaryzation with a small value $Threshold_{binary}$ is first used to get the candidate area of road intersection according to the fact that road intersection appears as the darkest region in closing transform result (Fig. 4(a)). "8-connected neighbourhood" is then employed to calculate connected component on binary image. If a connected component has large numbers of pixel, it would be classified as road wider than structuring element. While if it has too little pixel, it would be seen as noise. Both wider roads and noise are discarded according to the threshold $Threshold_{large}$ (threshold for deleting wider roads) and $Threshold_{small}$ (threshold for deleting noise). Then enclosing rectangle is calculated for each connected component and geometric center of it is defined as the position center for candidate road intersection (Fig. 4(b)).

Other objects such as buildings are deleted from candidate road intersections by spectral criterion, which is provided by prior knowledge (as shown in Fig. 4(d)).

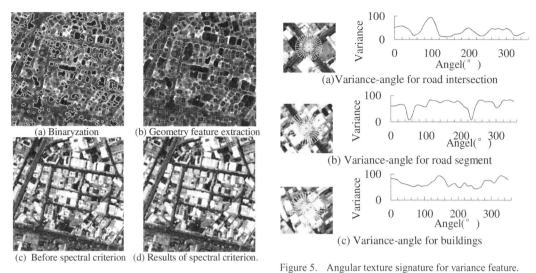

(a) Binaryzation (b) Geometry feature extraction

(c) Before spectral criterion (d) Results of spectral criterion.

Figure 4. Central position extraction.

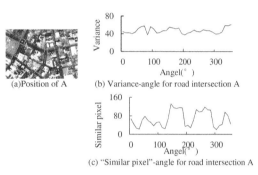

(a)Variance-angle for road intersection

(b) Variance-angle for road segment

(c) Variance-angle for buildings

Figure 5. Angular texture signature for variance feature.

(a)Position of A

(b) Variance-angle for road intersection A

(c) "Similar pixel"-angle for road intersection A

Figure 6. Comparing between angular texture signature for variance and for similar pixel.

5 SHAPE IDENTIFICATION

The propose of shape identification is to refined the extraction result further based on the model that the center of road intersection usually connects several road branches as mentioned in Section 2. AST extraction can provide a graph illustrated the connected characteristic for road intersection. The number and direction of branches are then defined by valley-finding algorithm.

5.1 *Angular texture signature extraction*

Angular texture signature algorithm derives a rectangle set with evenly spaced angel θ around the central point and calculates a value represents the feature within the rectangle. A feature-angle graph is obtained as the result of ATS which shows the shape feature around road intersection.

Variance within the rectangle is a good descriptor for road intersection because intensity homogeneity along road is better than other direction. As shown in Fig. 5, road segment has two valleys in ATS and the angle between them is about $180°$. As for road intersection, there are about four valleys in graph, whereas other objects do not have dominating valleys.

As shown in Fig. 5, variance within the rectangle can illustrate the characteristic of small-scale road well when there were no evident interference near road intersection, such as sidewalk and overpass. Whereas in large-scale road context, many traffic facilities appear around road intersection leading no dominating valleys in variance-angle angle graph, as shown in Fig. 6(a). Therefore, in this paper, we proposed a new descriptor for feature within the rectangle, namely, "similar pixel". More details are described as follows.

Define l and w as the length and width of a rectangle, respectively. Let *color_center* represents spectral value of the central point, then we calculate the number of pixel $num(\theta_i)$ in each rectangle which satisfy the function $|point\_temp_j - color\_center| <$ $Threshold_{color}$ $(0 \leq i < 360/\theta, 0 \leq j < w \times l)$, where i is the index of the ith rectangle, $point\_temp_j$ is the spectral value of the jth point in each rectangle and $Threshold_{color}$ is provided by prior knowledge.

We defined $f(\theta_i) = w \times l - num(\theta_i)$ as the feature within the rectangle for further processing in valley-finding. This feature can generally show the characteristic of road when interference exist near the intersection (Fig. 6(b)(c)). This method is more flexible and adaptable for spectral differences caused by different material and age of road, because it extracts road intersection based on each central point respectively which does not use a enforced consistent threshold to segment road information [17].

5.2 *Valley-finding*

Based on feature-angle graph obtained by ATS, valley-finding algorithm is designed to identify the number of branches connected to central position of road

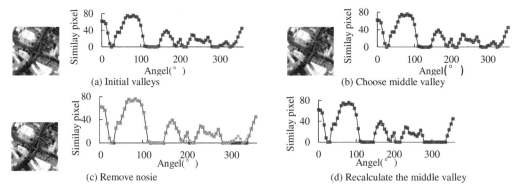

(a) Initial valleys (b) Choose middle valley

(c) Remove nosie (d) Recalculate the middle valley

Figure 7. Valley-finding.

Table 1. Experimental parameters.

| | D | Threshold$_{binary}$ | Threshold$_{large}$ | Spectral Criterion | Revolving Rectangle | | | |
					l	w	θ	Threshold$_{color}$
Figure 8	9	20	260	0–68	20	4	5	–
	15		710	0–69	20			
Figure 9	11	45	450	0–110	40	4	10	–
	21		1800		55			40

intersection and the angle between them. The method consists of five steps as follows:

1) Find all the valleys that satisfy ① $f(\theta_i)=0$ or ② $f(\theta_i)\leq f(\theta_{i+1})$ and $f(\theta_i)\leq f(\theta_{i-1})$ and $f(\theta_i)\leq$ median$(f(\theta i))/2$, and defined as $v(\theta_i)$. median$(f(\theta i))$ is the median value of all the $f(\theta_i)$.
2) Find all the peaks which satisfy $f(\theta_i)\geq$ median$(f(\theta_i))/2$ and $f(\theta_i)\geq f(\theta_{i+1})$ and $f(\theta_i)\geq f(\theta_{i-1})$, and defined as $p(\theta_i)$.
3) Remove false valleys: we define the peaks on the left and right side of $v(\theta_i)$ are $p(\theta_{left})$ and $p(\theta_{right})$, and $p(\theta_{max})=max(p(\theta_{left}),p(\theta_{max}))$. If $v(\theta_i)/p(\theta_{max})\geq 0.6$, we consider $v(\theta_i)$ is not significant enough and remove it from the valleys.
4) Modify consecutive valleys for "similar pixel"-angle graph: there always more than two consecutive valleys in feature-angle graph derived from large-scale road context. Normally, these valleys have similar value and approach to zero. We choose the middle one as the modified valley. At the same time, if the internal between two consecutive valleys is small, less than 30° for example, we regard the peaks between them as noise and recalculate the position of valley after remove the noise (Fig. 7).
5) Merge the valleys that close: $v(\theta_i)$ and $v(\theta_j)$ are two neighbouring valleys, if $|\theta_i-\theta_j|\leq 30°$ or $|\theta_i-\theta_j|\geq 330°$, we merge the two valleys into one, where min$(p(\theta_i),p(\theta_j))$ is the new position of valleys.

We can identify road intersection base on the number and direction of branches as follows:

1) If the number of branches smaller than 2 or larger than 5, we do not consider the central position as a road intersection.
2) If there exists two valleys $v(\theta_i)$ and $v(\theta_j)$, and $||\theta_i-\theta_j|-180°|\geq 30°$, we identify the central position as a road intersection.
3) If the number of valleys larger than 3 and smaller than4, the central position is identified as road intersection.

6 RESULTS AND DISCUSSION

The procedure is tested in two representative high-resolution remote sensing images (Fig. 8 and Fig. 9) with resolution about 0.6–0.7 m. We utilize multi-scale structuring element to extract road intersections based on the fact that different classes of roads exist in images. In Fig. 8, there were no evident interference exists near wide road intersections, so we extract candidate central points with D = 9 and D = 15, and calculate variance within the rectangle for ATS in shape identification. As for more complicated images, we use variance and "similar pixel" features to calculate ATS in Fig. 9, which the size of structuring element are 11, 12. Tabel 1 shows the summary of parameters in three images, and the results of experiment are presented in Fig. 8 and Fig. 9, which the red

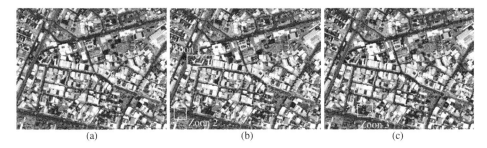

(a)	(b)	(c)

Figure 8.   Experiment 1.

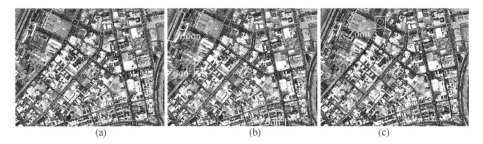

(a)	(b)	(c)

Figure 9.   Experiment 2.

crosses represent the road intersections removed by shape identification and the green ones are the final results of extraction. The final result is computed as a logical AND across the results at all scales.

The extraction result in Fig. 8 and Fig. 9 suggest that the method we proposed can extract road at different scales successfully. Almost all the possible position centers of road intersections are separated by homogeneous circular Area detection and centeral position extraction. Shape identification is an effective means eliminating interference, such as buildings in Zoon 1 in Fig. 8(a) and Fig. 9(a). The example of false-positive results in Zoon 2 (as shown in Fig. 8(a) and Fig. 9(a)) are deleted in shape identification. As for large-scale road in Fig. 9(b) (Zoon 3), the feature of "similar pixel" in ATS can make a correct recognition in interference of traffic transportation.

The buildings near the road sometimes create interference in shape identification. The building appeared as "L" in Zoon 3 (Fig. 8(b)) and the one perpendicular to road in Zoon 4 (Fig. 9(a)) are considered as road intersections in our method.

7   CONCLUSION

Aiming at extracting road intersections in high-resolution panchromatic images, this paper has proposed an automatic method which neither needs extracting road in advanced nor geospatial databased. The results show that our method performs well in urban situation and is robust to various interferences. The future work will be devoted to a more robust method in order to fit complicate situation. It would also need a more adaptively strategy to set parameters rather than provided by prior knowledge. Meanwhile, a proper clustering algorithm is required to process the road intersections fused from different scales.

REFERENCES

[1] T.M. Talal, A. El-Sayed, M. Hebaishy, I.D. Moawad, A.A. Saleh and E.A. El-Samie Fathi, "Extraction of roads from high-resolution satellite images with the discrete wavelet transform," Sensing and Imaging: An International Journal, vol. 14, 2013, pp. 29–55.

[2] S. Wang, and G. Cao, "New method for road extraction based on modified path opening algorithm," Computer Science, vol. 41, 2014, pp. 285–289 (in Chinese).

[3] W.Z. Shi, Z.L. Miao, Q.M. Wang and Z. Hua, "Spectral–Spatial Classification and Shape Features for Urban Road Centerline Extraction," Geoscience and Remote Sensing Letters, vol. 11, 2014, pp. 788–792.

[4] S.G. Zhou, C. Chen and J.P. Yue, "Extracting roads from high-resolution RS Images based on shape priors and graph cuts," Acta Geodaeticaet Cartographica Sinica, vol. 1, 2014, pp. 60–65 (in Chinese).

[5] J.C. Trinder and Y. Wang, "Knowledge-based road interpretation in aerial images," International Archives of Photogrammetry and Remote Sensing, vol. 32, 1998, pp. 635–640.

[6] P. Gamba, F. Dell'Acqua and G. Lisini, "Improving urban road extraction in high-resolution images exploiting directional filtering, perceptual grouping, and simple topological concepts," Geoscience and Remote Sensing Letters, vol. 3, 2006, pp. 387–391.

[7] I. Laptev, T. Lindeberg, W. Eckstein, C. Steger, A. Baumgartner and H. Mayer "Automatic extraction of roads from aerial images based on scale space and snakes," Machine Vision and Applications, vol. 12, 2000, pp. 23–31.

[8] Y.Y. Chiang, C.A. Knoblock, C. Shahabi and C.C. Chen, "Automatic and accurate extraction of road intersections from raster maps," Geoinformatica, vol. 13, 2009, pp. 121–157.

[9] X.F. Chen, F. Xue and R.S. Wang, "Intersections automatic detection in aerial photos," Pattern Recognition and Artificial Intelligence, vol. 13, 2000, pp. 83–86.

[10] A. Barsi and C. Heipke, "Detecting road junctions by artificial neural networks," Remote Sensing and Data Fusion over Urban Areas, 2nd GRSS/ISPRS Joint Workshop on IEEE, Berlin: Germany 2003, pp 129–132.

[11] D. Haverkamp, "Extracting straight road structure in urban environments using IKONOS satellite imagery," Optical Engineering, vol. 41, 2002, pp. 2107–2110.

[12] S.G. Zhou, J.J. Liu and R.X. Chen, "New method to extract roads in urban area from high-resolution remote sensing imagery," Computer Engineering and Applications, vol. 46, 2010, pp. 216–219 (in Chinese).

[13] Y.C. Wan, S.H. Shen, Y. Song and S.F. Liu, "A Road Extraction Approach Based on Fuzzy Logic for High-Resolution Multispectral Data," Fourth International Conference on Fuzzy Systems and Knowledge Discovery IEEE, Haikou 2007: 203–207.

[14] R. Zhang, J.X. Zhang and H.T. Li, "Semi-automatic extraction of ribbon roads from high resolution remotely sensed imagery based on angular texture signature and profile match," Journal of Remote Sensing, vol. 12, 2008, pp. 224–232 (in Chinese).

[15] J.X. Hu, A. Razdan, J.C. Femiani, M. Cui and P. Wonka, "Road network extraction and intersection detection from aerial images by tracking road footprints," Geoscience and Remote Sensing, vol. 45, 2007, pp. 4144–4157.

[16] Z. Chen, H.C. Ma and Y.F. Li, "Extraction of road intersection from LiDAR point cloud data based on ATS and Snake," Remote Sensing For Land & Resources, vol. 25, 2013, pp. 79–84 (in Chinese).

[17] J.H. Cheng, J. Tian, X.S. Ku and J.X. Sun, "Road junction extraction in high-resolution SAR images via morphological detection and shape identification," Remote Sensing Letters, vol. 4, 2013, pp. 296–305.

Multimedia Technology IV – Farag, Yang & Jiao (Eds)
© 2015 Taylor & Francis Group, London, ISBN: 978-1-138-02794-7

FPGA implementation of the encoding and decoding of an LDPC code for deep space applications

Xiaoming Liu, Kunbao Cai, Xiancheng Tang & Haowei Wu
College of Communication Engineering, Chongqing University, Chongqing, P.R. of China

ABSTRACT: Based on understanding a set of Low-density parity-check codes recommended by CCSDS and studying their encoding and decoding principles, we concentrate our experimental research on the encoding and decoding of an (1280, 1024) LDPC code with code rate 4/5. Firstly, an encoder for this code is implemented by using an FPGA device. Next, several decoding algorithms for the LDPC code over an additive white Gaussian noise channel are extensively simulated and their error performances are compared, through using MATLAB software. From our experimental research, it shows that the Normalized BP-based decoding algorithm possesses the best comprehensive property for its lower computational complexity and for the feasibility to be efficiently implemented via FPGA devices. Then, a decoder for the (1280, 1024) code is successfully designed and implemented on an FPGA device in which the realization complexity and the savings of hardware resources are carefully considered. In our experimental research, the design correctness of the encoder and decoder are verified through hardware and software simulations, as well as practical measurement.

Keywords: Low-density parity-check codes; encoding and decoding; Normalized BP-based decoding; FPGA; CCSDS

1 INTRODUCTION

It is well known that Low-density parity-check (LDPC) codes were originally invented by Gallager in the 1960s [1]. Might be restricted by the availability of powerful digital computers used for further theoretical research and of high-speed microprocessors applied for encoding and decoding implementation, this pioneering work was almost forgotten for more than three decades. With the development of theory and implementation technique in the field of channel coding, and especially with the discovery of an iterative decoding algorithm which is now called Belief Propagation (BP) decoding, the LDPC codes were rediscovered by MacKay and Neal in 1990s [2] and [3]. And they showed that the error performance of these codes is almost as close to the Shannon limit as that of turbo codes. Since then, the theoretical research on LDPC codes with their encoding and decoding implementation has being rapidly progressed.

In September 2007, an instructive and steering document about the experimental specification on low-density parity-check codes for use in near-earth and deep space applications was released under approval of the Consultative Committee for Space Data Systems (CCSDS) [4]. This CCSDS experimental specification is mainly composed of two parts. In the first part, the construction of an LDPC code with code rate 7/8 and its encoding are described in detail, which can be used for many near-earth missions. In the second part, a set of LDPC codes was designed and optimized for the characteristics and requirements of many typical Deep-Space missions. In this set, there are nine LDPC codes that are all the linear and systematic binary block codes.

In this paper, we concentrate our experimental research on the encoding and decoding of an (1280, 1024) LDPC code with code rate 4/5, for which an encoder is implemented by using an FPGA device. For efficiently decoding the (1280, 1024) LDPC code, several decoding algorithms over an additive white Gaussian noise (AWGN) channel are extensively simulated and corresponding error performances are compared, through using MATLAB software. Base on simulation results, the Normalized BP-based decoding algorithm is selected for our implementation of the decoder on an FPGA device [5]. The design correctness of the encoder and decoder in this paper is verified through hardware and software simulations as well as practical measurement.

2 CODE SPECIFICATION AND ENCODING

As described in [4], the set of LDPC codes contains nine AR4JA LDPC codes that are all the systematic and possess relatively large minimum distance for their block length and undetected error rates lie several orders of magnitude below detected frame and bit error rates for any given operating signal-to-noise

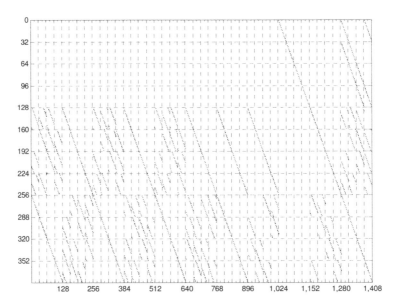

Figure 1. Scatter chart of the parity-check matrix H.

ratio. Thus, these codes are suitable for the deep space applications.

2.1 Code specification

One of these LDPC codes is the (1280, 1024) code whose information block length is $k = 1024$ and code-block length is $n = 1280$. Thus, its code rate is exactly equal to $r = k/n = 4/5$. The code is indirectly defined by a 384-by-1408 parity-check matrix H which is constructed from $M \times M$ submatrices with $M = 128$. More precisely speaking, the parity-check matrix H is formed by using a 3×11 array of square submatrices with dimension $M = 128$, including 12 identity matrices denoted as I_M, 11 zero matrices written as $\mathbf{0}_M$ and 10 submatrices which are, respectively, formed by permutation matrices Π_k for $k = 1, 2, \ldots, 26$. A scatter chart of the parity-check matrix H is shown in Fig. 1 where every '1' bit in the matrix is represented by a point. The dashed gridlines in Fig. 1 are equally spaced with interval $m = M/4$. In other words, every $M \times M$ submatrix is equally divided into 16 square submatrices with dimension $m = 32$. Since the matrix H has 1408 columns, the last M symbols in an encoded codeblock may need to be punctured (not transmitted).

2.2 Encoding implementation

The (1280, 1024) code is a member of the AR4JA code family. For a given information block, its corresponding codeblock can be obtained by performing a multiplication of the information block by a block-circulant generator matrix G. The matrix G can be analytically derived out from the above parity-check matrix H, as shown in [4]. Explicitly, the generator matrix has a form of $G = [I_{MK} \ W]$, where I_{MK} is an identity with dimension MK for $K = 8$, and W is a

dense matrix of circulants that has size $MK \times 3M$ if punctured columns are described in the encoding, or $MK \times 2M$ if punctured columns are omitted. Especially, the matrix G is block-circulant and is composed of sets of superimposed size $m = M/4$ circulants so that the encoding realization is very efficient.

In our experimental research, we use an FPGA (EP3SL150F780I4) in Altera Stratix III family as an implementation platform of the encoder. Considering that the punctured columns are kept in encoding, the matrix W contained in the generator matrix G can be represented by a 32×12 array of square submatrices as follows.

$$W = \begin{bmatrix} B_{1,1} & B_{1,2} & \cdots & B_{1,12} \\ B_{2,1} & B_{2,2} & \cdots & B_{2,12} \\ \vdots & \vdots & \cdots & \vdots \\ B_{32,1} & B_{32,2} & \cdots & B_{32,12} \end{bmatrix} \quad (1)$$

Here, $B_{i,j}$ is such a 32×32 circulant that is uniquely specified by its first row [4], and its remainder 31 rows can be obtained by successively performing one-bit right cyclic shift. Thus, the desired encoder can be efficiently implemented in a bit-serial manner using 12 linear feedback shift 32-bit registers denoted as A1 to A12. The schematic for implementing the encoder is shown in Fig. 2.

The encoding process begins with loading the first rows of $B_{1,1}, B_{1,2}, \ldots, B_{1,12}$ into corresponding registers A1, A2, ..., A12, and then performs the computations for the first bit of the input information. After finishing the computations for the first 32 bits of the input information, the first rows of $B_{2,1}, B_{2,2}, \ldots, B_{2,12}$ are loaded into the corresponding registers and the encoder repeats the same computations for the second 32 input information bits. When 32 cycles of such manipulations are completed, a desired 1408-bit

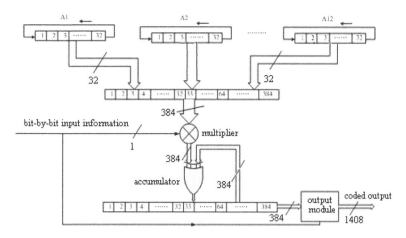

Figure 2.   Schematic for the encoder implementation.

codeblock is obtained at the encoder output. By the hardware and software simulations as well as the operation performed in the FPGA encoder, it is verified that the encoder design is correct, and it shows that for the 80 MHz system clock and the 4 MHz information input clock, the total time for obtaining one codeblock is about 0.3 μs.

3   DECODING ALGORITHM SELECTION

Roughly speaking, the decoding algorithms for LDPC codes can be classified into two types. One is Belief Propagation (BP) based algorithms and the other is check-bit flipping based Bit Flipping (BF) algorithms [5], [6], [7], [8] and [9]. Although the computational complexity of BP-based soft decision algorithms is comparatively higher, the decoding performance for longer codeblocks can approach Shannon limit. On the other hand, several simplified algorithms such as UMP-BP and Normalized BP-based algorithms as well as others have been invented, which can obtain a good tradeoff between the decoding error performance and the implementation complexity. The BF-based algorithms belong to a kind of hard decision decoding methods that are suitable to realize in hardware. Because their lower implementation complexity, several improved algorithms have been proposed, such as weighted bit flipping (WBF), modified weighted bit flipping (MWBF) and improved modified weighted bit flipping (IMWBF) algorithms [1], [9] and [10].

Using MATLAB software, the decoding performances of 6 algorithms for the (1280, 1024) LDPC code are compared, as shown in Fig. 3. Here we have assumed that the BPSK modulation scheme is used that maps a codeblock $c = (c_1 c_2 \ldots c_n)$ into a transmitted sequence $x = (x_1 x_2 \ldots x_n)$ in terms of $x_i = 1 - 2c_i$, and the additive noise in the AWGN channel has zero mean and variance $\sigma^2 = N_0/2$. At the receiver, the sequence to be decoded can be represented as $y_i = x_i + n_i$, where n_i is the ith sample of the noise, and thus y_i is a Gaussian random variable whose

mean value is 1 or -1 and variance is $\sigma^2 = N_0/2$. As expected, the bit error performance of BP-based and UMP-APP algorithms is entirely better than that of BF-based algorithms. Particularly, the Normalized BP-based algorithm shows the best bit error rate (BER) performance. The performance of UMP BP-based algorithm is very close to that of the Normalized BP-based algorithm, and both of them have a sharp-dropping waterfall property at the SNR near 2.5 dB, which is close to the Shannon limit by 0.5 dB only. The UMP-APP algorithm is a simplified version of the minimum sum-product decoding algorithm, and thus its performance is not as good as that of the previous BP-based algorithms. It is worth noting that the performance of Normalized BP-based algorithm is superior to that of UMP BP-based algorithm, which is achieved by introducing a normalization factor [5]. However, the computational amount of the former is only slightly greater than that of the latter.

In the scope of our research, we think of that the Normalized BP-based algorithm has a best tradeoff between the error performance and the computational complexity for the above 6 decoding algorithms. Here, we have used a good value of the normalization factor α. Through the simulation shown in Fig. 4, the optimum value of the factor for the (1280, 1024) LDPC code should be about 0.69. Considering the implementation efficiency in FPGA, we select $\alpha = 0.75$.

4   DECODER REALIZATION IN FPGA

4.1   *Decoding Algorithm Description*

For the (1280, 1024) LDPC code, its parity-check matrix H has 384 rows and 1408 columns that correspond to 384 check nodes and 1408 variable nodes, respectively. We now define the notation $C(i)$ as the set of check nodes connecting with the ith variable node, $R(j)$ as the set of variable nodes connecting with the jth check node, $q_{ij}(b)$ as the external probabilistic information at the jth check node that is passed from the ith

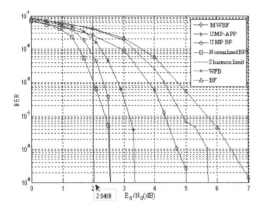

Figure 3. Performance Comparison for 6 decoding algorithms.

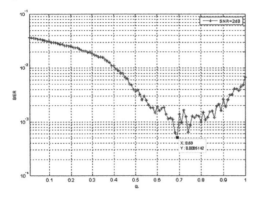

Figure 4. Selection of the normalization factor value.

variable node, and $r_{ji}(b)$ as the external probabilistic information at the ith variable node that is passed from the jth check node. The computational procedure for the Normalized BP-based algorithm can be concluded as follows [5]:

Step 1: Information Initialization

1) Determine the log-likelihood ratios $L(P_i)$ for $i = 1, 2, \ldots, n$ that depend on initial information received from the channel.

2) For every variable node i with its connecting check node j for $j \in C(i)$, set the initial information sent from the variable node to the check nodes, that is,

$$L^{(0)}(q_{ij}) = L(P_i) = \ln(\frac{1+exp(2y_i/\sigma^2)}{1+exp(-2y_i/\sigma^2)}) = 2y_i/\sigma^2 \quad (2)$$

Step 2: Iterative Process

1) Check-node information processing at the lth iteration, that is, for every check node j with its connecting variable nodes i for $i \in R(j)$, compute the transmission information $L^{(l)}(r_{ji})$ that is sent from the variable nodes to the check node, by using the following formula

$$L^{(l)}(r_{ji}) = \alpha \prod_{i' \in R_j \setminus i} sign(L^{(l-1)}(q_{i'j}))[\min_{i' \in R_j \setminus i} |L^{(l-1)}(q_{i'j})|] \quad (3)$$

where $\alpha = 0.75$.

2) Variable-node information processing at the lth iteration, i.e., for every variable node i with its connecting check nodes j for $j \in C(i)$, compute the transmission information that is sent from the check nodes to the variable node, through using the formula below.

$$L^{(l)}(q_{ij}) = L(P_i) + \sum_{j' \in C_i \setminus j} L^{(l)}(r_{j'i}) \quad (4)$$

3) Decoding decision at the lth iteration, that is, for every variable node i make decision in terms of

$$L^{(l)}(q_i) = L(P_i) + \sum_{j \in C_i} L^{(l)}(r_{ji}) \quad (5)$$

If $L^{(l)}(q_i) > 0$, then set the ith bit in an estimated codeblock $\hat{c}$ to be $\hat{c}_i = 0$, otherwise, $\hat{c}_i = 1$.

Step 3: Stopping Criterion

If the estimated codeblock $\hat{c}$ satisfies $H\hat{c}^T = 0$ or the iterative number has arrived at a prescribed maximum value, then stop the iteration, otherwise transfer to the step 2 and continue to iterate.

4.2 Decoder structure

According to the above decoding algorithm, we use a half-parallel decoding method to realize the decoder of the (1280, 1024) LDPC code with an FPGA (EP3SL150F780I4) of Altera Stratix III, where the block-circulant property of the check matrix H is successfully exploited. The decoder structure in the FPGA consists of the data buffers, the check-node processing array, the variable-node processing array, the global-state control and address generating array, and the information memory array, which are shown in Fig. 5. The datain_buffer shown in Fig. 5 is the memory space with size 1408×7 bits that is divided into 44 subspaces with size 32×7 bits. The dataout_buffer is the buffer memory space with size 1024×1 bit, whose final output is the decoded 1024-bit codeword. The variable-node processing array consists of several variable-node processing units that are used for computing the variable-node information of individual variable nodes and the result is used to update the corresponding information stored in the information memory array, and make the decoding decision and the estimated codeword is sent to the dataout_buffer. The check-node processing array consists of several check-node processing units that are used for computing the check-node information of individual check nodes and the result is used to update the corresponding information stored in the information memory array [9], [11] and [12].

The functional modules in Fig. 5 can be further described as follows.

1) Information Memory Array

As shown in Fig. 1, the check matrix H consists of a 12×44 array of square circulant submatrices with dimension 32. According to the above decoding algorithm, the intermediate information computed for the

100

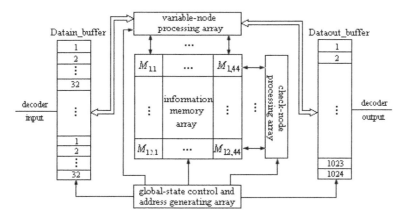

Figure 5. Schematic for the decoder structure.

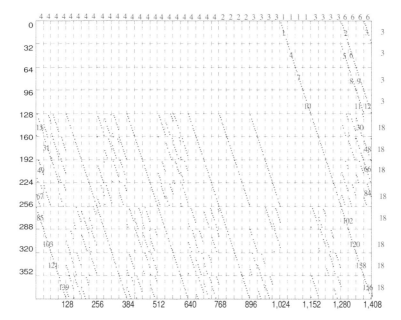

Figure 6. Numbering for nonzero submatrices in check matrix.

variable and check nodes corresponding to the nonzero entries in H needs to be stored in the information memory array. We number the 156 nonzero submatrices sequentially, as shown in Fig. 6. In the decoding process, only the variable-node information and check-node information corresponding to these nonzero submatrices are used to update the contents stored in the information memory array, with the result that the storage space can be reduced by more than 50%.

As shown in Fig. 6, 156 storages with size of 32×32 are needed to store the intermediate information data. Considering that we set the width of information data to be 10 bits, the size of a single storage is 1024×10 bits. Considering that the check matrix H possesses block-circulant property and every row in any circulant submatrix has only one nonzero entry, one row in a circulant submatrix only needs 1×10 bits, and thus one storage needs 32×10 bits only. Keeping

the relative position of the nonzero entry to its corresponding check and variable nodes from change (i.e., hardware structure fixed), the computations for nonzero entries within a single submatrix can be performed by using the same variable-node processing unit or check-node processing unit. Therefore, the reading and writing of the 32 information data in a submatrix can be completed by cyclic method. Thus, the information memory array only needs 156 storages of size 32×10 bits, and thus the memory resources are reduced further.

2) Check-Node Processing Units

In Fig. 6, the numbers labeled at the right side and on the top of the check matrix H indicate the row weight and column weight of the matrix, respectively. A row weight represents the number of variable nodes that take part in the information processing of a corresponding check node, which determines the

101

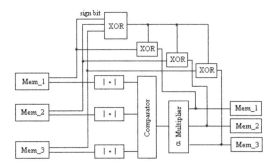

Figure 7. Check-node processing unit for 3 variable nodes.

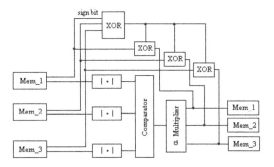

Figure 8. Variable-node processing unit for the column weight with 6.

computational structure for its corresponding check-node processing unit. As shown in Fig. 6, there only are two different computational structures. One is for 3 variable nodes and the other is for 18 variable nodes. Thus, only two different check-node processing units need to be designed in terms of (3). For example, the structure of the check-node processing unit for 3 variable nodes is shown in Fig. 7, where Mem_1 to Mem_3 represent 3 storages for the variable nodes which connecting with the check node. Considering that the value of the normalization factor α has been selected as 0.75, the multiplier for the factor can be implemented by shifting its input to right by 1 bit and 2 bits, respectively, and then adding these two shifted values.

3) Variable-Node Processing Units

In Fig. 6, there are five different numbers labeled on the top of H. It means that only five types of variable-node processing units need to be designed in terms of (4) and (5). Thus, for the variable nodes whose column weight is 6, we only need to design one variable-node processing unit that is shown in Fig. 8.

The design correctness of the decoder is carefully verified through simulation and practical measurement. It shows that for the 80 MHz system clock and the 4 MHz information input clock, the total decoding time is about 0.5 μs.

5 CONCLUSION

In this paper, the encoder and decoder for the (1280, 1024) LDPC code over the AWGN channel are successfully designed on the FPGA devices, where the block-circulant properties of the check and generator matrices are sufficiently considered. In the design of the decoder, we classified the check-node and variable-node processing units into a few different types, with the result that the structure complexity of the decoder is substantially reduced. On the other hand, the saving of hardware resources is also considered. Thus, the designed decoder shows a good property, that is, it is easy to implement and consume less hardware resources.

ACKNOWLEDGMENT

The authors wish to thank Lecturer Yuanhong Zhong of Chongqing University for his some valuable suggestions in the design of electronic circuits.

REFERENCES

[1] R.G. Gallager. Low-density parity-check codes. IRE Trans. on Inform. Theory, Vol. 8, pp. 21–28, Jan. 1962.
[2] D.J.C. MacKay and R. M. Neal. Near Shannon Limit Performance of Low density Parity check Codes. Electronics Letters, Vol. 33, pp. 457–458, Mar. 1997.
[3] D.J.C. MacKay. Good error correcting codes based on very sparse matrices. IEEE Trans. On Inform. Theory, Vol. 45, pp. 399–431, Mar. 1999.
[4] CCSDS. CCSDS 131.1-O-2. Low Density Parity Check Codes for Use in Near-Earth and Deep Space Applications. Experimental Specification, Orange Book, Issue 2 [S], Washington DC, USA, Sep. 2007.
[5] Jinghu Chen, Marc P.C. Fossorier. Near optimum universal belief propagation based decoding of low-density parity check codes. IEEE Trans. Commun. Vol. 50, pp. 406–414, Mar. 2002.
[6] Robert J. McEliece, David J.C. MacKay and Jung-Fu Cheng. Turbo decoding as an instance of pearl's "belief propagation" algorithm. IEEE Journal on Selected Areas in Communications, Vol. 16, pp. 140–152, Feb. 1998.
[7] Xiao-Yu Hu, Evangelos Eleftheriou, Dieter–Michael Arnold and Ajay Dholakia. Efficient implementations of the sum-product algorithm for decoding LDPC codes. GLOCOM, pp. 1036–1036E, 2001.
[8] J. Chen, A. Dholakia, E. Eleftheriou, M. Fossorier, and X.-Y. Hu. Reduced-complexity decoding of LDPC codes. IEEE Trans. Commun. Vol. 53, pp. 1288–1299. July 2005.
[9] Dongfeng Yang and Haigang Zhang. Theory and Applications of LDPC Codes. People's Posts and Telecommunications Press, China, 2008.
[10] Ming Jiang, Chunming Zhao, Zhihua Shi, and Yu Chen. An improvement on the modified weighted bit flipping decoding algorithm for LDPC codes. IEEE Commun. Lett., Vol. 9, pp. 814–816, Sept. 2005.
[11] Xing Wang. FPGA-based design and implementation of a high-throughput QC-LDPC Decoder. Master's Thesis, Xidian University, China, 2011.
[12] Fei Cao. Research and implementation of LDPC codes over COFDM communication systems. Master's Thesis, University of Electronic Science and Technology of China, 2010.

Multimedia Technology IV – Farag, Yang & Jiao (Eds)
© 2015 Taylor & Francis Group, London, ISBN: 978-1-138-02794-7

The research on dim moving target detection algorithm in deep space

Yonghui Xu & Yinong Mao
Department of Automatic Test and Control, Harbin Institute of Technology, Harbin, China

ABSTRACT: After analyzing the image characteristic of the surveillance equipment, a real-time dim moving target detection algorithm in deep space is put forward. It uses row high pass filter to suppress background and multi-frame addition to improve contrast between stars and targets. Then, cross projection is used to confirm the star's position. Most disturbances of stars are eliminated through the star-point matching. Data association based on logic principle and the characteristic of target are adopted to detect the target. Practical application approves that the system perfectly meets the requirements of the real-time dim moving target detection and recognition in deep space.

Keywords: deep space; background suppresion; star-map matching; target detection

1 INTRODUCTION

Moving target detection is one of the important subjects of applied vision research. It is also regarded as an important ability in computer vision system and has broad prospects for application such as in the intelligent monitoring, military and industrial areas [1]. With the development of modern satellite technology, for consideration of improving the country's space airpower, the problem of satellite detection, identification and tracking in deep space background has more and more important significance. When the satellite is in the far away location, it shows the point target in the surface of the image. The pixels are few, and the signal noise ratio (SNR) is low. The number of stars is huge in the start map. The target is completely submerged in the map. It is the hot spot of space science and technology research at home and abroad to overcome the influence of the stars and noise and to extract motion trajectory of space target accurately. Some representative algorithms of sequence image point target detection are 3D filter theory [2] raised by REED and dynamic programming method [3] proposed by Barniv. The shortcoming of the two methods mentioned above is that, when the target location, speed, and direction are all unknown, the calculation is huge, which makes it difficult to realize real-time processing. Other methods are neural network method and wavelet transform method, and optical flow field method, etc. The advantages, disadvantages and performances of the various methods are analyzed in reference [4]. Based on the CCD image data of the monitoring equipment as the research background, this article uses "column high-pass filter" for background suppression and uses the sequence image multi-frame accumulation to increase contrast of goals and star,

extract local sky map, and then uses local map matching to eliminate stars interference. Finally, based on the logic of the nearest neighbor correlation method, isolated noise point is eliminated, and target track is extracted according to the candidate target size and gray characteristics. The simulation results of CCD image for the monitoring equipment show that this algorithm meets the requirement of the real-time dim moving target detection and recognition in deep space.

2 DESCRIPTION OF THE ALGORITHM

2.1 Image preprocessing

Formula (1) shows an image:

$$f(i,j) = f_B(i,j) + f_T(i,j) + n(i,j). \tag{1}$$

In this formula, $f_B(i,j)$ is background image, $f_T(i,j)$ is point target, $n(i,j)$ is high frequency noise. For point target detection, image sequence can be used for only target gray value and target speed. To visible light target detection, since the target gray level may be either lower than that of the background or higher than the background, we can't use single threshold to detect the target. Small target detection mainly relies on the gray mutation between it and the background. For space background, the gray level change of the whole background is slow, and it can be regarded as accumulating large blocks of the low-frequency background and the image high-frequency portion. High frequency part more contains small target information, so a high-pass filter is used to isolate gray singular point. The rest is the target, noise and interference target (stars or synchronous satellite).

(a) Original image

Figure 2. Image difference results.

(b) High pass filter image

Figure 1. Image preprocessing results figure.

Figure 1 (a) shows CCD image acquired by monitoring equipment. A lot of the stars have long bright stripes below, the larger the stars the wider the bright stripes are. In addition, the bottom part of the image is getting brighter; therefore, column high-pass detection or column CFAR detection is needed to detect the entity, as shown by formula (2) and (3).

$$T_h = \max\left(\frac{1}{n-1}\sum_{i=2}^{n} f(x-i), \frac{1}{n-1}\sum_{i=2}^{n} f(x+i)\right) \quad (2)$$

$$f(x,y) = \begin{cases} f(x,y) & f(x,y) > \alpha \times T_h \\ 0 & f(x,y) < \alpha \times T_h \end{cases} \quad (3)$$

In this formula, T_h is segmentation threshold, $f(x,y)$ is gray value of pixel (x,y), α is weighted coefficient. As shown in figure 1, (a) is the original star image, (b) is its high pass filter image; hence, the use of "column high-pass filtering" can remove the background,

and the rest is the target, noise and interference target (stars or synchronous satellite). It is thus clear that, using "column high-pass filtering" can remove the background, and the rest is the target, noise and interference target (stars or synchronous satellite).

2.2 Target detection

Deep space background mainly is the stars. The position of stars in the image should be basically unchanged; their gray scale and shape are difficult to distinguish from goals. We can only detect the target with the motion characteristics. The main methods of moving target detection are difference image method [5] and optical flow method [6]. Optical flow method spends much time, its real-time and practicality is poor. Difference image method is simple, easy to real-time. Ideally, the simple image subtraction in different time can get moving target. In fact, for deep space image, due to the atmospheric disturbance, the brightness of the stars has differences in the image at different frames. As shown by figure 2, difference results cannot effectively eliminate stars interference.

In view of this situation, the literature [7] proposed a stars background eliminating method based on map matching. Using star catalog, this method selects matching features, matching on the map between point in the images of the scene and star point, based on Least Trimmed Square Hausdorff Distance (LTS-HD), so as to determine one to one corresponding relation, to eliminate point matched successfully, and to realize the purpose of removing stars. The disadvantage of this kind of map matching method is the star matching in the whole sky, which requires huge amount of computation, making it difficult to meet the requirements on the higher processing speed requirements situation.

Based on the analysis of the monitoring equipment characteristics of the CCD image, this article put forward a kind of small moving target detection method based on local star background extraction. The sky local star map extraction method is the use of

(a) Star point diagram   (b) Vertical direction   (c) Horizontal
                   projection   projection

Figure 3.   Cross projection diagram.

multi-frame accumulation. Because the place of star is fixed in the space sequence image, stacked image can enhance the contrast of stars and moving target. After high-pass filter, we can extract the sky local star map, and thus eliminate stars interference by using the local map matching.

2.2.1 *The algorithm in locating the stars*

To extract the position of the star point in star map, the literature [8] introduces the cross projection segmentation algorithm. The specific process is that, first, the map vertical direction projection is made, the area projection gray level greater than 0 is detected, the column coordinate range in the starpoint existing area is determined, as shown by figure 3(b). The horizontal projection image is detected on the basis of the vertical projection, and then stars are determined like the row coordinate range. After the vertical and horizontal projection detection, four vertex coordinates of each star image point external rectangular are obtained, hence at once determining the star point distribution range, as shown by figure 3(c).

Star segmentation localization method can be divided into two types based on gray level and edge. Method based on the gray is suitable for smaller goals, and method based on the edge is suitable for large target.

Another gray value weighted method is especially applicable to the center calculation of symmetric image, and its advantage is that it makes full use of every bit of gray level information of symmetrical image, and at the same time calculation can meet the star point positioning accuracy and real-time requirements. The star diameter in the actual map is less than 5 pixels and belongs to a small goal; therefore, the star image point segmentation positioning uses the gray value weighted method. The formula for gray value weighted centroid coordinates computation is as follows.

$$\bar{x} = \frac{\sum_{i=1}^{m} x_i f(x_i, y_i)}{\sum_{i=1}^{m} f(x_i, y_i)}$$

$$\bar{y} = \frac{\sum_{i=1}^{m} y_i f(x_i, y_i)}{\sum_{i=1}^{m} f(x_i, y_i)}$$

(4)

Among them, $\bar{x}$ and $\bar{y}$ are centroid coordinates; m is the number of pixels occupied by the star point, and $m \geq 2$, $f(x_i, y_i)$ is the gray value in the i pixels [9].

2.2.2 *Local map matching procedure*

The position of the stars is fixed in the space sequence image, the target motion trajectory is the continuous stripe across the scene in continuous several frames synthetic image; the experiment uses sequence image for 10 frames. Figure 5 (1), (2) show part of the image. Based on the local map matching method for moving object extraction, the main steps are as follows.

In the first step, the image sequence is multi-frame accumulated. We enhance the contrast of stars, star background and moving target, as shown in figure 5 (3). In fact, due to the randomness of the noise, after multi-frame accumulation, the magnitude of the noise is also greatly reduced, and the signal-to-noise ratio of the stars improves approximately $\sqrt{n}$ times.

In the second step, superimposed star has been greatly enhanced, with the contrast of the moving target. Using column high-pass filtering discussed earlier, target point and bright line are eliminated; local sky map is extracted, as shown in Figure 5 (4). The average gray level and centroid position are calculated for each star and recorded to a local map database.

In the third step, column high-pass filtering is used again for the image detection, in order to segment the suspected target (star or moving target), and match the database of the local map in front. If the suspected target split out and the characteristics of a star (position and average gray) in the star atlas is consistent, we regard the suspected goal as a star and eliminate the star directly. That is, assuming that the map database has a star, the gray level is g_{star}, the centroid position is (p_{star_x}, p_{star_y}), one of the split out target is T, the gray level is g_T, the centroid position is (p_{T_x}, p_{T_y}). Meeting formula (5) relationship, we think that the split out goal T is star interference, which can be directly removed.

$$\left| f_{star} - f_T \right| < \varepsilon_g$$
$$\left| p_{star\_x} - p_{T\_x} \right| < \varepsilon_d$$
$$\left| p_{star\_y} - p_{T\_y} \right| < \varepsilon_d$$

(5)

ε_g or ε_d is a small positive number in formula (5).

In the fourth step, the image is eliminated after background stars and the random noise by local map matching method. An obvious character of the noise point is that it occupies fewer pixels. The width filtering mode filter can be used. The map matching can remove most of the stars, but there may be some stars that failed to match. In view of this situation, according to the characteristics of the continuous moving targets, filtering is done by the frame relevant way (details will be discussed later in the section of this chapter), and final detection results obtained are shown in figure 5 (9) and (10).

2.2.3 Frame correlation filtering

The target follows the law of motion, whose trajectory has certain continuity and relevance. Conversely, the noise is a random fluctuation, having no particular movement law. The motion law of the target decides that it can only appear in the surrounding area in the subsequent image, and gray level keeps continuous in a short time. Assuming that time series is $C(t)$, $t = 0, 1, \ldots, T$, in the $C(t)$ and $C(t+1)$, there is a connected domain $D(t)$ and $D(t+1)$ respectively. The small target image formed by the connected domain $D(t)$ is $P_t = \{p_t(m,n)\}, [m,n] \in D(t)$. The small target image formed by the connected domain $D(t+1)$ is $P_{t+1} = \{p_{t+1}(m,n)\}, [m,n] \in L(t+1)$, their centroids are $(c_{x(t)}, c_{y(t)})$ and $(c_{x(t+1)}, c_{y(t+1)})$, respectively. The average gray level are $\bar{f}(t)$ and $\bar{f}(t+1)$ respectively. If $|x(t+1) - x(t)| \leq \varepsilon_1$, $|y(t+1) - y(t)| \leq \varepsilon_1$ and $|\bar{f}(t+1) - \bar{f}(t)| \leq \varepsilon_2$ (ε_1 and ε_2 are set threshold), we think that P_{t+1} and P_t are related, denoted:

$$P_{t+1} \cap P_t \geq 1 \tag{6}$$

That is, a small target in the t frame and the $t+1$ frame is related. If a small target is related in consecutive u frame images, denoted:

$$P_{t+1} \cap P_t \geq 1$$
$$P_{t+2} \cap P_{t+1} \geq 1 \tag{7}$$
$$P_{t+u-1} \cap P_{t+u} \geq 1$$

We think that the small targets are related u times. Assuming that the threshold is λ, if $u \geq \lambda$, it is recognized as the goal that you want to detect.

3 IMPLEMENTATION OF THE ALGORITHM

3.1 Hardware block diagram

In the real-time image processing system, the image preprocessing algorithm has large computation and high processing speed requirements. But the operation structure is relatively simple. It is suitable for using the FPGA hardware to realize. We choose EP2S30F672 produced by Altera Company as FPGA chip. Target detection and tracking algorithm are about the characteristics of target. There are many criteria, and the algorithm control is complex. So it is suitable for using DSP software to realize. We choose TMS320C6416 produced by TI Company. The highest basic frequency is 720 MHz. Peak processing speed is 5760MIPS. Deep space background weak target real-time detection system block diagram is showed by Figure 4.

3.2 Algorithm verification

The sequence image used in the experiment is 10 frames 1024 × 1024 image taken from the CCD image data of the monitoring equipment. Figure 5 shows the

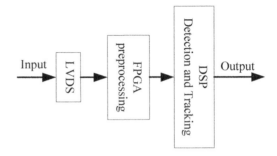

Figure 4. Weak target real-time detection system composition.

simulation test results. Actual joint debugging proves that, when the DSP basic frequency is set to 720 MHz, the whole target detection identification process can finish in 25 milliseconds.

(1) and (2) are part of the CCD image for monitoring equipment.

(3) and (4) are multi-frame accumulation results and the star map extracted by accumulation results after "column high-pass filtering".

(5) and (6) are the results of (1) and (2) after "column high-pass filtering", respectively, so we can see that column high-pass can effectively suppress background interference and remove the bright lines in the background.

(7) and (8) are the results of (5) and (6) after star map matching, respectively, so we can see that star map matching can remove the star interference effectively, leaving just a small amount of targets and the noise points.

(9) and (10) are the results of (5) and (6) after target detection.

4 CONCLUSION

Based on the characteristics of CCD imaging for monitoring equipment, the paper puts forward a kind of algorithm for deep dim moving target detection. The main idea of this algorithm is using column high-pass filter to remove background and bright line interference, using the map matching to get rid of stars interference, using the width of the filter to remove isolated noise, and finally combining the features of candidate targets and using the nearest neighbor correlation method based on the logic to complete the target detection. The method improves the efficiency of target detection and has strong robustness for slight shaking to the system. But since the map is generated by the superposition of sequence images and has global features, if in one frame image targets overlap with the stars in sports, map matching will weed out the target, causing target point location error, which requires forecasting combining target tracking algorithm to solve this problem. Practical application

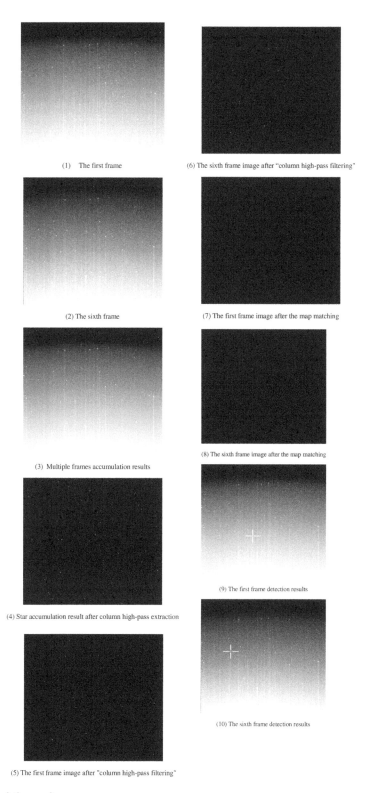

(1) The first frame

(6) The sixth frame image after "column high-pass filtering"

(2) The sixth frame

(7) The first frame image after the map matching

(8) The sixth frame image after the map matching

(3) Multiple frames accumulation results

(4) Star accumulation result after column high-pass extraction

(9) The first frame detection results

(10) The sixth frame detection results

(5) The first frame image after "column high-pass filtering"

Figure 5.   The simulation results.

shows that the algorithm adapts to the starry background target detection; the test results meet actual work requirements.

REFERENCES

[1] S. Wang L, Hu W, Tan T. Visual Analysis of human movement, Journal of Computers, 2002. 25(3) 225–237.

[2] T. Reed I. S., Gagliardi R. M., Shao H M. Application of three-dimensional filtering to moving target detection. IEEE Transactions on Aerospace and Electronic Systems, 1983, 19(6), pp. 898–905.

[3] T. Barniv Y. Dynamic programming solution for detecting dim moving targets. IEEE Transactions on Aerospace and Electronic Systems, 1985, 21, pp. 144–156.

[4] T. Fu S, Zhang X. Real-time detection method based on the sequence of images moving target, Optical Technology, 2004, 30(2), pp. 215–217.

[5] T. Milan Sonka, Vaclav Hlavac, Roger Boyle. Image Processing, Analysis, and Machine vision. Ai Hai-zhou, translate. Beijing: Post & Telecom Press, 1999, pp. 471–473.

[6] T. Fennema C L, Thomp son W B. Velocity determination in scenes containing several moving objects. Computer Graphics and Image Processing, 1979, 9(4), pp. 301–315.

[7] S. Liu ZY. Deep space background small target detection technique based on the star chart matching, Journal of Beijing University of Aeronautics and Astronautics. 2007.

[8] T. Wang ZK, Zhang YL. A CCD star map star point fast positioning algorithm, Chinese Journal of Space Science, 2006, 26(3), pp. 209–214.

[9] S. Zhao Y, Zhang Y. Research of star pattern recognition centroid extraction algorithm. Space Electronic Technology, 2004, (4), pp. 5–8.

Multimedia Technology IV – Farag, Yang & Jiao (Eds)
© *2015 Taylor & Francis Group, London, ISBN: 978-1-138-02794-7*

An adaptive multi-scale lattice vector quantization and its application in low bit rate speech coding

Weijun He & Qianhua He
School of Economics and Information, South China University of Technology, Guangzhou, China

ABSTRACT: The codebook design is a critical component of low bit rate speech coding. This paper proposed an improved Pyramid Lattice Vector Quantization (PLVQ) based on Adaptive Multi-Scale (AMS), abbreviated as AMS-PLVQ. The AMS-PLVQ employs a novel lattice structure of Global Nonuniform and Local Uniform (GNLU) aiming at improving the PLVQ performance. Based GNLU lattice structure, discriminating VQ scheme is introduced and implemented with multiple sub-quantizers defined by dynamic scale. The AMS-PLVQ is utilized in VQ-PLVQ and P-PLVQ, which is used in replacement of MSVQ in 2.4 kbps MELP encoding approach. Experimental results, on TIMIT database, demonstrated the VQ-AMS-PLVQ and P-AMS-PLVQ achieved the transparent quality at 36 bits/frame and 35 bits/frame respectively and offer an compromise option for coding applications.

Keywords: speech coding; lattice; vector quantization; low bit rate

1 INTRODUCTION

In recent years, military application and satellite communication have increased the interest in speech coding below 2.4 kbps because of limitation of bandwidth. Among various novel low bit rate speech coding schemes [1–3], Mixed Excitation Linear Prediction (MELP) speech-coding algorithm [4] and its evolutions [5–7] are very important representatives, in which vector quantization (VQ) techniques and super-frame architecture are used.

The VQ techniques based on the Linde-Buzo-Gray (LBG) algorithm [8] has little discernible structure and is optimal for nonuniform source. This unstructured VQ yields high computational complexity and large storage requirement. Both drawbacks deteriorate due to the super-frame architecture in low bit rate speech coding [6, 9]. Multistage vector quantization (MSVQ) [10] divides the quantization task into several successive stages, resulting in a reduction of codebook search complexity and a significant increase of encoding distortion. Structured VQ algorithms are proposed to avoid these drawbacks and lattice vector quantization (LVQ) [11–14] is one of the most studied method. In LVQ coding, a source vector x, is first mapped to the minimal distortion lattice code vector y, and then code vector is lossless encoded into an integer index for transmission or storage. Various LVQ algorithms have been developed for speech or audio encoding in recent years [15, 16]. Two-stage vector quantization-pyramid lattice vector quantization (VQ-PLVQ) was introduced by Pan et al [17], where the first stage

uses an unstructured VQ codebook and the second-stage LVQ uses a pyramidal lattice codebook [18]. The structure of VQ-PLVQ depends on the assumption of a laplacian source from first-stage VQ encoding error. Based on predictive vector quantization (PVQ) [19], Adriana [20] et al studied predictive PLVQ(P-PLVQ). For fixed-rate coding, a PLVQ quantizer has a finite support [21] and is composed of a subset lattice points. Although the complexity of PLVQ is much lower than that of unstructured VQ for large dimension, there is also the difficult question of how to quantize a source vector lying outside the support region (i.e. overload distortion). Overload distortion is still an issue in practical applications. PLVQ deals with this problem by making some decrement or increment to component of vector at the cost of introducing extra distortion, what is called truncation.

The lattice structure of PLVQ is global uniform. Global uniform quantization can't give an optimum average distortion for nonuniform input. Further more, for fixed-rate coding, all source has to be quantized through a lattice quantizer, which has a finite support region. Vectors lying outside the region have to be quantized through truncation, which is inevitable to introduce extra distortion. In order to improve the PLVQ performance, an improved pyramid lattice vector quantization (PLVQ) based on adaptive multi-scale (AMS) method is proposed and abbreviated as AMS-PLVQ in this paper. The method is based on a novel lattice structure, which is named global nonuniform and local uniform (GNLU). In structure of GNLU, lattice quantizer is composed of multiple sub-quantizers with the same rate. Although the density of lattice point is varying with sub-quantizers, the lattice points distribute uniformly in the finite region of each sub-quantizer. Then source in space can be quantized discriminatingly. In addition, the amount of code vectors in each sub-quantizer is identical, which corresponds to the fixed-rate so that truncation process is alleviated. In our experiment, it is utilized in both LVQ schemes (VQ-PLVQ and P-PLVQ), which is used in replacement of MSVQ of 2.4 kbps low bit rate speech encoding approach.

The rest of this paper is organized as follows:, PLVQ algorithm is formulated in Section 2 and GNLU structure is developed in Section 3, along with an AMS method. In Section 4, experiment results and performance analysis is given. Finally, conclusion is provided in Section 5.

2 PYRAMID LATTICE VECTOR QUANTIZATION

LVQ can be viewed as a vector generalization of uniform quantization. It constrains the reproduction codebook, which is a subset of a regular lattice.

2.1 Regular lattice

Given l linear independent vectors $a_1, a_2, \ldots, a_l$ in R^n ($l \leq n$), a n-dimensional lattice Λ_n is formulated as:

$$\Lambda_n = \left\{ y \mid y = u_1 \cdot a_1 + u_2 \cdot a_2 + \cdots + u_l \cdot a_l \right\}$$

where $u_1, u_2, \ldots, u_l$ are integers.

The simplest lattice is the integer lattice Z_n, in which all the n components of the lattice points are integers. Some of the most frequently used lattices in LVQ are A_n, D_n, E_n and their duals, which consist of the lattice points of Z_n and are given by Conway and Sloane in [11]. Their fast quantization algorithms were given in [22]. The D_n lattice is used in this paper, which have integer components with even-component sum.

For fixed-rate coding, the lattice must be scaled and a subset lattice points must be identifies as the code vectors of a quantizer, which is usually chosen according to the distribution of the source so that the resulting quantizer support region has most probability. For example, pyramid lattice vector quantization (PLVQ) [18] is optimal for Laplacian source and the quantizer is composed of the finite integer lattice lying on a pyramid surface region.

2.2 Pyramid lattice vector quantization

PLVQ is optimal for Laplacian source with probability density function as (1):

$$p(x_i) = \frac{\lambda}{2} \exp(-\lambda |x_i|)$$ (1)

where λ is the scale parameter, $\{x_i\}$ is a sequence with independent and identical distribution, assembled

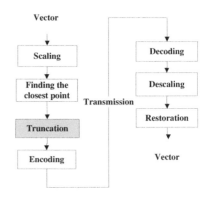

Figure 1. The flowchart of PLVQ

into vector x of length L. The codebook of PLVQ is arranged in variable pyramid surface $S(L, k)$ as (2):

$$S(L, k) = \left\{ x : \sum_{i=1}^{L} |x_i| = \|x\|_1 = k \right\}$$ (2)

where $\|x\|_1$ is L_1-norm. The number of lattice points $N(L, k)$ in each pyramid surface $S(L, k)$ can be computed by (3):

$$N(L, k) = N(L-1, k) + N(L, k-1) + N(L-1, k-1)$$ (3)

For fixed-rate coding, the PLVQ is executed as follows:

a) *Finding the closest lattice point*: A source vector x is first scaled to $\widehat{X}$ by a fixed scale s and mapped to the minimum distortion lattice code vector $\widetilde{X}$ through rounding each component of $\widehat{X}$ to the nearest integer.

b) *Trucation*: Compute the L1-norm of $\widetilde{X}$ as (2) and execute truncation according to the fixed-rate.

c) *Computing the index*: Use the enumeration encoding algorithm [18] to find the transmission index and transmit to receiver.

The flowchart of PLVQ is summarized in Fig. 1.

As mentioned in section 1, there is a difficult question of how to quantize a source vector lying outside the support region for fixed-rate coding (i.e. overload distortion). In PLVQ, vector truncation is a method to deal with the problem of overload distortion. In truncation process, a lattice vector outside the pyramid support region is truncated through some decrement or increment to the local components [18]. However, any adjustments not only introduces intolerable distortion, but also destroys the correlation of the components in a vector.

3 ADAPTIVE MULTI-SCALE METHOD

In fixed-rate coding of PLVQ, there are 2 steps in the procedure of finding the closest integer vector on $S(L, K)$ to the input source. Firstly, round the scaled input vector $\widehat{X}$ to the nearest lattice point $\widetilde{X}$. Secondly,

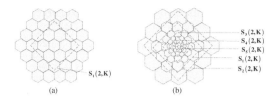

(a)   (b)

Figure 2. Lattice A2 for traditional lattice and GNLU lattice: (a) Traditional lattice, (b) Global nonuniform and local uniform lattice

if $\widetilde{X}$ is not on pyramid surface $S(L,K)$ (i.e. the support region), find the closest lattice point y on $S(L,K)$ to $\widetilde{X}$. On the one hand, the first step is a uniform VQ process because interval of lattice is identical in the whole space. It's not appropriate for the source of nonuniform distribution. Assume that the nonuniform input is quantized with different intervals, a better performance can be achieved. On the other hand, the second step is a truncation process. The process is aiming at finding the closest code vector y in the quantizer to $\widetilde{X}$ at the cost of extra distortion. Assume that the nearest lattice point $\widetilde{X}$ lies on the region of a quantizer at the fixed-rate, the truncation process can be neglected and $\widetilde{X}$ can be encoded into an integer index directly. We consider designing a nonuniform lattice structure from a perspective of discriminating quantization for the purpose of improving the performance.

From the above analysis, a GNLU (global nonuniform and local uniform) LVQ structure is proposed in this paper. On GNLU, the lattice quantizer is composed of multiple sub-quantizers. The density of lattice point is varying with different sub-quantizers. As a result, differential intervals are used for source in different areas according to the fixed-rate. Furthermore, number of code vector in each sub-quantizer is identical, which responds to the fixed-rate. No matter which sub-quantizer the nearest lattice point $\widetilde{X}$ locates on, the truncation is neglected.

3.1 Global nonuniform and local uniform

Take hexagonal lattice A2 [12] for example, the difference of structure between traditional lattice and GNLU lattice is described as Fig. 2.

In traditional lattice structure (fig. 2(a)), distribution of lattice is global uniform and all sources in space are quantized with the equal interval. For fixed-rate coding, the lattice subset is chosen from an pyramid surface $S_1(2,K)$ and compose the quantizer, which has a finite support region. Source vectors lying outside the support region have to be quantized through truncation mentioned in section 2.

In GNLU structure (fig. 2(b)), lattice quantizer is composed of multiple sub-quantizers of identical rate. Although the density of lattice point is varying with sub-quantizers, distribution of the lattice points is uniform in the finite region of each sub-quantizer. Thus it is a global nonuniform and local uniform structure. The amount of code vectors in different pyramid

surface $S_i(2,K)$ is identical, which correspond to the fixed-rate as (4) so that truncation can be neglected:

$$N_{S_1} = N_{S_2} = N_{S_3} = N_{S_4} = N_{S_5} \qquad (4)$$

where N_{S_i} is the amount of code vectors pyramid surface $S_i(2,K)$.

3.2 Scale analysis in PLVQ

In PLVQ, pyramid surface region is distinguished by L_1-norm of vectors. We define $\|\widetilde{X}\|_1 = r$. it's obvious that statistics of r is a decisive factor for choosing the subset lattice of a quantizer. The probability density function of r is calculated as (5) [18]:

$$f(r) = \frac{\lambda^L r^{L-1} e^{-\lambda r}}{\Gamma(L)} \qquad (5)$$

where $\Gamma(L) = (L-1)!$. The mean and variance of r are

$$E[r] = \frac{L}{\lambda}$$

$$\mathrm{var}[r] = \frac{L}{\lambda^2}$$

Since the scaling factor s is correlate with λ as (6):

$$s = \frac{K\lambda}{L} \qquad (6)$$

Then

$$E[r] = \frac{L}{\lambda} = \frac{K}{s} \qquad (7)$$

$$\mathrm{var}[r] = \frac{L}{\lambda^2} = \frac{K^2}{s^2 L} \qquad (8)$$

According to (7) and (8), there's a nonlinear relationship between statistics of r and scale s. Thus we consider controlling r as close to K (correspond to the fixed-rate) as possible with a dynamic scale. As a result, it is equal to quantize source with sub-quantizers of the same rate, which is mentioned in GNLU lattice structure.

3.3 Adaptive multi-scale method

Now the key is how to search a appropriate scale for each sub-quantizer. In this paper, an adaptive multi-scale method is proposed. We define four additional bits for transmission of scale information. Bit assignment is described as table 1.

There are 4 bits for encoding the scale adjustment information, 1st bit is indication of adjustment, 2nd to 4th bits indicate the magnitude of adjustment, the rest are assigned for the vector index. Where $bit_K = [\log_2 N(L,K)]$.

Table 1. Bits assignment for scale.

	Indication	Magnitude	Index
Bits (bit)	1	3	$bit_K - 4$

Given a vector x, s_0 and Δ_s, search scale upwards or downwards by step Δ_s on the basis of s_0 before the truncation procedure, where $s_0 = K\lambda/L$:

a) *Compute the L_1-norm and search the scale*: compute: $\widetilde{X} = s_i x$ and $r = \|\widetilde{X}\|_1$: If $bit_r < bit_K - 1$, then go to b), else if $bit_r > bit_K - 1$, go to c); Otherwise, go to d).

b) *Search the scale upwards*: If $bit_r \geq bit_K - 4$, go to d); Otherwise, $s_{i+1} = s_i + \Delta_s$ and $\widehat{X}'_s = s_{i+1} \cdot x$, find the closest point $\widetilde{X}'$ to $\widehat{X}'_s$. Compute $k = \|\widetilde{X}'\|_1$ and bit_k, $bit_r = bit_k$, $s_i = s_{i+1}$, go to b);

c) *Search the scale upwards*: If $bit_r \leq bit_K - 4$, go to d); Otherwise, $s_{i+1} = s_i - \Delta_s$ and $\widehat{X}'_s = s_{i+1} \cdot x$, find the closest point $\widetilde{X}'$ to $\widehat{X}'_s$. Compute $k = \|\widetilde{X}'\|_1$ and bit_k, $bit_r = bit_k$, $s_i = s_{i+1}$, go to c);

d) *Trucation and encoding*: Execute truncation and the enumeration encoding procedure as described in [18].

4 EXPERIMENT

The proposed algorithm is implemented on Intel processor 2.80 GHz, 2GB RAM machine and TIMIT [23] database is used to evaluate its performance, from which 40 speakers (20 males and 20 females) were selected. The speech were sampled at 16 kHz, 10 LSF parameters were extracted from $L = 10$ LPC parameters, with window length of 22.5 ms. About 50,000 vectors were collected. The D_{10} lattice is used in fast quantization algorithms. Set $\Delta_s = 2$. The AMS-PLVQ is utilized in VQ-PLVQ and P-PLVQ schemes, which is used in replacement of MSVQ of 2.4 kbps MELP encoding approach.

Distribution of first-stage VQ encoding error in VQ-PLVQ and distribution of prediction error in P-PLVQ are depicted in Fig. 3 and Fig. 4 respectively, which approximately obey Laplacian Distribution (10 dimension).

The performances are evaluated by the average spectral distortion (ASD) which is often used as an objective measure of the LSF encoding performance. The spectral distortion for frame is given in [24].

Table 2 presents a comparison on performance between the improved scheme(VQ-AMS-PLVQ and P-AMS-PLVQ) and the universal scheme(VQ-PLVQ and P-PLVQ). It shows that VQ-AMS-PLVQ and P-AMS-PLVQ achieve the transparent quality at 36 bits/frame and 35 bits/frame respectively, compared with 40 bits/frame and 43 bits/frame of the original schemes. Howerer, the percentage of Outliers having SD between 2 and 4 dB of the both methods are a slightly larger the origins. The chief cause is that a

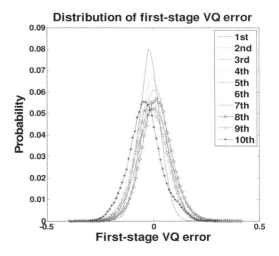

Figure 3. Dstribution of first-stage VQ encoding error.

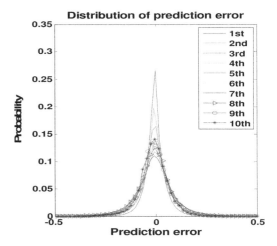

Figure 4. Distribution of prediction error.

Table 2. ASD of LSF (Transparent quality).

Method	Bit rate (bit/frame)	ASD (dB)	$2 < SD < 4$ (%)	$SD > 4$ (%)
VQ-PLVQ	40	1.1257	0.21	0
VQ-AMS-PLVQ	36	1.0486	0.23	0
P-PLVQ	43	1.1309	0.32	0
P-AMS-PLVQ	35	0.9479	0.83	0.01

few source are quantized with larger interval in GNLU structure.

For practical applications the transparent quality is too costly and recent standards have settled the trade-off cost-performance at lower than transparent quality requirements. VQ-AMS-PLVQ and VQ-AMS-PLVQ are used in replacement of MSVQ of 2.4 kbps MELP encoding approach. A comparison of performance at 25 bit/frame in MELP vocoder is given in Table 3. It showed that the proposed method which is utilized

Table 3. ASD of LSF (25 bit in 2.4 kpbs MELP).

Method	Bit rate (bit/frame)	ASD (dB)	$2 < SD < 4$ (%)	$SD > 4$ (%)
MSVQ	25	1.5003	17.07	0.24
VQ-PLVQ	25	1.6867	25.97	0.55
VQ-AMS-PLVQ	25	1.6362	25.38	0.50
P-PLVQ	25	2.5183	52.09	9.41
P-AMS-PLVQ	25	1.9801	38.53	2.28

Table 4. 2.4 kpbs MELP Vocoder (PESQ-MOS, Delay, Memory).

Method	PESQ		Delay (ms)	Memory of codebook (words)
	20 (male)	20 (female)		
MSVQ	2.93	2.69	7.5	$128 \times 10 + 64 \times 10 + 64 \times 10 + 64 \times 10$
P-PLVQ	2.41	2.35	1	0
P-AMS-PLVQ	2.73	2.54	3.3	0
VQ-PLVQ	2.83	2.65	1.5	128×10
VQ-AMS-PLVQ	2.84	2.62	3.1	128×10

in VQ-PLVQ and P-PLVQ schemes, has an reduction of 3% and 21% in ASD compare with the origins respectively.

Performance is improved as a result of releasing distortion generated in truncation process in GNLU lattice structure. Howerer, the improvement of VQ-AMS-PLVQ is not so great as P-AMS-PLVQ. The main reason is that the rate of AMS-PLVQ in VQ-AMS-PLVQ is lower than that of P-AMS-PLVQ.

The comparison of PESQ, delay and codebook memory requirement are given in Table 4. The encoding delay and storage requirement of PLVQ methods are greatly improved compare to MSVQ. Among the LVQ methods, the encoding peformance of proposed P-AMS-PLVQ is superior (2.73 for male and 2.54 for female) to original P-PLVQ (2.41 for male and 2.35 for female), even still lower than MVSQ (2.93 for male and 2.69 for female). Further more, the encoding peformance of VQ-AMS-PLVQ (2.84 for male) is a bit better than the original VQ-PLVQ (2.83 for male). However, according to the encoding delay, addition complexity is introduced due to the scale searching process in the proposed method.

On the one hand, there is significant reduction of complexity and storage requirement for PLVQ methods compare to MSVQ even with a bit worse encoding performance. On the other hand, the proposed PLVQ algorithm gives a further improvement in encoding compare with the original PLVQ method at the cost of introducing some tolerable computational complexity.

5 CONCLUSION

In low bit rate speech coding, complexity and codebook storage are drawbacks due to unstructured VQ

and super-frame architecture. Although the original PLVQ gives lower complexity and storage requirement, encoding performance is still an obstacle. An improved pyramid lattice vector quantization (PLVQ) algorithm based on adaptive multi-scale (AMS) method is proposed for fixed-rate coding in this paper. The method bases on GNLU lattice structure, which generalized the idea of nonuniform quantization in scalar quantization, aiming at quantizing source discriminatingly and alleviating the overload distortion problem in PLVQ. Experimental results showed the proposed method not only keep the advantage of PLVQ (i.e. lower complexity and storage requirement), but also improve the encoding performance against to the traditional PLVQ. The proposed method offer an compromise option for coding applications.

ACKNOWLEDGMENT

This work is supported by science and information technology of Guangzhou 2060503 and 4500001.

REFERENCES

[1] W. Jiang, R. Ying, and P. Liu, "Speech reconstruction for MFCC-based low bit-rate speech coding," in Multimedia and Expo Workshops (ICMEW), 2014 IEEE International Conference on, 2014, pp. 1–6.

[2] A. Liutkus, R. Badeau, and G. Richard, "Low bitrate informed source separation of realistic mixtures," in Acoustics, Speech and Signal Processing (ICASSP), 2013 IEEE International Conference on, 2013, pp. 66–70.

[3] B. Sisman, U. Guz, H. Gurkan, and B. S. Yarman, "A new speech coding algorithm using zero cross and phoneme based SYMPES," in Signals, Circuits and Systems (ISSCS), 2013 International Symposium on, 2013, pp. 1–4.

[4] A. V. McCree and T. P. Barnwell, III, "A mixed excitation LPC vocoder model for low bit rate speech coding," Speech and Audio Processing, IEEE Transactions on, vol. 3, pp. 242–250, 1995.

[5] G. Di and Z. Xiaoqun, "A 600bps MELP-Based Speech Quantization Scheme for Underwater Acoustic Channels," in Computational and Information Sciences (ICCIS), 2013 Fifth International Conference on, 2013, pp. 1983–1986.

[6] Z. Jiyong, W. Jingyuan, Z. Xia, and X. Zhiyong, "Research and implementation of an improved 800BPS speech coding algorithm," in Information Theory and Information Security (ICITIS), 2010 IEEE International Conference on, 2010, pp. 794–797.

[7] M. Saidi, B. Boudraa, M. Bouzid, and M. Boudraa, "Multiple descriptions coding in MELP coder for voice over IP," in Systems, Signals and Devices (SSD), 2012 9th International Multi-Conference on, 2012, pp. 1–7.

[8] Y. Linde, A. Buzo, and R. M. Gray, "An Algorithm for Vector Quantizer Design," Communications, IEEE Transactions on, vol. 28, pp. 84–95, 1980.

[9] G. Guilmin, F. Capman, B. Ravera, and F. Chartier, "New Nato Stanag Narrow Band Voice Coder at 600 Bits/s," in Acoustics, Speech and Signal Processing,

2006. ICASSP 2006 Proceedings. 2006 IEEE International Conference on, 2006, pp. I–I.

[10] B. H. Juang and A. Gray, Jr., "Multiple stage vector quantization for speech coding," in Acoustics, Speech, and Signal Processing, IEEE International Conference on ICASSP '82., 1982, pp. 597–600.

[11] J. Conway and N. Sloane, "Voronoi regions of lattices, second moments of polytopes, and quantization," Information Theory, IEEE Transactions on, vol. 28, pp. 211–226, 1982.

[12] J. Conway and N. Sloane, "A fast encoding method for lattice codes and quantizers," Information Theory, IEEE Transactions on, vol. 29, pp. 820–824, 1983.

[13] G. Fuchs, "Embedded Voronoi codes for successive refinement lattice vector quantization," in Acoustics, Speech and Signal Processing (ICASSP), 2013 IEEE International Conference on, 2013, pp. 5805–5809.

[14] W. Patchoo, T. R. Fischer, and C. Maddex, "L1-norm-based coding for lattice vector quantization," in Signal and Information Processing Association Annual Summit and Conference (APSIPA), 2013 Asia-Pacific, 2013, pp. 1–4.

[15] X. Kai, H. Ruimin, and Z. Yuanyuan, "Mobile audio coding using lattice vector quantization based on Gaussian mixture model," in Multimedia Technology (ICMT), 2011 International Conference on, 2011, pp. 412–415.

[16] M. Xie, "Lattice Vector Quantization Applied to Speech and Audio Coding," ZTE Communications, pp. 25–33, 2012.

[17] P. Jianping and T. R. Fischer, "Vector quantization-lattice vector quantization of speech LPC coefficients," in Acoustics, Speech, and Signal Processing, 1994. ICASSP-94., 1994 IEEE International Conference on, 1994, pp. I/513-I/516 vol.1.

[18] T. R. Fischer, "A pyramid vector quantizer," Information Theory, IEEE Transactions on, vol. 32, pp. 568–583, 1986.

[19] J. Skoglund and J. Linden, "Predictive VQ for noisy channel spectrum coding: AR or MA?," in Acoustics, Speech, and Signal Processing, 1997. ICASSP-97., 1997 IEEE International Conference on, 1997, pp. 1351–1354 vol.2.

[20] A. Vasilache, M. Vasilache, and I. Tabus, "Predictive multiple-scale lattice VQ for LSF quantization," in Acoustics, Speech, and Signal Processing, 1999. Proceedings., 1999 IEEE International Conference on, 1999, pp. 657–660 vol.2.

[21] R. M. Gray and D. L. Neuhoff, "Quantization," Information Theory, IEEE Transactions on, vol. 44, pp. 2325–2383, 1998.

[22] J. Conway and N. Sloane, "Fast quantizing and decoding and algorithms for lattice quantizers and codes," Information Theory, IEEE Transactions on, vol. 28, pp. 227–232, 1982.

[23] DARPA-TIMIT, "Acoustic-Phonetic Continuous Speech Corpus," Speech Disc 1.1-1 ed, 1990.

[24] S. E. Cheraitia and M. Bouzid, "Reduced complexity system for robust encoding of wideband speech LSF parameters," in Electronics, Communications and Photonics Conference (SIECPC), 2013 Saudi International, 2013, pp. 1–5.

Multimedia Technology IV – Farag, Yang & Jiao (Eds)
© 2015 Taylor & Francis Group, London, ISBN: 978-1-138-02794-7

Sparse coding based kinship recognition

Yunfei Chen, Hongwei Hu, Shujuan Cao & Bo Ma
Beijing Laboratory of Intelligent Information Technology,
School of Computer Science and Technology, Beijing Institute of Technology, Beijing, China

ABSTRACT: Image based kinship recognition is a challenging problem since finding the subtle features that are reliable across a large span of ages (e.g., father and son) and gender difference (e.g., father and daughter) is very difficult. In this paper, we tackle the problem using sparse coding method, automatically classifying pairs of face images as "related" or "unrelated" (in terms of kinship). First , the face images are divided into overlapping patches. Each patch is represented by its gray values. In order to capture the spatial information of the patch, the center coordinates of the patch is used. Second, we use the sparse coding based algorithm to capture more salient properties of visual patterns than vector quantization (VQ). Here, the Locality-constrained Linear Coding (LLC) scheme is used to solve the sparse coding problem. Finally, the linear SVM classifier is used for kinship recognition since the linear SVM pays less computation complexity than nonlinear SVM. Experiments results have shown that, in terms of recognition accuracy, the suggested method outperforms the NRML [6] on the challenging database KinFace-I (KFW-I) and KinFaceW-II (KFW-II).

Keywords: kinship recognition; sparse coding; local features; LLC

1 INTRODUCTION

Facial images convey a lot of human characteristics, such as age, skin color, and gender. In the last few decades, facial image analysis has attracted a number of researchers in computer vision and many representative methods have been proposed for practical applications such as face recognition, facial expression recognition, gender classification, human age estimation and ethnicity recognition. While great successes have been made in these fields, there have few researches on kinship recognition, possibly due to its great challenges and lacking of publicly available database.

During the past decades some benchmark databases, e.g., Yale B, AR, and CMU PIE had been designed for basic research. However, many of them were collected under controlled conditions and suffered from great natural variations in factors. Later, a new unconstrained face dataset called Labeled Faces in the Wild (LFW) was designed for face identification. For kinship verification, two major components are needed: (1) inherited facial features extraction and (2) kinship measurement based on the extracted familial traits. However, due to the large span of age difference and the inevitable natural factors such as pose, lighting, there still exist room for improvement on kinship recognition.

In this paper, we focus our study on the uncontrolled dataset KinFace-I and KinFace-II [6] for kinship recognition. Since the database images we used only contain a frontal face with few background information or context clues, how to obtain the kinship clues from the facial images decides the recognition accuracy. To address this problem, the sparse representation theory [1], [2], [3], [13], [14], [15] is used to find the kinship clues between kinship members. The sparse coding (SC) strategy, instead of the traditional hard quantization or soft quantization, uses a linear combination of a small number of code words to approximate the input features. The approach is naturally derived by relaxing the restrictive cardinality constraint of vector quantization (VQ). The strong restraint of VQ leads to a larger reconstruction error than sparse coding in terms of the final obtained code. Next, the max pooling [13] and the spatial information of the block are concerned to stand up to the local spatial translations and viewpoints changes. The robust facial features can be extracted after sparse coding and max pooling. Finally, the linear SVM classifier is used for classification. Experiment results show that our method outperforms the state-of-the-art on KFW-I and KFW-II.

2 RELATED WORK

The pioneer work in [4] attempted to discriminate kinship based on a list of facial features that potentially encompass genetic information passed down from parents to descendants. They evaluated a set of image features to select the most discriminative inherited facial features. After that, they used the K-Nearest-Neighbors for kinship verification. A database containing 150 frontal image pairs was used for training and testing. However, the database in [4] was collected in controlled environment; this implied a severe limitation-it was nontrivial to apply it to the real-world application.

In [7], an image was divided into several salient parts. To match the two salient parts, the DAISY descriptor was used to represent each part. They argued that familial traits were 'special' for each family pair, so they selected different salient parts for different kinship pair independently for final kinship verification. In [16], they performed Gabor wavelet on each face image to obtain a set of Gabor magnitude (GM) feature images from different scales and orientations. Then, they extracted the Gradient Orientation Pyramid (GOP) feature of each GM feature image and performed multiple feature fusion for kinship verification. In [19], the Self Similarity Representation of Weber face (SSRW) algorithm was proposed for kinship classification. Each face was represented by its own reflectance and difference of Gaussian filters. Xiuzhuang Zhou et al. in [5] presented an automatic kinship verification system based on Viola-Jones face detector and spatial pyramid learning-based (SPLE) feature descriptor under uncontrolled conditions. Xia Siyu et al. in [8] proposed to take advantage of some intermediate data, e.g. young parents, to abridge the great discrepancy between children and their old parents. Their core idea was based on the assumption that faces of parents captured when they young were more alike their children's compared with images captured when they old. The aforementioned methods mainly depend on classifier such SVM or KNN in the final verification. In [6], a metric learning approach was adopted. They proposed a new neighborhood repulsed metric learning (NRML) method for kinship verification inspired by the observation that interclass image pairs (without kinship relationship) with higher similarity were more easily misclassified than those with lower similarity. So they aimed to learn a distance metric to settle the situation. The method had better result on KinFace-II database than KinFace-I, possibly due to that the KinFace-I has more discrepancy than KinFace-II. Ming Shao et al. in [9] extended the [8] with the metric learning method. They extracted two typical features; one was based on appearance and extracted by Gabor filters. Another one was based on the anthropometric model which considered structure information of faces. Besides, they considered the metric learning approach to generate proper distance metric to learn the potential rules for kinship verification.

While promising results have been obtained from the previous methods, the inherited characteristics which mainly influences the recognition accuracy cannot extracted effectively. How to find the familial clues shared by a pair of family members is of great importance. To address this problem, we adopt the sparse

coding and max pooling to obtain the similarities between a pair of images.

3 SPARSE CODING BASED KINSHIP RECOGNITION

3.1 Sparse representation

The perception to the real world of the human visual system is based on the effective coding of the world according to the research of neurologists. This inspired researchers to simulate the human visual system to deal with the complicated signals. Olshausen in [15] presented the sparse representation model for the first time. Compared with the other coding schemes (hard quantization, soft quantization), the result in [13] shows that the sparse coding is better than the vector quantization. Possibly due to that the sparse representation can capture the saliency of an image and reduce the impact of the interference information.

Let $y = (y_1, y_2, \ldots, y_m)^T \in R^m$ and $D \in R^{m \times N}$ be a dictionary. If we can reconstruct y use only a few elements contained in D, we call that y can be sparse represented based on dictionary D. In specially, the sparse coding [1], [2], [3] needs to solve the following problem:

$$\min_X \| X \|_0 \quad s.t. \quad y = DX \tag{1}$$

where $X = (x_1, x_2, \ldots, x_N)^T$ is the corresponding coefficient of $y \cdot \| \bullet \|_0$ denotes the l_0 norm. However, the l_0 norm optimization problem is NP-hard. In practice, we can gain the approximate result by relaxing the l_0 norm to l_1 norm. This is because l_1 norm is a close form of l_0 considering the convex optimization problem. Furthermore, l_1 norm is equal to the l_0 norm when the result is sparse enough. Then the optimized formula becomes:

$$\min_x \| X \|_1 \quad s.t. \quad y = DX \tag{2}$$

Considering that there exists noise in the observed signals, appropriate error should be taken into account to obtain more precise result. We then have the following formula:

$$\min_x \| X \|_1 \quad s.t. \quad \| y - DX \| \leq \varepsilon \tag{3}$$

where $\varepsilon \geq 0$ represents the error during the observation. We can rewrite the above formula as:

$$\min_x \| y - DX \|_2^2 + \tau \| X \|_1 \tag{4}$$

where τ is the control coefficient that balances the reconstruction error and the sparsity. The larger τ indicates that we take more attention on sparsity, the smaller τ means that we take more attention on reconstruction error.

We use the Locality-constrained Linear Coding (LLC) method to solve the sparse coding problem. Specifically, the LLC needs to solve the following problem:

$$\min_X \sum_{i=1}^m \| y_i - Dx_i \|^2 + \lambda \| d_i \odot x_i \|$$
$$s.t. \mathbf{1}^T x_i = 1, \forall i \tag{5}$$

where $\odot$ indicates the inner product, and $d_i \in R^C$ is used to represent the similarity between each atom and the input y_i.

Since the LLC solution only has a few significant values, or in other words it just like features selection. The bases actually provide a set of anchor points to form a local coordinate system, such that each data point can be approximated by a linear combination of its nearby anchor points. This means that we can directly select the nearest neighbors of the y_i in the dictionary to speed up the encoding process. We can simply use the K (K<C) nearest neighbors of y_i as the local bases D_i, and solve a much smaller linear system to get the codes:

$$\min_{\bar{x}} \sum_{i=1}^m \| y_i - \bar{x}_i D_i \|^2$$
$$s.t. \mathbf{1}^T x_i = 1, \forall i \tag{6}$$

As K is usually very small, solving the above equation can be very fast.

3.2 Sparse representation for kinship recognition

This section focuses on the kinship recognition [4], [5], [6], [7], [8] based on sparse coding. Take the face image as a whole for global facial feature extraction is commonly used in face recognition. However, it focuses few on the detailed information. In the real world, we often hear phrases such as "Jack has his father's nose" or "Lucy has her mother's eyes". This implies that local feature is of great important during the kinship recognition. Besides, various local features proposed during the last few decades have gained encouraging performance in many applications such as face detection, image classifications etc. In this paper, the local features are extracted firstly and effective organization of the local features is executed to obtain the whole image representation. The method contains the advantage of local features and global features, which can represent an image well.

Firstly a facial image is divided into multiple patches according to fixed size to extract the local features. Fig. 1 shows an example of dividing an image into four patches. The partition of the image can avoid illumination variation and expression changes to some extent. Then an over-complete dictionary is learned for the sparse representation of the image patches. After the pooling function on the sparse coding, linear SVM [17] [18] classifier is used to judge whether a pair of images has kinship or not.

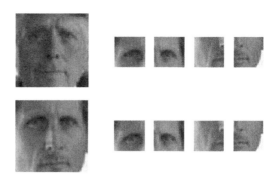

Figure 1. A pair of images with father-son kinship and corresponding patches. The first row corresponding the father's face image and the patches, second row is the son's image face and the patches, respectively. The image is divided into four patches for convenience.

Let I be a facial image with the size of $N \times N$ we perform the division on the two-dimensional image space. The image is divided into overlapping patches with the size of $n \times n$ and the step size is d where $d < n$ along the x-axis and y-axis of the image to ensure that the patches are overlapping. The choice of d and n should make the patches meet the fully division of facial image. The overlapping patches can efficiently obtain the traits implicated in the image. Original image information is reserved by expand the patch into a $1 \times n^2$ feature vector and a set of local descriptors $\{f_i\}_{i=1}^{Num}$ is obtained after the normalization, Num is the total number of patches in an image. In order to capture the spatial information of an image, the patch center coordinates are used to obtain the structure information. Then each patch is represented by a $1 \times (n^2 + 2)$ vector. After that an over-complete dictionary D is learned through k-means method.

We now perform the kinship recognition based on the aforementioned local feature extraction and dictionary learning. Denote $y^{(1)}, y^{(2)}, \ldots, y^{(m)}$ as a set of local features, the sparse coding of the local features is known as:

$$\min_{x^{(j)}, D_i} \sum_{j=1}^m \| y^{(j)} - \sum_{i=1}^C x_i^{(j)} D_i \|^2 + \lambda \sum_{i=1}^C \| x_i^{(j)} \|_1 \quad st. \; x_i^{(j)} \geq 0 \tag{7}$$

where $x^{(j)}$ is the sparse coding corresponding to $y^{(j)}$. The first item is the data fitting function; the second item is sparsity penalty function where the l_1 norm is used instead of the l_0 norm. C is the number of dictionary atoms. The constraint $x_i^{(j)} \geq 0$ means that all the elements of $x^{(j)}$ are nonnegative.

We then compute the holistic image feature through a pre-chosen pooling function on the obtained sparse coding. Here we use the max pooling function aforementioned to obtain the coding vector of each image $(s_1, s_2, \ldots, s_{Num})^T$.

Suppose each patch of an image has obtained its corresponding sparse code. All the sparse codes form

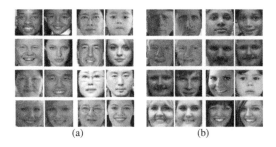

     (a)   (b)

Figure 2. Several examples contained in the kinship database. (a) and (b) are some images from KFW-I and KFW-II respectively. From top to bottom are face images with the Father-Son (F-S), Father-Dau (F-D), Mother-Son (M-S), and Mother-Dau (M-D) kinship relationship respectively.

a matrix S with *Num* rows and *C* columns. The max pooling is conducted as follows:

$$\begin{bmatrix} s_{0,0} & \cdots & s_{0,C} \\ \cdots & \cdots & \cdots \\ s_{Num,0} & \cdots & s_{Num,C} \end{bmatrix} \xrightarrow{\text{Each column take maximum}} \max \left(\begin{bmatrix} s_{0,i} \\ \cdots \\ s_{Num,i} \end{bmatrix} \right) \rightarrow \begin{bmatrix} s_1 \\ \cdots \\ s_{Num} \end{bmatrix} \quad (8)$$

For a pair of images s_i and s_j with kinship relationship, the representation of the pair images is obtained by the absolute difference between s_i and s_j, namely: $S_{i,j}^d = |s_i^d - s_j^d| (d = 1, \ldots, Num)$. The obtained image pair feature and the corresponding label is used to train the SVM classifier. Finally, the trained SVM is used to classify the test set.

4 EXPERIMENTS AND RESULTS

We have evaluated the proposed methods by conducting a number of kinship verification experiments on two datasets: KFW-I and KFW-II [6]. The following describes the details of the experiments and results.

4.1 Data set

We conduct the experiments on two dataset called KFW-I and KFW-II. The datasets were collected by J. Lu et al. in [6]. The databases have no restrictions on pose, lighting, background, expression, age and ethnicity. Each image in the database has normalized to 64×64. The difference of KFW-I and KFW-II is that each pair of kinship facial images in KFW-I is collected from different photo while in KFW-II it is collected from the same photo.

There are four kinship relations in the KFW-I and KFW-II datasets: Father-Son (FS), Father-Daughter (FD), Mother-Son (MS) and Mother-Daughter (MD). Some examples from the KEW-I and KFW-II dataset are shown in Fig. 2 respectively.

4.2 Experiments settings

In our experiments, the images are converted to grayscale. We adopt the 5-fold cross validation strategy for experiments. The positive samples are the true

Table 1. Verification accuracy (%) of different methods on different subsets of the KFW-I dataset.

Method	Feature	F-S	F-D	M-S	M-D	Mean
CSML	LE	61.1	58.1	60.9	70.0	62.5
NCA	LE	62.1	57.1	61.9	69.0	62.3
LMNN	LE	63.1	58.1	62.9	70.0	63.3
NRML	LE	64.1	59.1	63.9	71.0	64.3
OURS	Gray Value	**80.0**	**75.0**	**77.4**	**81.6**	**78.5**

Table 2. Verification accuracy (%) of different methods on different subsets of the KFW-II dataset.

Method	Feature	F-S	F-D	M-S	M-D	Mean
CSML	LE	71.8	68.1	73.8	74.0	71.9
NCA	LE	73.8	70.1	74.8	75.0	73.5
LMNN	LE	74.8	71.1	75.8	76.0	74.5
NRML	LE	76.8	73.1	76.8	77.0	75.7
OURS	Gray Value	**82.6**	**73.8**	**82.8**	**84.0**	**80.8**

pairs and the negative samples are each parent with the selected child from the children images who is not his/her true child stochastic. The patch size n is empirically set to be 20; the step size d is set to be 5. The experiment results show that the choice of d and n can meet the fully division of facial image. The neighborhood size k is empirically set to be 3.

Since our kinship verification is a binary classification problem and the support vector machine (SVM) has excellent performance for such tasks, we here apply SVM for classification. In our experiments, the RBF kernel is used for similarity measure between images since we find that this kernel can yield higher verification accuracy than others.

We have compared our method with four other face verification algorithms which could also address the kinship verification problem, including CSML [20], NCA [10], LMNN [11] and NRML [6].

4.3 Results and analysis

In our experiments, we have compared our method with CSML [20], NCA [10], LMNN [11], NRML [6]. The LEarning-based (LE) feature which is demonstrated to be the best feature representation in [6] is used for the four methods. The best recognition accuracy of each method are recorded for a fair comparison.

Table 1 & 2 list the verification accuracy of different methods on the four subsets of the kinship databases. The results shows that the proposed methods outperforms the NRML [6] on the four subsets 15.9%, 15.9%, 13.5%, 10.6% respectively and 14.2% on the mean accuracy of the KFW-I dataset, 5.8% on the F-S subset, 0.7% on the F-D subset, 6% on the M-S subset, 7% on the M-D subset and 5.1% on the mean accuracy of the KFW-II dataset, respectively.

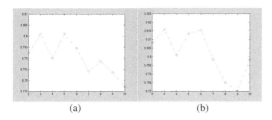

(a)   (b)

Figure 3. Mean verification accuracy versus different values of parameter k on the KFW-I(a) and KFW-II(b) dataset, respectively.

Besides, our method outperforms the NRML in that the NRML method has a big accuracy difference on the two different databases, while ours has a smaller difference. This suggests that our method can adapt to the image changes well.

Then, we investigate the effect of the parameter k in our method. Figure 3 shows the mean kinship verification accuracy versus different values of k, where Figure 3(a) and Figure 3(b) are the results obtained on the KFW-I and KFW-II database, respectively.

The Figure 3 shows that the value of k has a relative small influence on the final recognition accuracy on the database KFW-I and KFW-II respectively. Hence suitable k value can obtain encouraging results in the kinship recognition.

5   CONCLUSION AND FUTURE WORK

In this paper we propose a new representation of facial image for kinship verification. Experiments results have shown that the performance of our proposed method is better than the state-of-art algorithms. How to further combine the structure information with our proposed method may lead to the future research on kinship recognition.

REFERENCES

[1] J. Wright, A.Y. Yang, A. Ganesh, S.S. Sastry, and Y. Ma, "Robust face recognition via sparse representation", IEEE PAMI, 31(2):210–227, 2009.

[2] I. Theodorakopoulos, I. Rigas, G. Economou and S. Fotopoulos, "Face recognition via local sparse coding", In ICCV 2011.

[3] M. Yang, L. Zhang, J. Yang and D. Zhang, "Robust sparse coding for face recognition", In CVPR 2011.

[4] R. Fang, K. Tang, N. Snavely and T. Chen "Towards computational models of kinship verification", In ICIP, pages 1577–1580, 2010.

[5] X. Zhou, J. Hu, H. Lu and Y. Guan, "Kinship verification from Facial Images Under Uncontrolled Conditions", In ACM Multimedia, pages 953–956, 2011.

[6] J. Lu, J. Hu, X. Zhou, Y. Shang, "Neighborhood repulsed metric learning for kinship verification", In CVPR 2012.

[7] G. Guo, X. Wang, "Kinship Measurement on Salient Facial Features", IEEE Transactions on Instrumentation and Measurement, 2012.

[8] S. Xia, M. Shao, and Y. Fu, "Kinship verification through transfer learning", In IJCAI, 2011.

[9] M. Shao, S. Xia, and Y. Fu, "Genealogical face recognition based on UB kinface database", In CVPR 2011.

[10] J. Coldberger, S. Roweis, G. Hinton and R. Salakhutdinov, "Neighborhood component analysis", In NIPS, pages 2539–2544, 2004.

[11] K.Q. Weinberger, J. Blitzer, L. Saul, "Distance metric learning for large margin nearest neighbor classification", In NIPS 2005.

[12] S. Lazebnik, C. Schmid, J. Ponce, "Beyond bags of features: spatial pyramid matching for recognizing natural scene categories", In CVPR 2006.

[13] J. Yang, K. Yu, Y. Gong and T. Huang, "Linear spatial pyramid matching using sparse coding for image classification", In CVPR 2009.

[14] J. Wang, J. Yang, K. Yu, F. Lv, T. Huang and Y. Gong, "Locality-constrained linear coding for image classification", In CVPR 2010.

[15] B.A. Olshausen and D.J. Field, "Emergence of simple-cell receptive field properties by learning a sparse code for natural images", Nature, 1996.

[16] X. Zhou, J. Lu, J. Hu and Y. Shang, "Gabor-based gradient orientation pyramid for kinship verification under uncontrolled environments", In ACM Multimedia, pages 725–728, 2012.

[17] D. Boswell, " Introduction to Support Vector Machines", 2002.

[18] G. Dai and C. Zhou, "Face recognition using support vector machines with the robust feature", In Proc. IEEE Workshop Robot and Human Interactive Communication, 2003.

[19] N. Kohli, R. Singh, and M. Vatsa, "Self-similarity representation of Weber faces for kinship classification", In IEEE BTAS, pages 245–250, 2012.

[20] H. Nguyen, L. Bai, "Cosine similarity metric learning for face verification", In ACCV 2011.

Multimedia Technology IV – Farag, Yang & Jiao (Eds)
© 2015 Taylor & Francis Group, London, ISBN: 978-1-138-02794-7

Sparse representation and random forests based face recognition with single sample per person

Tao Xu, Hongwei Hu, Qiaofeng Ma & Bo Ma
Beijing Laboratory of Intelligent Information Technology, School of Computer Science and Technology, Beijing Institute of Technology, Beijing, China

ABSTRACT: Traditional face recognition methods usually require a large number of training samples. In some specific applications, however, we can only obtain one facial image as training sample for each person, which is usually referred to as single sample per person face recognition. The recognition rates will decrease dramatically using traditional methods in such situations, and some may even fail to work. To address this problem, we propose in this paper a novel face recognition approach based on sparse representation and random forests. We first divide each face image into multiple patches. And then we employ sparse coding to obtain local image features and random forests to acquire global features. Finally, we use L1 based nearest neighbor classifier to identify the unknown face image. Experiments are carried on two widely used face databases AR and FERET. The experimental results demonstrate our proposed approach is effective and promising.

Keywords: face recognition; single sample per person; sparse representation; random forests

1 INTRODUCTION

Face recognition refers to the problem of identifying one or more individual faces from a known face database with static or dynamic scenes. Due to its non-invasive and user-friendly, it plays an important role in file management system, public security work, customs monitoring, etc. After years of research and development, researchers have proposed many effective face recognition algorithms. Representative algorithms include principal component analysis (PCA) [1], linear discriminant analysis (LDA) [2], etc.

Traditional face recognition method is based on the system has a large number of training samples, often referred to as multiple sample per person (MSPP) [3] face recognition. Its recognition rate is greatly affected by the number of training samples of each person. However, in some practical applications, such as identity verification, passport verification, law implementation, etc. there is usually only one single sample per person (SSPP) [3] can be used because it is generally expensive to store large training set or difficult to collect additional samples under these scenarios. In such situations, most of traditional methods will suffer serious performance drop or even fail to work, such as LDA, due to the lack of samples, the within-class scatter cannot be computed.

The SSPP problem is defined as follows: given a stored database of faces with only one image per person, the goal is to identify a person from the database later in time in any different and unpredictable poses, lighting, etc. from the individual image [4]. Roughly speaking, previous SSPP face recognition approaches can be mainly classified into three categories: generic learning [5, 6], virtual sample generation [7], and image partitioning based methods [3, 8, 9].

Generic learning based methods collect an additional generic training set with multiple samples per person to extract discriminative features, which are then used to make up the lack of interclass information in SSPP problem. Su et al. [5] proposed an adaptive generic learning method to estimate the discriminative information of SSPP sample set by learning a robust model from the generic training set. Even if generic learning based methods can improve the recognition accuracy on addressing the SSPP problem, the performance of these methods is heavily influenced by the collected generic training set, which is still very difficult to obtain in practical applications. Virtual sample generation based methods generate some additional training samples for each person so that the SSPP problem turns to be MSPP problem. One main drawback of these methods is that there is high correlation between the virtual samples and original facial images, while MSPP methods assume the samples are independent with each other. Just as its name implies, image partitioning based methods first partition each facial image into several local patches and then we can acquire more discriminative features from the segmented patches.

Tang et al. [10] proposed an efficient algorithm for image classification by combining sparse coding with random forests. They used sparse coding to extract image SIFT features and random forests to classify. Motivated by Tang's work, we propose in this paper a sparse representation and random forest based method (SR-RF, in what follows we refer to our approach as SR-RF) to address SSPP face recognition problem. Firstly, we divide each face image into multiple over-lapped patches. Secondly, employ sparse coding to obtain local image features and random forests to acquire global features. Finally, use L1 based nearest neighbor classifier to identify the unknown face image. We compare SR-RF algorithm with several classic SSPP face recognition algorithms on two widely used face databases AR and FERET. Experimental results demonstrate our proposed approach is effective and promising.

The remainder of this paper is organized as follows: in section 2, we briefly illustrate the sparse coding and random forest theory; Section 3 elaborates our proposed SR-RF algorithm; Section 4 is the experiments and result analysis; Finally, we conclude our work in section 5.

2 PRELIMINARIES

2.1 Sparse coding

In recent years, sparse coding theory has achieved remarkable results in face recognition, image denoising and object tracking fields. One particularly simple and effective approach of employing sparse coding for face recognition models the samples from a single class as lying on a linear subspace. For a new face image to be identified, we represent it as a linear combination of all training face images. From the linear coefficients, we can correctly determine the class to which the test sample belongs.

Assuming a training database contains n face images with k distinct classes person, we arrange the given n_i training samples from the i-th class as columns of a matrix $D_i = [u_{i,1}, u_{i,2}, \ldots, u_{i,n_i}] \in R^{m \times n_i}$, where $u_{i,j} \in R^m$ denotes the column vector form of each face image. Then the over-complete dictionary D composed by the entire training set can be represented by concatenating the n training samples of all k classes: $D = [D_1, D_2, \ldots, D_k] \in R^{m \times n}$.

Then, the linear representation of any test face image y belonging to i-th class can be rewritten in terms of the dictionary D as

$$y = D\alpha \tag{1}$$

where $\alpha = [0, \ldots, 0, \beta_{i,1}, \ldots, \beta_{i,n_i}, 0, \ldots, 0] \in R^n$ is a coefficients vector whose entries are zero except those corresponding to i-th class.

2.2 Random forest

Random forest was proposed by Leo Breiman in 2001. It can be seen as a multi-classifier consisting of a series

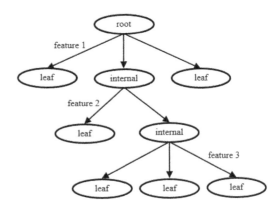

Figure 1. Schematic diagram of a decision tree.

of decision trees. When entering a test sample, each decision tree will give a classification result. Then the category of the test sample will be acquired by integrating all the classification results. The randomness of random forest is mainly embodied in the following two points: 1) choosing training samples randomly. 2) choosing features of training samples randomly.

Decision tree is a prediction model of tree structure. Its nodes can be divided into three categories: root node, internal node and leaf node. Root node contains all the training samples. Internal node splits sample set according to one of their feature. Leaf node labels the sample in itself (i.e., acquires the final classification result). In a decision tree, each path from root to leaf node represents a kind of classification procedure. An example of decision tree is shown in Fig. 1.

Taking the local image feature acquired by sparse coding as the input of random forest, we can get a vector by integrating the classification results of all decision trees. We refer to this vector as voting vector. Then we can obtain the global feature for a facial image by concatenating the voting vectors of all sub-images in it.

3 SR-RF

In this section, we first illustrate how to solve the problem of lack of samples by partitioning face image into overlapped patches. Next, we describe the procedure of sparse coding local sub-images. Then, we learn a random forest to acquire the global facial image feature and finally employ an l1 based nearest neighbor classifier to recognize the given face image.

3.1 Image partition

In order to solve the problem of lack of samples in the SSPP, we partition each enrolled image into several overlapped patches to form an image set for each sample per person, which can take full advantage of the local image information contained in each sub-image.

Given a training set $Z = \{z_1, z_2, \ldots, z_N\}$ with single sample per person, where z_i denotes the face image

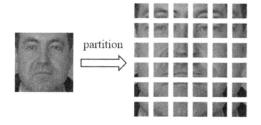

Figure 2. Image partition.

of the i-th person. The size of each face image is normalized into $m \times n$. For each training image z_i, we divided it into t overlapped patches. Assuming the size of each patch is $a \times b$, the number of overlapped pixels is d, then the number of the patch in each image is $t = \lceil (m-a)/(a-d) + 1 \rceil \times \lceil (n-b)/(b-d) + 1 \rceil$.

Let $M_i = \{z_{i1}, z_{i2}, \ldots, z_{it}\}$ denote the patches set of the i-th person. After image partition processing, the whole training set can be denoted as a matrix form $Z = [M_1, M_2, \ldots, M_N] = [z_{11}, \ldots, z_{1t}, \ldots, z_{N1}, \ldots, z_{Nt}]$, where $z_{ij} \in R^{(a*b) \times 1}$ is a vector given by stacking the columns of the j-th patch of i-th person.

For example, in AR face image database, each face image size is normalized into 60×60. We set patch size to 15×15, and the number of overlapped pixels to 5, then we can acquire 36 patches for each training image.

3.2 Sparse coding local sub-images

In the case of MSPP, its generic training set contains so rich inter-class and intra-class information that we can construct sparse coding dictionary directly by using the entire training set. In the SSPP problem, however, each person has only one training sample, the dictionary constructed in the same way cannot linearly code the test sample.

Due to the local similarities and global differences of distinct face images, we can use the image patches set related in the previous section to construct dictionary. We apply K-means clustering algorithm on the patches set, and consider the cluster centers as sparse coding dictionary. Then we code all patches based on this dictionary.

As mentioned above, the training set is denoted as $Z = [z_{11}, \ldots, z_{1t}, \ldots, z_{N1}, \ldots, z_{Nt}]$. We cluster it into k classes, and arrange the k cluster centers as columns of a matrix $D = [d_1, d_2, \ldots, d_k]$, $D \in R^{(a*b) \times k}$, the corresponding label of all patches can be represented by a column vector $X = [x_{11}, \ldots, x_{1t}, \ldots, x_{N1}, \ldots, x_{Nt}]^T$, $x_{ij} \in [1, k]$, $X \in R^{(N*t) \times 1}$.

For each image patch, we can compute its sparse code by minimizing the following object function:

$$\min_{\alpha_{ij}} \left\| z_{ij} - D\alpha_{ij} \right\|_2^2 + \lambda \left\| \alpha_{ij} \right\|_1, \tag{2}$$
$$i = 1, 2, \cdots N, j = 1, 2, \cdots, t$$

where z_{ij} denotes each image patch, D is the dictionary acquired by K-means clustering, and $\alpha_{ij} \in R^{k \times 1}$ is the sparse code of each image patch. Then we define a new matrix A for the entire sparse codes as the concatenation of the sparse code of all image patches: $A = [\alpha_{11}, \ldots, \alpha_{1t}, \ldots, \alpha_{N1}, \ldots, \alpha_{Nt}]$. In this paper, we use Basis Pursuit algorithm to solve the sparse coding problem.

3.3 Random forest voting

We take the sparse code matrix A and corresponding label matrix X as input to train a random forest model. In this model, we randomly select training data using Bagging algorithm, and construct a random forest containing 500 decision trees by CART method.

Entering a sparse code into random forest, each decision tree will give a classification to it. Integrating all the classification results we will get the voting vector of each image patch. For the j-th patch of i-th person, we denote its voting vector as a $k \times 1$ vector $vote_{ij} = [v_{ij1}, v_{ij2}, \ldots, v_{ijk}]^T$, where k is the total number of categories, each element represents the number of decision tree which classifies the image patch to the corresponding label.

Voting vectors indicate the similarities and differences between the image patches, and distinct facial image contains local similarities and global differences. To robustly represent facial image, we stack all voting vectors of a facial image in a column as the global image feature, which is denoted as $vote_i = [vote_{i1}, vote_{i2}, \ldots, vote_{it}]$, where t is the number of the patches in each image.

3.4 Classification

Given a test face image z_{test}, as the training process does, we first partition it into t patches with overlapping segmentation, denoted as $\{z_{test\ 1}, z_{test\ 2}, \ldots, z_{test\ t}\}$; secondly, sparse coding all patches with the same dictionary using in the training process, we represent the acquired sparse code matrix as $A_{test} = [\alpha_{test\ 1}, \alpha_{test\ 2}, \ldots, \alpha_{test\ t}]$; and then using the learned random forest model to compute the voting vector of each patch, stacking all the voting vectors in a column we will get the global feature $vote_{test} = [vote_{test\ 1}, vote_{test\ 2}, \ldots, vote_{test\ t}]$; at last, we employ the l1 based nearest neighbor classifier to recognize the identifier of the test image.

We classify the test image into c class when

$$c = \arg\min_i \left\| vote_{test} - vote_i \right\|_1, \quad i = 1, 2, \ldots, N \tag{3}$$

where N is the number of training images (i.e. the identifier of the test image is same as the c-th training image).

4 EXPERIMENTS

To evaluate the performance of our SR-RF method, we compare it with several representative methods on two widely used face databases namely AR and FERET. For more details about this two databases please refer to [3]. The following describes the details of the experiments and results.

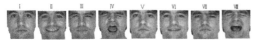

(a) AR. The first four images are collected in the first session, and the last four images are collected in the second session. Four images in each session are with expressions: neural, smile, anger, scream.

(b) FERET. The firsr row are fa images, and the second row are fb images

Figure 3. Sample face images from the (a) AR, (b) FERET database.

Table 1. The highest recognition rate (%) of different methods on AR and FERET databases.

SSPP Methods	AR							FERET
	II	III	IV	V	VI	VII	VIII	
PCA	93	85	60	77	75	65	35	84.0
2DPCA	95	87	60	76	76	67	37	85.0
PCA+ DCT+2DPCA	95	88	62	77	76	68	38	85.5
Block PCA	95	85	60	77	76	67	37	84.5
Block LDA	85	79	29	73	59	59	18	86.5
DMMA	99	93	69	90	85	79	45	93.0
SR-RF	99	95	73	95	90	80	50	93.0

4.1 Experimental settings

In our experiments, we select the subset of AR and FERET databases as our experimental data. In AR database, we randomly select 100 different persons (50 males and 50 females), and for each person, select 8 images which are taken from different sessions and with different expressions. Then we get a dataset of 800 images, and then we divide it into 8 subsets according to their sessions and expressions. Fig. 3(a) shows 8 images of one person from 8 subsets named I to VIII. We use subset I for training and others for testing. In FERET database, we use a subset including 400 images, which consists of 200 distinct persons, and each of who has two images (fa and fb, fa for training and fb for testing). Fig. 3(b) shows several sample images from our choosing subset.

We manually normalize all selected facial images into 60×60 pixels according to the eyes' positions. We compare our method with 6 SSPP approaches, including PCA [1], 2D-PCA [11], PCA+DCT+2DPCA [12], Block PCA [13], Block LDA [8], DMMA [3]. For a fair comparison, in our experiments these methods use their own parameter settings, and for our algorithm, we set $a \times b$, d, k to 15×15, 5, 80, and set the number of decision tree to 500.

4.2 Result and analysis

Table 1 records the best recognition accuracy of different methods on the AR and FERET databases. Intuitively, simply from the quantitative level of the experimental results listed in Table 1, our method outperforms all the compared methods, on the test subsets III-VIII of the AR database, the lowest gains in rate are 2%, 4%, 5%, 5%, 1%, 5%, respectively. Although DMMA achieves the same accuracy as our algorithm on the subset II of AR database and FERET database, our method wins a higher recognition rate on other 6 test sets.

By analyzing the experimental results, we will get the following observations: 1) From the results of PCA and Block PCA, we can draw a conclusion that there is no significant difference on the performance of representing image as global feature or local feature by unsupervised learning technique. 2) DMMA and our methods results are far better than other 5 methods', which explains that integrating local and global image features can actually improve the recognition accuracy. 3) Our algorithm obtains the highest recognition rate, which implies that using sparse coding and random forest can acquire better discriminative features to recognize face image more accurately.

5 CONCLUSION

We proposed a new SSPP face recognition method based on sparse representation and random forest in this paper. To solve the lack of samples problem, we first partition each image into several image patches. Specially, when a face image is partitioned into several local patches, they represent different local semantics of the original face image. Then, we employ sparse coding to represent the local image patches and random forest to acquire global image features. At last, L1 based nearest neighbor classifier will give the identifier of the image to be recognized based on the global image features. Experimental results shows our proposed method achieves best performance on two widely used face databases AR and FERET.

REFERENCES

[1] M. Turk and A. Pentland. Eigenfaces for recognition. Journal of Cognitive Neuroscience, 3(1): 71–86, 1991.
[2] P.N. Belhumeur, J. Hespanha, and D.J. Kriegman. Eigenfaces vs. fisherfaces: recognition using class specific linear projection. IEEE Transactions on Pattern Analysis and Machine Intelligence, 19(7): 711–720, 1997.
[3] J. Lu, Y.P. Tan, and G. Wang. Discriminative Multi-manifold Analysis for Face Recognition from a Single Training Sample per Person. IEEE Trans on Pattern Analysis and Machine Intelligence, 35(1): 39–51, 2013.
[4] X.Y. Tan, S.C. Chen, Z.H. Zhou, et al. Face Recognition from a Single Image per Person: A Survey. Patten Recognition, 39(9): 1725–1745, 2006.
[5] Y. Su, S. Shan, X. Chen, et al. Adaptive Generic Learning for Face Recognition from a Single Sample per Person. IEEE Conference on Computer Vision and Pattern Recognition, 2010, pp. 2699–2706.

[6] D.A. Huang, Y.C.F. Wang. With One Look: Robust Face Recognition using Single Sample per Person. In Proceedings of the 21st ACM International Conference on Multimedia, 2013, pp. 601–604.

[7] Q. Gao, L. Zhang, and D. Zhang. Face Recognition Using FLDA with Single Training Image per Person. Applied Mathematics and Computation, 205(2): 726–734, 2008.

[8] S. Chen, J. Liu, and Z.H. Zhou. Making FLDA Applicable to Face Recognition with One Sample per Person. Pattern recognition, 37(7): 1553–1555, 2004.

[9] K. J. Wang, G. F. Zou. A Sub-Pattern Gabor Features Fusion Method for Single Sample Face Recognition. Pattern Recognition & Artificial Intelligence, 26(1): 50–56, 2013.

[10] F. Tang, H. Lu, T. Sun, et al. Efficient Image Classification using Sparse Coding and Random Forest. Image and Signal Processing, 5th International Congress on. IEEE, 2012, pp. 781–785.

[11] J. Yang, D. Zhang, A.F. Frangi, et al. Two-dimensional PCA: a New Approach to Appearance-based Face Representation and Recognition. IEEE Trans on Pattern Analysis and Machine Intelligence, 26(1): 131–137, 2004.

[12] J.R. Hernandez, M. Amado, and F. Perez-Gonzalez. DCT-domain Watermarking Techniques for Still Images: Detector Performance Analysis and a New Structure. IEEE Transactions on Image Processing, 9(1): 55–68, 2000.

[13] R. Gottumukkal, V. K. Asari. An Improved Face Recognition Technique based on Modular PCA Approach. Pattern Recognition Letters, 25(4): 429–436, 2004.

Multimedia Technology IV – Farag, Yang & Jiao (Eds)
© *2015 Taylor & Francis Group, London, ISBN: 978-1-138-02794-7*

Practice and thinking of the bilingual teaching for undergraduate digital signal processing course

Kunbao Cai

College of Communication Engineering, Chongqing University, Chongqing, P.R. of China

ABSTRACT: The internationalization of higher education has already become an inevitable trend of China's higher education reform. The international perspective and communicative ability have become the basic requirement of talent cultivation. The students graduated from the programs in electronic information engineering and communication engineering must have a firm foundation on two aspects of the specialty knowledge and the specialty English, and a strong ability to adapt future science and technology development. The author of this paper has practiced for bilingual teaching course of digital signal processing about 10 years. To achieve the aim of mutual exchanging and learning with other colleagues teaching similar courses, the author, hereby, authentically introduced some intuitive experiences and thinking problems that arise from the teaching reform process of the course of Digital Signal Processing that is lectured by using Chinese and English alternately.

Keywords: undergraduate education; bilingual teaching; teaching reform; digital signal processing

1 INTRODUCTION

The 21st century is an internationalization era of knowledge-driven economy. The modern science and technology education has made profound changes. The new theories and techniques for a great variety of specialties almost change everyday. The innovation for science and technology largely depends, to a great extent, on acquiring information in time and utilizing efficiently [1], [2]. The research on the theory and algorithm of digital signal processing, the development of applications and implementation techniques, as well as its great importance and potential in the modern information and communication technology have surpassed the estimation and prediction that were made in early development stage. At the same time, the demand of modern society for high-quality talents in the field of information technology has proposed higher and higher requirements on the teaching quality of professional basic courses in universities. However, the teaching hours assigned for Digital Signal Processing with its associated fundamental courses in China's universities of science and technology is generally reduced. A well-known expert and scholar in China has concluded such a tough teaching reform as that the contradiction between the infinite accumulation of human knowledge and the limited personal learning ability and time has become increasingly sharp [3].

In recent years, computers and high-speed digital signal processors are updated more and more rapidly. At the same time, new theories and methods of signal analysis and processing as well as sophisticated algorithms have emerged in endlessness. The development of these two aspects are mutually dependent and promoted with each other, with the result that the field of signal analysis and processing has explosively progressed toward a new high-tech subject. At present, the course of Digital Signal Processing is not only the required course for undergraduate students in electronic information engineering and communication engineering in China's universities, but also has become a compulsory or optional course in other related disciplines. With the rapid development of modern science and technology, the trend of the interdisciplinary penetration and fusion is sharply unstoppable. "Digital signal Processing", as the most common and universal technique and its extremely extensive applicability in modern science and technology, is bound to open up more and more wide application fields. It has become a basic requirement for modern information and communication engineers to master the basic theory as well as analysis and design techniques of signals and systems, and to implement electronic systems using digital method flexibly.

It is worth noting that a batch of famous professors with high academic attainment in worldwide first-rank universities, such as MIT, Harvard and Stanford, offers high-quality video open courses for global undergraduate students. In China, a batch of famous experts and scholars lectures video open courses for Chinese students at an undergraduate level. Some video open courses provided by key universities in China have been broadened from previous humanistic philosophy courses to science and engineering courses. Facing the huge impact coming from worldwide education and teaching reform tide, the author has deeply felt that the urgent affairs are, by referencing international advanced teaching idea, teaching method and means, to construct the bilingual teaching course of digital signal processing that conforms to China's national conditions.

2 CONSTRUCTION OF BILINGUAL TEACHING COURSE

In early 2001, the Ministry of Education of the People's Republic of China issued a document about the construction of bilingual or full English teaching courses with the emphasis on several points as follows: the colleges and universities must actively promote the use of English and other foreign languages in teaching common required courses and specialty courses; especially, in the specialties of information technology, biotechnology, new materials, financial, law and others, and in the specialized fields urgently needed for national development should carry out bilingual teaching; the national key construction universities should strive for offering bilingual teaching courses which are required to occupy 5% to 10% of all courses, within three years. Considering that there is a comparatively larger gap between China and foreign countries on information technology personnel training, in order to catch up with the rapid development of information technology, one of the most effective measures is to introduce abroad excellent textbooks of original editions on information science and technology. The schools with good conditions should carry out lecturing with full English or bilingual method.

2.1 Preliminary practice

Since the end of 20th century, the author of this paper had started trying the bilingual teaching in an undergraduate course titled as Fundamentals of Signal Processing and two graduate courses named as Digital Control of Dynamic Systems and Modern Filtering, respectively. For these courses, several excellent textbooks in English edition, written by worldwide famous professors, were used in classroom teaching, including Signals & Systems [4], Discrete-Time Signal Processing [5], Digital Control of Dynamic Systems [6], Digital Control Systems [7] and Modern Filters [8]. Under the effort of two sides of teaching and studying, the teacher and students agreed that the bilingual teaching is benefit to improve specialty English proficiency while studying professional knowledge.

2.2 Practice for teaching digital signal processing

The professor Oppenheim of MIT, a well-known scholar enjoying worldwide reputation in signal processing society, as a chief author, has published several editions of Signals & Systems and Discrete-Time Signal Processing that have been used as textbooks or reference books in many famous universities in the world. In China, his masterpieces have been translated into Chinese already and used as textbooks or teaching reference books in some universities.

Since entering the 21st century, two aspects on production and scientific research in China's information industry have progressed rapidly, which has become one of pillar industries of national economy development. Since that time, several famous presses in China have started considering and carrying out the introduction of a set of foreign electronic and communication textbooks series from world famous publishing companies. A batch of excellent English-edition textbooks concerning with Circuit Theory and Applications, Signals and Systems, Digital Signal Processing and other fields are reprinted and published in China. All of the above works supply rich teaching resources for Chinese teachers to carry out and further improve bilingual teaching.

In 2004, the author of this paper started lecturing the course of Digital Signal Processing for undergraduate students in the College of Communication Engineering, Chongqing University. By summarizing the experiences accumulated from practical teaching and research on signal analysis and processing, and after repeated comparison and careful thinking, the masterpieces in English edition were not directly used as textbooks. Although our teachers can arrange, through carefully selecting teaching contents from thick books, the teaching task of 68 (64 now) teaching hours, for most undergraduate students, they will face the double pressure coming from the specialty English and the knowledge basis, and also have no such an ability to extract key knowledge points from very thick textbooks in English. Therefore, in the teaching process of Digital Signal Processing, the author, by referencing dozens of excellent textbooks both at home and abroad, wrote lecture notes in English that have been used in classroom teaching. Since then, the textbooks of Signals & Systems and Discrete-Time Signal Processing written by Professor Oppenheim et al. have been used as the main teaching reference books, while the Chinese-edition textbook of Digital Signal Processing written by Professor Peiqing Cheng of Tsinghua University in China has been used as teaching reference textbook [9], with the result that the students taking the course obtain an improvement on the reading ability of the original English books as well as specialty knowledge.

2.3 Textbook construction

In has been recognized that the internationalization of higher education has already become an inevitable trend of China's higher education reform. The international perspective and communicative ability have become the basic requirement of talent cultivation. The students graduated from the programs in electronic information and communication engineering must have a firm foundation on two aspects of the specialty knowledge and the specialty English, and a strong ability to adapt future science and technology development. In order to adapt to such a trend of higher education reform in our country, my lecture notes on digital signal processing for undergraduate level course, through summarizing more than twenty-year teaching and research practice on signal analysis and processing, were repeatedly promoted by revisions and fueled by many excellent textbooks published at home and abroad, which leads to that my English-edition textbook "Digital Signal Processing" was published in 2007 [10]. On this basis, the simplified-version English-edition textbook of Digital Signal Processing was published in 2010 [11].

In writing the second-edition textbook, the selection of contents and the organization and arrangement of knowledge system were carefully considered, which leads to that the textbook comparatively adapts to the actual situation of course setting and teaching in china's universities. Facing up to the contents of digital signal processing being rapidly expanded and the factor of reduced teaching hours, the basic idea which is always kept in wring process is that the readers of this textbook can systematically grasp the basic analysis and design theory of discrete-time signals and systems. In two kinds of commonly used digital signal processing techniques, i.e. the DFT-based spectrum analysis of continuous-time signals and the design of digital signal processing systems such as IIR and FIR filters, it strives to make readers have a thorough understanding and grasp of analysis and design principle and methods. The author hopes that the contained contents, concerning with finite-wordlength effects in digital signal processing systems and multirate digital signal processing, can help readers to lay a good foundation on these two aspects. The author also hopes that through further self-study or studying followed higher-level courses, students can more easily expand theoretic knowledge and practical skills of digital signal processing.

The teachers who use the above books as teaching textbooks in classroom can obtain a free set of multimedia electronic courseware, course outline, detailed solution manual for many end-of-chapter problems and experimental instructor manual, from the Publishing House of Electronics Industry in China. The author carefully prepared this set of auxiliary teaching materials, which is expected that these materials are helpful for the improvement of teaching quality, and especially make teachers who are preliminary to open the bilingual teaching course of digital signal processing improve the efficiency in preparing the course. The feedback messages coming from users show that dozens of universities in China, including key universities, have adopted the textbooks as a bilingual teaching textbook for the course of digital signal processing.

2.4 Teaching reform

Under the guidance of the idea of learning and absorbing advanced teaching modes as much as possible, the author of this paper investigated the course setting and teaching modes for digital signal processing in many famous or key universities at home and abroad. On this basis, a substantial reform for bilingual teaching course of digital signal processing has been carried out at multiple aspects, including the teaching material construction, the teaching content selection, the implementation of teaching method and means, the assessment of student course grades, and etc. The teaching outline, the examination outline and the teaching plan have been revised. Several key points of the reformed bilingual teaching course are as followings:

- The 64-hour course is set for 4-year schooling undergraduate students in Electronic Information Engineering, Communication Engineering and other related disciplines.
- It is lectured for the students in the first semester of the third year.
- The prerequisites are Circuit Theory, Complex Variables and Continuous-Time Signals and Systems.
- Now, the textbook used in classroom is the second-edition Digital Signal Processing [10].
- The main reference textbooks are those masterpieces written by the famous professors [4], [5] and [9].
- The key teaching objective of the course is to make students systematically grasp a relatively complete set of the basic theory and analysis techniques on discrete-time signals and systems and gain basic training on the design of fundamental digital signal processing systems such as FIR and IIR filters.
- This course puts emphasis on making students firmly grasp the basic principles of digital signal processing and promoting students' ability using the theory to solve practical engineering problems.
- The main contents and hours distribution are designed as: 1) Brief Introduction to Digital Signal Processing, 3 hours; 2) Discrete-Time Signals and Systems, 7 hours; 3) Transform-Domain Analysis of Discrete-Time Signals and Systems, 13 hours; 4) The Discrete Fourier Transform, 12 hours; 5) The Fast Fourier Transform Algorithms, 4 hours; 6) Basic Structures of Digital Filters, 4 hours; 7) Design Techniques of IIR Digital Filters, 12 hours; 8) Design of FIR Digital Filters, 6 hours; 9) Finite-Wordlength Effects in Digital Systems, 3 hours.
- This course is parallelly accompanied by a practical course titled Laboratory Course of Digital Signal Processing in which students will accept fundamental training on the topics in digital signal processing based-on MATLAB.
- In order to improve the teaching quality and objectively assess student course grade, the course is graded according to the items shown in Table 1. It may be a useful measure that every student is required to submit a course study report before the end of the course, which includes an extracurricular literature reading report and a course study summary. All of the course study reports are corrected and evaluated by the lecturer, and then commented on and appraised in classroom.

Table 1. Course grading.

Items	Weight	Remark
assignment	20%	submit in time
examination 1	5%	randomly arranged
examination 2	5%	randomly arranged
course study report: extracurricular literature reading report; course study summary	5%	submit before the last lecture
accumulated score: classroom discussion; tutorial; attendance record	5%	absent without cause 2 times or more, the score is zero
final examination	60%	must obey the examination discipline and relevant provisions
Total score	100%	100 points

- The final examination for this course is closed-book. Students must complete the examination within 120 minutes. Generally, the test questions include the basic concept part, analysis or calculation part, and the essay questions or brief statement questions. It emphasizes that the basic structure of the examination paper is in favor of testing the understanding and grasp degrees of important fundamental concepts contained in the course, and testing the comprehensive ability for analyzing and solving problems. Particularly, it emphasizes that students can further enhance, through the examination, the integrated concepts of the course.

Due to the adoption of the above teaching method and measures, the teaching quality is continuously improved. The students taking this course can receive a comprehensive training in learning specialty knowledge, English listening, reading, writing and expression. Through the network platform for teaching evaluation by students that is designed by the Academic Affairs Office of Chongqing University, the bilingual teaching course always gets a higher evaluation.

3 THINKING AND EXISTING PROBLEMS

Since the bilingual teaching course of Digital Signal Processing was first offered for students in the College of Communication Engineering of Chongqing University, the teaching reform of the course has been continuously performed. A set of comparatively rich teaching materials has been accumulated, including formally published English-edition textbooks with auxiliary teaching materials. With the progress of course construction, the author is more and more clearly aware of that the development of modern information and communication technology is more and more rapid, which puts forward higher and higher requirements

on the teaching quality for a batch of courses concerning with signal analysis and processing. Up to now, the knowledge and skills of digital signal processing has formed a vast storehouse. For students at the undergraduate stage, the key teaching objective should aim at such a direction that is to improve students' ability for analyzing and solving problems, to cultivate students' habit good at thinking, and to improve students' self-study ability further. The students graduated from the information and communication discipline must have a good foundation at both specialty knowledge and skills and specialty English, so as to lay a basis of lifetime learning.

The author is also aware of that there is a comparatively big gap between our teaching mode and that of the first-rank universities in the world. The author presents some thinking and existing problems in our education and teaching reform below.

- In China, a technology basic course is usually performed by one teacher. Thus, the lecturer must complete all teaching links of the course, except that a graduate teaching assistant helps the lecturer to correct students' assignments and answer some questions. In addition, teachers' and students' English proficiency may be a factor which restricts the further improvement of teaching quality.
- Generally speaking, the classroom teaching efficiency at the first-rank universities in the world is much higher than ours.
- The course teaching reform should be performed by simultaneously combining with the reform of the whole course system in the discipline.
- The international first-rang universities have the first-class teachers, studious students and strict management system.

4 CONCLUSION

The 21st century is an internationalization era of knowledge-driven economy. The modern science and technology education has made profound changes. In the reform of the bilingual teaching course of digital signal processing, if there is some difference among the teaching content selection, the teaching method and means adopted due to the different teaching environment and the academic background of course outline makers, it can be understood. However, to lay a basis of lifetime learning for students should become a basic idea to guide the teaching reform.

ACKNOWLEDGMENT

The author wishes to thank the Academic Affairs Office of Chongqing University for the financial support during textbook construction.

REFERENCES

[1] Kunbao Cai, Gaoke Ying and Yusheng Jiang, "Practice and exploration in teaching specialty English for postgraduate students," Journal of Architectural Education in Institutions of Higher Learning, China, Vol. 19, No. 3, pp. 95–98, 2010.

[2] Kunbao Cai, "Exploration and thinking of the bilingual teaching method for signal courses," International Journal of Modern Education Forum, Vol. 3, pp. 13–16, 2014.

[3] Yue Wang, "Thinking of the times development of electronic and electrical courses," Keynote report on the Fourth Report Forum on Electronic and Electrical Courses, Xian, China, 2008.

[4] A.V. Oppenheim, A.S. Willsky and S.H. Nawab, "Signals and Systems (Second Edition)," Prentice-Hall, Inc., 1997.

[5] A.V. Oppenheim, R.W. Schafer and J.R. Buck, "Discrete-Time Signal Processing (Second Edition)," Prentice-Hall, Inc., 1999.

[6] G.F. Franklin, J.D. Powell and M. Workman, "Digital Control of Dynamic Systems (Third Edition)," Addison Wesley Longman, Inc., 1998.

[7] B.C. Kuo, "Digital Control Systems (Second Edition)," Saunders College Publishing, 1992.

[8] S. Haykin, "Modern Filters," Macmillan Publishing Company, 1989.

[9] Peiqing Cheng, "A Course in Digital Signal Processing (Second Edition)," Tsinghua University Press, China, 2001.

[10] Kunbao Cai, "Digital Signal Processing," Publishing House of Electronics Industry, China, 2007.

[11] Kunbao Cai, "Digital Signal Processing (Second Edition)," Publishing House of Electronics Industry, China, 2011.

Multimedia Technology IV – Farag, Yang & Jiao (Eds)
© 2015 Taylor & Francis Group, London, ISBN: 978-1-138-02794-7

Interactive random music using breath control for entertainment application

Tsung-Ching Liu
Electrical Engineering Department, Chinese Culture University, Taipei, Taiwan

Chia-Chien Tu
Graduate Institute of Electronic Engineering, National Taiwan University of Science & Technology, Taiwan

ABSTRACT: This paper deals with random music generation in a Max/Msp environment to follow players' heart beat rate (HBR), meanwhile, the other people use his breath to interact the generated music. For HBR part, each of the two players wears an infrared sensor connected to an Arduino microcontroller with on-board Xbee to measure their heart beat rate. The measured data is then wirelessly sent to the Max/Msp, one for the parameter control of a chaotic system described by difference equations and the other for the MIDI duration control. We choose the 2-D Hénon map for generating the chaotic process where equations are solved graphically in Max/Msp. Controlled by increasing the player's HBR, the system is entering into the chaotic behavior once the system's parameter value passes over certain critical point. The output data is mapped into pitch in Max/Msp where rhythm is generated automatically. For breath control part, the third person uses his breath input into a microphone. The output is rectified and filtered to create dc voltage change to the Arduino's input. The data reading is used to fly the pitch level while the automatic music is running in the Max/Msp.

Keywords: random music; non-haptic interactive music; breath sensor; chaos system, Max/Msp

1 INTRODUCTION

Haptic or non-haptic technology has been used in inter-active computer music application for a while [1], [2] [3], [4]. Among them physiological signals are used to control the MIDI parameters via Max/Msp environment to create music change. The simplest physiological signals to acquire are HBR (Heart Beat Rate) and breath. However, the HBR data is pretty much monotonic rising or falling that cannot create reasonable music directly. Therefore, Liu [5] had adopted a chaos system with its parameter varied by HBR, then let system itself evolves to generate a random data output. Those data is then collected by Max/Msp to create pitch, intensity or tempo. The players don't need to have any music background but can create colorful music; however, their music interaction is indirect or light, i.e., they first change their HBR by exercise, the data then vary the parameter inherently inside the system. They can change the music evolution style but not the instant response. In order to create instant or salient real-time interactive response, we have to add other elements. The breath we thought is a good candidate for this purpose. It could be the other people or the HBR players themselves that use their breath to conduct a more prominent change of music. Fig. 1 depicts the whole system we proposed for interactive random music generation using breath control.

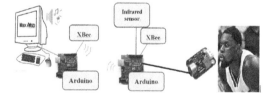

Figure 1. The system setup for interactive random music generation using breath control for entertainment application.

In Section 2 we briefly review our previous work on automatic music generation by HBR. Then Section 3 will introduce our work of a self-made breath sensor tested and applied to the HBR automatic music generation system. The combined system is demonstrates in Section 4 where discussions and comments are made.

2 AUTOMATIC MUSIC GENERATION BY HBR

Once started, the HBR cannot be irregularly jumping between data. So the data process is more or less a deterministic monotone function of time. With this simple behavior, direct mapping of data into MIDI data cannot generate colorful music. Therefore, we need to add some uncertainty by passing the data through certain systems, and let the output to control the change.

This then directs to the random music category, a more randomized data development to follow a pre-set parameter. To achieve this goal we choose chaos system as the candidate for music generation, due to its inherent nature is closely resemble the music evolution. Four pioneers of this method are Jeff Pressing, Michael Gogins, Rick Bidlack, and Jeremy Leach [6].

In Section 2.1, we will briefly review the chaos system. We also describe how we relate heart rate to the controlling parameters of such system. Section 2.2 describes the sensor board and the related Max/Msp patch design where an Arduino with the add-on Xbee and infrared sensor is used to monitor the HBR in real-time. The value is sent to the Max/Msp patch layout to solve the chaos equation dynamically. The data output then is mapped to create music.

2.1 Chaos system

Chaos has been already studied and discovered in a wide range of natural phenomena such as the weather, population cycles of animals, the structure of coast-lines and trees and leaves, bubble-fields and the dripping of water, weather and also acoustical systems such as that of woodwind multi-phonics. A dynamic system can be used to emulate this behavior is called the chaotic system. A chaotic system must have the following properties: (1) it must be sensitive to initial conditions; (2) it must be topologically mixing; and (3) its periodic orbits must be dense. With this chaotic nature, the data generated by this system is adequate for music composition, particularly automatic computer music generation. There are different specific nonlinear dynamic equations that composers have experimented with: including, but not limited to, (1) the 1-D **logistic map**—traditionally used to model a species' change in population, (2) the 2-D **Hénon map**—originally introduced as a simple and efficient model of chaotic systems in general, and (3) the 3-D **Lorenz system**—developed from a simplified model of atmospheric turbulence. Composers have then applied these equations to their compositional process in which chaos is employed as an algorithm for making choices having to do with note events—pitch, dynamic level, rhythm, and instrumentation. They use nonlinear dynamic systems iteratively to generate chaotic sequences of numbers that are then mapped to various note parameters (pitch, dynamic, rhythm, duration, tempo, etc.). In this paper, we choose the 2-D **Hénon map** for HBR music with add-in breath control due to it is simple to realize and has adequate behavior. We briefly review our previous work on HBR random music below.

The 2-D **Hénon map** was introduced by Michel Hénon as a simplified model of the Poincaré section of the Lorenz model. It is characterized by the following system's equation [7]:

$$x_{n+1} = y_n + 1 - ax_n^2$$
$$y_{n+1} = bx_n$$
(1)

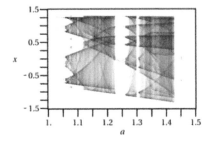

Figure 2. Orbit diagram for the Hénon map with $b = 0.3$. Higher density (darker) indicates increased probability of the variable x acquiring that value for the given value of a.

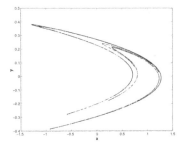

Figure 3. Plot of $[x_n, y_n]$ (*Hénon* attractor for $A = 1.4$, $b = 0.3$).

Fig. 2 shows the plot of x_n as a function of a if we fix $b = 0.3$ and allow a to vary. As a passes over 1.05 the system enters into chaos. At this value, the $[x_n, y_n]$ would generate the attractor. Fig. 3 shows that $[x_n, y_n]$ is plotted for $a = 1.4$, $b = 0.3$, and x_n ranges from -1.5 to 1.5 and y-axis ranges from -0.4 to 0.4.

We can let a be controlled by the HBR scaled to effective range and the generated process of x_n for pitch control.

2.2 System setup for HBR random music: Infrared sensor, XBEE, arduino and MAX/MSP

As in Fig. 1, the transmitter part has an infrared sensor attached to the Arduino microcontroller to test the transparency change of one's index finger related to blood flow rhythm contracted by heart. The detected pulse then is recorded and calculated by the Arduino for the HBR value. The number is transmitted to the receiver side by Xbee which is then interfaced to Max/Msp environment running on a PC. The Max/Msp uses *ctlin* object to receive data input into chaos system to generate music.

Fig. 4 is the completed infrared sensor module, Fig. 5 is the Arduino board, and Fig. 6 is the Arduino with loaded Xbee module.

The 8 bit Microcontroller Arduino board has 14 analog I/O and 6 analog I/O, and USB is supported. The board can be powered through USB or with adaptor of 5V~9V. The infrared sensor module output is connected to the Digital I/O for measuring pulse rate. The extension board allows Xbee be add-on to the Arduino

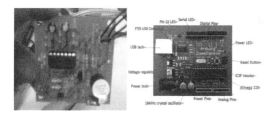

Figure 4. Infrared circuit module. Figure 5. Arduino board layout.

Figure 6. Arduino with Add-on Xbee.

Figure 7. The setup for multiple (four) testers.

Figure 8. The program code for Arduino in transmitting end (left) and receiving end (right).

with a preset baud rate 9600. It is also possible to change this baud rate according to one's need. Fig. 7 is the setup for receiving data simultaneously from multiple testers. Fig. 8 is the program code for Arduino in transmitting and receiving end with receiving data recorded in TeraTerm (Fig. 9) (an open source software implemented for terminal (Communication) emulator program).

2.3 HBR random music generation by 2-D Hénon map

Two people's heart rate are recorded simultaneously, and their data are used to control the parameter a and the initial condition of x_n in (1), where x_n is to control pitch and allows tempo stay in constant. The Max patch design for Hénon map music generation is in

Figure 9. Four testers' heart rate recorded in TeraTerm.

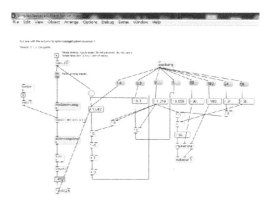

Figure 10. The Max patch for music generation by Hénon map.

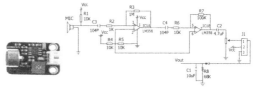

Figure 11. Microphone (left) and breath detector circuit (right).

Fig. 10. The leftmost branch is for receiving data from Arduino, and the implement of dynamic equation is by the blocks (the three columns) on its right. The rightmost part (five columns) is for MIDI note event generation.

3 BREATH SENSOR DESIGN

In here, our goal is to detect the breath intensity by microphone and convert the intensity to a DC voltage level sent to the Arduino.

3.1 Breath sensor circuit design

The microphone we used is depicted in Fig. 11 (left) and the related combined detector circuit is in Fig. 11 (right).

3.2 Breath control system test in Max/Msp

Fig. 12 and 13 shows the breath control test in Max/Msp.

Figure 12. Circuit test for the breath detector with the designed Max/Msp Patch in Fig. 13.

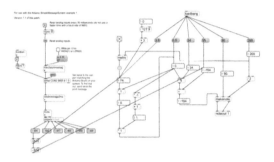

Figure 13. Pitch flies as a function of breath intensity, the random music generated with fixed parameter. Arduino has only the breath input data.

4 DEMONSTRATION HBR + BREATH CONTROL

Fig. 14. shows the combination of the HBR random music generation with breath interactive control. The leftmost bottom shows two HBR data, one with HBR 91 and the other with HBR 78, and the breath intensity is 450. The first HBR controls the parameter a, and second HBR controls the duration of *makenote*. This design creates a feeling that rhythm flies as one blow the microphone with his breath while the automatic music is generated by the HBR's. It could be presented by an episode that at the beginning when the parameter a controlled by one person's HBR has not yet driven the parameter a into the chaos region the rhythm is a pure step increased monotone; however, when his HBR is increased (by exercise) and drives the parameter a across the critical point where system enters into the chaos region, the music starts jumping randomly up and down but with an attractor behavior. And when the third person blows the microphone with his breath we have a paragraph of music is flying in the pitch domain with transposed effect that creates amazing effect. The system may support a large group of people into the interactive scenario just with minor adjustment of the system setup and Max/Max patch design. In here, we had only used x_n, one of the 2-D data $[x_n, y_n]$ for the pitch control. When more people are to play, we can extend the control by the 2-D data and allow y_n control other note events such as intensity or another rhythm in MIDI. In fact, the episode design is also a key issue for a successful music performance on our system that remains further development.

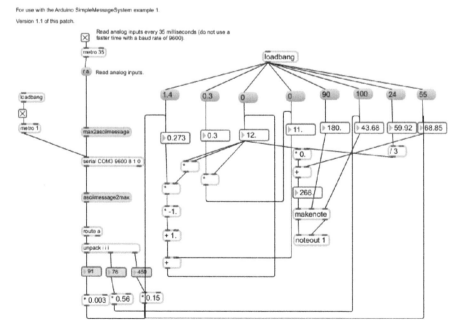

Figure 14. The combination of the random music generation with breath interactive control. The leftmost bottom shows two HBR data, one with HBR 91 and the other with HBR 78, and breath intensity is 450. The first HBR controls the parameter a in Hénon map and the second HBR controls the duration of *makenote* object in Max/Msp.

REFERENCES

[1] Arslan, B., et al., From Biological Signals to Music, Proceedings of ENACTIVE05 2nd International Conference on Enactive Interfaces Genoa, Italy, November 17th–18th, 2005.

[2] Knapp, R.B., Lusted, H.S.: A bioelectric controller for computer music applications.Computer Music Journal 14(1) (1990) 42–47.

[3] Mann, S., Fung, J., Garten, A.: DECONcert: bathing in the light, sound, Jones, and waters of the musical brain-baths. In: ICMC 2007: International Computer Music Conference. (2007) C.D., A.B. Smith, and E.F. Roberts, *Book Title*, Publisher, Location, Date.

[4] Le Groux, S., Manzolli, J., Verschure, P.F.M.J.: Disembodied and collaborative musical interaction in the multimodal brain orchestra. In: NIME'10: Proceedings of the International Conference on New Interfaces for Musical Expression. (2010).

[5] Tsung-Ching Liu, Jia-Chien Du (2013, Dec). Automatic Music Generation by Heart Beat Rate. WOCMAT 2013 (Workshop on Computer Music and Audio Technology 2013), B103: International Conference Hall Kainan University.

[6] Bidlack, Rick (1992), Chaotic systems as simple (but complex) compositional algorithms. *Computer Music Journal*. 16(3): 33–47.

[7] Hénon map (1976), http://en.wikipedia.org/wiki/H%c3%a9non_map. Acessed 21 Oct 2014.

Multimedia Technology IV – Farag, Yang & Jiao (Eds)

A high efficient and feature lossless image compression approach for image retrieval

Ping Lu
SISE, Southeast University, Nanjing, China

Yong Yang & Ming Liu
ZTE Cooperation, Shenzhen, China

Zhenjiang Dong
SEIEE, Shanghai Jiaotong University, Shanghai, China

ABSTRACT: Image retrieval is a key technology in the mobile multimedia applications, such as mobile augmented reality. In most scenarios, the mobile terminal needs to upload a photo to the application server. Considered the large size of the photo, the weak computing capability and the limited bandwidth, those factors will lead to a poor user experience. In this paper, an efficient image compression approach is proposed, and in which the DCT coefficient quantization table is optimized with the genetic algorithm based on the massive image library, and then, according to the feature distribution of the picture generated in the mobile multimedia applications, the quantization table is adjusted again. After that, the normal JPED image compression steps are proceeding. The experimental results show that, this kind of method can achieve a high compression ratio, JPEG-compatible and features lossless in for the image retrieval. Using the CDVS (Compact Descriptors for Visual Search) image data and the SCFV image retrieval algorithm, the JPEG file size reduced 42.7%, and the image retrieval accuracy has a slight improvement.

Keywords: image compression, feature lossless, image retrieval

1 INTRODUCTION

With the development of mobile internet technology, a lot of mobile multimedia applications appeared, such as photo sharing, mobile augmented reality and so on. It is known that, the image search and cognition is a key technology in these applications. In specifically, considered the limit of computing capability and wireless bandwidth of the mobile terminal, and the large size of a photo taken by the mobile terminal, a normal picture uploading from the terminal to the application will spend a long time, so as to lead to a poor user experience. Therefore, a new JPEG image compression is studied, and which not only should have a low complexity and high compression ratio, but also should keep the main features of an image for image retrieval.

Many domestic and foreign universities and research institutions have carried out a study of this kind of approach. In which, Region Of Interest (ROI) based image coding is one of the research topic. Paul G Ducksbury [1] proposed a wavelet image compression approach based on ROI detection and the corresponding ROI masks. Yan Liang [2] proposed a new ROI coding method called generalized partial

bitplanes shift, which can get better visual quality at low bit rates. Loganathan and Kumaraswamy [3] proposed a fuzzy based adaptive active contour for segmentation of Region of Interest and then a novel biorthogonal wavelet image compression technique is used to achieve higher compression rate. Uma Vetri Selvi [4] proposed a new rapid method for the compression of coronary angiogram video sequences, and which uses a wavelet-based contourlet transform coder based on the set partitioned embedded block coder combined with a region-of-interest (ROI) detection technique.

As we know, the accuracy of ROI is not so good in some special circumstances, and also it need large amount of computation in the mobile terminal, so that it is not suitable for the mobile applications.

In this paper, an efficient image compression approach is studied, and it will support some characteristics required by the mobile multimedia applications, including high compression ratio, JPEG-compatible and features lossless in for the image retrieval.

Our works will focus on the optimization of the table and adjusting the quantized DCT coefficient, which includes two kinds of aspect. The first is the formation of a feature losses DCT coefficient quantization table,

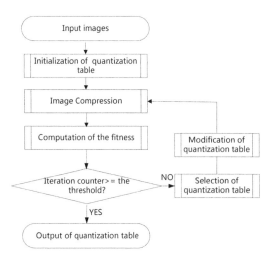

Figure 1. The flow of feature lossless quantization table training.

(1,16)	(1,64)	(1,64)	(1,64)	255	255	255	255
(1,64)	(1,64)	(1,64)	(1,64)	255	255	255	255
(1,64)	(1,64)	(1,64)	(1,64)	255	255	255	255
(1,64)	(1,64)	(1,64)	(1,64)	255	255	255	255
255	255	255	255	255	255	255	255
255	255	255	255	255	255	255	255
255	255	255	255	255	255	255	255
255	255	255	255	255	255	255	255

Figure 2. Rules of quantization table initialization.

and the second is the reset of DCT coefficient. More details will be given in the following.

2 FEATURE LOSSLESS QUANTIZATION TABLE

It is known that, for the image compression, high compression ratio and the loss of image details are contradictory in the normal cases. If high compression ratio is required, mean while which means the loss of image details, and vice versa. Therefore, we will look for a balance point between the image compression ratio and the loss of image detail. Normally, the main feature of an image concentrates on the part of low frequency, and the details are defined by the part of high frequency. For the image retrieval in a natural scene, partial loss of image details does not affect the result of the image retrieval greatly. If the balance point can be found, we can get a suitable DCT coefficient quantization table. By this table, not only the high compression ration can be achieved, but also those features for image retrieval will be kept. In order to achieve this goal, the genetic algorithm is introduced, and the processing flow is shown in Figure 1.

1. A large amount of pictures in the natural scene is captured.
2. Several groups quantization tables are initialized as the first generation quantization table according to the rules: The DC coefficients are set to a random value between 1 to 16, and the first 15 AC coefficients are set to a random value between 1 to 64, and the left are set to 255, shown in Figure 2.
3. The image is compressed with the former quantization tables;
4. A value is defined to meter the fitness of a quantization table, that is,

$$F(D, R) = D + \lambda R$$

In which, $F(D, R)$ is the fitness, D is the matching ratio of some random image feature pixels. R is the weight factor,

$$\lambda \approx \frac{\Delta D(Q)|_{Q \to qQ}}{\Delta R(Q)|_{Q \to qQ}}$$

$\Delta D(Q)|_{Q \to qQ}$ and $\Delta R(Q)|_{Q \to qQ}$ represent the change of matching ration and the compression ratio respectively when the quantization table is adjusted.
The Function F represents both the impact of the loss of image features and image compression ratio comprehensively. A bigger F means a lower loss of image features and a higher compression ratio.
5. The fourth step is to control the iteration numbers threshold K, and in this paper, K is set to be 50. If the iteration counter is smaller than K, then go to the next step;
6. One of the quantization tables with higher fitness value are selected randomly to act as the new quantization tables.
7. According to the genetic algorithm, some small mutation and cross-breeding actions are introduced, wherein the former means the replacement of quantization coefficients with a random value, and the latter means the exchange between two quantization coefficients at the same location.
8. Repeated the step from 3 to 7 until the iteration counter equal to the threshold K, the quantization tables with the highest fitness value is obtained, and that is the optimized quantization table.

3 RESET OF THE DCT COEFFICIENT

In this section, we will consider the effect of human behavior on the photo taken by their mobile terminal. In most cases, people used to place the interested object in the center of a photo in the mobile multimedia applications. Therefore, we can set the DCT coefficients of a block according to the distance between the center of an image and it. The rules is as the following, shown in Figure 3:

- For the region I, the DC coefficients are kept while the others are set to be zero;

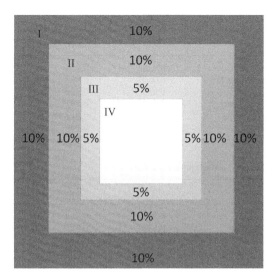

Figure 3.   Rules of reset of DCT coefficients.

Figure 4.   Experimental datasets.

- For the region II, the DC coefficients are kept, and the top four AC coefficients after ZIG-ZAG scanning are also kept, while the others are set to be zero;
- For the region III, the DC coefficients are kept, and the top eight AC coefficients after ZIG-ZAG scanning are also kepted, while the others are set to be zero;
- For the region IV, there is no adjustment;

4   EXPERIMENT AND VALIDATION

4.1   Datasets

The result of our proposed image compression scheme is validated based on the MPEG CDVS benchmark datasets [5–9]:

- Mixed graphic dataset depicts 5 product categories including CDs, DVDs, books, text documents and business cards. There are 1,500 queries and 1,000 reference images.

Table 1.   Comparison in file size of image compression.

Dataset	JPEG (kB)	Proposed method (kB)
Mixed	22.51	13.68
Paintings	18.87	12.17
Frames	20.48	13.25
Landmarks	32.86	15.00
Commons	24.14	14.00
Avg.	23.77	13.62

- Paintings dataset contains 400 queries and 100 reference images for paintings, such as history, portraits, landscapes and modern art.
- Video frames dataset contains 500 video frames, with a range of contents like movies, news reports and sports. There are 400 queries taken by a mobile phone, capturing the screen of laptop, PC and TV, which involves typical secular distortions.
- Landmarks dataset contains 2,302 queries and 6,367 reference images from 3 benchmarks
- Common dataset contains 2,550 objects, each with 4 images taken from different viewpoints. All the 10,200 images are indexed as reference images and used as queries.

Besides that, another 1 million images are used as distracters in retrieval experiments.

4.2   Resource consumption

In mobile visual retrieval applications, the image compression algorithm mostly runs on the mobile terminal, which leads to a worse performance due to the computing power and memory limitation. In this paper, we test resource consumption in the mobile terminal consumption on CDVS datasets. For VGA images, the average memory consumption is 1.87 MB in around 200 ms on HTC T328 (Memory 512 MB, CPU frequency 1024 MHz). The results show that, the approach proposed in this paper has a lower memory consumption and lower computing complexity; hence, it is suitable for mobile visual retrieval application.

4.3   Compression ratio

As shown in Table 1, for VGA images, the image file size reduced 42.7% in the proposed method compared to the standard JPEG image compression algorithm.

4.4   The extent of the image feature loss

Four kinds of image features are used to check the extent of the image feature loss, including color, texture, local feature and MAP (Mean Average Precision) factor are used to evaluate the feature loss.

4.4.1   Color feature

The color histogram feature L2 distance is used as the indicator to evaluate the extent of the color feature loss in the image compression algorithm. The lower L2 is,

Table 2. Comparison in color feature loss.

Dataset	JPEG	Proposed method
Mixed	50.85	56.55
Paintings	62.48	65.27
Frames	35.18	39.41
Landmarks	20.20	25.50
Commons	56.80	60.27
Avg.	45.10	49.80

Table 3. Comparison in texture feature loss.

Dataset	JPEG	Proposed method
Mixed	5.10	5.54
Paintings	4.92	5.17
Frames	5.93	6.16
Landmarks	2.43	2.57
Commons	5.90	6.14
Avg.	4.86	5.12

Table 4. Comparison in local feature loss.

Dataset	JPEG	Proposed method
Mixed	0.974	0.975
Paintings	0.950	0.962
Frames	0.985	0.992
Landmarks	0.840	0.841
Commons	0.897	0.912
Avg.	0.929	0.936

Table 5. Image retrieval results.

Dataset	JPEG	Proposed method
Mixed	0.851	0.874
Paintings	0.810	0.886
Frames	0.921	0.948
Landmarks	0.587	0.607
Commons	0.687	0.714
Avg.	0.771	0.801

the compressed image is more similar to the original image, and the less the loss of the color feature is.

As shown in Table 2, there is no large difference between our image compression method and the standard JPEG image compression algorithm, hence, color feature can be considered nearly lossless with our compression algorithm.

4.4.2 *Texture feature*

The CEDD (Color and Edge Directivity Descriptor) feature Tanimoto coefficient [10] is used as the indicator to evaluate the extent of the texture feature loss in the image compression algorithm. The lower the Tanimoto coefficient is, the compressed image is more similar to the original image, and the less the loss of the texture feature is.

As shown in Table 3, there is no large difference between our image compression method and the standard JPEG image compression algorithm, hence, texture feature can be considered nearly lossless with our compression algorithm.

4.4.3 *Local feature*

The SIFT (Scale-invariant feature transform) Feature matching percentage is used as the indicator to evaluate the extent of the local feature loss in the image compression algorithm [11], which is widely used in the image retrieval, image classification, image registration and so on. The higher the percentage is, the compressed image is more similar to the original image, and the less the loss of the local feature is.

As shown in Table 4, there is a small difference between our image compression method and the standard JPEG image compression algorithm, hence, local feature can be considered nearly lossless with our compression algorithm.

4.4.4 *Image retrieval performance*

SCFV (Scalable Compressed Fisher Vector) algorithm is used to evaluate the image retrieval performance [12], and in which MAP is the evaluating indicator.

As shown in Table 5, the MAP factor in our approach is higher than that in the standard JPEG compression algorithm. This is because the optimization of Quantization table and DCT coefficient reset method is introduced into image compression procedure, and after the compression procedure, the main feature of an image is retained while the noise is removed, therefore, a better retrieval result is achieved.

5 CONCLUSION

In this paper, an efficient image compression approach is proposed. Firstly, a scheme to optimize the DCT coefficient quantization table in JPEG image compression is proposed based on the genetic algorithm. According to it, we got an optimized quantization table by the training in the genetic algorithm based on the massive image dataset. And then, according to the feature distribution of the pictures generated in the mobile multimedia applications, the quantization table is adjusted again. After that, the normal JPEG image compression steps are proceeding. The experimental results are shown that, this kind of method can achieve a high compression ratio, JPEG-compatible and features lossless in for the image retrieval. Using the CDVS image data and the DCFV image retrieval algorithm, the JPEG file size reduced 42.7%, and the image retrieval accuracy has a slight improvement.

REFERENCES

[1] Paul G Ducksbury. "Target detection and intelligent image compression", Proceedings of SPIE Conference on Automatic Target Recognition X, pp. 86–97, 2000.

[2] Yan Liang, Wenyao Liu. "A new JPEG2000 region of interest coding method: generalized partial bitplanes shift", Electronic Imaging and Multimedia Technology, 2005.

[3] Loganathan, Kumaraswamy. "Medical Image Compression with Lossless Region of Interest Using Fuzzy Adaptive Active Contour", International Conference on Computational Techniques and Mobile Computing, 2012.

[4] Uma Vetri Selvi, Madarajan. "Coronary angiogram video compression using wavelet based contourlet transform and region-of-interest technique", J. Image Process. Inst. Eng. Technol., 2012.

[5] ISO/IEC JTC1/SC29/WG11/N12201 Call for Proposals for Compact Descriptors for Visual Search. 2011

[6] ISO/IEC JTC1/SC29/WG11/N12202 Evaluation Framework for Compact Descriptors for Visual Search. 2011

[7] ISO/IEC JTC1/SC29/WG11/N12735 Description of Core Experiments on Compact descriptors for Visual Search. 2012

[8] ISO/IEC JTC1/SC29/WG11/M25929 CDVS CE2: Local Descriptor Compression Proposal. 2012

[9] SO/IEC JTC1/SC29/WG11/N12929 Test Model 3: Compact Descriptors for Visual Search. 2012

[10] Sawas A. Chatzichristofis, Yiannis S. Boutalis. CEDD: Color and Edge Directivity Descriptor. A Compact Descriptor for Image Indexing and Retrieval [J], Department of Electrical & Computer Engineering Democritus University of Thrace. 67100, 2009

[11] David G. Lowe, "Distinctive image features from scale-invariant keypoints", International Journal of Computer Vision, 2004.

[12] Lin J., Duan L.Y., Chen J., et al. Peking Univ.Response to CE1: A scalable low-memory global descriptor [S]. M26726, ISO/IEC JTC1/SC29/WG11, Shanghai 2012.

Multimedia Technology IV – Farag, Yang & Jiao (Eds)
© 2015 Taylor & Francis Group, London, ISBN: 978-1-138-02794-7

Automatical face beautification based on near-infrared image

Qiang Zhang, Fei Zhou, Fan Yang & Qingmin Liao
Department of Electronic Engineering/Graduate School of Shenzhen, Tsinghua University, Shenzhen Key Lab. of Information Sci & Tech/Shenzhen Engineering Lab. of IS & DRM, Shenzhen, China

ABSTRACT: In this paper, we propose a framework for capturing visible and near-infrared (NIR) images as well as a new algorithm fuses the two captured images into a beautiful one. Three steps are used for fusion part. Firstly, face detection is utilized for segmenting the interested area and reducing the time cost. Secondly, the gradient in the interested area is estimated for image recovery with three masks. Thirdly, the output image is obtained by solving the Poisson equation. The approach has been tested under various illumination conditions, and the results are satisfactory.

Keywords: Harr-like features; gradient; descent iterative; Poisson equation

1 INTRODUCTION

Skin beautification is a technique to smooth the skin of a photographed portrait. There are two main constraints of such an approach, i.e., realistic skin tones and high-frequency details of original images. Many consumer cameras have contained the function of skin beautification. However, most of these techniques cannot beautify the face automatically and the result always looks distorted.

Related research has made approach on skin beautification. In [1], Lee *et al.* proposed an automatic skin smoothing algorithm, which is based on smoothing filter. The algorithm segments the skin automatically, while the drawback is that it cannot segment the skin area precisely under different capture conditions and thus, may cause artificial effect and a lot of high-frequency details will loss. In [2], Chen *et al.* proposed a skin smoothing algorithm based on face detection and bilateral filter, but it could not preserve the details of the face organs well and was sensitive to luminance. Additionally, relying on 3D face model can be precision limited and usefulness when confronted with different capture conditions [4].

The research on spectral image and the optical properties of human skin have been developed rapidly [5], [6], and [7]. Comparing the same portrait in the visible and near-infrared (NIR) bands that is shown in Fig. 1, we can find that the skin appears much smoother in the NIR. Meanwhile most high-frequency details are effectively preserved. In [6], Chen *et al.* offers a new camera sensor to reach the visible and NIR image simultaneously, which can be used in many devices such as smart-phone, personal computer, and so on.

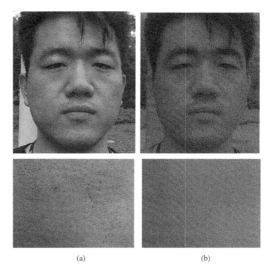

(a)   (b)

Figure 1. Visible and NIR representation of a portrait. Parts of the portrait are segmented to show the detail. While the skin appears much smoother in the NIR, most of the high-frequency details are effectively preserved. (a) Visible image, (b) NIR image.

This is why the algorithm is convenient for human daily life.

In [3], Fredembach *et al.* proposed an approach that needs no skin segmentation to fuse near-infrared image and visible image by bilateral filter. The algorithm does not need skin segmentation either. However the filter's parameters cannot adapt to various capture conditions and it has badly robust for different luminance. Fredembach [8] proposed that one could obtain color images with a NIR "look" simply by treating the NIR channel as luminance-related information and substituting it to the original visible image's. While the method performs well on the little difference luminance between NIR and visible image which is always very large because of the device limits, it always cannot get realistic looking images. Indeed, fusion methods generally aim to maximize the amount of information present in the fused image, whereas our goal here is to preserve the relevant details and remove unwanted ones.

In this paper, a new algorithm is proposed which fuses visible and NIR information in an appropriate manner to obtain smooth yet realistic color image. The approach is as follows: considering the background details cannot be detected for the power of device and time cost, we need to segment face area. A face detection method which can adapt to luminance variation is proposed. In order to avoid artificial effects caused by inaccurate face segmentation and large difference luminance between NIR and visible image, a novel gradient domain fusion approach is adopted and a descent iterative is employed to reduce time consumption. A gradient based image reconstruction by solving the Poisson equation approach is used to get the final result. Results show that our approach can be robust to different luminance between NIR and visible image and various scenes for portrait. Additionally the realistic results are obtained across various skin types.

The rest of the paper is organized as follows. Section 2 presents the details of the proposed algorithm. Section 3 is about the experiments and Section 4 is the conclusion of the paper.

2 PROPOSED ALGORITHM

2.1 Face detection

There are several skin color detection algorithms proposed to extract the skin parts from given image [11]. Most of these approaches utilize statistical method to find out the boundary of human skin in specific color space. However, skin color is sensitive to color temperature, which will affect the experiment's robustness. Viola *et al.* proposed an efficient face detection approach [12], which makes the face detection in real time and has been used in a lot of smart phones as a camera feature. The face detection approach adapts to the types of skin. Take advantage of this, our algorithm does not need considering the types of skin. Furthermore, Lienhart *et al.* proposed Haar-like features for object detection [13], which has a high hit rate in many conditions and owns the advantage of [12]. Because of our algorithm reconstruct image from the estimated gradient, there is no need to consider the blocking artifacts. Based on this advantage, Lienhart's approach is used to detect face area, which is a rough skin area data. This will enhance the efficiency of the proposed algorithm. The result is shown in Fig. 2 (a), (b).

2.2 Adaptive gradient reconstruction

In this section, the estimation of the gradient in the area which is obtained in section 2.1 is introduced. In the study of skin optical properties, it can be concluded that in NIR image the skin area is much smoother than visible image. For the big difference of illumination between NIR and visible image which is always happened in real conditions, it is impossible to use the NIR image to substitute the visible image in pixel domain directly. Color distortion and blocking artifacts will be produced by the direct substitution. With the development of the gradient based image reconstruction [14], the gradient in horizontal and vertical direction can be estimated by the information of NIR and visible image. NIR image shows the information under the epidermis and this phenomenon leads to smaller gradient in NIR image than visible image not only in skin area but also in organ area. The NIR image can preserve some details of the face but the contrast of these details is much smaller than visible image. Fig. 3 shows this phenomenon. In Fig. 3, the curve represents the distribution of the pixel value in vertical direction and the average pixel value in horizontal direction in the red rectangle is calculated firstly. With this situation, the direct substitution is difficult for visible image not only in pixel domain but also in gradient domain directly. To produce a realistic image, three masks are abstracted firstly to adjust the gradient in face area. The masks are produced based on the assumption that the edge with big contrast is easy to detect. The first mask is called "h-mask" which is extracted by NIR image's horizontal gradient with a small threshold which can filter some small gradients. The second mask is called "v-mask" which is generated by NIR image's vertical gradient with a small threshold. The third mask called as "e-mask" is produced by visible image's edge detection. In this paper, canny operator is utilized to detect the edge of visible image with a big threshold which can preserve continuous large edges and ignore small edges. The details of calculating the three masks are shown in Fig. 4 *Lorig* denotes the visible image, and *NIRorig* denotes the NIR image. *Yorig* is the Y channel of the visible image. *NIRGxorig* and *NIRGyorig* denote the original gradients of NIR image in two directions. V is a small value to erase pixels with small gradients. The formulas to get the two directions gradient are shown as (1), (2). $Gx = G_h(m,n)$ is the gradient in horizontal direction. $Gy = G_v(m,n)$ represents the gradient in vertical direction. (m,n) is the coordinate of pixel. $p(m,n)$ is the pixel value in (m,n).

$$G_h(m,n) = p(m+1,n) - p(m,n) \tag{1}$$

$$G_v(m,n) = p(m,n+1) - p(m,n) \tag{2}$$

The reason for using the three masks is that the "e-mask" can give the location of the big edges, the "h-mask" and "v-mask" can give some small details' locations and these locations will be used to enhance the fidelity of the result. In the estimated gradient image, we assume that these locations are the

146

Figure 2. Result for face detection. (a) original visible image, (b) face detection result.

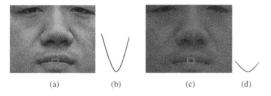

Figure 3. Difference of the contrast between visible and NIR image is obviously. (a) visible image in Y channel, (c) NIR image.(b) and (d) are the distribution of pixel value in vertical direction in the red rectangle. We calculate the average pixel value in horizontal direction in the red rectangle, and then draw the curve in vertical direction. (b) the distribution of visible image, (d) the distribution of NIR image.

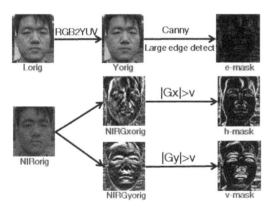

Figure 4. Details for calculating three masks. They can be used for face reconstruction in gradient domain.

place where we should keep the gradient of the visible image. Because these masks are got from gradient domain which means it will be robust to illumination. The threshold of these masks' dynamic range is little for their mutual complementation. In the experiment, the value of the threshold is fixed, also the situation is found that it is robust to various conditions. The thresholds of these masks in our experiment are 1 for "h-mask" and "v-mask", and 0.15 for "e-mask".

Once the mask is extracted, the gradient will be estimated adaptively. Firstly, in the area where the three masks with non-zero values, the new gradients are determined by the gradient of visible image. Secondly,

in the area where three masks' values are zero, the new gradients are determined by the gradient of NIR image with a coefficient α. For the big different luminance between NIR image and visible image, the reconstruction image will be distortion in color domain. That is why a coefficient is multiplied the NIR image' gradient to adjust the illumination intensity in Y channel. Multiplicative coefficient has little effect on small gradient which means the coefficient will not affect the smooth of the skin, and will make the result more realistic. The coefficient will be same in horizontal gradient and vertical gradient just because of the similar property in the two directions. The formulas to calculate α is showed in (3), (4), and (5).

$$CG = \frac{\sum_{x,y}(|G_{l-h}(x,y)|+|G_{l-v}(x,y)|)}{\sum_{x,y}(|G_{NIR-h}(x,y)|+|G_{NIR-v}(x,y)|)} \tag{3}$$

$$CP = \frac{\sum_{x,y}P_{l-orig}(x,y)}{\sum_{x,y}P_{NIR}(x,y)} \tag{4}$$

$$NewCP = \frac{\sum_{x,y}P_{l-orig}(x,y)}{\sum_{x,y}P_{l-res}(x,y)} \tag{5}$$

where $G_{l-h}(x,y)$ and $G_{l-v}(x,y)$ are the gradient value in visible image. $G_{NIR-h}(x,y)$ and $G_{NIR-v}(x,y)$ are the gradient value in NIR image. $P_{l-orig}(x,y)$ is the pixel value in original visible image. $P_{l-res}(x,y)$ is the pixel value in the reconstructed visible image. $P_{NIR}(x,y)$ is the pixel value in NIR image. (x, y) denotes the area where the three masks have zero value. CG denotes the ratio of the average gradient in visible and NIR image. CP denotes the ratio of the average pixel value in visible and NIR image. Two properties can be found in CP and CG. First, CP is bigger than CG. Second, CG is bigger than CP. What does this mean? The first property means that in the correspond areas visible image has the same texture as the NIR image. In this condition, the roughly multiplicative coefficient α is determined by CG. The second property means that in the correspond areas visible image's texture is different from that of the NIR image (specifically speaking, the former is always bigger than the latter). In this condition, CG cannot be the same as α because of the nonlinear correlation, but CG can be used as the maximum coefficient because of the relationship between visible and NIR image's gradient. For the two properties, CG will be used as the maximum coefficient and zero is set as the minimum coefficient to find the precise coefficient α. In the interval, α is the value to make sure $NewCP$ is closest to one. $NewCP$ denotes the ratio of the average pixel value in original and new reconstructed visible image. $NewCP$ is the function of the coefficient. Gradient descent iterative algorithm is used to calculate the precise coefficient α Using α

and three masks, the gradient in horizontal and vertical direction can be estimated adaptively. The flowchart of the proposed algorithm is presented in Fig. 5: *Vis_orig* is the original visible image and *NIR_orig* denotes the original NIR image. *Vis_gx* is the original gradient in horizontal direction of the visible image and *Vis_gy* is the gradient in vertical direction. *NIR_gx* denotes the gradient in horizontal direction of the NIR image and *NIR_gy* is the gradient in vertical direction. *masks* denotes the three masks that are gotten from Y channel of the visible image and NIR image. *NEW_gx* denotes the estimated gradient in horizontal direction. *NEW_gy* represents the estimated gradient in horizontal direction. *NEW_vis* is the reconstructed image in Y channel. *RESULT* denotes our final result.

2.3 Reconstruction of the image

This section will introduce a method of obtaining images by using the result of part C. Image reconstruction from gradient fields is a quite active research area. In 2D, a modified gradient vector field $G' = [G'_x, G'_y]$ may not be integrable. I' denotes the accomplished image reconstructed from G'. We adopt one of the methods proposed in [15] to minimize $||\nabla I' - G||$. I' can be confirmed by solving Possion differential equation [16], and [17], with both the Laplacian and divergence operator. The Poisson equation has been used extensively in computer vision. It arises naturally as a necessary condition in the solution of certain variational problems.

$$\nabla^2 I' = div([G'_x, G'_y]) \tag{6}$$

A solution of linear equation is employed to approximate the solution of (6), since Laplacian ∇^2 and *div* are both linear operators. In [18], Jia *et al.* proposed a method based on Gaussian-Seidel iterations, i.e., full multigrid method, to solve Laplacian equation. The solution complexity reached $O(n)$, where n represents the number of pixels in the face region. This will certainly improve the efficiency of the new algorithm.

In order to improve the efficiency, a rapid Poisson solver is used to make Poisson approximation. Based this method [18], a sine transform is used to invert Laplacian operator, which improves solver complexity to $O(N(\log(N)))$. The new solver is utilized in our implementation.

Since we utilize the Dirichlet boundary condition instead of Neumanm boundary condition to reconstruct the image I', the region is fully zero-padded on all sides. Therefore, the scale-shift ambiguity is avoided.

3 EXPERIMENTS

This section will give a detailed explanation about the experimental protocol that was used in obtaining

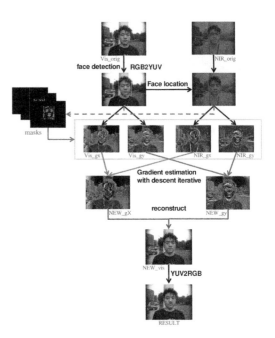

Figure 5. Flowchart of the proposed algorithm.

the images, as well as the processing steps undertaken. The smoothing is done by adopting the gradient reconstruct method described in the previous section.

The experiment is carried out in the natural condition, rather than in the lab. The VIS-NIR sensor is used in our own camera with a NIR flash at 850 nm. The white balancing of the camera is set to automatic and designed to capture faithful visible images. By using the camera, NIR and visible images are gotten simultaneously which means that the registration of the face does not need to be considered. It is highly possible to apply this advanced camera module to smart phone, computer and so on. Brightness does not need to be adjusted in our experiment, even though there is a big difference between NIR and visible image. Luminance information is easier to be perceived by human visual system than color information. Visible image is separated into YUV channel. Y channel is used to estimate gradient and reconstruct image. Every step is automatic, and the quality of the results does not depend on the type of skin, the gesture and the number of person. The values of the three masks are set to 1 for "h-mask" and "v-mask", and 0.15 for "e-mask". A small value is always added to the result of the precise coefficient, which will make the skin white and beautiful. The results are shown in Fig. 6 (a), (b) and Fig. 7 (a), (b). Other algorithm is compared with our own algorithm in Fig. 8. From the results, we can observe that realistic and smooth human faces (even with uneven lighting, Fig. 7 (a), (b)) are generalized by the proposed algorithm. Result from the algorithm of Fredembach is blurred because of the using of bilateral filter and it must adjust the luminance as image preprocessing. Compared with fredembach's result, the proposed algorithm can produce much smoother skin,

(a)

(b)

Figure 6. Experiment result. (a) orignal image, (b) our result.

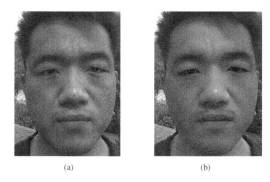

(a)   (b)

Figure 7. Result with non-uniform lighting. (a) orignal image, (b) our result.

and sharper edges because the gradient is preserved in the high frequency part. The speed of the two algorithms is compared under the same hardware condition (on a PC with single Pentium 4 2.8 GHz CPU and 2 G of memory). The result is shown in TABLE I. From the result, we can find that our algorithm is faster than fredembach's with the same condition.

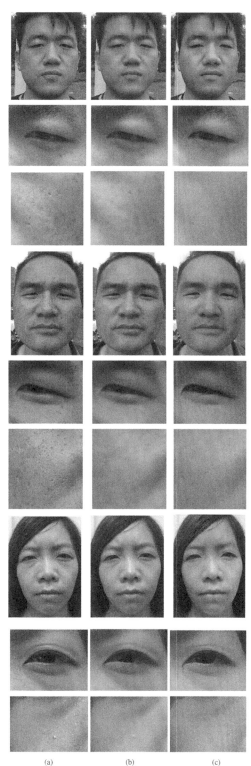

(a)   (b)   (c)

Figure 8. Visual comparison. The parts of portrait are listed under the portraiture to show the detail. (a) original image, (b) fredembach's result, (c) our result.

149

Table 1. Comparison of the algorithm speed.

Algorithm	Image Size	Time
ours	1632*1224	4.355 s
fredembach	1632*1224	10.133 s

4 CONCLUSIONS

With the images captured by NIR-VIS sensor, a beautiful portrait image can be obtained by the new algorithm. Near-infrared wavelengths are not as much scattered or absorbed by skin as visible ones. NIR skin images therefore exhibit much fewer unwanted "features" than their visible counterparts. Face detection gives us the opportunity to control the cost of time, and the type of skin needs no consideration. The brightness can be adjusted adaptively with the help of the estimated gradient, and this will make the algorithm robust to various luminance conditions. This method achieves results that are realistic and beautiful. The enhanced portraits are visibly better, as wrinkles, blemishes and other skin imperfections are significantly reduced. With the fast speed of the algorithm, people can use this algorithm in smart phone in the future for convenient in human daily life.

ACKNOWLEDGEMENT

This work was supported in part by the National Natural Science Foundation of China under Grant (No. 61271393 and 61301183) and in part by China Postdoctoral Science Foundation under Grant 2013M540947 and 2014T0083.

REFERENCES

[1] C. Lee, M.T. Schramm, M. Boutin, and J.P. Allebach, "An algorithm for automatic skin smoothing in digital portraits" in ICIP'09: Proceedings of the 16th IEEE international conference on Image processing, New Jersey, 2009, pp. 3113–3116.

[2] C.W. Chen, D.Y. Huang, C.S. Fuh, "Automatic skin color beautificaiton" Arts and Technology, Taiwan, vol. 30, pp. 157–164, 2010.

[3] C. Fredembach, N. Barbuscia, and S. Süsstrunk, "Combining visible and near-infrared images for realistic skin smoothing," in Proc. IS&T/SID 17th Color Imaging Conference, Albuquerque, NM, 2009, pp. 242–247(6).

[4] C. Dubout, M. Tsukada, R. Ishiyama, C. Funayama, and S. Süsstrunk. "Face image enhancement using 3d and spectral information," in IEEE International Conference on Image Processing, Cairo, 2009, pp. 697–700.

[5] S.B. Kusse, "Spectral imaging and analysis of human skin," Master Thesis, University of Eastern Finland, 2010.

[6] Z. Chen, X. Wang, and R. Liang, "RGB-NIR multispectral camera," Optics Express, vol. 22, pp. 4985–4994, 2014.

[7] H. Steiner, O. Schwaneberg, and N. Jung, "Advances in active near-infrared sensor systems for material classification," in Imaging Systems and Applications, Monterey, California United States, 2012.

[8] C. Fredembach and S. Süsstrunk, "Colouring the near-infrared," in Proc. Of the 16th IST/SID Color Imaging Conference, Portland, OR, 2008, pp. 176–182.

[9] Skin Anatomy. http://dermatology.about.com/cs/skinanatomy (Updated May 2014).

[10] M.J.C. van Gemert, S.L. Jacques, H.J.C.M. Sterenborg, W.M. Star, "Skin optics," Biomedical Engineering, IEEE Transactions on, vol. 36, pp. 1146–1154, Dec. 1989.

[11] P. Kakumanu, S. Makrogiannis, and N. Bourbakis, "A survey of skin-color modeling and detection methods," Pattern Recognition, vol. 40, pp. 1106–1122, March 2007.

[12] P. Viola, and M.J. Jones, "Robust Real-Time Face Detection," International Journal of Computer Vision, vol. 57, pp. 137–154, May 2004.

[13] R. Lienhart, and J. Maydt, "An extended set of Haar-like features for rapid object detection," In: Proceedings of 2002 International Conference on Image Processing, 2002, pp. I-900–I-903.

[14] J. Shen, X. Jin, C. Zhou, and C.C.L. Wang, "Gradient based image completion by solving the Poisson equation," Computers & Graphics, vol. 31, pp. 119–126, January 2007.

[15] R. Fattal, D. Lischinski, and M. Werman. "Gradient domain high dynamic range compression," ACM Transactions on Graphics, New York, vol. 21, pp. 249–256, 2002.

[16] R. Raskar, K. Tan, R. Feris, J. Yu, and M. Turk, "Non-photorealistic camera: depth edge detection and stylized rendering using multi-?ash imaging," ACM Transactions on Graphics, New York, vol. 23, pp.679-688, 2004.

[17] A. Agrawal, R. Raskar, S.K. Nayar, and Y. Li, "Removing flash artifacts using gradient analysis," ACM Transactions on Graphics, New York, vol. 24, pp. 828–835, 2005.

[18] J. Jia, and C.K. Tang, "Image repairing: Robust image synthesis by adaptive tensor voting," In: Proceedings of Conference on Computer Vision and Pattern Recognition '03," Madison, WI, 2003, pp. 643–650.

Multimedia Technology IV – Farag, Yang & Jiao (Eds)
© 2015 Taylor & Francis Group, London, ISBN: 978-1-138-02794-7

Learning semantic correlations of images and text by automatic image annotation

Ying Xia, YunLong Wu & JiangFan Feng
Research Center of Spatial Information System, Chongqing University of Posts and Telecommunications, Chongqing, China

ABSTRACT: Recently probabilistic model of automatic image annotation (AIA) has been usually utilized to solve problems of cross-media retrieval due to its advantage of learning semantic correlations of images and text efficiently. However, some AIA models may ignore correlations among keywords used to annotate images. In this paper, we propose a kind of probability-based cross-media relevance model (PBCMRM). In our approach, not only the joint probability of keywords and segmented image regions is considered, also correlations of annotation keywords. In the model, a kind of vocabulary called blob is used to represent images in training dataset. The effectiveness of the probability-based cross-media relevance model is verified by several experiments conducted on Corel dataset.

Keywords: automatic image annotation, semantic correlations, cross-media retrieval

1 INTRODUCTION

In current time, with the growth of multimedia data, content-based retrieval is proposed to retrieve the multi-modality information precisely. Murala S. and Maheshwari [1] propose a novel image indexing and retrieval algorithm using local tetra patterns for content-based image retrieval. Yildizer E. and Balci A.M. [2] propose an extremely fast CBIR system which uses Multiple Support Vector Machines Ensemble applying Daubechies wavelet transformation to extracting the feature vectors of images. However, most methods of content-based retrieval only focus on features of single modality data. Correlations among multimedia data with different modalities are ignored, so cross-media retrieval is put forward to solve this problem. Zhuang and Wu [3], [4] introduce an isomorphic subspace constructed based on Canonical Correlation Analysis (CCA) to learn cross-modal correlations of multimedia data. Lu and Wang [5] propose a multi-modality semantic relationship graph (MSRG) to map media objects onto an isomorphic semantic space and an efficient indexing MK-tree to manage the media objects. These methods concentrate on low-level features and solve the problems of cross-media retrieval to some extent, but a great deal of annotation information may be ignored. Nowadays, there exist myriad variety of Web images with manual annotations, such as anchor text and labels. These annotations are very significant for mining the semantic correlations between images and text. As a result, to avoid labor intensive procedure and improve the efficiency, automatic image annotation may be appropriate way to learn semantic correlations between images and text.

The most intrinsic problem for automatic image annotation is how to improve the accuracy of annotation. To tackle the problem of automatic image annotation, various machine learning algorithms have been utilized. Some approaches apply supervised learning methods to automatic image annotation. Other approaches take advantage of unsupervised learning methods including parametric models and non-parametric models to represent correlations between images and annotation keywords. However, these methods neglect the correlations among annotation keywords. This word-to-word correlation may make contributions to improve the accuracy of automatic image annotation.

To make use of context information of annotation keywords to improve automatic image annotation with the aim to research the correlations between images and text, this paper proposes a probability-based cross-media relevance model combining two kinds of correlations. One is between keywords and segmented image regions, another is among annotation keywords. In the model, we estimate the joint probability of keywords and image regions to get image-to-word correlations and use the co-occurrence of all keywords in training dataset to get word-to-word correlations.

2 RELATED WORK

Recently, many models use machine learning methods to annotate images automatically. Burdescu and Mihai [6] present a system used in the medical domain for three tasks: image annotation, semantic based image retrieval and content based image retrieval. Pan and Yang [7] propose a novel, graph-based approach to discover multi-modal correlations. Researchers take advantage of automatic image annotation to mine the correlations among media objects of different modalities also in [8], [9]. Duygulu and Barnard [10] propose a model of object recognition used to annotate image regions with keywords. Normalized Cuts [11] is used to segment images into discrete regions and afterwards these image regions are clustered into special image vocabularies called blobs using K-Means algorithm. Then, like one kind of language in a lexicon corresponding to another kind of language, a unique number of a blob corresponds to an image region. EM algorithm is utilized to compute probability of adding keywords to a new image's blobs in [10]. Hiemstra [12] introduces a variety of information retrieval models, especially probabilistic model, thus we assuming that there existing some probability distribution for an image. Lavrenko and Croft [13] propose a novel technique for estimating probabilities of keywords in the relevant class using the query alone. These methods require a training dataset to predict correlations between keywords and visual image features.

3 PROBABILITY-BASED CROSS-MEDIA RELEVANCE MODEL

In this section, we will illustrate the Probability-Based Cross-Media Relevance Model (PBCMRM). PBCMRM can associate an image with relative keywords. Actually, our model annotates images by predicting the probability of assigning keywords w_i ($i = 1, \ldots, n$) into an un-annotated image I_Q. We formulate PBCMRM as follow:

$$P\left(w_i \mid I_Q\right) = \lambda P\left(w_i \mid I_Q\right) + (1 - \lambda) \sum_{j=1, j \neq i}^{n} P\left(w_i \mid w_j\right) P\left(w_j \mid I_Q\right) \quad (1)$$

In equation (1), the conditional probability $P(w_i|I_Q)$ represents the probability of annotating image I_Q by keyword w_i and it can be calculated by Improved Cross-Media Relevance Model. The conditional probability $P(w_i|w_j)$ indicates the correlation of these two keywords, it can be calculated by its co-occurrence matrix. And λ is the smoothing parameter.

3.1 *Improved cross-media relevance model*

Jeon and Lavrenko [8] propose the Cross-Media Relevance Model (CMRM) to solve the problem of cross-media retrieval. In CMRM, a special image vocabularies called blobs [11] is used to represent images. There exists a training dataset T, in which every image $K \in T$ has been segmented and annotated, that is, K has a set of blobs $\{b_1 \ldots b_m\}$ and a set of words $\{w_1 \ldots w_n\}$. They assume that there is no correspondence between the blob $b_m \in K$ with the keyword $w_n \in K$ in the same image. Given an un-annotated test image I, which only has a set of blobs $\{b_1 \ldots b_z\}$,

there exists the probability distribution $P(\bullet|I)$ according to [12]. Based on this relevance model $P(\bullet|I)$, the process of image annotation is actually sampling several words having highest probability from the model. So they calculate the probability of any word appearing in the training dataset T when sampling from $P(\bullet|I)$ and then they estimate the probability $P(w|I)$ for every word w. Given $P(\bullet|I)$ is unknown, image I can be expressed as $\{b_1 \ldots b_z\}$, that is, the probability of assigning words into image I is approximated by the conditional probability of w given $b_1 \ldots b_z$:

$$P\left(w \mid I\right) \approx P\left(w \mid b_1 \text{⦚⦚}b_z\right) \quad (2)$$

They compute the joint probability of the word w and blobs $b_1 \ldots b_z$ in the same image using the training dataset T. The joint distribution can be calculated as the expectation over images K in the training dataset T:

$$P\left(w, b_1 \text{⦚⦚}b_z\right) = \sum_{K \in T} P\left(K\right) P\left(w, b_1 \text{⦚⦚}b_z \mid K\right) \quad (3)$$

They assume that variables w and $b_1 \ldots b_z$ are independent, so are events of observing w and $b_1 \ldots b_z$. Equation (3) can be represented as follows:

$$P\left(w, b_1 \text{⦚⦚}b_z\right) = \sum_{K \in T} P\left(K\right) P\left(w \mid K\right) \prod_{i=1}^{z} P\left(b_i \mid K\right) \quad (4)$$

The prior probabilities $P(K)$ are kept uniform over all images in T. The probability of drawing the word w or the blob b from relevance model of K is formulated as:

$$P\left(w \mid K\right) = \left(1 - \alpha_K\right) \frac{N\left(w, K\right)}{|K|} + \alpha_K \frac{N\left(w, T\right)}{|T|} \quad (5)$$

$$P\left(b \mid K\right) = \left(1 - \beta_K\right) \frac{N\left(b, K\right)}{|K|} + \beta_K \frac{N\left(b, T\right)}{|T|} \quad (6)$$

In formula (5) and (6), $N(w, K)$ refers to the actual number of times that the word w is attached to the image K. $N(w, T)$ describes the total number of times that the word w occurs in the training dataset T. Similarly, $N(b, K)$ denotes the actual number of times that the blob appears in the image K and $N(b, T)$ is the number of occurrences of blob b in dataset T. $|K|$ represents count of occurrences of words and blobs occurring in the image K and $|T|$ stands for total size of training dataset T. The smoothing parameters α_K and β_K determine the degree of interpolation between the maximum likelihood estimates and the background probabilities for words and the blobs.

However, this model may not overcome the uneven distribution of blobs in training dataset. If some blobs are much more than others, the results annotation may be affected. So we need to provide another two smoothing parameters γ_w and γ_b. Equations (5) and (6) can be represented as follows:

$$P'\left(w \mid K\right) = \gamma_w P\left(w \mid K\right), \gamma_w = \frac{|K| + |T|}{N\left(w, K\right) + N\left(w, T\right)} \quad (7)$$

$$P'\left(b \mid K\right) = \gamma_b P\left(b \mid K\right), \gamma_b = \frac{|K| + |T|}{N\left(b, K\right) + N\left(b, T\right)} \quad (8)$$

3.2 Correlations among annotation keywords

Some keywords appearing in the same image contain important context information and it can be used to annotate images. The static correlations among annotation keywords contain semantic similarity and can be calculated by its co-occurrence matrix.

In our work, we get the co-occurrence matrix by counting number of times that every keyword-pair used to annotation appearing in the same image over the training dataset.

$$P\left(w_i \mid w_j\right) = \frac{P(w_i, w_j)}{N(w_i, T)} \qquad (9)$$

In equation (9), $P(w_i, w_j)$ denotes the number of times these two keywords occurring in the same image and $N(w_i, T)$ represents the total number of times that the word w_i occurs in the training dataset T. Thus in the equation (1), image-to-word correlations $P(w_j|I_Q)$ and word-to-word correlations $P(w_i|w_j)$ can be computed both. So the process of image annotation has two steps:

- For an un-annotated image I_Q in test dataset, we translate it into several blobs using Normalized Cuts [11] and cluster algorithm.
- PBCMRM is used to predict the conditional probability $P(w_i|I_Q)$ over all keywords and then annotate image I_Q using some keywords having highest probability.

4 EXPERIMENTAL RESULTS

In this section the details of dataset used will be discussed in section 4.1 and experimental results will be showed through comparing our model with other different models of [8], [9] in section 4.2.

4.1 Dataset

The Corel dataset is a public and widely used dataset in evaluating image annotation methods. It is composed of 3 sections and every section is grouped into training dataset and test dataset. It contains about 700 training images and 340 test images. Each image is segmented into 1 to 20 regions using Normalized Cuts [11]. 16 kinds of visual features including color and shape are extracted for each image region. All image regions are grouped into 55 visual blobs using K-Means algorithm. Each training image is annotated with 1 to 5 words. A total number of 42 keywords are used to annotate the entire dataset.

4.2 Automatic image annotation results and analysis

The PBCMRM can be applied to annotate images. To evaluate the accuracy of this model, single keyword appearing in the training dataset will be used to retrieve images in the test dataset (note that this is not ranked retrieval). We can get the relevance degree of

Table 1. Some keywords used to retrieve images.

Keywords				
airplane	bear	building	church	crab
elephant	fish	goat	grass	ground
horse	log	polarbear	road	coral
earth	rock	person	sky	water

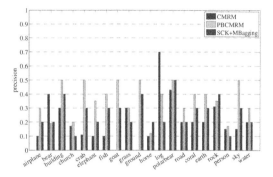

Figure 1. Precision of image retrieval using some high-frequency keywords.

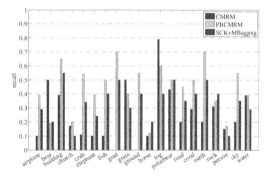

Figure 2. Recall of image retrieval using some high-frequency keywords.

retrieved images by comparing with images' original annotation, specifically the precision and recall. The precision denotes the number of correctly retrieved images divided by the number of retrieved images and the recall represents the number of correctly retrieved images divided by the number of relevant images in the test dataset. Our model has three smoothing parameters. These parameters are estimated through the training dataset. We concentrate on the average precision and recall to pick the best parameters out. The experiment shows that $\alpha_K = 0.1$, $\beta_K = 0.9$ and $\lambda = 0.7$ are the best.

Here we compare the results of three models, the CMRM [8], SCK+MBagging [9] and our model. All these models annotate images with different numbers of keywords according to the number of image's blobs. There are 42 kinds of query word in the dataset and Table 1 shows 20 high-frequency keywords used for

Table 2. Average precision and recall.

| Models | Average precision and recall | |
	Precision	Recall
CMRM	0.24	0.32
PBCMRM	0.37	0.45
SCK+Mbagging	0.27	0.34

Table 3. Automatic annotation examples.

| Images | Annotation Information | |
	True annotations	Automatic annotations
	rock tree water sky	rock water sky ground
	airplane cloud grass road	airplane grass rock earth
	elephant ground trees sky	elephant ground road coral

image retrieval. The Figure 1 and Figure 2 show the precision and recall using a set of high-frequency keywords as single word query. Table 2 shows the average precision and recall of these three models. Obviously, the CMRM has 0.24 mean precision and 0.32 mean recall, the PBCMRM has 0.37 mean precision and 0.45 mean recall, the SCK+MBagging has 0.27 mean precision and 0.34 mean recall. In terms of recall and precision, our approach PBCMRM is better to some extent. In addition, some examples of automatic image annotation using our model are showed in Table 3.

5 CONCLUSION AND FUTURE WORK

In this paper, we have proposed a new approach for cross-media retrieval using probability-based cross-media relevance model. Compared to other models, the proposed model has shown better annotation and retrieval results, suggesting the importance of PBCMRM. But some major challenges still remain: the appropriate semantic features for more precise retrieval are difficult to be extracted and our model mainly depends on image segmentation.

After assigning the keywords into every image, we may take advantage of the spatial information among these blobs in the same image. The spatial contextual information may access to semantic scene more accurately, thus we getting more accurate results of cross-media retrieval. We believe that other areas of possible research for the use of captions will get progress.

ACKNOWLEDGMENT

We would like to thank to the reviewers for their helpful comments. This work was financially supported by the Natural Science Foundation of China (41201378), Natural Science Foundation Project of Chongqing CSTC (cstc2012jjA40014), and Doctoral Startup Foundation of Chongqing University of Posts and Telecommunications (A2012-34).

REFERENCES

[1] S. Murala, R.P. Maheshwari, and R. Balasubramanian, "Local tetra patterns: a new feature de-scriptor for content-based image retrieval," Image Processing, IEEE Transactions on, vol. 21, pp. 2874–2886, 2012.
[2] E. Yildizer, A.M. Balci, M. Hassan, and R. Alhajj, "Efficient content-based image retrieval using multiple support vector machines ensemble," Expert Systems with Applications, vol. 39, pp. 2385–2396, 2012.
[3] F. Wu, H. Zhang, and Y. Zhuang, "Learning semantic correlations for cross-media retrieval," In: Image Processing, 2006 IEEE International Conference on. IEEE. pp. 1465–1468, 2006.
[4] H. Zhang, Y. Zhuang, and F. Wu, "Cross-modal correlation learning for clustering on image-audio dataset," In: Proceedings of the 15th international conference on Multimedia. ACM, pp. 273–276, 2007.
[5] B. Lu, G.R. Wang, and Y. Yuan "A novel approach towards large scale cross-media retrieval" Journal of Computer Science and Technology, vol. 27, pp. 1140–1149, 2012.
[6] D.D. Burdescu, C.G. Mihai, L. Stanescu, and M. Brezovan, "Automatic image annotation and semantic based image retrieval for medical domain," Neurocomputing, pp. 33–48, 2013.
[7] J.Y. Pan, H.J. Yang, C. Faloutsos, and P. Duyqulu, "Automatic multimedia cross-modal correlation discovery," In: Proceedings of the tenth ACM SIGKDD international conference on Knowledge discovery and data mining. ACM, pp. 653–658, 2004.
[8] J. Jeon, V. Lavrenko, and R. Manmatha, "Automatic image annotation and retrieval using cross-media relevance models," In: Proceedings of the 26th annual international ACM SIGIR conference on Research and development in informaion retrieval. ACM, pp. 119–126, 2003.
[9] J. Guo, and X. Liao, "Cross-Media Image Retrieval via Latent Semantic Indexing and Mixed Bagging," In: Computer Science and Information Engineering, 2009 WRI World Congress on. IEEE, pp. 187–193, 2009.
[10] P. Duygulu, K. Barnard, J.F.G. de Freitas, and D.A. Forsyth, "Object recognition as machine translation: Learning a lexicon for a fixed image vocabulary," In: Computer Vision—ECCV 2002. pp. 97–112. Springer Berlin Heidelberg, 2006.
[11] J. Shi, and J. Malik, "Normalized cuts and image segmentation," Pattern Analysis and Machine Intelligence, IEEE Transactions on, vol. 22, pp. 888–905, 2000.
[12] D. Hiemstra, "Using language models for information retrieval," Taaluitgeverij Neslia Paniculata, 2001.
[13] V. Lavrenko, and W.B. Croft, "Relevance based language models," In: Proceedings of the 24th annual international ACM SIGIR conference on Research and development in information retrieval. ACM, pp. 120–127, 2001.

Multimedia Technology IV – Farag, Yang & Jiao (Eds)
© 2015 Taylor & Francis Group, London, ISBN: 978-1-138-02794-7

Chinese character recognition based on 8-direction feature extraction

Ping Lu
School of Information Science and Engineering, Southeast University, Nanjing, China

Yi Yang & Bin Sheng
Department of Computer Science and Engineering, Shanghai Jiao Tong University, Shanghai, China

Ping Li
Department of Mathematics and Information Technology, Hong Kong Institute of Education, Hong Kong

Mingang Chen
Shanghai Key Laboratory of Computer Software Testing & Evaluating,
Shanghai Development Center of Computer Software Technology, Shanghai, China

Dan Wu
Information Center, China Southern Power Grid Co. Ltd., Guangzhou, China

ABSTRACT: The field of practical character recognition has seen great advances these years, owing the to proposition of effective new method and progress in computer hardware. However, lots of problems like precision and progressing speed remain to be solved. This paper proposes a useful practical optical character recognition method of both Chinese character and English character. Given a photo randomly taken, we pre-progress it to undo the influence of light and tilt. Then we separate each word to extract 8-direction chain-code feature of it. When faced with complex scene, the method we propose achieve relatively high precision and fast speed.

Keywords: OCR; formatting; 8-direction; chain-code feature; tilt correction

1 INTRODUCTION

The area of machine-printed Chinese charter has been the subject of many research studies in the past decades. Lots of methods aiming at solving practical problems, such as blurring [1], direction pattern matching [2,3], hierarchical classification [4,5] and multiple classifiers combination [6,17], have been proposed in the past few years.

The obstacles in practical character recognition are the pre-progress and separation. When dealing with randomly taken photos, the paper containing characters are usually tilt and vague, sometimes mixed with spots. The complex scene is hard to handle.

The result of pre-progress determines the final result to a certain extent. In order to maintain a relatively clean background, we employ tilt correction and shadow removal to undo the influence of tilt and light. Repeated test results prove the effectiveness of our pre-progress method. In the second, we separate each single word to extract its 8-direction chain-code feature. At last, we identify the certain character according to the 8-direction chain-code.

The result of this paper is organized as follow: some related work are introduced in the second part; the details of our method are presented in the third part; in

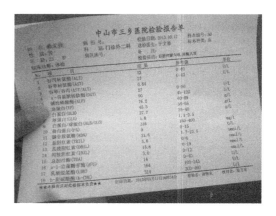

Figure 1. Example of randomly taken photo.

the fourth part, we compare the results of our method and the others'.

2 RELATED WORK

Optical Character Recognition is classified into two types, Offline recognition and online recognition. In offline recognition, the source is either an image or a scanned form of the document whereas in online recognition the successive points are represented as a function of time and the order of strokes are also available [8,9]. Here in this paper only offline recognition is dealt.

In 1929 Gustav Tauschek obtained a patent on OCR in Germany, followed by Handel who obtained a US patent on OCR in USA in 1933. In 1935 Tauschek was also granted a US patent on his method. Tauschek's machine was a mechanical device that used templates and a photo detector. RCA engineers in 1949 worked on the first primitive computer-type OCR to help blind people for the US Veterans Administration, but instead of converting the printed characters to machine language, their device converted it to machine language and then spoke the letters. It proved far too expensive and was not pursued after testing.

As for Chinese character recognition, the methods proposed up to now can be roughly grouped into two types: feature matching and structure analysis. Based on feature vector representation of character patterns, feature matching approaches usually compute a simple distance measure (Euclidean or Manhattan distance) between the test pattern and class prototypes. Sophisticated classification techniques [10,11,12], including statistical classifiers, neural networks, support vector machines (SVM), can yield higher recognition precision. Our method belong to the former type.

The methodology of Chinese character recognition is largely affected by such techniques: blurring, directional patter matching [2,3,13], modified quadratic discriminate function (MQDF) [14], etc. These techniques and their variations are still widely used in many character recognition systems.

Many methods based on feature extraction are proposed in the past few decades: normalization-cooperated chain-code feature (NCCF) [15], and gradient direction feature [16]. These feature have yielded good performance due to the sensitivity to stroke-direction variance and in sensitivity to strike-width variance.

3 OUR METHOD

Our method consists of three steps: first, we convert the input color photo into corrected black-and-white picture to undo the influence of tilt and shadow; secondly, we detect Chinese character in the progressed photo and separate them into single word; at last, we extract the 8-direction chain-code feature of each single word and identify them according to the feature we get. The procedures of our algorithm are presented in Figure 2.

3.1 *Pre-progress*

Given a certain photo, we deal with the tilt and light first. Almost all the randomly taken photo are accompanied by shadow and tilt which impact recognition of characters. To undo the influence the these

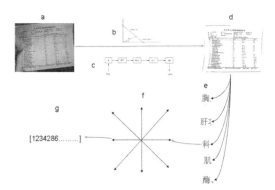

Figure 2.   Procedures of our method. Give a input photo (a); we use Hough Transform (b) to detect the lines in this photo, which are used in the tilt correction; then homomorphic filter (c) is used to undo the influence of light; the black-and-white picture (d) is maintained; secondly, we separate the picture (d) into single Chinese word (e); the 8-direction chain-code feature vectors (g) are calculated via the 8-direction chain-code feature filter (f).

bias, we convert the input color photo into corrected black-and-white picture.

At first, we convert the input color photo to gray scale, for the reason that Hough Transformation and homomorphic filter can be only applied to gray scale image.

When dealing with the tilt of input photo, we use Hough Transform to detect the lines in the picture, which are used to determine the slope of the whole picture. The parameter formula we use is:

$$p = x \times \cos(\theta) + y \times \sin(\theta)$$

In which p represent a point on the line. In average, we select longest five longest straight lines in a picture and take the average of the slope of the five lines as the slope of the picture.

Then, we use homomorphic filter to undo the light bias influence of given photo. An image can be represented by the product of illuminance and reflection.

$$f(x,y) = i(x,y) \times r(x,y)$$

Thus, we can use homomorphic filter in frequency domain to compress the illuminace part, removing the influence of light and improve the quality of input image.

3.2 *Separation*

Given the clean image generated by pre-progress procedure, we detect the words blocks in the whole image and divide them into single Chinese words.

The blank between printed Chinese characters is the key to extract words block or single word in the input image. We start from the left-top corner of the image and take the black pixel as foreground while the white pixel as background. All the connect foreground pixel

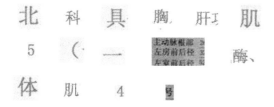

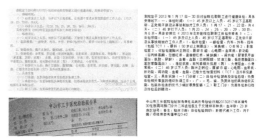

Figure 3. Separated blocks and single words.

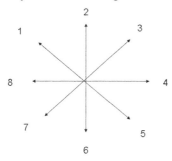

Figure 4. Example of 8-direction chain-code.

Figure 5. Brief presentation of our result.

Table 1. Average CPU times (ms) of feature extraction on CASIA database.

	Direction	Blurring
chn	0.121	0.439
nccf	0.458	0.752
grd-g	0.329	1.276
ours	0.217	0.533

are regard as a block respectively. When it comes to the right-bottom corner, we end the search of the image and save all the blocks we find.

After that, we get several blocks and many single words. We judge a divided image part a block or a single word according to its size. As for the big blocks, we divide them into several smaller image parts that contain only a single Chinese word respectively by using stricter filter.

3.3 Recognition

Given the separated single words, we extract the 8-direction chain-code feature of each Chinese word respectively.

Start from the left-top corner of image that contain only a single word, we set the first foreground pixel as start, and there are eight pixels around it. The eight pixels are numbered by numbers one to eight. When we find the next foreground pixel on the detect direction, we save its number as a part of the chain-code. This progress ends when it returns to the start pixel. The chain-code we get can be used to identify the single Chinese word. When it is compared with ground truth, we judge the word that the image contains as the nearest one in ground truth.

To put it in another way, we extract the contour of single Chinese word as its feature. To make the recognition procedure faster, we use 8-direction chain-code as our feature but not 12-direction chain-code.

4 RESULT COMPARATION

4.1 Brife presentation

Our method gets 100 percent precision when dealing with simple scene. When faced with complex scene, we still maintain high precision.

Table 2. Average CPU times (ms) of normalization on CASIA database. Binary normalized image involves smoothing.

	Coordinate	Binary	Grayscale
LN	0.002	0.318	0.133
NLN	0.115	0.331	0.143
MN	0.017	0.321	0.126
BMN	0.024	0.332	0.135
MCBA	0.032	0.336	0.137
LDPI	0.266	1.512	1.282
P2DMN	0.143	1.514	1.236
P2DBMN	0.147	1.536	1.274
Ours	0.107	0.401	0.137

4.2 Computation time comparation

To compare the computational complexity of different methods, we profile the processing time in two tasks: coordinate mapping and normalized image generation. Smoothing is involved in binary normalized image, but not for gray scale image. On the test samples of CAISA database, we counted the CPU time on Pentium-4.3 GHz processor. The average time per sample are shown in Table 1. We can see that our method outperform NCCF and grd-g methods.

In the tables below, the NCCF method is denoted by nccf, and the gradient direction feature by grd-g. For the chn method and our method, the normalized binary image is smoothed using a connectivity-preserving smoothing algorithm. Gradient feature is extracted from gray scale normalized image.

4.3 Precision rate comparation

We compared our method with other methods on error rate on two large datasets of handprinted characters (constrained writing). We use two classifiers for classification: the Euclidean distance to minimum distance classifier and the MQDF. To reduce the classifier complexity and improving classification accuracy, the feature vector is transformed to a lower dimensionality by Fisher linear discriminant analysis (FLDA). The dimensionality is set to 160 for all feature types. Result shows that we exceed most contemporary methods.

	Euclidean			MQDF		
	chn	nccf	grd-g	chn	nccf	grd-g
LN	6.36	5.94	5.97	2.38	2.09	2.11
NLN	2.56	2.06	2.30	1.00	0.77	0.86
MN	2.35	2.07	2.12	0.95	0.83	0.82
BMN	2.33	2.04	2.09	0.92	0.81	0.80
MCBA	2.52	2.19	2.27	1.00	0.84	0.86
OURS	2.92	2.27	2.14	1.02	0.80	0.83

5 CONCLUSION

We propose a practical method of printed Chinese character recognition. We pre-progress the input image to remove the light and correct the tilt of image; then we precisely divide the image into small parts that contain only a single word; after the 8-direction chain-code feature of characters are extracted respectively, we recognize each character according to their feature vector.

The results prove that our method outperform some existing methods. And our method has good trade-off between precision and algorithm complexity. Its accuracy and fast speed suggest its wide application in practical.

ACKNOWLEDGEMENTS

This work was supported by the National Natural Science Foundation of China (No. 61202154, 61133009), the National Basic Research Project of China (No. 2011CB302203), Shanghai Pujiang Program (No. 13PJ1404500), the Science and Technology Commission of Shanghai Municipality Program (No. 13511505000), the Open Projects Program of National Laboratory of Pattern Recognition, and the Open Project Program of the State Key Lab of CAD&CG (Grant No. A1401), Zhejiang University, the HKIEd-Internal Research Grant (ref. RG 77/2013-2014R).

REFERENCES

[1] T. Iijima, H. Genchi, K. Mori, A theory of character recognition by pattern matching method, Proc. 1st IJCPR, 1973, pp. 50–56.

[2] M. Yasuda, H. Fujisawa, An improved correlation method for character recognition, Systems, Computers, and Controls, 10(2): 29–38, 1979 (Translated from Trans. IEICE Japan, 62-D(3): 217–224, 1979).

[3] Y. Yamashita, K. Higuchi, Y. Yamada, Y. Haga, Classification of handprinted Kanji characters by the structured segment matching method, Pattern Recognition Letters, 1: 475–479, 1983.

[4] R. Casey, G. Nagy, Recognition of printed Chinese characters, IEEE Trans. Electronic Computers, EC-15(1): 91–101, 1966.

[5] S. Yamamoto, A. Nakajima, K. Nakata, Chinese character recognition by hierarchical pattern matching, Proc. 1st IJCPR, 1973, pp. 183–194.

[6] L. Xu, A. Krzyzak, C. Y. Suen, Methods of combining multiple classifiers and their applications to handwriting recognition, IEEE Trans. System, Man, and Cybernetics, 27(3): 418–435, 1992.

[7] J. Kittler, M. Hatef, R.P.W. Duin, J. Matas, On combining classifiers, IEEE Trans. Pattern Analysis and Machine Intelligence, 20(3): 226–239, 1998.

[8] C.-L. Liu, S. Jaeger, and M. Nakagawa, Online recognition of Chinese characters: the state-of-the-art, IEEE Trans. Pattern Anal. Mach. In-tell. 26(2)(2004) 198–213. inria-00120408, version 1–14 Dec 2006.

[9] A. Kawamura, K. Yura, T. Hayama, Y. Hidai, T. Minamikawa, A. Tanaka, and S. Ma-suda, On-line recognition of freely handwrit-ten Japanese characters using directional feature densities, inProc. 11th Int'l Conf. on Pattern Recognition, The Hague, 1992, Vol. 2, 183–186. inria-00120408, version 1–14 Dec. 2006.

[10] K. Fukunaga, Introduction to Statistical Pattern Recognition, 2nd edition (Academic Press, 1990).

[11] R.O. Duda, P.E. Hart, and D.G. Stork, Pattern Classification, 2nd edition (Wiley Interscience, 2001).

[12] A.K. Jain, R.P.W. Duin, and J. Mao, Statistical pattern recognition: a review, IEEE Trans. Pattern Anal. Mach. Intell. 22(1)(2000), 4–37.

[13] H. Fujisawa and C.-L. Liu, Directional pattern matching for character recognition revisited, in Proc. 7th Int'l Conf. on Document Analysis and Recognition, Edinburgh, Scotland, 2003, 794–798.

[14] F. Kimura, K. Takashina, S. Tsuruoka, and Y.Miyake, Modified quadratic discriminant functions and the application to Chinese character recognition,IEEE Trans. Pattern Anal. Mach. Intell. 9(1)(1987), 149–153.

[15] Y.X. Gu, Q.R. Wang, C.Y. Suen, Application of a multilayer decision tree in computer recognition of Chinese characters, IEEE Trans. Pattern Analysis and Machine Intelligence, 5(1): 83–89, 1983.

[16] F. Kimura, T. Wakabayashi, S. Tsuruoka, and Y. Miyake, Improvement of handwritten Japanese character recognition using weighted direction code histogram, Pattern Recognition, 30(8)(1997), 1329–1337.

Multimedia Technology IV – Farag, Yang & Jiao (Eds)
© *2015 Taylor & Francis Group, London, ISBN: 978-1-138-02794-7*

Visual tracking via discriminative random ferns

Hui Wen
Beijing Key Laboratory of IOT Information Security Technology,
Institute of Information Engineering, CAS, Beijing, China
University of Chinese Academy of Sciences, Beijing, China

Shuixian Chen, Shiming Ge & Limin Sun
Beijing Key Laboratory of IOT Information Security Technology,
Institute of Information Engineering, CAS, Beijing, China

ABSTRACT: This paper presents a method for long-term tracking in unconstrained environments. It provides discriminative random fens that integrated into the tracking by detection framework as the object detector for improving the capability of tracking appearance variation. The proposed random ferns method aims to adapt the discriminative ferns with better normalized cross correlation score and discard the weak discriminative ferns that may cause the drift error by online updating and feature space regeneration. Besides, the tracking by detection framework considers the compressive tracker as a short-term tracker for improving the robustness and effectiveness of the approach. Experiments on public datasets demonstrate that the proposed method have a better performance while comparing with several tracking algorithms.

Keywords: Random ferns; Discriminative ferns; Object tracking; Online updating

1 INTRODUCTION

As one of the most important areas in computer vision, visual tracking has made great strides in recent years. However, visual tracking still have a number of problems that needed to be addressed. The key problem is the long-term tracking issues: the object becomes occluded, significantly change scale or leave the field-of-view. In order to address the problems of the long-term tracking, training a discriminative model with self learning mechanism is considered as an effective method and has becomes popular recently [1–3].

Consider that the long-term tracking can be benefit from combine tracking and detection technology, a class of tracking algorithms called tracking by detection [4] method has been proposed to overcome the long-term tracking issues. According to the preliminary researches, the tracker and detector have their own weakness while tracking the target object in a long-term. Tracking algorithms aim at estimating the object motion [5] or finding the candidate object from neighbor patches. During the tracking, trackers accumulate the drift error and would fail if the object disappears from the camera view. Detection based algorithms aim at estimating the object location in every frame independently [6]. Different from the trackers, detectors do not drift and not fail if the object disappears from the camera view, but the detector cannot handle the

situation such as illumination changes, object deformation and object occlusion. It is potential to benefit one from another if they operate simultaneously. Based on this idea, tracking by detection method solves the long-term tracking task by combining the tracker and the detector with a self learning mechanism. The tracker can provide weakly labeled data for training the detector and the detector can reinitialize the tracker for eliminating the tracking drift error.

Researches on tracking by detection method suggest that training the target object's appearance by two processes in different views is benefit for robust tracking. As the co-training framework proposed by Blum and Mitchell [7], training two classifiers on two conditionally independent views of the data provide a better accurate and help to avoid the error accumulation problem. From this point of view, the tracking by detection algorithms training the object in tracking and detection process separately. In addition, it provides a self learning mechanism to overcome the problems caused by variation of the target object. The self learning mechanism build a connection with tracking components for labeling and learning the variation of the target object's appearance. However, these tracking by detection methods also have their drawbacks. A weak tracker would cause drift for the self-learning of detection by accumulating the slight inaccuracy tracking results. On the other hand, a weak discriminative detector would fail to reinitialize the tracker with the correct object's position. For these reasons, the tracking by detection framework should contain a discriminative detector, a robust tracker and a self learning mechanism with sample constraint.

For fast and robust visual tracking, the tracker and the detector should be processed in real time with good performance. Ozuysal et al. [8] demonstrated that fern-based classifier outperforms the combination of the trees and achieves impressive detection results. The greatest advantage of random ferns is its speed and simplicity while compared to the other detection methods. Compressive tracking [9] algorithm shows its fast speed and performs better compared to several tracking algorithms in terms of efficiency, accuracy and robustness.

In this paper, we present a tracking by detection method with a discriminative detector and a robust tracker, which is based on discriminative random ferns and compressive tracking. The proposed method attempts to update discriminative ferns online for separating the object from its background and use a robust short-term tracker for labeling the positive samples with normalized cross correlation constraint.

2 APPROACH

In this section, we briefly introduce the random ferns and compressive tracker for better understands the proposed method, which is an enhanced tracking algorithm that based on these methods. After that, we present the details of the proposed method in the final subsection.

2.1 Random ferns

Random ferns is a Semi-naive Bayesian classifier for fast classification, which provides a set of binary features for modeling the appearance of the target object and uses Bayesian method for classification. Instead of the random forest, random ferns uses Bayes to model the feature of the patch by replace the trees with non-hierarchical ferns. let c_i, $i = 1, \ldots, H$ be the set of classes and let $f_i, j = 1, \ldots, H$ be the set of binary features. The process of classification aims to assign a set of feature for a similar class. The conditional probability of selecting class c_i based on bayesian theorem can be expressed as:

$$\hat{c}_i = \arg\max_{c_i} P(C = c_i | f_1, f_2, ..., f_N)$$
$$= \arg\max_{c_i} \frac{P(f_1, f_2, ..., f_N | C = c_i) P(C = c_i)}{P(f_1, f_2, ..., f_N)} \quad (1)$$

Assuming that the probability $P(C)$ is the uniform prior over classes, we consider it as a constant and ignore it. The denominator does not depend on C, so it also can be taken as a constant and the formula can be written as:

$$\hat{c}_i = argmax_{c_i} P(f_1, f_2, ..., f_N | C = c_i) \quad (2)$$

Since it is not practical to model the joint distribution of all features, they are grouped into sets of small size which defined as *ferns*. The joint distribution of all features in each fern is computed and conditional probability becomes

$$P(f_1, f_2, ..., f_N | C = c_i) = \prod_{k=1}^{M} P(F_k | C = c_i) \quad (3)$$

where $F_k = \{f_{\sigma(k,1)}, f_{\sigma(k,2)}, \ldots, f_{\sigma(k,S)}\}, k = 1, \ldots, M$ represent kth fern and $\sigma(k, j)$ is a random permutation function with range $1, \ldots, N$. For each fern F_m, its conditional probability can be written as:

$$P_{k,c_i} = P(F_m = | C = c_i) \quad (4)$$

and thus F_m can take $K = 2^S$ values. According to the maximum likelihood estimate from the training samples, p_{k,c_i} can be computed as:

$$P_{k,c_i} = \frac{N_{k,c_i}}{N_{c_i}} \quad (5)$$

where N_{k,c_i} is the number of training samples of class c_i that evaluates to fern value k and N_{c_i} is the total number of samples for class c_i. Therefore, p_{k,c_i} can be estimated for each fern independently.

Note that the random fern method use randomization not only in feature selection but also in grouping. S features forms a group for representing a fern and each group is independent from each other with random selection. Although its performance is proved to be better than several detection algorithms, the fern feature shows its weakness while detecting the object with variation. The reason is that the discriminative performance of the ferns relies on the randomization, which is not uncertain for detection.

2.2 Short-term tracker

The short-term tracker is used for providing tracking information in a different view to improve the performance of the long-term detector. We choose a robust tracker named compressive tracker (CT) to implement the task of the short-term tracker.

CT considers tracking as classification. As the most of the tracking method, it assumes that the location and size of object in first frame is known for initialing. The classifier is constructed in the beginning and updated during the process of the tracking. At each frame, the samples from current frame are used to train the tracking classifier. Positive samples are sampled near current object location, while negative samples are sampled far away from current object location. Due to the assumption that object location is not changed notably, the object location at the next frame is searched around the object location at current frame. The location with the maximal confidence is considered as the tracking result. Besides,

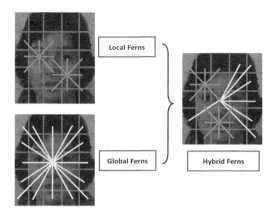

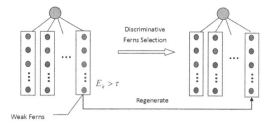

Figure 2. The process of selecting discriminative ferns by regenerating the ferns and discarding the weak ferns.

Figure 1. Two types of the ferns: local ferns and global ferns. Local ferns is the pixel pair that generated in random neighbour patch. Global ferns is the pixel pair that generated in center patch and the patch that away from the center.

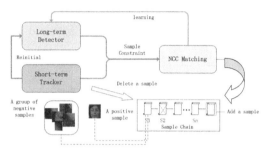

Figure 3. The framework of the proposed tracking method.

CT compresses the feature of the object from high dimension space to random low dimension space for real time tracking. Specifically, the high-dimensional feature used in compressive tracking is a series of rectangle features which have different locations and sizes within the region of interest, just like haar features. The large set of features is then compressively sensed using a very sparse measurement matrix with random projection method. After that, CT use them to train an appearance bayes model for estimating the probability of the positive samples for classification.

2.3 Learning with Discriminative Ferns

As mentioned in section 3.1, the ferns are a set of the binary code trained by random pixel-pair, the design of the binary feature is important for classifying the object from the others. For improving the robustness of the long-term tracking, we design two types of the binary feature called local ferns and global ferns. Fig. 1 shows that the intuitive concept of the ferns designed by our approach. The proposed binary feature is designed to reduce the less discriminative ferns that generated by picking the pixel-pair randomly. Specifically, we divide the initial object into 5×5 parts. Each part called grid is used for generating the proper ferns. The local ferns is considered as the random pixel-pair that generated by picking the pixel-pair from the random neighbor grids. The global fern is considered as the random pixel-pair by picking a pixel in the center grid and another pixel in the grids that away from the center. The final random ferns take random combinations of the local ferns and global ferns called hybrid ferns to train and detect the object.

Despite of designing the binary feature ferns, we proposed a feedback mechanism to adapt the discriminative ferns and discard the less discriminative ferns

for improving the robustness of the long-term detector. The architecture is similar to the other tracking by detection method, but the proposed method providing an additional error learning mechanism. During the tracking, the discriminative random ferns focuses on the detection performance of each fern F_k. While updating positive sample for online learning, the proposed method records the detection error E_k for each fern F_k. As Fig. 2 shows, While a branch of the random ferns always fails to detect the true object (accumulated detection error E_k is larger than the error threshold τ), the random ferns will regenerate a new ferns to replace the weak ferns and train it with the online samples. The online detection ground truth is judged by NCC scores with recorded online samples and the tracked result achieved by short-term tracker. Besides, the online samples need the extra information to evaluate its confidence. Therefore, compressive tracker is used as the short-term tracker that provides the spatio-temporal constraint for choosing the reliable samples to update the random ferns.

Additionally, for managing the increased online samples, we proposed sample chain architecture for saving the online samples. The sample chain only save the object sample from first frame in node S_1 and recent $n - 1$ frame samples in nodes $\{S_2, \ldots, S_n\}$. Each node in sample chains contains a group of negative samples and a positive sample. While the number of samples is more than n, sample chain delete the node S_2 and move the nodes after S_2.

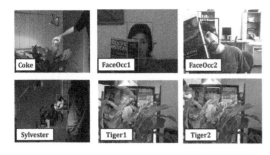

Figure 4. Snapshots of our approach on the public tracking sequences.

The proposed algorithm can be expressed as follows:

Algorism 1: Our Tracking Approach
Input: Detection error threshold τ, the length of samples chain n, the object bounding box in first frame
1: Get the first frame in image sequence;;
2: Initial the random ferns detector;
3: Initial the compressive tracker;
4: Save the first positive sample and negative samples in sample chain S_1;
5: Repeat
2 | Get the current frame in image sequence;
2 | Get the object bounding box from previous frame;
2 | Track the object in current frame;
2 | Detect the object in current frame;
2 | Calculate the tracked object NCC scores NCC_t and detected object NCC scores NCC_d with the samples in sample chain;
10 | **If** $NCC_t > 0.5$&&$NCC_d < NCC_t$ **Then**
11 | | Add the tracked sample and the corresponding negative samples to the sample chain
12 | | **If** the length of samples chain $> n$ **Then**
11 | | | remove the node S_2 in sample chain;
12 | | **End If**
11 | | | record the decision error E_k for each fern;
11 | | **If** $E_k > \tau$ **Then**
11 | | | regenerate the fern F_k with online samples;
11 | | **End If**
11 | | Updating the random ferns detector;
11 | **End If**
11 | Compare NCC_t and NCC_d, choosing the object bounding box with larger scores;
11 | Updating the compressive tracker;
24: Until
25: Get no more frame in image sequence;

---

3 EXPERIMENTS

All of the video sequences come from the public tracking database and the ground truth of the object location is obtained from manual labels at each frame. The experiments use the number of the successfully tracked subsequences to evaluate the tracking results. This criterion is used in the PASCAL VOC challenge and the score is defined as:

$$score = \frac{area(G \cap T)}{area(G \cup T)} \tag{6}$$

where G is the ground truth bounding box and T is the tracked bounding box. We consider the object to be tracked correctly if the score is greater than 0.5. In the experiments, we set the number of the sample chain to 50 and error threshold $\tau = 30$.

In terms of the accuracy of tracked frames, table i shows the experimental results compared with several recent state-of-the-art approaches, including OAB [10], ORF [11], FT [12], MILT [2], and PNT [5]. The proposed method outperforms the other tracking methods and achieves 30fps in PC with i5-530M CPU, 4G memory.

Video Sequence	Frames	OAB	ORF	FT	MILT	PNT	Ours
Coke	292	18.4	17.0	11.6	44.5	40.3	**63.8**
Face1	888	72.9	97.5	97.5	89.6	95.6	**98.8**
Face2	820	76.3	68.9	63.7	92.9	94.5	**98.1**
Sylvester	1345	56.1	69.2	82.6	82.4	87.6	**94.7**
Tiger 1	354	31.6	27.3	26.5	73.8	69.4	**83.3**
Tiger 2	365	35.5	20.8	23.5	76.5	72.9	**86.7**

4 CONCLUSION

We have presented a new tracking by detection method which combines the discriminative random ferns and the compressive tracker in our tracking framework. In order to overcome the less discriminative ferns problem, we design local ferns and global ferns for better feature representation and providing online ferns regeneration mechanism for improving the detection performance. We also proposed sample chain architecture for managing the increased online samples. Experimental results demonstrate that the satisfying tracking performance can be obtained by automatic selecting proper ferns. Comparison with several approaches shows the superior performance of our method.

For future work, we will study more sophisticated learning methods for accurate detection and design more reliable constraints for robust tracking. As the development of the sparse coding or dictionary learning technology, we plan to use this technology for robust tracking with better feature representation.

ACKNOWLEDGMENT

This work was supported in part by the Strategic Priority Research Program of CAS (No. XDA06040101).

REFERENCES

[1] L. Cehovin;ehovin, M. Kristan, and A. Leonardis, "Robust visual tracking using an adaptive coupled-layer visual model," IEEE Transactions on Pattern Analysis and Machine Intelligence, vol. 35, no. 4, pp. 941–953, 2013.

[2] B. Babenko, M.-H. Yang, and S. Belongie, "Robust object trackingwith online multiple instance learning," Pattern Analysis and Machine Intelligence, IEEE Transactions on, vol. 33, no. 8, pp. 1619–1632, Aug 2011.

[3] S. Duffner and C. Garcia, "Pixeltrack: A fast adaptive algorithm for tracking non-rigid objects," in Computer Vision (ICCV), 2013 IEEE International Conference on, Dec 2013, pp. 2480–2487.

[4] Z. Kalal, K. Mikolajczyk, and J. Matas, "Tracking-learning-detection," Pattern Analysis and Machine Intelligence, IEEE Transactions on, vol. 34, no. 7, pp. 1409–1422, July 2012.

[5] Z. Kalal, J. Matas, and K. Mikolajczyk, "P-n learning: Bootstrapping binary classifiers by structural constraints," in Computer Vision and Pattern Recognition (CVPR), 2010 IEEE Conference on, June 2010, pp. 49–56.

[6] S. Avidan, "Ensemble tracking," Pattern Analysis and Machine Intelligence, IEEE Transactions on, vol. 29, no. 2, pp. 261–271, Feb 2007.

[7] A. Blum and T. Mitchell, "Combining labeled and unlabeled data with co-training," in Proceedings of the eleventh annual conference on Computational learning theory. ACM, 1998, pp. 92–100.

[8] M. Ozuysal, P. Fua, and V. Lepetit, "Fast keypoint recognition in ten lines of code," in Computer Vision and Pattern Recognition, 2007. CVPR '07. IEEE Conference on, June 2007, pp. 1–8.

[9] K. Zhang, L. Zhang, and M. Yang, "Fast compressive tracking," Pattern Analysis and Machine Intelligence, IEEE Transactions on, vol. 36, no. 10, pp. 2002–2015, Oct 2014.

[10] H. Grabner and H. Bischof, "On-line boosting and vision," in Computer Vision and Pattern Recognition, 2006 IEEE Computer Society Conference on, vol. 1, June 2006, pp. 260–267.

[11] A. Saffari, C. Leistner, J. Santner, M. Godec, and H. Bischof, "Online random forests," in Computer Vision Workshops (ICCV Workshops), 2009 IEEE 12th International Conference on, Sept 2009, pp. 1393–1400.

[12] A. Adam, E. Rivlin, and I. Shimshoni, "Robust fragments-based tracking using the integral histogram," in Computer Vision and Pattern Recognition, 2006 IEEE Computer Society Conference on, vol. 1, June 2006, pp. 798–805.

Multimedia Technology IV – Farag, Yang & Jiao (Eds)
© *2015 Taylor & Francis Group, London, ISBN: 978-1-138-02794-7*

Classifying collaborative behavior in the form of behavioral stereotypes in collaborative mobile applications

Rhys Tague, Anthony Maeder & Jim Basilakis
School of Computing, Engineering and Mathematics, University of Western Sydney, Australia

ABSTRACT: Online Social networks empower users to collaborate with other users through complex interfaces. They enable users to take on various behaviors to achieve an objective or goal together. However, with the rise of smart devices and their small view ports these interfaces have been restricted. This results in the user having to wait until they have access to a desktop version before they can interact with these complex interfaces again. This paper presents a framework for classifying collaborative behavior in the form of Behavioral Stereotypes. In addition it presents initial results of a implementation of the framework in a collaborative mobile application to demonstrate its ability to help understand user behavior and how it changes from social ties users establish.

Keywords: classifying behaviour; collaborative envrionment; user modelling; mobile computing

1 INTRODUCTION

Actions speak louder than words. This old proverb can be mapped to a user's interactions with an interface. When a user clicks, slides, scrolls, or manipulates an interface their actions not only result in system feedback, but also behaviors and intentions to achieve an overall goal or desire.

Today, with Online Social Networks (OSNs) making up 66% of online usage within Australia alone [1], users are able to create new behaviors and have new intentions with other users through interfaces. This has derived from OSNs enabling users to connect and collaborate together through interfaces to carry out collaborative tasks together. Users are encouraged to create social ties with other users or nodes, such as media. For example, GitHub, an online programming code sharing and publishing environment, enables users to achieve code production and maintenance through the use of various interfaces [2]. In this environment users are able to take on varying stereotypical behaviors you would normally associate within a software development company. For instance, a user is able discuss future development releases, identify bugs, provide patches and also create documentation. In addition, they are able to do this for multiple projects with different subsets of users.

Although these environments can provide such interfaces, their ability to provide the same variance through smart devices is limited. The viewport smart devices possess can be a fraction of the size of its desktop counterpart. For this reason, interfaces are more focused and sub-level interactions are found deeper within the interface or don't exist at all. It is up to the designer of the interface to choose the most crucial or important features for their environment [3]. Therefore, the capability of the user to carry out stereotypical behavior, like that found in complex interfaces, diminishes. Instead, they are left only with simplistic behaviors that may or may not coincide with their normal behavior and current needs.

By understanding a user's stereotypical behavior within a smart device environment, users could be provided with personalized and frictionless interfaces to overcome this barrier found within smart device environments.

This paper presents initial results for classifying stereotypical collaborative user behavior within a smart device environment. It demonstrates this through the use of a collaborative mobile application for the capture of user interactions with other users or social ties. These interactions were classified through the use of a framework implemented within the mobile application environment.

2 BACKGROUND

Today with OSNs the type of information that can be collected is endless. This information can consist of user preferences or their interactions within an environment. This information though can be difficult to understand without a formal approach. One approach is user modeling [4]. It provides methods and theories on how to understand user behavior and capture data in a meaningful way to create a model that represents a user. Although effective, a user model's characteristics are based on the purpose of the user model's existence, which leaves it open for interpretation. For this reason, in recent times there have been many approaches to user modeling, and more importantly, classifying user behavior, or roles, within OSNs [5][6]. These approaches focus on singular users and their overall behavior within an OSN as an entity, or their position within the user population, or a sub-set of users. The behaviors, or roles, used for these studies are general role or *status* based, which is dependent on their content types and the number of items published. There are other approaches for classifying which exists using online social network analysis and is more aligned with this work [7]. Instead of how much content a user publishes, it focuses on the connections made and actions taken on those to find patterns of behavior and usage. The approach is after the interaction has taken place, and therefore, can only be used as future steering instead of assisting the user at the point of interaction.

Many user-adaptive techniques have been used to prevent this lag time seen with these approaches to OSNs and other collaborative environments [8][9]. They achieve this through machine learning techniques and other logic based systems. However, their focus is either on a individual user or the whole population, such as in collaborative filtering [9].

3 METHOD

3.1 *Environment*

This study involved the development of an online collaborative environment focusing on tools and actions towards collaboration. The resulting environment was a mobile application built using the PhoneGap Software Developer Kit. The mobile application was provided in the Google Play Store as a free download with public access. Upon installation a basic registration form with personal details, such as email address, was presented to all participants before they could be part of the environment. The only criteria for users to enter the environment were that they were 18 years of age or older.

Within the environment the tools available promoted social interaction and collaboration for the purpose of content creation and discovery. The theme for content was around establishments that served coffee or food. The tools provided in this collaborative environment were simple traditional tools found in other similar environments such as Yelp [10]. Every tool within the environment had three major objectives, one, to promote collaboration between users for the purpose of content creation, two, awareness of other users and locations and their interactions, and finally, social tie creation. This involved users being able to communicate with each other and also be notified when a user carried out an action towards a social tie that is relative to another. Users were also able to favorite other users and locations to "keep tabs" on their interactions.

Figure 1.   Screenshot of content publication tools.

The sets of tools available to users were: *content publication, content reply, content annotation, expanding views, location creation.*

Content publication empowers users to create new and original content for a geographical location. In addition, they were also able to create new geographical locations for other users to interact with. Fig. 1 presents a screenshot of the tools available for this category. They allowed a user to segment their publication into one of five service areas an establishment possesses: Coffee, Food, Price, Customer Service, and Location. They were also able to compound the publication with images and a review of 140 characters or less. Upon completing the content publication the content created is accessible globally within the environment for others to discover. This is shown in Fig. 2. A global stream of all user content is presented for user's to discover and be aware of other user behavior and interactions.

Content annotation is the annotation in the form of content replies to and tagging content published. Annotation allowed users to establish a dialogue around content a user may have published. Users were also able to annotate locations in the form of small brief summary statements so others users could discover when finding a new location. Fig. 3 provides a screenshot of tagging user content. The tags result in hyperlinks allowing users to *"follow breadcrumbs"* to discover new content. This category of tools also allowed user's to add comments to existing content in the form of additional 140 character replies.

Expanding views enabled users to explore additional content for user publication or geographical location. Expanding views are a common element used in smart device applications to cater for the small view port they possess [3]. Fig. 4 gives an example of an expanded view for the user to investigate additional content about a location.

Figure 2. Screenshot of global status stream.

Figure 3. Screenshot of available annotation tools.

Location creation was the final tool set available. It allowed users to use their geographical location to generate new locations within the environment for other users to annotate and publish new content to.

3.2 Framework

Fig. 5 presents the model of the framework and its components implemented within the application. The framework extends between client and server side of the application environment to achieve classification. Having the framework on the client enables real time logging of user interaction that may or may not result in content publication. For instance, a user carries out large amounts of content scrolling that doesn't result in content creation or manipulation.

Figure 4. Screenshot of an expanding view.

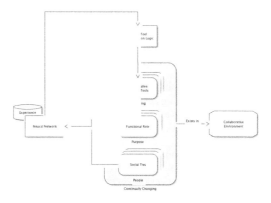

Figure 5. A simple representation of the framework components.

Although the framework extends to the client, or smart device, it is limited to meta-data and basic interaction identification data. The meta-data consists of the tool's identification, and the stereotypical behaviors the tool are categorized in. The behaviors used are derived from behavioral stereotypes a representation of common behavior when interacting with social ties [11]. Only three behavioral stereotypes were chosen for this environment: *publisher, annotator,* and *lurker.* These three behavior stereotypes align with the tool sets used through out the environment. A *Publisher* stereotype results when a user predominantly creates content with or for a common social tie. For instance, when they continually visit a particular coffee location or user profile and publish new content for that particular user or location. An *Annotator* stereotype results when a user predominantly annotates a common social tie's interactions or content. The final stereotype, *Lurker,* is a result of a user consuming or discovering content that a social tie creates or annotates, yet does not interact with.

The server side of the framework composes of a dynamic node neural network for the purpose of generalizing behavior towards social ties and user collaboration. This type of artificial neural network was chosen because of its ability to be trained over a period of time, and also the ability to not know and adapt to the environment's social network that will exist in the future.

To maintain performance, the training of the neural network was carried out for every user session that was 24 hours old or more. The training consisted of back propagating the cached interaction packages sent from the client. Below is an example of such an interaction package as a JSON string:

```
{'inputs':    [1,    'review-creator',    'u3'],
'outputs': ['publisher', 'annotator', 'lurker'],
'train-key': 'publisher']}
```

From this example the package is made up of three objects: Inputs, outputs and a training key. These objects are used for the neural network during back propagation (training). Inputs consist of a user id, interface tool id, and social tie id. The nature of the dynamic node neural network enables the outputs to be any number of behaviors. This flexibility enables new tools that may present new behaviors to be integrated in the environment without having to alter the environment or framework in the future. Finally the last segment of the package is the training key. This is the behavior stereotype shown by the user during the interaction with the tool, and it has to be one of the elements within the output object.

The final component of the framework is the use of the classification returned by the framework. This is in the form of a behavior weighting. Each behavior that a user can undertake with a social tie is given a weighting from −1 to +1. This weighting can be used to personalize the interface based on the social tie and current interface present.

4   RESULTS

The recruitment of participants involved the posting of brochures and dissemination of material for the purpose of downloading the application from the Google Play Store. Registration was open to anyone who was able to download and install the application on a compatible device. Upon registration users were asked for their email address, and basic details. These details were used to provide daily emails to remind them to use the app.

The initial recruitment phase resulted in 22 participants downloading and registering for the application. Of these 22 participants, 16 have carried out initial interaction in the environment. This initial interaction ranges from browsing to content creation. They have also created 54 geographical locations for others to review and interact with. This has lead to 185 content producing interactions. For instance, location reviews and annotation of those reviews.

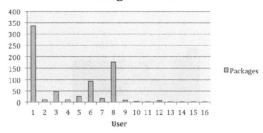

Figure 6.   Distribution of behaviour packages created by the framework for each user.

Table 1.   Results created by the framework for behaviuoral stereotype.

User	Publsiher	Lurker	Annotator
1	0.2695	0.7133	0.0608
2	0.286	0.6489	0.0335
3	0.239	0.6281	0.0271
4	0.3796	0.6761	0.0659
5	0.1664	0.7048	−0.0158
6	0.3821	0.5998	0.0386
7	0.054	0.7625	−0.0327
8	0.1134	0.7154	0.1057
10	0.2508	0.6109	0.0569
11	0.0771	0.5476	−0.0045
12	0.3017	0.5127	−0.0073

From these standard interactions the framework has created 745 interaction packages with an average of 46.56 packages per user. Although the average number of packages per user is high the standard deviation is 87.12. This is a result of dominant users within the environment producing the majority of the interactions.

Figure 6 shows the distribution of these packages. The users are ordered in the date of the registration. The first user, being the user who has been in the system the longest has the largest number of packages. This is a result of continual use over the period of time. The most recent users, 13, 14, 15, and 16 only have one behavior package consisting of lurking. For this reason they were not passed through the neural network for classifying.

Table 1 presents the results produced by the framework of the dominant behavioral stereotype each user presented when interacting in the environment with no social ties. These results represent the weighting of behavior between −1 and +1. The closer the value is towards +1 the more dominant the behavior. After analyzing these results the users have shown a dominant behavioral stereotype of *Lurker* consistently throughout the environment. This coincides with many other studies when users enter a new environment where they *lurk* and explore before they participate [12].

168

Although all users present *Lurker* globally, each user's behavioral stereotype changes when the framework uses a user's social tie to determine their behavioral stereotype. For brevity, analysis of only a few examples is given.

User 1, User 6 and User 8 have the most behavior packages. These users have established social ties amongst each other. When analyzing User 1 to User 6, User 1's behavioral stereotype remains as a *Lurker*, however their *Publisher* value increases considerably; *Publisher:* 0.5431, *Lurker:* 0.7268, *Annotator:* 0.0400. The inverse to this relationship though, User 6 to User 1, results in User 6's dominate behavioral stereotype changing to *Publisher*; *Publisher:* 0.7007, *Lurker:* 0.6613, *Annotator:* −0.092. User 1 to User 8 results in a similar to that of User 1 to User 6: *Publisher:* 0.5014, *Lurker:* 0.6759, *Annotator:* 0.0419.

5 CONCLUSION

This paper has presented a framework for classifying user behavior in a collaborative mobile application in the form of behavioral stereotypes. In addition, initial results have been presented showing early stages of generalized stereotypical behavior and more personalized interactions with social ties changing such behavior. These results will help establish direction for future work in using the framework to provide personalized collaborative environments within smart devices.

REFERENCES

[1] "8146.0 Household Use of Information Technology, Australia, 2012–2013." Australian Bureau of Statistics, 2014.

[2] L. Dabbish, C. Stuart, J. Tsay, and J. Herbsleb, "Social coding in GitHub: transparency and collaboration in an open software repository," *Proc. ACM 2012 ...*, 2012.

[3] L. Findlater and J. McGrenere, "Impact of screen size on performance, awareness, and user satisfaction with adaptive graphical user interfaces," *Proc. SIGCHI Conf. ...*, 2008.

[4] P. Brusilovsky, A. Kobsa, and W. Nejdl, *The adaptive web: methods and strategies of web personalization.* 2007.

[5] S. Angeletou, M. Rowe, and H. Alani, "Modelling and analysis of user behaviour in online communities," *Semant. Web–ISWC 2011*, 2011.

[6] M. Forestier, J. Velcin, and D. Zighed, "Analyzing Social Roles using Enriched Social Network on On-Line Sub-Communities.," *ICDS 2012, Sixth Int. ...*, 2012.

[7] U. Pfeil, K. Svangstu, C. S. Ang, and P. Zaphiris, "Social Roles in an Online Support Community for Older People," *Int. J. Hum. Comput. Interact.*, vol. 27, no. 4, pp. 323–347, Feb. 2011.

[8] E. Friasmartinez, G. Magoulas, S. Chen, and R. Macredie, "Modeling human behavior in user-adaptive systems: Recent advances using soft computing techniques," *Expert Syst. Appl.*, vol. 29, no. 2, pp. 320–329, Aug. 2005.

[9] J. Linden, G. and Smith, B. and York, "Amazon.com recommendations: Item-to-item collaborative filtering," *IEEE Internet Comput.*, vol. 7, no. 1, pp. 76–80, 2003.

[10] M. Luca, "Reviews, reputation, and revenue: The case of Yelp. com," 2011.

[11] R. Tague, A. Maeder, and J. Basilakis, "Adaptive Web Framework for Online Collaborative Environments," *Aust. J. Intell. Inf. Process. Syst.*, vol. 13, no. 4, 2014.

[12] B. Nonnecke and J. Preece, "Online lurkers tell why," in *Proceedings of the 10t Americas Conference on Information Systems*, 2004, no. August, pp. 1–7.

Multimedia Technology IV – Farag, Yang & Jiao (Eds)
© *2015 Taylor & Francis Group, London, ISBN: 978-1-138-02794-7*

DOA estimation of array radar via compressive sampling and matrix completion

Wei Wang, Xin Bi & Jinsong Du
Shenyang Institute of Automation, Chinese Academy of Science, Key Laboratory on Radar
System Research and Application Technology of Liaoning Province, Shenyang, China

ABSTRACT: With the requirement of high-precision and high-resolution, the huge data greatly increases data transmission and storage load. Compressive sampling and Matrix completion have received considerable attention recently, and has been applied successfully in diverse field. In this paper, we propose the application of compressive sampling (CS) and matrix completion techniques for the signal processing of array radar. Spatial compression reduces the number of front-end units and the random interval sampling method via matrix completion reduces the sampling rate. The system via Compressive Sampling and Matrix Completion can be used for direction of arrival (DOA) estimation of targets.

Keywords: Array Radar; Compressive Sampling; Matrix Completion; DOA estimation

1   INTRODUCTION

With the requirement of high-precision and high-resolution, the huge data greatly increases data transmission and storage load.

Compressive sampling/Compressive sensing (CS) [1, 2] has received considerable attention recently, and has been applied successfully in diverse field. The approach of [3] is proposed to achieve the superior resolution of MIMO radar with far fewer samples via CS. The approach of [4] proposed a space-time compressive sampling method for DOA estimation of targets. The CS array with spatial compression can reduce the number of front-end chains for DOA estimation. The application of analog-to-information conversion (AIC) [5] system can sample with a sub-Nyquist-rate. The input signal must be mixed by a pseudorandom sign waveform which alternates at the Nyquist rate. The high-speed mixing process enhances the system implementation difficulty.

Matrix completion [6, 7] is a new technique which can be applied to recover a low-rank matrix from subset of the matrix entries. Thus the work of [8] propose the use of matrix completion to conquer the challenge of huge nu mber of front-end units. The uniform spatial sampling method in the paper is difficult for hardware implementation and it increase the complexity of the data storage. We have propose the random interval sub-Nyquist-sampling method for array radar [9]. The method can be used for direction of arrival (DOA) estimation of targets for array radar via the MUSIC algorithm by the completing data.

In this paper, we propose the application of CS and matrix completion techniques for signal processing of array radar. Spatial compression reduces the number of front-end units and the random interval sampling method via matrix completion reduces the sampling rate. The system via Compressive Sampling and Matrix Completion can be used for direction of arrival (DOA) estimation of targets.

2   SIGNAL MODEL FOR ARRAY RADAR

Supposing the receiver is a uniform linear array (ULA) of L antennas with element spacing d. Let us assume that there are K point targets present. The azimuth angle of the kth target is θ_k.

The continuous-time waveform transmitted by the transmit antenna under the narrowband assumption is denoted

$$s(t) = u(t)e^{j(2\pi ft + \varphi(t))} \tag{1}$$

where $u(t)$ is the complex amplitude, $\varphi(t)$ is the phase, f is the carrier frequency. The first antenna as the reference element, the received signal at the lth antenna

$$z_l(t) = \sum_{k=1}^{K} s_k(t - \tau_{lk}) + \varepsilon_l(t) \tag{2}$$

where τ_{lk} is the time delay difference between each element to the reference element when the target is at the azimuth angle θ_k. $\varepsilon_l(t)$ represents noise, which is assumed to be independent and identically distributed (i.i.d.) Gaussian with zero mean and variance σ^2.

The relationship bewteem the azimuth angle θ_k and the time delay difference τ_{lk} are as follows

$$\tau_{lk} = \frac{(l-1)d\sin\theta_k}{c} \tag{3}$$

As a result, the received signal can be described as

$$Z(t) = \begin{bmatrix} z_1(t) \\ z_2(t) \\ \vdots \\ z_L(t) \end{bmatrix} = \begin{bmatrix} \sum_{k=1}^{K} s_k(t-\tau_{1k}) \\ \sum_{k=1}^{K} s_k(t-\tau_{2k}) \\ \vdots \\ \sum_{k=1}^{K} s_k(t-\tau_{Lk}) \end{bmatrix} + \begin{bmatrix} \varepsilon_1(t) \\ \varepsilon_2(t) \\ \vdots \\ \varepsilon_L(t) \end{bmatrix} \tag{4}$$

Equ. (4) can be expressed in a matrix form

$$\mathbf{Z} = \mathbf{S} + \mathbf{E} \tag{5}$$

where $\mathbf{Z}$ of size $L \times N$ is the received signal of array radar. N is the length of signal.

3 COMPRESSIVE SAMPLING AND MATRIX COMPLETION

3.1 Compressive sampling

Recent results in Compressive Sampling state that it is possible to reconstruct a $\mathbf{K}$-sparse signal of length N from M measurements via l_1-optimization. Let $\mathbf{\Psi}$ denote the basis matrix that spans this sparse space, and let $\mathbf{\Phi}$ denote the measurement matrix. The convex optimization problem arising from CS is formulated as follows:

$$\min\|\mathbf{x}\|_1 \quad s.t \quad \mathbf{y} = \mathbf{\Phi z} = \mathbf{\Phi\Psi x} \tag{6}$$

where $\mathbf{x}$ is a sparse vector with K non-zero elements; $\mathbf{\Phi}$ is an $M \times N$ matrix with $M << N$, that is incoherent with $\mathbf{\Psi}$.

Dividing the DOA search range into N_θ angles denoted θ_p and $p = 1, 2, \ldots, N_\theta^{[4]}$. We can define the basis matrix $\mathbf{\Psi}_\theta$ in the angle domain of size $L \times N_0$ as

$$\mathbf{\Psi} = [\mathbf{\psi}_1, \mathbf{\psi}_2, \cdots, \mathbf{\psi}_{N_\theta}],$$
$$\mathbf{\psi}_i = [1, e^{-j2\pi(d/\lambda)\sin(i\bullet\theta_p)}, \cdots, e^{-j2\pi(d/\lambda)\sin(i\bullet\theta_p)(L-1)}]^T \tag{7}$$
$$i = 1, 2, \cdots N_\theta$$

The process of spatial compression can be represented as

$$\mathbf{M} = \mathbf{\Phi Z} = \mathbf{\Phi\Psi}_\theta\mathbf{X} \tag{8}$$

where $\mathbf{X}$ of size $N_\theta \times N$ and each column of $\mathbf{S}$ is a sparse vector with K non-zero elements. $\mathbf{\Phi}$ of size $M \times L$ denote the measurement matrix. $\mathbf{M}$ of size $M \times N$ is the measurement result.

3.2 Matrix completion

The work of [6, 7] suppose $\mathbf{M} \in \mathbf{R}^{n_1 \times n_2}$ is a matrix we would like to know as precisely as possible. We use r to denote the rank of $\mathbf{M}$. However, the only information available about $\mathbf{M}$ is a sampled set of entries M_{ij}, $(i,j) \in \Omega$, where Ω is the randomly chosen subset of the complete set of entries of the matrix.

The sampling operator $\mathcal{P}_\Omega: \mathbf{R}^{n_1 \times n_2} \to \mathbf{R}^{n_1 \times n_2}$ is defined by

$$[\mathcal{P}_\Omega(\mathbf{Y})]_{ij} = \begin{cases} Y_{ij}, & (i,j) \in \Omega \\ 0, & \text{otherwise} \end{cases} \tag{9}$$

In principle, if the singular vectors of $\mathbf{M}$ are sufficiently spread, one could recover the unknown matrix by solving

$$\begin{aligned} &\text{minmize} \quad \text{rank}(\mathbf{Y}) \\ &\text{subject to} \quad \mathcal{P}_\Omega(\mathbf{Y}) = \mathcal{P}_\Omega(\mathbf{M}) \end{aligned} \tag{10}$$

where $\mathbf{Y} \in \mathbf{R}^{n_1 \times n_2}$ is the decision variable matrix. A popular alternative is the convex relaxation

$$\begin{aligned} &\text{minmize} \quad \|\mathbf{Y}\|_* \\ &\text{subject to} \quad \mathcal{P}_\Omega(\mathbf{Y}) = \mathcal{P}_\Omega(\mathbf{M}) \end{aligned} \tag{11}$$

where $\|\mathbf{Y}\|_* := \sum_{k=1}^{r} \sigma_k$ is the nuclear norm and $\sigma_1, \ldots, \sigma_r \geq 0$ are the singular values of $\mathbf{Y}$.

If the matrix $\mathbf{M}$ obeys the strong incoherence property. Suppose we observe m entries of $\mathbf{M}$ with locations sampled uniformly at random. Then there is a positive numerical constant C and c such that if

$$m \geq Cn^{5/4}r\log n \tag{12}$$

The minimizer to the problem is unique and equal to $\mathbf{M}$ with probability at least $1 - cn^{-3}\log n$, $n := \max(n_1, n_2)$. Nuclear-norm minimization recovers all the entries of $\mathbf{M}$ with high probability.

3.3 MC-CS for Array Radar

The work of [8] proves the received signal as a matrix obeys the strong incoherence property. The signal after spatial compression satisfies the low-rank matrix model. Spatial compression reduces the number of front-end units and the random interval sampling method via matrix completion reduces the sampling rate. The structure of the MC-CS system is shown in Fig. 1.

Taking into account the sub-Nyquist-rate for each channel sampling' we propose a random interval sampling method.

1. Generating a random delay

$$\Delta T = \{nT_s | 0 \leq n \leq N_{Sub} - 1\}$$

where T_s is the Nyquist sampling time, N_{Sub} is the Desampling ratio.

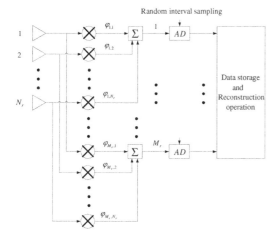

Figure 1. Schematic diagram of MC-CS.

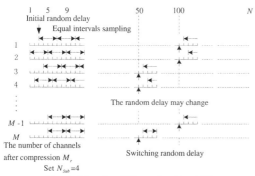

Figure 2. Random interval sampling. Supposing $N_{Sub} = 4$.

2. Outputing the sampling clock

$f_{Sub} = f_s / N_{Sub}$

where f_{Sub} is the output clock frequency, f_s is the Nyquist frequency.

The random delay of the clock can ensure that there is at least one channel data to be sampled at the Nyquist sampling moment. In order to obtain a higher accuracy, switching random delay in a certain time interval to increase the randomness. The lack of data may be caused by the hardware implementation of random delay switching, each channel can switch random delay asynchronously to ensure that each column of the matrix elements can be get. The method of random interval sampling (RIS) is shown in Fig. 2.

Candes, Recht and Plan put forward independent sample model, namely Bernoulli model. Bernoulli model meets the condition that there are samples from each row and column. Randomly generates a matrix, $n_1 = 100$, $n_2 = 1000$ and $r = 5$, N_{Sub} changes from 2 to 10. On the other hand, randomly generates a matrix, n_1 changes from 50 to 15, $n_2 = 1000$ $r = 5$ $N_{Sub} = 4$. The

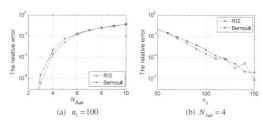

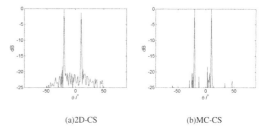

(a) $n_1 = 100$ (b) $N_{Sub} = 4$

Figure 3. The relative error of RIS model and Bernoulli model.

(a)2D-CS   (b)MC-CS

Figure 4. The results of DOA estimation.

maximum number of iterations is 100. As shown in Fig. 3, the effect of RIS model and Bernoulli model is basically the same. RIS model can be used for Matrix Completion data acquisition. When N_{Sub} changes from 3 to 6, the relative error increases 10^4 times. When the number of rows increases, the relative error varies linearly.

The reconstruction process divides into two parts.

1. Completing the the signal after spatial compression by the sampling data $\mathcal{P}_\Omega(\mathbf{M})$ via Matrix Completion.

minmize $\mathrm{rank}(\mathbf{Y})$

subject to $\mathcal{P}_\Omega(\mathbf{Y}) = \mathcal{P}_\Omega(\mathbf{M})$

2. Reconstructing the sparsity vector of angle domain via Compressive Sampling.

minmize $\|\mathbf{x}_i\|_1$ subject to $\mathbf{y}_i = \mathbf{\Phi}\mathbf{z} = \mathbf{\Phi}\mathbf{\Psi}\mathbf{x}_i$

Where $\mathbf{x}_i$ and $\mathbf{y}_i$ are the ith column of $\mathbf{X}$ and $\mathbf{Y}$.

The normalization of integration by the N times reconstruction results is the DOA estimation denoted by $\hat{\boldsymbol{\theta}}$. We use the OPTSPACE algorithm [10] and FOCUSS algorithm [11] to solve the problem.

4 SIMULATION

Supposing a array radar system, the number of receive antennas is $L = 64$. The length of signa is $N = 300$. The range starts from $-90°$ and ends at $89°$. The step of search is $1°$. Two targets are located at angles $\theta_1 = -20°$ and $\theta_2 = 10°$. The vector of angle is $\boldsymbol{\theta}$.

When SNR of input is 0, the results of DOA estimation are shown in Fig. 4. It turns out that both of two kinds structures obtain precise estimations of DOA. The method of MC-CS uses singular value $\sigma_1, \ldots, \sigma_r$

Table 1. The average computation time.

	MC-CS	2D-CS
Time	2.270937s	1.091425s

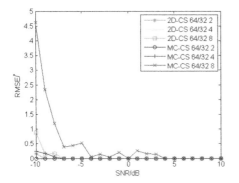

(a) The RMSE under different desampling ratio

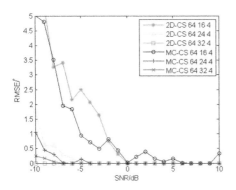

(b) The RMSE under different compression ratio

Figure 5. The RMSE under different situation.

and the corresponding singular vectors. The process can effectively reduce noise and make the estimate spectrum more discrete.

The estimation process of MC-CS consists of Matrix Completion and sparsity reconstruction' while 2D-CS is implemented by angle domain sparsity reconstruction. The method of 2D-CS needs a little calculation. The maximum number of iterations is 50 and the length of signa is $N = 300$. The average computation time as shown in Table 1.

The the root mean square error (RMSE) of DOA estimation under different SNR are show in Fig. 5 (a) and (b). 2D-CS represent the 2-dimensional space-time compressive sampling method. The numbers mean compression ratio and desampling ratio.

In general, the simulation results indicate that the DOA estimation has high accuracy. The RMSE of DOA estimation reduce with the increase of SNR. When the desampling ratio increases, the RMSE increases. If the desampling ratio equals to 2 or 4, the results of the two structures are basically identical. If the desampling ratio increases to 8, the result of 2D-CS is better than MC-CS. The RMSE of 2D-CS is below 1°. The effect is superior to MC-CS. It means the AIC structure has advantages in time-domain desampling. In practice, when the desampling ratio equals 4, the signal has largely reduced the requirements for AD. Because the structure of MC-CS is simpler, so that the structure has a more practicality.

Supposing desampling ratio equals to 4, considering the influence of compression ratio on the results, MC-CS performances in general better than 2D-CS. The RMSE of DOA estimation reduce with the increase of SNR. When the number of channels equals to 16, the robustness of MC-CS reduces. The theory of Matrix Completion requirements $M_r >> r$. Fig. 2 (b) also proves the point. For the same amount of data, the number of channels has more important influence on the effect of DOA estimation.

5 CONCLUSIONS

The solution results prove that the system via Compressive Sampling and Matrix Completion can be used for DOA estimation of targets. The method of MC-CS uses the r largest singular value and the corresponding singular vectors. The process can effectively reduce noise and make the estimate spectrum more discrete. The structure of 2D-CS has advantages in terms of time-domain down-sampling. The structure of MC-CS is simpler and the structure has a more practicality. The structure of the MC-CS system can be applied to other field, e.g., the SAR imaging. The more in-depth work is to derive more efficient algorithms exploiting the features of the matrix with joint sparsity and low-rank.

ACKNOWLEDGMENT

This research is supported by the Innovation Subject of the Shenyang Institute of Automation, Chinese Academy of Science (NO: YOF5150501).

REFERENCES

[1] E. J. Candès, "Compressive sampling," in *Proceedings oh the International Congress of Mathematicians: Madrid, August 22–30, 2006: invited lectures*, 2006, pp. 1433–1452.
[2] R. G. Baraniuk, "Compressive sensing," *IEEE signal processing magazine*, vol. 24, 2007.
[3] A. C. Gurbuz, J. H. McClellan, and V. Cevher, "A compressive beamforming method," in *Acoustics, Speech and Signal Processing, 2008. ICASSP 2008. IEEE International Conference on*, 2008, pp. 2617–2620.
[4] Y. Wang and G. Leus, "Space-time compressive sampling array," in *Sensor Array and Multichannel Signal Processing Workshop (SAM), 2010 IEEE*, 2010, pp. 33–36.

[5] M. Mishali and Y. C. Eldar, "From theory to practice: Sub-Nyquist sampling of sparse wideband analog signals," *Selected Topics in Signal Processing, IEEE Journal of*, vol. 4, pp. 375–391, 2010.

[6] E. J. Candès and B. Recht, "Exact matrix completion via convex optimization," *Foundations of Computational mathematics*, vol. 9, pp. 717–772, 2009.

[7] E. J. Candes and Y. Plan, "Matrix completion with noise," *Proceedings of the IEEE*, vol. 98, pp. 925–936, 2010.

[8] Z. Weng and X. Wang, "Low-rank matrix completion for array signal processing," in *Acoustics, Speech and Signal Processing (ICASSP), 2012 IEEE International Conference on*, 2012, pp. 2697–2700.

[9] M. Wang and W. Wang, "DOA estimation of array radar via random interval sub-Nyquist-sampling," in *Signal Processing, Communication and Computing (ICSPCC), 2013 IEEE International Conference on*, 2013, pp. 1–4.

[10] R. H. Keshavan and A. Montanari, "Regularization for matrix completion," presented at the in Information Theory Proceedings (ISIT), 2010 IEEE International Symposium on, 2010.

[11] B. D. Rao, "Analysis and extensions of the FOCUSS algorithm," presented at the in Signals, Systems and Computers, 1996. Conference Record of the Thirtieth Asilomar Conference on, 1996.

Multimedia Technology IV – Farag, Yang & Jiao (Eds)

An improved non-linear ARED algorithm based on queue length

Ying Zhou & Jihong Zhang
College of Information Engineering, Shenzhen University, Shenzhen, China

Wei Liu, Yongsheng Liang, Tao Hu & Xianyi Ren
Shenzhen Key Laboratory of Visual Media Processing and Transmission,
Shenzhen Institute of Information Technology, Shenzhen, China

Xiaoping Chen
SZMOBI Shenzhen Company, Shenzhen, China

ABSTRACT: Active queue management algorithm can effectively control the network congestion, among which ARED and its improved algorithm has been widely used in recent years. In order to timely response to unexpected network congestion and match the non-linear relationship between packet loss rate and queue length, this paper improved ARED algorithm and proposed a queue length based nonlinear ARED algorithm. This algorithm was analyzed and compared with others in NS2 simulation environment. Experimental results show that compared to other ARED algorithm, this algorithm can guarantee the stability of the queue, respond to unexpected network congestion timely, reduce drop rate and improve network throughput.

Keywords: congestion control; active queue management; ARED; queue length; non-linear; NS2

1 INTRODUCTION

In recent years, with the development of Internet and multimedia technology, computer users and Internet applications grow explosively. However, the traditional "best effort" network service mechanism has been unable to meet the users' needs to access huge amounts of data. When transmitted packets increase and network resources (such as buffer size, link bandwidth, etc.) are limited, the network congestion will happen. The network congestion will result in network throughput degradation, a large of packet loss, network performance and efficiency degradation. Therefore, network congestion control has become a research hotspot of computer network.

Network congestion can be effectively controlled depending on the router queue management algorithms. The Active Queue Management (AQM) is an important congestion control mechanism. It can decide how many packets should be discarded in accordance with certain strategy before the queue expiry, so that the sending nodes can respond effectively before the link buffer overflow and avoid network congestion[1].

Since 1993 S. Floyd and V. Jacobson advanced Random Early Detection (RED) algorithm, RED algorithm has become the unique AQM strategy, which is recommended by IETF (Internet Engineering Task Force). Due to the deficiencies of RED algorithm in the parameter setting, many domestic and foreign researchers have proposed a number of improved algorithm, such as ARED[2], Gentle-RED[3], self-configuring RED[4], NewARED[5] and so on. Reference [6]–[8] modified nonlinear function of packet loss rate based on ARED algorithm to make it more conform with the relationship with average queue length. The authors avoided congestion by modifying the maximum drop rate in ARED algorithm in [9]–[10]. Fumihiko N. et al.[11], [12] and FAN Jisong et al.[13] reduced queue oscillation by re-calculating the queue length.

In this article, we also optimized RED algorithm and proposed a nonlinear ARED algorithm based on queue length. This algorithm modified the parameters in real time by monitoring the current buffer occupancy, so that the queue length changes more smoothly. It can response more rapidly for the sudden network congestion, meanwhile reducing the packet loss rate, improving network throughput and maximizing the effectiveness of the network transmission.

The rest paper is organized as follows: Section 2 provides an overview of the main improved ARED algorithms. Deficiencies of these algorithms are listed, then the Queue Length Based non-Linear Adaptive RED (QnLARED) algorithm is proposed and analyzed in section 3. Section 4 presents the simulation experiments conducted to evaluate the efficiency of the proposed algorithm. Conclusions and some improving directions can be found in Section 5.

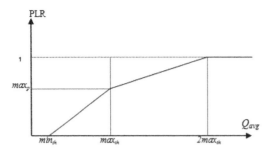

Figure 1. The relationship between packet loss rate and Q_{avg}.

2 IMPROVED RED ALGORITHM REVIEW

2.1 Gentle-RED algorithm

In RED algorithm, when the average queue length $Q_{avg} > max_{th}$, the arrived packets are directly discarded. This jumping packet loss rate will cause severe queue length vibration. Gentle-RED algorithm improves the original RED algorithm[1]. It inherits the main idea of the RED algorithm, when $max_{th} < Q_{avg} < 2max_{th}$, probability P_b is calculated with linear relationship and drop rate P_a is the same as the RED algorithm. Probability P_b is calculated as follows:

$$P_b = \begin{cases} 0 & Q_{avg} \leq min_{th} \\ max_p \cdot \dfrac{Q_{avg} - min_{th}}{max_{th} - min_{th}} & min_{th} < Q_{avg} < max_{th} \\ (1 - max_p) \cdot \dfrac{Q_{avg} - max_{th}}{max_{th}} + max_p & max_{th} \leq Q_{avg} < 2max_{th} \\ 1 & 2max_{th} \leq Q_{avg} \leq buffersize \end{cases} \quad (1)$$

Until $Q_{avg} > 2max_{th}$, the arrived packets are directly discarded. This method can better maintain the stability and robustness of queue length, control congestion and reduce the packet loss rate more effectively.

The relationship of packet loss rate and Q_{avg} in Gentle-RED algorithm is shown in Figure 1.

2.2 NewARED algorithm

The basic idea of improved adaptive newARED algorithm is to adaptively adjust the maximum drop rate max_p to maintain the queue length between the low and high threshold. It is for reducing network latency and improving network throughput[4]. By monitoring the average queue length, newARED algorithm determines whether RED should be more aggressive or conservative. If the average queue length oscillates around min_{th}, which indicates that congestion control is too aggressive, the algorithm should reduce max_p; if the average queue length oscillates around max_{th}, which indicates that congestion control is too conservative, the algorithm should increase max_p. The maximum drop rate max_p can be dynamically adjusted

according to the detected average queue length. The algorithm is described as follows:

Every *interval*:
  if (Q_{avg}>*target* and max_p<0.5)
    increase max_p;
    max_p= max_p +α;
  elseif (Q_{avg}<*target* and max_p>0.01)
    decrease max_p;
    max_p= max_p×β;

Wherein, *interval* is the time interval, that is how often max_p is changed. *target* is target range of Q_{avg}, *target* $\in [min_{th} + 0.4 \times (max_{th} - min_{th})$, $min_{th} + 0.6 \times (max_{th} - min_{th})]$; α is the increasing factor, $\alpha = min(0.01, max_p/4)$; β is the decreasing factor, the default value is 0.9.

Unlike RED algorithm changing max_p when each data packet arrives, newARED algorithm calculates max_p at some intervals. This enhances the robustness of the algorithm. But when network congestion changes dramatically, max_p will take some time to adapt with it. The max_p is limited in [0.01,0.5], which can ensure ARED does not excessively decrease at this interval and global synchronization caused by excessive max_p is avoided.

3 QUEUE LENGTH-BASED NON-LINEAR ADAPTIVE RED (QNLARED)

3.1 Deficiencies of other algorithms

Analyzed as in section 2, Gentle-RED and newARED improved RED algorithm in various degrees. They both enhanced algorithm robustness and ensured the network transmission performance. However, these algorithms still exist some shortcomings:

1) In newARED algorithm, max_p changes periodically according to Q_{avg} changing between high and low threshold. This non-real-time adjustment is more suitable for stable network state. For the mutational network status, this algorithm requires a certain time to make the network performance stable.

2) In order to filter the short term burst stream, two algorithms mentioned in section 2 use the exponentially weighted moving average of the current instantaneous queue length to calculate the average queue length by, calculations are as follows:

$$Q_{avg} = (1 - \omega_q) \cdot Q_{avg} + \omega_q \cdot q(t) \quad (2)$$

$$\omega_q = 1 - e^{-1/C} \quad (3)$$

ω_q is the weight value, C is the link capacity, $q(t)$ is the current queue length.

This calculation method reflects the packet arrival rate instead of the current buffer occupancy. Since ω_q is small, Q_{avg} changes little. The instantaneous queue length growth caused by sudden increase in the network data or transient congestion will not be reflected. This method is hysteretic for monitoring the queue length, prone to the global synchronization and increases the delay jitter.

3) As known in [6] and [14], the relationship between drop rate P and average queue length L is non-linear, but exponential as the following formula:

$$P = 1/(1+1/L)^{\tilde{N}} \cdot [1/(1+L)] \qquad (4)$$

Two algorithms mentioned in section 2 calculate the drop rate as a linear function of average queue length. Although the linear function is simple for calculation, it is not quite up to the non-linear nature of the RED algorithm.

3.2 QnLARED algorithm description

Based on the above considerations, this paper proposes a queue length based non-linear ARED algorithm (QnLARED). This algorithm combines Gentle-RED and newARED algorithms and make further improvements. max_p and ω_q are modified according to the current queue length. This algorithm makes the RED more sensitive for the mutational network status and avoids global synchronization. According to the non-linear relationship between drop rate and average queue length, P_b is modified to make the queue length grow smoothly. It can increase network utilization and ensure the stability of the queue length.

1) *Improvement of max_p*
Supposing the current queue length is S_q, buffer size is S_b, we define the current buffer occupancy rate as B_o, then:

$$B_o = S_q / S_b \qquad (5)$$

Greater B_o indicates the more transmitted packets in current queue and the greater probability of congestion. Original algorithm is modified as follows:

if (Q_{avg}>target and max_p<0.5)
   increase max_p:

$$max_p = max_p + \frac{\delta}{max_{th} - min_{th}} \cdot B_o ;$$

elseif (Q_{avg}<target and max_p>0.01)
   decrease max_p:

$$max_p = max_p \cdot \frac{\gamma}{max_{th} - min_{th}} \cdot B_o .$$

δ, γ are the variable to control max_p's amplitude of increasing and decreasing.
   Thus, max_p can be dynamically adjusted according to the current queue status. It will adapt mutational network and improve the transmission efficiency.

2) *Improvement of ω_q*
ω_q of original algorithm is modified as follows:

$$\omega_q = (1 - e^{-1/(10*RTT*T_d)}) \cdot (1/B_o) \qquad (6)$$

RTT is the round-trip transmission time, T_d is the transmission delay.
   Thus, ω_q can be dynamically adjusted according to the current buffer occupancy. It is more sensitive to the queue length changes caused by sudden network congestion. This algorithm also avoids the

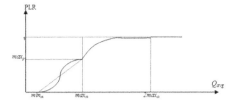

Figure 2. The relationship between packet loss rate and Q_{avg}.

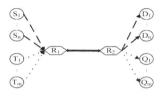

Figure 3. Network simulation topology.

following phenomena: ω_q is too large to filter transient congestion, while ω_q is too small to reflect changes of the queue length.

3) *Improvement of P_b*
When the average queue length oscillate around min_{th}, it indicates the queue is relatively idle, so the packet loss rate should be relatively small in order to increase network throughput. When the average queue length oscillates between min_{th} and max_{th}, it indicates the queue buffer is far from overflow, so the packet loss rate can be increased in a smooth way in order to improve network utilization. When the average queue length is greater than max_{th}, it indicates the queue buffer is near overflow and system utilization is close to the ceiling, so packets should be dropped quickly and smoothly in order to ensure the stability of the queue. In order to match the non-linear relationship between packet loss rate and the queue length, to ensure steady growth of P_b, and timely response to average queue length changes, P_b is calculated as follows:

$$P_b = \begin{cases} 0 & Q_{avg} \leq min_{th} \\ \dfrac{(Q_{avg} - min_{th})^2 \cdot max_p}{1 + \dfrac{(max_{th} - min_{th})^2 - 1}{(max_{th} - min_{th})^2}(Q_{avg} - min_{th})^2} & min_{th} < Q_{avg} < max_{th} \\ \dfrac{1 - max_p}{\sqrt[3]{max}} \cdot \sqrt[3]{Q_{avg} - max_{th}} + max_p & max_{th} \leq Q_{avg} < 2max_{th} \\ 1 & 2max_{th} \leq Q_{avg} \leq buffersize \end{cases} \qquad (7)$$

The relationship of packet loss rate and Q_{avg} in QnLARED algorithm is shown in Figure 2.

4 SIMULATION AND RESULTS ANALYSIS

4.1 Simulation model and parameter settings

In order to verify QnLARED algorithm's advance, the simulation experiment is made using NS 2.28 simulation software in this paper. The algorithm results are analyzed and compared with ARED algorithm. The Network simulation topology is shown in Figure 3.

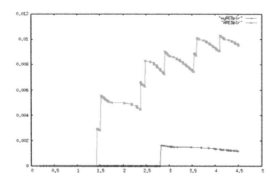

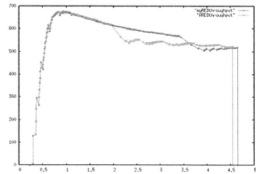

Figure 4. Comparison of PLR of ftp stream with different algorithms.

Figure 5. Comparison of throughput of ftp stream with different algorithms.

As shown in Figure 3, the sender S1 ... Sn generate TCP streams, T1 ... Tm generate UDP traffic. Via the middle node R1 and R2, the sender transmit n pieces of FTP streams and m pieces of CBR streams to the receiver D1...Dn, Q1...Qm. The bandwidth of bottleneck between R1 and R2 is 1.5 Mbps, and the delay is 20 ms. During simulation, CBR streams start at 0.1 s and end at 5.0 s; FTP streams start at 0.2 s and end at 4.5 s. The parameters are set as follows: $min_{th} = 5$, $max_{th} = 15$, $\delta = 0.1$, $\gamma = 9$, Each packet is 1 kB and maximum of buffer length is 50 packets.

4.2 Experimental results and analysis

In the experiments, the sender sends one TCP data and one UDP data, that making n = m = 1. The bandwidths from sender and receiver nodes to the middle node are 10 Mbps. The transmission delay from S1 to R1 is 2 ms, that from T1 to R1 is 3 ms. The transmission delay from R1 to D1 is 4 ms, that from R2 to Q1 is 5 ms. newARED and QnLARED algorithm are used on the link between R1 and R2 for packet scheduling. The simulation results are as follows:

1) *Packet Loss Rate Analysis*
   The Packet loss rate (PLR) of FTP streams in newARED and QnLARED are shown in Figure 4.
   The packet loss rate of FTP stream in newARED is 0.009490, that in QnLARED is 0.001195. The latter protects the reliable TCP data and reduces the packet loss rate of FTP stream.

2) *Throughput Analysis*
   Throughput refers to the successfully transmitted data in unit interval, which reflects the bandwidth utilization. The higher throughput indicates the greater bandwidth utilization and better network performance. The throughput of FTP streams in newARED and QnLARED are shown in Figure 5.
   The throughput of FTP stream in newARED is 525.9182 bps, that in QnLARED is 71.5125 bps. The latter improves reliable throughput of FTP stream and network transmission efficiency.

3) *Queue Length Analysis*
   The queue length of FTP streams in newARED and QnLARED are shown in Figure 6.

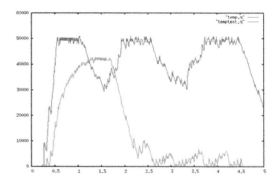

Figure 6. Comparison of queue length of ftp stream with different algorithms.

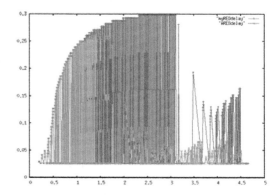

Figure 7. Comparison of delay of ftp stream with different algorithms.

As shown in Figute 6, QnLARED algorithm maintains the stability of queue length, thus increases the robustness of the packet scheduling.

4) *Delay Analysis*
   The delay of FTP streams in newARED and QnLARED are shown in Figure 7.
   The delay of FTP stream in newARED is 72.25 ms, that in QnLARED is 119.22 ms. Unlike the fixed ω_q and max_p in newRED, QnLARED algorithm updates ω_q and max_p according to

the current buffer occupancy at setting intervals. Although it improves the queue stability and throughput and reduces the drop rate, QnLARED algorithm increases more transmission delay than newRED at the same time. So proposed QnLARED algorithm is more suitable for the applications that require less real-time demand, while high video transmission quality.

5 CONCLUSIONS

This paper analyzes the advantages and disadvantages of various existing ARED algorithms. These algorithms can not make a timely response to explosive network congestion and likely cause global synchronization. In order to overcome the above shortcomings and conform better to the non-linear relationship between packet loss rate and queue length, this paper proposes a queue length based non-linear ARED algorithm (QnLARED). This algorithm is compared with other ARED algorithms in NS2 simulation environment. Experimental results show that the proposed algorithm can better ensure the stability of the queue length, reduce the packet loss rate and increase the throughput and network utilization. However, due to updating parameters according to the queue occupancy, this algorithm could be improved further in the transmission delay.

ACKNOWLEDGMENT

This paper is supported by National Natural Science Foundation of China (61172165) and National Natural Science Foundation of Guangdong (S2011010006113).

REFERENCES

[1] Adams, R. "Active Queue Management: A Survey", IEEE Communications Surveys & Tutorials, vol. 15, 2013, pp. 1425–1476. doi:10.1109/SURV.2012.082212. 00018

[2] Floyd S. and Jaeobson V. "Random early detection gateways for congestion avoidance", IEEE/ACM Transaction on Networking, vol. 1, Aug 1993, pp. 397–413, doi: 10.1109/90.251892.

[3] Hussein Abdel-jaber, Fadi Thabtah, et al "Performance Invsetigations of Some Active Queue Management Tchniques Using Simulation" International Journal on New Computer Architectures and Their Applications, vol. 2, Mar. 2012, pp. 286–301.

[4] Feng W, Kandlur D, Saha D, et al. "A Self-configuring RED Gateway" Proc of IEEE INFOCOM, vol. 3, Mar. 1999, pp. 1320–1328 doi: 10.1109/INF-COM.1999.752150.

[5] Floyd S, Ramakrishna Gummadi and Scott Shenker "Adaptive RED: An Algorithm for Increasing the Robustness of RED's Active Queue Management", Berkeley, USA: ACIRI, 2001, pp. 324–336

[6] Zhang Yan-ping, MA Jun, Wang Yong-cheng and CHEN Xiao-yan "Improved nonlinear random early detection algorithm" Journal of Computer Applications, vol. 31, Apr. 2011, pp. 890–892.

[7] Wu Bo and Li La-yuan "An Improved RED Routing Queue Algorithm Analysis and Research" Microcomputer Information, vol. 26, Mar. 2010, pp. 131–133.

[8] Ma Jun "Researches on Active Queue Management with Network Simulator Version 2" Anhui University, 2011.

[9] Cao Zhibo "Simulation and Optimization of RED Algorithm" Computer Technology and Development, vol. 20, Aug. 2010, pp. 188–191.

[10] Yunqi Luo, Hong Chen, et al "BO-ARED: A New AQM Algorithm with Adaptive Adjustment of Parameters" Proceedings of the 8th World Congress on Intelligent Control and Automation (WCICA10), Jul, 2010, pp. 1852–1857, doi: 10.1109/WCICA.2010.5554486.

[11] Nakamura F. and Nakashima T., "Multiple Active Queue Management within Input/Output buffers" 7th International Conference on Broadband, Wireless Computing, Communication and Applications (BWCCA), Nov. 2012, pp. 656–661, doi: 10.1109 /BWCCA.2012.114.

[12] Nakamura F. and Nakashima T., "Active Queue Management with the Stable Unit Average Calculation" International Conference on Broadband and Wireless Computing, Communication and Applications (BWCCA), Oct. 2011, pp. 567–572, doi: 10.1109/ BWCCA.2011.92

[13] Fan Jisong, Wu Xinrong and Liu Jie "Modified RED Stability Research" Journal of System Simulation, vol. 22, Jul. 2010, pp. 1711–1715

[14] Starkova, O. and Andrushko, D. "Mathematical description of TCP-sessions using AQM-algorithms for nonlinear packet drop model" 2012 International Conference on Modern Problems of Radio Engineering Telecommunications and Computer Science (TCSET), Feb. 2012, pp. 358.

Multimedia Technology IV – Farag, Yang & Jiao (Eds)
© *2015 Taylor & Francis Group, London, ISBN: 978-1-138-02794-7*

Frontier approach research on the detection of early breast tumor

Yang Gao, Xin Bi, Jinsong Du, Rui Su & Wei Wang
Shenyang Institute of Automation, Chinese Academy of Science,
Key Laboratory on Radar System Research and Application Technology of Liaoning Province,
Liaoning Province, Shenyang City, China

ABSTRACT: The accident and mortality ratio of various cancers are increasing continually reported by a lot of medical literatures in every year, and that more early diagnose more surviving is also the truth in the breast cancer detection and therapy field. Developing a detection instrument about the early breast cancer is the aim of this paper. The microwave-induced thermoacoustic tomography (MITAT) is an innovative technology for tumor detection. Under the microwave irradiation condition, the rapid increase in temperature causes the instantaneous pressure, resulting in the ultrasonic signal, therefore the method has both advantages of high-contrast in microwave image and high-resolution in ultrasonic image. In this paper, with the circular scanning probe method, the system achieves the thermoacoustic images of the different size tumor phantom and the complex tumor phantom of different conductivity, and the experimental results show that the system can carry out the above test samples with high contrast and high resolution imaging.

Keywords: early detection of tumor; Microwave induced thermoacoustic; image reconstruction

1 INTRODUCTION

Breast cancer is a common malignancy tumor which endangers women's life and health [1]. With the global industrial development and the living environment deterioration, the global incidence of breast cancer is increasing year by year [2]. The previous medical study shows that the patient's long-term survival rate drops to 95% in the case of that breast cancer can be detected and treated [1, 2]. Therefore, early detection of breast cancer is an important way to reduce mortality ratio.

X-ray, CT, ultrasound imaging and MRI are the traditional detection approaches for breast cancer [3]. However, because of the low contrast and the lionizing radiation, the above detection method cannot be an effective method for routine detection [2]. In recent years, there have been other detection methods, e.g. photo acoustic imaging technology [4], which don't become the safe use of conventional detection methods for the detection range and cost factor. Based on the limitations of the above methods, more and more people begin to focus on microwave-induced thermoacoustic tomography technology for the detection of the early breast cancer [4, 5]. The technology makes use of the difference in electrical characteristics between normal breast and malignant tissue in microwave frequency. The biological tissue can release the ultrasonic signal, because its absorbing microwave energy causes thermal expansion. Our system can obtain microwave energy distribution image which reflects characteristics of biological tissue with

the ultrasonic signal. Compared with the conventional method of breast tumor detection, the technology has several advantages as follows: non-ionizing radiation, free extrusion, non-invasive, high contrast and etc.

There are two main microwave imaging methods currently: the tomography and confocal imaging ways [4, 5, 6]. The former one, as an electromagnetic inverse scattering method, which reconstructs electromagnetic distributed parameter properties of the imaging field by scatter electromagnetic fields, can determine the target position, shape and size information, however its ill-condition and nonlinear are not resolved [5]. The latter method can obtain reconstructed image which distinguishes between the poor and strong scattering region, based on electromagnetic parameter differences [6]. The current microwave confocal imaging algorithm includes delay-and-sum (DAS), space-time beam forming and Capon beam forming method. This paper uses DAS with the stability.

The previous study has found the microwave absorbing contrast between normal and malignant tissues is 1:6, in addition, the penetration depth for the muscle is 1.2 cm in 3 GHz microwave, and it is 9 cm for adipose tissue. Combined with the characteristics of early detection of breast cancer, the system uses S-band frequency microwave as the source which irradiates tumor phantoms. The experiment results show the excellent imaging performance of the system, furthermore the image contrast and resolution can meet the requirement of early detection for breast cancer, which have advanced domestic and international.

2 THEORETICAL BASIS AND ALGORITHMS

In the case of thermal confinement, the acoustic wave at point r and time t, $p(r,t)$ is related to the microwave absorption $H(r,t)$ by the following wave equation:

$$\left(\nabla^2 - \frac{1}{c_s^2}\frac{\partial^2}{\partial t^2}\right)p(r,t) = -\frac{\beta}{c_p}\frac{\partial}{\partial t}H(r,t) \qquad (1)$$

where c_s is the acoustic speed, c_p is the specific heat, and β is the coefficient of the volume thermal expansion. $H(r,t)$ can be written as a product form of space absorption function and an instant pulse function:

$$H(r,t) = A(r)I(t) \qquad (2)$$

where $I(t)$ is the instant pulse function, $A(r)$ is the space absorption function.

In the microwave pulse irradiation period, the tissue inhomogeneity leads to pressure wave unevenly distributed. Every non-zero sound pressure can be regarded as a heat source which propagates sound waves outwards. The initial sound pressure depends on the electromagnetic parameters of biological tissue, the source frequency and amplitude of the field intensity.

3 EXPERIMENTAL INTRODUCTION

The experimental platform uses an array consisted of four ultrasonic sensors to acquire 180-positions sample signal whose interval is 2 degree in a circular scan, and reconstructs the electrical field image which reflects the tissue character. The principle pattern is shown in Figure 1, S-band power microwave is radiated to sample via the circuit and the horn antenna (The peak power is 60 kW, the carrier frequency is 3 GHz, the pulse width is 400 ns. The average amount of electromagnetic radiation is 0.097 mW/cm², and the value is less than 20 mW/cm² which is body electromagnetic radiation safety standard in 2005 IEEE). The sample is immersed into transformer oil to prevent the microwave signal attenuation and the air absorption for ultrasonic signal. With the absorption of microwave pulse energy causing the instantaneous expansion, the sample generates ultrasonic pressure wave which

carries the physical information of the sample. The signal is received by ultrasonic sensors, and processed to obtain the image reflecting the electromagnetic characteristics.

4 RESULTS AND DISCUSSION

4.1 Samples of different sizes

The system uses different size tumor phantoms which are formed from the colloid hybrid heating solidified with water and agar by a certain percentage to validate the detection ability. Figure 2 shows the different size square colloids (2×5 mm, 2×10 mm and 1×15 mm), which contains ink to be distinguish clearly and does not affect the physical properties. Figure 3(a) shows the imaging results of five different size tumor phantoms, and it can be distinguished from the background, which proved the high-contrast performance of the imaging system. The energy amplitude of the 5 samples of the same physical characteristics exist difference, because of the larger size sample absorbs the more energy. From the result, the system can detect the 5mm square phantom clearly, and it is enough for the early detection of breast cancer.

The paper selects imaging results of three different size samples (15 mm, 10 mm, 5 mm) to verify the precision of the system, Figure 3(b) shows the three profiles, and the extreme points of half are used as the threshold point. The corresponding reconstructed size of the 15 mm phantom is 14.8 mm, the one of 10 mm is 9.8 mm, and the one of 5 mm is 5.2 mm, so the reconstructed size is consistent with the actual one.

4.2 Samples of different conductivity

In practice, the growth of the tumor is a gradual process. Even for the same tumor, the different locations will exhibit different physical characteristics, and which provides a reference for the grasp of tumor growth phase and the judgment of the development state. In this paper, we use the complex tumor phantom composed from the sample superimposed by the three different conductivity phantoms, to verify the ability to distinguish between complex objects. Figure 4(a)

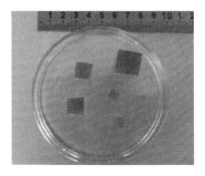

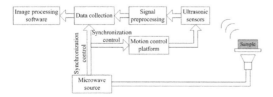

Figure 1. System block diagram.

Figure 2. 5 colloids of different sizes.

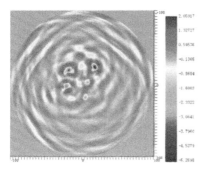

(a): Image reconstruction of 5 tumor phantoms

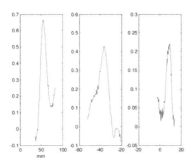

(b): profiles of three sizes

Figure 3. Experimental results of different size phantoms.

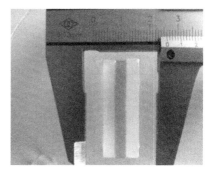

(a): Complex tumor phantom

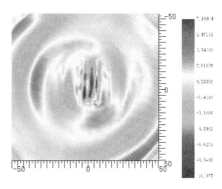

(b): Image reconstruction of different conductivity

Figure 4. Experimental results of different conductivity phantoms.

shows the photo of the experiment sample, where the green one's conductivity is the lowest, and the black is the lowest. Figure 4(b) shows the imaging result, which clearly distinguish differences in the physical characteristics of the sample at different locations, and the location of a large electrical conductivity, energy amplitude is large. The energy magnitude difference accords with the actual conductivity difference, so that the system can distinguish the physical characteristic difference at the different locations of the same tumor.

for the grasp of tumor growth phase and the judgment of the development state.

In summary, the system for early detection of breast cancer has the potential advance of high contrast ratio, non-invasive, and etc. The experiment results can provide a reliable safeguard for the next vivo animal and clinical studies, as well as the next phase of quantitative microwave thermoacoustic tomography reconstruction of the conductivity distribution to form a solid foundation.

5 CONCLUSION

Based on the theory and thermoacoustic imaging system, this article assesses the multifaceted performance of the 3 GHz microwave thermal acoustic imaging system, and uses different sizes and conductivity to achieve microwave-induced thermoacoustic tomography image. From the experimental results, the image reconstruction errors are control less than 5%, and the resolution is enough for early detection of the early breast tumor. This paper use the complex tumor phantom composed from the sample superimposed by the three different conductivity phantoms, to verify the ability to distinguish between complex objects, which clearly distinguish differences in the physical characteristics of the sample at different locations. It helps

ACKNOWLEDGMENT

This research is supported by the Innovation Subject of the Shenyang Institute of Automation, Chinese Academy of Science (NO: YOF5150501).

REFERENCES

[1] Nie L.M., Xing D., Yang D.W., "Detection of foreign body using fast termoacoustic tomography with a multi-element linear transducer array," Appl Phys Lett, vol. 90, pp. 1–3, 2007.
[2] Zeng L.M., Xing D., Gu H.M., "Fast microwave-induced thermoacoustic tomography based on multi-element

phase-controlled focus technique". Chin Phys Lett, vol. 23, pp. 12125–1218, 2006.

[3] Rachel Bitton, Roger Zemp, Jesse Yen, Lihong Wang, "A 3-D high-frequency array based 16 channel photoacoustic microscopy system for in vivo micro-vascular imaging". IEEE Trans on Medical Imaging, vol. 28, pp. 1190–1197, 2009.

[4] Huang L., Yao L., Liu L.X., "Quantitative thermoacoustic tomography: recovery of conductivity maps of heterogeneous media" Appl Phys Lett, vol. 101, pp. 1–3, 2012.

[5] Yao Xie, Bin Guo, Geng Ku, Lihong Wang, "Adaptive and Robust Methods of reconstruction for thermoacoustic tomography" IEEE Trans on Biomedical Engineering, vol. 55, pp. 2741–2752, 2008.

[6] Yao L., Guo G.F., Jiang H.B., "Quantitative microwave-induced thermoacoustic tomography. Med Phys," vol. 37, pp. 3752–3759, 2010.

Multimedia Technology IV – Farag, Yang & Jiao (Eds)
© 2015 Taylor & Francis Group, London, ISBN: 978-1-138-02794-7

An invisible watermark algorithm including embedding and detection for color image based on internet

Xin-long Chen & Guo-qing Hu
College of Communication Engineering, Chongqing University, Chongqing, China

ABSTRACT: This paper presents an invisible watermark algorithm including embedding and detection for color image based on .NET GDI+. By visiting the web site (http://dgdz.ccee.cqu.edu.cn/watermark/invisiblewatermarkb.aspx) and uploading the original image and watermark image, the color image with the invisible watermark can be gained. By converting color image from RGB to YUV, the algorithm, based on DCT domain, is carried out by modifying some coefficients according to the characteristics of Human Visual System. By detecting or modifying some coefficients, the detection of watermark, which doesn't need original watermark image, also can be done on web and the algorithm is very simple and quite suitable for running on internet.

Keywords: Invisible Watermark; watermark removal; Color Image; internet

1 INTRODUCTION

The intellectual property right, which is the concentrated expression of the core competitiveness of enterprises, is the important wealth and resource of factors of production in the knowledge times. More and more problems of intellectual property rights infringement are generated by digital image transmission. The copyright protection and content authentication method and its application system for digital image, based on the Internet, has important significance. Digital image watermarking technology, a powerful tool for digital image copyright protection and content authentication, has been widely concerned by scholars.

There digital image watermark technology includes visible and invisible watermarks. The invisible watermark requires that the embedded watermark should be not only transparent to observers, but also robust enough so that it cannot be easily destroyed or removed after some digital image processing or attacks [1–2]. According to the watermark embedding technology, the digital watermark is divided into spatial domain and transform domain [3]. The existing frequency transformation methods for watermark embedding include discrete cosine transform (DCT) [4], discrete Fourier transform (DFT) [5], and discrete wavelet transform (DWT) [6]. In recent years, watermarking techniques have been improved using optimization algorithms such as genetic algorithm (GA) which is a popular evolutionary optimization technique invented by Holland [7]. In the field of watermarking, GA is mainly used in the embedding procedure to search for locations to embed the watermark [8–11].

As humans entered twenty-first century, the internet has changed people's life. Designing a color image watermark scheme and its application system, based on internet, are of great significance to the further promotion of digital watermarking technology. In this paper, the digital watermark scheme, which has been authorized Chinese invention patent (Patent No.: ZL200910104746.6), is a transform domain algorithm, and the texture complexity and edge feature of the carried image is not considered.

2 WATERMARK EMBEDDING

DCT (discrete cosine transform) is an orthogonal transformation method and proposed by Ahmed, etc. in 1974. The real part of the Fourier transform has many advantages, such as a high compression ratio, a small bit error rate, concentrate information and low computational complexity.

The scheme of watermark embedding, considering the need to use by Internet platform, is based on DCT transform and described in Figure 1.

The original image and the original watermark are obtained by File Upload component of ASP.Net. Considering the need to use by Internet platform, the original image, supporting JPG, PNG, GIF, BMP format, is color image. When its width has more than 800 pixels, or the height has more than 600 pixels, the application system adjusts it to 800 pixels or 600 pixels automatically.

The original watermark, supporting JPG, PNG, GIF, BMP format, is a two value image. Its width and height

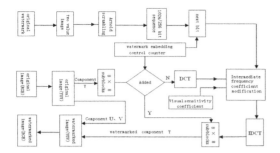

Figure 1. The scheme of watermark embedding.

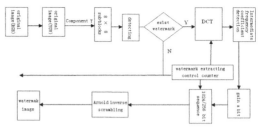

Figure 2. The scheme of watermark extracting.

are 32 pixels. When the image has more than 2 colors, or the width and height is not equal to 32 pixels, the application system adjusts it to two value images with 32 pixels width and height automatically.

When the width of original image has less than 256 pixels, or the height has less than 256 pixels, the application system adjusts the image of watermark to two value images with 16 pixels width and height automatically.

The application system also uses the.NET framework of GDI+ technology to obtain the original watermark. The original watermark is a two value image and scrambled by Arnold transformation.

Follows the steps of using .NET framework GDI+ technique to obtain the image and finish the processing of the image.

Using the bitmap class of the.NET GDI+ to object a new instance of the Bitmap object box, the Width, Height and other attribute information of the original image and original watermark will be obtained. Creating a new instance of the Color object, then you can gain the original image pixels and the original watermark image pixels of RGB component.

After that, the RGB image of the original image is converted to YUV space.

Y: brightness

U, V: color difference

The relationship from RGB color space to YUV color space as follows:

$$\begin{cases} Y = 0.299R + 0.587G + 0.114B \\ U = 0.147R + 0.289G + 0.436B \\ V = 0.615R - 0.515G + 0.100B \end{cases} \quad (1)$$

The Y component data is extracted from the original image and divided into many 8*8 subblocks. Each subblock does not overlap each other and performs DCT transform respectively.

Follows the DCT transform and inverse DCT transform:

$$X_{uv} = \alpha_u \alpha_v \sum_{i=0}^{N-1} \sum_{k=0}^{N-1} x_{ik} \cos\left[\frac{(2i+1)u\pi}{2N}\right] \cos\left[\frac{(2k+1)v\pi}{2N}\right] \quad (2)$$

$$x_{ik} = \sum_{u=0}^{N-1} \sum_{v=0}^{N-1} \alpha_u \alpha_v X_{uv} \cos\left[\frac{(2i+1)u\pi}{2N}\right] \cos\left[\frac{(2k+1)v\pi}{2N}\right] \quad (3)$$

The watermark is embedded by modifying two intermediate frequency coefficients, which is named D1 and D2.

Following the reference of the two intermediate frequency coefficient:

$DCT\_block(4,3), DCT\_block(5,2)$.

The method for modifying the middle frequency coefficients is amended as follows.

$Water(m,n)$=0, D1=N、D2=-N; （4）

$Water(m,n)$=1, D1=-N、D2=N;

The value of N is greater, the robustness of watermark image is better, but more distortion will come. According to the actual situation to set the value of N, maybe 10 is the right value of N.

Y component will be gained by performing inverse DCT transform for each sub watermarked block. Using Y component, U components and V components, converted them to RGB space, the invisible watermarked image has gained.

The relationship from YUV color space to RGB color space as follows:

$$\begin{cases} R = Y + 1.140V \\ G = Y - 0.395U - 0.581V \\ B = Y + 2.032U \end{cases} \quad (5)$$

3 WATERMARK EXTRACTING AND RECOVERING

The algorithm of watermark extracting as shown in Figure 2, explained briefly as follows.

The application system uses the.NET framework of GDI+ technology to obtain the Y component of the original image with watermark, divides the Y component into many 8*8 subblocks, and performs DCT transform for each subblock.

Got the values of the D1 and D2 and compared them with the threshold of T, if the image has embedded watermark, got the bit of watermark image.

The method for getting the bit of watermark image is amended as follows.

D1>T、D2<-T: $Water(m,n)$=0;

D1<-T、D2>T: $Water(m,n)$=1;

188

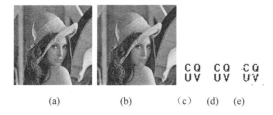

(a)   (b)   (c)   (d)   (e)

Figure 3. The test images.
A: original image   b: watermarked image
C: original watermark   d: watermark extracting

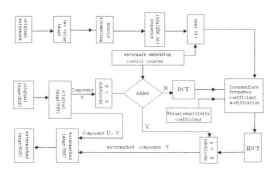

Figure 4. The gray watermarked image.

According to the actual situation to set the value of T, maybe 4 is the right value of T.

The bit sequences, extracted from the D1 and D2, are scrambled inversely by Arnold transformation, the watermark, which has embedded in the original image, can be obtained.

4   RESULTS AND CONCLUSIONS

When you have uploaded the original image and watermark image to the server, you can click the Embedding button to add a watermark into the original image. You can also click the extracting button to extract the watermark from the watermarked image.

You can click the default button to get the default original image (Fig. 3a) and the default watermark image (Fig. 3c).

Some test data is as shown in Figure 3. The test data shows that the method of watermark embedding has little influence on the original image and the image of watermark extracting is visible clearly.

This method can also be applied to gray image. The original gray image as shown in Figure 1, the watermarked image is shown in Figure 4, the watermark extracting is shown in Fig. 3e.

The experimental images from the attack of shearing are as shown in Figure 5.

Through the experiment site and test data, it is not difficult to get the conclusions as follows:

The recoverable color image blind watermark scheme, based on internet, has good imperceptibility. The effect on the color image is small and the watermark extracting is clearly visible. Furthermore, this

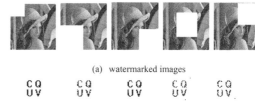

(a) watermarked images

(b)   The images of watermark extracting

Figure 5.   The experimental of the attack of shearing.

paper releases the algorithm for removal of watermark and the practicability of the scheme is very strong, so that the algorithm is very simple and quite suitable for running on internet.

REFERENCES

[1] Wei Wang, Chengxi Wang, "A Watermarking Algorighm for Gray-level Watermark based on Local Feature Region and SVD", International Congress on Image and Signal Processing, 2008, 650–654.

[2] W. Wang, W.H. Li, Y.K. Liu, Z. Borut," A SVD Feature based Watermarking Algorithm for Gray-level Image Watermark," Journal of Computers, vol. 9, pp. 1497–1502, 2014.

[3] R.B. Wolfgang, C.I. Podilchuk, E.J. Delp. Perceptual watermark for digital image and video. Pro. IEEE, 2007, 87(1): 1108–1126.

[4] W. Liu and C.H. Zhao, "Digital watermarking for volume data based on 3D-DWT and 3D-DCT," The 2nd International Conference on Interaction Sciences: Information Technology, Culture and Human, pp. 352–357, 2009.

[5] M. David, S.R. Jordi, and F. Mehdi, "Efficient selfsynchronised blind audio watermarking system based on time domain and FFT amplitude modification," Signal Processing. Vol. 90, pp. 3078–3092, 2010.

[6] B. Deepayan and A. Charith, "Video watermarking using motion compensated 2D+t+2D filtering," The 12th ACM workshop on Multimedia and security, pp. 127–136, 2010.

[7] J. Holland, "Adaptation in natural and artificial systems,"University of Michigan Press, Ann Arbor, MI, 1975.

[8] P. Kumsawat, K. Attakitmongcol, and A. Srikaew, "A new approach for optimization in image watermarking by using genetic algorithms," IEEE Transactions on Signal Processing, vol. 53, pp. 4707–4719, 2005.

[9] Y.T. Wu and F.Y. Shih, "Genetic algorithm based methodology for breaking the steganalytic systems," IEEE Transactions on Systems, Man, and Cybernetics, vol. 36, pp. 24–31, 2006.

[10] S.C. Chu, H.C. Huang, Y. Shi, S.Y. Wu, and C.S. Shieh,"Genetic watermarking for zerotree-based applications,"Circuits Systems Signal Process, vol. 27, pp. 171–182, 2008.

[11] H.C. Huang, J.S. Pan, Y.H. Huang, F.H. Wang, and K.C. Huang, "Progressive watermarking techniques using genetic algorithms," Circuits Systems Signal Processing, vol. 26, pp. 671–687, 2007.

Multimedia Technology IV – Farag, Yang & Jiao (Eds)
© 2015 Taylor & Francis Group, London, ISBN: 978-1-138-02794-7

A novel holistic approach for 3D face recognition from range images

Suranjan Ganguly, Debotosh Bhattacharjee & Mita Nasipuri
Department of Computer Science and Engineering, Jadavpur University, Kolkata, India

ABSTRACT: In this paper, a novel method is proposed for human face recognition from 2.5D range images using holistic approach. The proposed methodology extracts the edge image and mean curvature image from a range face image, which are then combined to form a new and efficient feature space for better recognition. With this kind of feature space, it has been observed that the similarities among intra-class members are much higher, whereas the interclass dissimilarities are also accountable. The measurement of similarities is carried out using Hausdorff distance and defined fuzzy rule for recognition purpose. The validation of the algorithm is doneon Frav3D as well as on GavabDB databases. The 3D face images from these databases deals with all frontal pose range images (expression, illumination and neutral) along with rotated faces about three axes (X, Y and Z). The databases are having synthesized dataset which have been considered by the authors during face recognition process. At first, the rotated face range images have been registered and then the proposed recognition methodology is applied on frontal face images along with registered face images. Thus, the synthesized dataset is consists of the original frontal as well as registered range face images. The recognition rates for Frav3D and GavabDB database have been reported in Section 4.

Keywords: 2.5D, Range face image, Holistic approach, Mean Curvature, Hausdorff distance, Frav3D, GavabDB

1 INTRODUCTION

Face image based biometric system has various applications in security, criminal identification, fraud detection, daily attendance etc. Face image is natural and it can be obtained without touching the sensor and for which it might not be an offensive issue for any culture as well as hygienic concerns are also addressed. There are some challenging tasks during face recognition due to illumination, expression, pose variation etc. Now a day's due to the availability of 3D sensor cameras, a new interest to 3D image based face recognition is growing among the researchers. The 3D face images are used to overcome some of the challenges like pose variation, illumination etc.

The aim of this work is to introduce a novel face recognition method, which is invariant to expression, illumination and pose variation. Here, mean curvatures from face images along with edge are combined and then holistic approach [1] is followed to carry out the recognition in newly generated feature space.

The rest of the paper has been organized as follows. In Section 2, some of the related works, in the research area, have been discussed. In Section 3, the proposed algorithm is described. Experimental results are reported in Section 4. Conclusions have been given in Section 5.

2 RELATED WORKS AND COMPARATIVE STUDY

Here an overview of related work on profile based 3D face recognition is discussed with a comparison to the proposed method.

Frank B. Haar et al. [2] presented a 3D face matching technique by facial curves. The algorithm is focused on profile and contour based face matching. Three curves collected from each of 45 face samples from SHREC2007 database are combined and achieved the maximum mean average precision (MAP) of 0.78. In [3], Chafik Samir et al. constituted a facial surface as a representation of indexed facial curves and that has been calculated from a surface distance function. Mahoor et al. [4] also introduced a recognition algorithm for range images in frontal pose. The algorithm is focused on ridge lines on surface from face images and then matching is done applying ausdorff distance and ICP. They have combined GavabDB and FRG V2.0 facedatabases for their work.

In comparison to the work on 3D face recognition from range images, we have established a new approach with following properties. In our method there is no training-testing phase. The algorithm is designed to take the recognition problem in real time. The proposed algorithm is invariant of expression and

Input Range Face Image

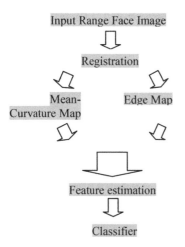

Registration

Mean-Curvature Map   Edge Map

Feature estimation

Classifier

Figure 1. Schematic diagram of the proposed method.

illumination problem without applying any normalization method. The poses have been corrected using novel face registration mechanism. The feature space that have been considered for matching purpose is new of its kind and incorporates all the local and surface features from face region. The ausdorff distance [5–6] is used to measure the dissimilarities which is used to recognize the probe image by the proposed fuzzy rule. This fuzzy rule is also invariant of databases.

3 PROPPOSED ALGORITHM

The proposed method is divided into four sub-mechanisms namely: range face image generation, pose registration, feature extraction, and classification. In Fig. 1 the schematic diagram of the proposed algorithm is depicted.

3.1 Range face image

For any 3D face image its corresponding range image [7] is created and such range images are also called as 2.5D images [16]. 3D face images that have been considered for our research work is collected from Frav3D database [8] and GavabDB database [9]. The face images for Frav3D database have been collected using Minolta VIVID 700 scanner.

Generated face range images for randomly selected single subject are shown in Fig. 2.

In GavabDB database, there is another challenge regarding face registration as well as recognition of face images that have been rotated along Y-axis. In Fig. 3, the range face images of a single person that is selected randomly from GavabDB database have been described.

3.2 Face registration

For robust face recognition, in an uncontrolled environment face registration is used to transform the

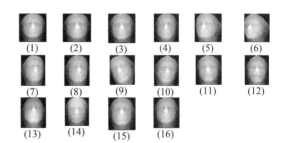

(1) (2) (3) (4) (5) (6)
(7) (8) (9) (10) (11) (12)
(13) (14) (15) (16)

Figure 2. Range face images generated from Frav3D database.

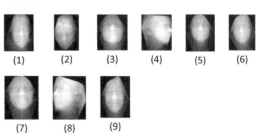

(1) (2) (3) (4) (5) (6)
(7) (8) (9)

Figure 3. Range face images generated from GavabDB database.

rotated face image oriented towards frontal pose. Face can be rotated in any direction along any axes (X, Y and Z). In the proposed method, 3D geometrical transformation about a reference point. The reference point can be any facial landmark such as: nose tip, eye corners, chin tip etc. Basically, there are three different types of registration methods [10], namely, one to all registration, registration by a model selected from a training face, and registration by facial geometric properties or reference point.

Proposed technique accomplishes registration of rotated face images using facial geometric property. The interest point i.e. the nose tip is detected from isolated nose region and for 3D geometric transformation. The transformation angle is derived from the position of the detected nose tips from neutral face and rotated face respectively. The mathematical computations that have been followed for angle computation are shown in equations (1) to (6).

The co-ordinate pairs (x_0, y_0) and (x_1, y_1) in X-Y plane is the detected nose tips for frontal and rotated face images respectively. If the face is rotated along X-axis in any direction (either left or right) then displacement along Y-axis has occurred. Here, the equation (1) is expressed as:

$$\alpha = \pm \tan^{-1}\left(\frac{(y_1 - y_0)}{(\text{depth})}\right) \quad (1)$$

When the face is rotated along Y axis then displacement is noted along X-axis. So, the formula for angle determination is shown in equation (2).

$$\beta = \pm \tan^{-1}\left(\frac{(x_1 - x_0)}{(\text{depth})}\right) \quad (2)$$

In both the equations (1) and (2) 'depth' is chosen as average depth value at nose tip from rotated and frontal pose face range images. But along Z-axis face rotation, equation 3 is followed.

$$\theta = \pm \tan^{-1}\left(\frac{(x_1 - x_0)}{(y_1 - y_0)}\right) \tag{3}$$

The 3D geometric rotation matrices for X, Y and Z are exhibited in equation (4), (5) and (6) respectively. Rotational matrix along X-axis is =

$$\begin{bmatrix} 1 & 0 & 0 & 0 \\ 0 & \cos\theta & -\sin\theta & 0 \\ 0 & \sin\theta & \cos\theta & 0 \\ 0 & 0 & 0 & 1 \end{bmatrix} \tag{4}$$

Rotational matrix along Y-axis is =

$$\begin{bmatrix} \cos\alpha & 0 & -\sin\alpha & 0 \\ 0 & 1 & 0 & 0 \\ \sin\alpha & 0 & \cos\alpha & 0 \\ 0 & 0 & 0 & 1 \end{bmatrix} \tag{5}$$

and Rotational matrix along Z-axis =

$$\begin{bmatrix} \cos\beta & \sin\beta & 0 & 0 \\ -\sin\beta & \cos\beta & 0 & 0 \\ 0 & 0 & 1 & 0 \\ 0 & 0 & 0 & 1 \end{bmatrix} \tag{6}$$

With the proposed methodology, the isolation of nose region and detection of nose tip can be done robustly and it is also invariant of pose. The nose region is isolated using Otsu's multilevel threshold method [11–13]. It is iterative in nature and unsupervised method. Authors have applied this method to maximize the goal to isolate the nose region for range face image registration. The depth values from range image are thresholded at level 13. From the isolated nose region, maximum depth based point is focused by scanning in row-major order to detect the nose tip for range face image registration purpose.

The accuracy for nose tip detection is measured as 98.91% for Frav3D and 94.44% for GavabDB. The accuracy is verified after validating it with manually detected nose tip.

With the depicted success rate for nose tip detection, 87.5% of the rotated faces have been successfully registered from Frav3D database and for GavabDB, the success rate of registration is 89.87%. Therefore, a partial synthesized face dataset from original Frav3D and GavabDB database have been proposed by the authors. The synthesized dataset consists of original frontal face images along with registered face range images. These datasets have been considered during our investigation for automatic face recognition. Some of the registered face images from Frav3D as well as GavabDB dataset is illustrated in Table 1.

3.3 Feature estimation

Feature selection is also a challenging issue for accurate recognition of face images. An efficient selection

Table 1. Randomly selected registered face images from databases.

Unregistered Face image	Registered Face image	Unregistered Face image	Registered Face image
Frav3D Database		GavabDB Database	

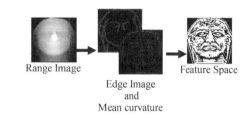

Range Image Edge Image and Mean curvature Feature Space

Figure 4. Pipeline process of feature selection.

of features will increase intra-class similarities as well as inter-class dissimilarities.

For our proposed 3D face recognition approach from range images uses a new logical image, which is designed from mean-curvature and edge images. This phenomenon is described in Fig. 4.

The accumulated points are then compared by the Hausdorff distance [6]. The face deformation during expression is handled by the proposed fuzzy rule. Due to the deformation, the dissimilarity between the members of its own class and members of the other classes' can be distinguished easily. The mean-curvature [14–15] points for any range face image are always preserved and some extra local edge points are combined with it to create a new feature space for better recognition purpose. The mean curvature denoted by (H) is computed from equation (7) and (8).

$$H = \frac{1}{2}\left(\frac{f_{xx} + f_{yy} + f_{xx}f_y^2 + f_{yy}f_x^2 - 2f_xf_yf_{xy}}{(1 + f_x^2 + f_y^2)^{3/2}}\right) \tag{7}$$

$$\text{where, } f_x = \frac{\partial f}{\partial x}, f_y = \frac{\partial f}{\partial y}, f_{xx} = \frac{\partial^2 f}{\partial x^2}, f_{yy} = \frac{\partial^2 f}{\partial y^2}, f_{xy}$$

$$= \frac{\partial^2 f}{\partial x \, \partial y} \tag{8}$$

Out of four curvatures such as: Gaussian curvature, mean curvature, maximum and minimum principal curvatures; mean curvature is considered due to its translation and rotation invariant component. Mean curvature is also having local properties from surface. There are also many edge operators [12] like 'Sobel', 'Prewitt' etc. But the edge from the depth based range image is calculated from canny edge detection mechanism. Due to the usage of Gaussian technique for smoothing along with upper and lower threshold value for preserving valid edge information, canny edge operator is chosen for our research work.

3.4 Classification

The problem of face recognition is very complex. In this context, a novel and effective classification algorithm is proposed, by which the probe image is assigned with its own class label. In our proposed algorithm, it is done using fuzzy-rule based classifier. The distance metric is also termed as max-min distance. It measures the minimum distances of a point from a set of points and then takes the largest value for determining final distance.

In brief, at first, the distance between probe image and all the gallery images are preserved. By the general perception, for the same person the distance between probe image and gallery images should be same. Hence the mismatched distance, measured by the Hausdorff distance, should be numerically zero (0). Due to the facial deformation, the zero perception does not make true sense for all. In this circumstance, for final classification purpose fuzzy rule is accomplished during class labelling step.

Based on the array of distances between probe and gallery face range images, a fuzzy rule is generated (shown in Fig. 5). Based on the fuzzy rule, every gallery range face images will vote for the probe image with respect to strongly acceptance, weakly acceptance, weakly rejection and strongly rejection. Thus, from distance metric, a 'vote matrix' is created by the system. Now, rather than only distance metric, 'vote metric' is used to label the class of the probe image. All the members from all the classes are allowed to match the probe image with their own and vote for the probe face range image and the maximum number of accepted members (i.e. the number of votes for strongly acceptance is added with the number of votes for weakly acceptance) from any class is privileged as destination class for the probe image.

The number of terms, shown in Fig. 5, is chosen empirically. The selection of distances that have been used for classification is executed by an iterative process. Similarly, changing number of terms may lead to poor recognition rate. Fuzzy disjunction method (described in equation (9)) is considered for our research work. Disjunction method selects the maximum of two selected probabilities ($p(d_1)$ and $p(d_2)$) as shown in Fig. 5.

4 EXPERIMENTAL RESULTS AND DISCUSSION

The research work has been carried out on Frav3D and GavabDB databases. The feature space generated for final distance matching is the combination of edge and mean-curve. As described earlier, the algorithm can

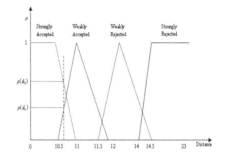

Figure 5. Four terms in distance fuzzification.

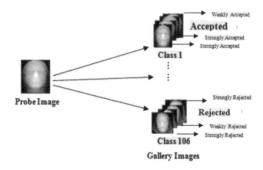

Figure 6. The matching phenomenon of the proposed algorithm.

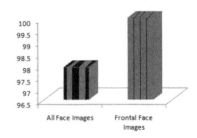

Figure 7. Summary of recognition rate for Frav3D database.

be used in real time classification purpose for probe image. The input probe image will be tested on all gallery images for selecting its own class correctly. The matching phenomenon is emphasized in Fig. 6.

The classification rate for synthesized Frav3D database is 97.89%. Another set of investigation for recognition purpose is performed by selecting only frontal pose face images which includes expression, illumination etc. from Frav3D database which gives 100% classification rate. The summary of accurate recognition rate is described in Fig. 7.

With this methodology, it is noticed that there are more than one class which are having the same probability for selecting the destination class of the probe image. Then, the class which will have a zero mismatch distance between any of its member and probe image is chosen as final destination class of the probe range

Recognition Rate(%)

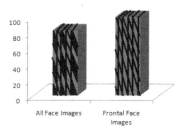

Figure 8. Summary of recognition rate for GavabDB database.

Table 2. Face recognition rate by proposed algorithm.

Database Name	Recognition rate from synthesized face dataset (frontal + registered)	Recognition rate for frontal face dataset
Frav3D	97.89%	100%
GavabDB	83%	100%

Recognition Rate(%)

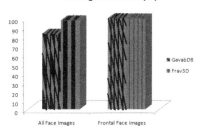

Figure 9. Comparison of the recognition rate from two different databases.

face image. It is further inspected that, there will be at least one face image from a particular class which will have the exactly same gallery image as probe image, then that class should have the better anticipation to adopt the probe image.

To validate our proposed algorithm, it has also been tested on GavabDB database. The fuzzy rule that has been designed for our algorithm for Frav3D database is also remained same for GavabDB database.

It is further noticed that, the algorithm for frontal face images from GavabDB is also securing 100% success rate, but when all the face image i.e. synthesized dataset is under investigation then success rate is reduced to 83% accurate classification rate. The summary of recognition rate from GavabDB database is explained in Fig. 8.

In Table 2, the accurate recognition rate for the databases by the proposed algorithm is reported.

A comparison of the recognition rates by our proposed mechanism on Frav3D and GavabDB databases has also been presented in Fig. 9.

5 CONCLUSION

Our proposed method is a novel solution to real time face recognition in un-controlled environment and the same is also tested on two datasets and therefore the validation and robustness of our algorithm is preserved.

It has a little drawback with a set of advantages as reported. The drawback is that with increasing number of classes, along with increase in the members of each classes, the matching phenomenon will be more time consuming. Testing of this algorithm with other datasets and minimization of the time complexity for those are currently under investigation.

ACKNOWLEDGMENT

Authors are thankful for a project supported by DeitY (Letter No.: 12(12)/2012-ESD), MCIT, Govt. of India, at Department of Computer Science and Engineering, Jadavpur University, India for providing the necessary infrastructure for this work.

REFERENCES

[1] Jennifer J. Richler, Olivia S. Cheung and Isabel Gauthier, 'Holistic Processing Predicts Face Recognition', Application for Psychological Science, 22(4), 464–471, DOI: 10.1177/0956797611401753.

[2] F.B. Haar and R.C. Veltkamp, "A 3D face matching framework," in Proc. IEEE Int. Conf. Shape Model. Appl., Oct. 2008, pp. 103–110.

[3] C. Samir, A. Srivastava, M. Daoudi, and E. Klassen, "An intrinsic framework for analysis of facial surfaces," Int. J. Comput. Vis., vol. 82, no. 1, pp. 80–95, 2009.

[4] M.H. Mahoor and M. Abdel-Mottaleb, "Face recognition based on 3Dridge images obtained from range data," Pattern Recognit., vol. 42, no. 3, pp. 445–451, 2009.

[5] Oliver Jesorsky, Klaus J. Kirchberg, and Robert W. Frischholz, "Robust Face Detection Using the Hausdor Distance", In Proc. Third International Conference on Audio- and Video-based Biometric Person Authentication, Springer, Lecture Notes in Computer, Science, LNCS-2091, pp. 90–95, Halmstad, Sweden, 6–8 June 2001.

[6] Dong-Gyu Sim, Oh-Kyu Kwon, and Rae-Hong Park, "Object Matching Algorithms Using Robust Hausdorff Distance Measures", IEEE Transactions On Image Processing, Vol. 8, No. 3, March 1999.

[7] Suranjan Ganguly, Debotosh Bhattacharjee and Mita Nasipuri, "3D Face Recognition from Range Images Based on Curvature Analysis", ICTACT Journal on Image and Video Processing, Volume: 04, Issue: 03, pages 748-753, ISSN Number (Print): 0976-9099, ISSN Number (Online): 0976-9102, February 2014.

[8] Frav3D details (http://www.frav.es/databases).

[9] GavabDB details (http://gavab.escet.urjc.es/recursos_en.html)

[10] Luuk Spreeuwers, "Fast and Accurate 3D Face Recognition", Int J Comput Vis (2011) 93: 389–414, DOI 10.1007/s11263-011-0426-2.

[11] Nobuyuki Otsu, "A Threshold Selection Method from Gray-Level Histograms",IEEE Transactions on Systems, Man, and Cybernetics, Vol. SMC-9, No. 1, January 1979.

[12] Rafel C. Gonzalez, Richard E. Woods; "Digital Image Processing", Third Edition, 2008.

[13] Ping-Sung Liao, Tse-Sheng Chen, Pau-Choo Chunga, "Fast Algorithm for Multilevel Thresholding", Journal Of Information Science And Engineering 17, 713–727 (2001).

[14] Zvi Har'el, "Curvature of Curves and Surfaces – A Parabolic Approach", January 16, 1995, URL: http://www.math.technion.ac.il/S/rl/docs/parabola.pdf.

[15] Michael Garman and Jessica Bonnie, "Curvature of Surfaces in 3-Space".

[16] Suranjan Ganguly, Debotosh Bhattacharjee and Mita Nasipuri, "2.5D Face Images: Acquisition, Processing and Application", Computer Networks and Security, International Conference on Communication and Computing, *Elsevier Science and Technology*, Pages: 36–44, ISBN: 9789351072447, June 2014.

Multimedia Technology IV – Farag, Yang & Jiao (Eds)
© 2015 Taylor & Francis Group, London, ISBN: 978-1-138-02794-7

Efficient SIMD acceleration of DCT and IDCT for high efficiency video coding

Lingyu Li, Xiaoyun Zhang & Zhiyong Gao
Institute of Image Communication and Network Engineering, Shanghai Jiao Tong University, Shanghai, China

ABSTRACT: The promising High Efficiency Video Coding (HEVC) standard aims at much higher coding efficiency, but the cost is the greatly increased computation complexity. Among all the coding modules, DCT and IDCT are frequently called and bring a lot of complexity burden. While, the Single Instruction Multiple Data (SIMD) technique has been widely used to speed up media data process. In this paper, we focus on SIMD acceleration of HEVC DCT and IDCT, and the implementation is conducted on 64-bit multicore platform. For DCT optimization, intermediate variables are processed in less bit width and parallel processing level is significantly improved with little compression efficiency loss. Experiment results on 64-bit Tilera multicore platform exhibit that the proposed SIMD implementation can greatly reduce about 40%–70% computational complexity of DCT and IDCT with negligible compression performance loss.

Keywords: simd; dct; idct; hevc; tilera

1 INTRODUCTION

The Joint Collaborative Team on Video Coding (JCT-VC) has published the next generation video coding standard referred to as High Efficiency Video Coding (HEVC). HEVC is expected to provide 200% compression efficiency over the current standard H.264. However, high compression efficiency is achieved at the cost of much more computational complexity, which has become a serious problem for the real-time video codec [1].

In video codec, Discrete Cosine Transform (DCT) plays a vital role in video compression. The transform tool in HEVC is far more complicated than the H.264 standard. HEVC can support various transform sizes ranging from 4×4 to 32×32. Besides, for the transform of 4×4 intra TU (transform unit) of luma component, an approximation to the discrete sine transform (DST) is applied [2]. Compared with H.264, the coefficients of DCT transform more complicated, which results in more multiplications instead of shifts and additions. In addition, the intermediate variables need more bit width, which reduces the parallel processing level.

In recent years, most modern processors provide media instructions to improve the computational performance. Single instruction multiple data (SIMD) is a very efficient tool in processing media data. By exploiting the data-level parallelism, SIMD technologies provide a series of effective approaches for fast algorithm implementation. On Intel platform, the MMX/SSE technology is a typical example of SIMD [10]. On popular Intel and ARM platforms, there

are some SIMD based algorithms for HEVC [5–6]. The TILE-Gx36 is a system-on-chip 36-core processor of Tilera family [12]. Each of the 36 processor cores is a full-fledged 64-bit processor. The processor instruction set architecture (ISA) includes a rich set of SIMD instructions. Due to the low power consumption and effective parallel processing ability, some HEVC codec implementation work has been done on Tilera platform [7–9].

We focus our work on the SIMD acceleration of HEVC DCT and IDCT modules on Tilera multicore platform. The rest of this paper is organized as follows. An introduction of HEVC DCT and IDCT is given in Section 2. Section 3 presents our proposed SIMD acceleration method of HEVC DCT and IDCT on Tilera platform. Section 4 provides the acceleration results. At last, Section 5 concludes the paper.

2 INTRODUCTION OF HEVC DCT AND IDCT

Similar to previous video coding standards, DCT and IDCT modules in HEVC are used to transform the prediction residues to eliminate spatial redundancy. Two-dimensional DCT and IDCT are calculated by applying horizontal and vertical one-dimensional DCT and IDCT. The DCT and IDCT of HEVC can support different TB (transform block) sizes: 4×4, 8×8, 16×16 and 32×32.

In H.264, the one-dimensional transform can be implemented by matrix multiplication and dot product. First, the multiplication of the input matrix and the kernel transform matrix is calculated. The coefficients of

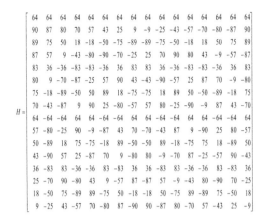

Figure 1. Coefficient matrix of 16 × 16 DCT.

Figure 2.   Process of one-dimensional HEVC DCT.

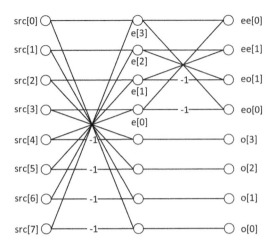

Figure 3. Process of partial butterfly computation of 8 × 8 DCT.

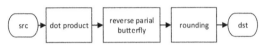

Figure 4.   Process of one-dimensional HEVC IDCT.

kernel transform matrix are $+1$, -1, $+2$, -2, which indicates the computation of the matrix multiplication can be done by addition and shift operations. Then, compute the dot product of the kernel transform result and a scaling matrix and this operation is embedded in quantization process [3]. The DCT and IDCT coefficient matrixes of HEVC are more complicated compared with previous standards. The matrix for the 16x16 DCT and IDCT is given in Fig. 1. [1]. The coefficient matrix has good even-odd symmetry property, which can be utilized to do partial butterfly process to reduce implementation complexity.

2.1   The process of one-dimensional HEVC DCT

Due to the symmetry and anti-symmetry of DCT coefficients, the matrix multiplication in transform can be done by partial-butterfly to reduce complexity [4]. The process of one-dimensional HEVC DCT can be presented in Fig. 2, in which src is the source input and dst is the destination output.

The first stage of one-dimensional HEVC DCT process is to do partial butterfly to calculate the even and odd intermediate variables. The partial-butterfly process is as shown in Fig. 3, in which src are the source input data. e/o is the even/odd intermediate variable. ee/eo is the even-even/even-odd intermediate variable, etc. The order of intermediate variables increases with the name length. The intermediate variables are computed by cascaded additions and subtractions of source input data.

Then the dot product of intermediate variables and the corresponding coefficients is computed to get the result of matrix multiplication.

Due to the 16-bit width limitation of one-dimensional DCT output, the 32-bit result of matrix

multiplication is rounded into 16-bit. The shift number varies with the DCT sizes and transform direction. In the rounding process, an offset number derived from shift number is added and then the result is right shifted. The rounding computation of DCT is as shown in (1), in which x is the input and y is the output. $offset$ is the offset number derived from shift number $shift$. The shift number varies with transform direction and size N. B is the pixel bit width (8 or 10) [2]. $error$ is the rounding error.

$$y = (x + offset) \gg shift$$
$$offset = (1 \ll (shift - 1))$$
$$shift = \begin{cases} \log_2(N) - 1 + (B - 8), (horizontol) \\ \log_2(N) + 6, (vertical) \end{cases}$$
$$error = 2^{shift - 1}$$

(1)

2.2   The process of one-dimensional HEVC IDCT

The process of one-dimensional HEVC IDCT is similar to that of HEVC DCT. In DCT, we add or subtract the source input to calculate the intermediate variables and then dot product the intermediate variables with coefficients. While in HEVC IDCT, partial butterfly process is in reverse. Dot product is processed first, then reverse partial butterfly, and finally rounding the results. The process is as shown in Fig. 4.

3   SIMD ACCELERATION OF HEVC DCT AND IDCT ON TILERA PLATFORM

In this section, we propose an acceleration method of HEVC DCT and IDCT using SIMD set on Tilera

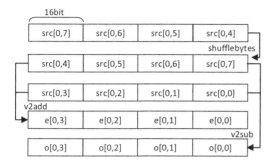

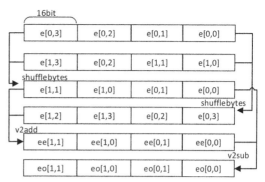

Figure 5.   Calculation of e/o intermediate variables.

Figure 6.   Calculation of ee/eo intermediate variables.

platform. The basic idea of SIMD is to utilize high-bit-width register to parallel process multiple low-bit-width data. Registers are considered as vectors of elements of the same data type: 8-bit, 16-bit, 32-bit and 64-bit signed/unsigned. In common computer architecture, multiplication instruction is more time-consuming than other mathematical computation instructions. High efficiency parallel multiplication related SIMD instructions is considered first and then other mathematical computation (i.e. addition, subtraction and shift) SIMD instructions. The data also need to be frequently rearranged according to the computation rule of those instructions. TILE Gx36 processor of Tilera has 64 64-bit registers and supports multiple vector mathematical operations such as vector dot product, addition, subtraction, shifting, multiplication and saturation etc. [11].

3.1   Acceleration of HEVC DCT

According to the process of one-dimensional HEVC DCT, we design the SIMD acceleration process as follows.

In one-dimensional HEVC DCT, partial butterfly is processed first to calculate the even-odd intermediate variables. Before partial butterfly, the source input data are loaded into 64-bit registers with instruction *ld* (for detailed description of all Tilera instructions, refer to [11]). The input data of DCT are stored in 16-bit, so four adjacent input data can be loaded into a four-word vector. We use *shufflebytes* instruction to rearrange the data in two registers. Then instruction *v2add* and *v2sub* is used to do four-word vector addition and subtraction to get the even-odd intermediate variables. The process is as shown in Fig. 5 and Fig. 6.

For the horizontal one-dimensional DCT transform, the input data are the residuals of 8-bit unsigned pixel data, so the residuals are 9-bit signed. The first-order even-odd intermediate variables are the sums or subtractions of source input data, so they are 10-bit signed data. The bit width increases with the intermediate variables order. The maximum order of intermediate variables is 4 in 32 × 32 DCT, so the maximum bit width of intermediate variables is 13 (9 + 4). They can be store in 16bits. However, the input of the vertical one-dimensional DCT is the output of the horizontal one-dimensional DCT, which are 16-bit data. If

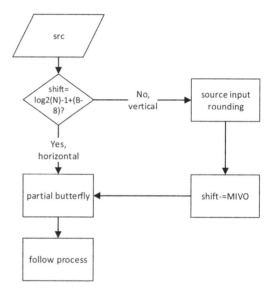

Figure 7.   Preprocess of one-dimensional DCT.

we still use 16bits to process intermediate variables, there would be serious bit overflow error. While the register bit width of Tilera platform is 64, the SIMD parallel processing level is limited compared with 128-bit Intel MMX/SSE. We tried using 32-bit to process intermediate variables, but the acceleration result is not good. In order to achieve reasonable parallel processing level, we consider rounding the input data to make the intermediate variables stored in 16bits.

We propose an approximate vertical one-dimensional DCT, in which the source input data are rounded to make the intermediate variables within 16-bit. This method is based on the strategy of maintaining parallel processing level at the cost of some compression performance loss. In order not to change the interface of one-dimensional DCT function, we add preprocessing before partial butterfly. The preprocessing of one-dimensional DCT is as shown in Fig. 7, in which $MIVO$ is the maximum intermediate variable order, and other variables are mentioned in (1). At the beginning of this preprocess, the direction of one-dimensional DCT is determined by the shift number. If it is the horizontal

Table 1. Error analysis in the vertical one-dimension DCT.

DCT Size	Max-order Intermediate Variable	Max Intermediate Variable Order	Maximum Error
4×4	e/o	1	1
8×8	ee/eo	2	2
16×16	eee/eeo	3	4
32×32	eeee/eeeo	4	8

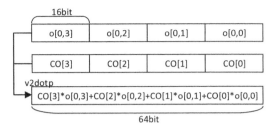

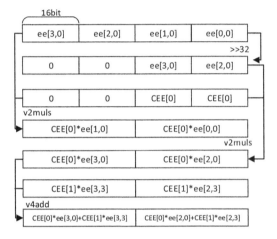

Figure 8. Computing the sum of four products.

one-dimensional DCT, we directly go to partial butter-fly process, or, we do the following process. First, the input data are rounded to make the intermediate variables be processed in 16-bit as shown in (2). In this rounding process, x is the source input, y is the rounding result. Then the shift number is decreased by $MIVO$ to compensate the right shift in source rounding. The parallel shift and addition can be done by using instruction $v2add$ and $v2shrs$. In one-dimensional DCT, the scaling effect of dot product with coefficients compensate that of the rounding of the final output, so the final output error equals to the source input rounding error. The detailed rounding error analysis is derived from (1), given in Table 1. We can see that the errors are limited and increases with the DCT size.

$$y = (x + (1 << (MIVO - 1))) >> MIVO \qquad (2)$$

As the even-odd intermediate variables are prepared, the dot product of the intermediate variables and coefficient vectors is to be computed. Instruction $v2dotp$ is used to get the dot product of two four-word vectors as shown in Fig. 8, in which CO is the coefficient of odd intermediate variable. As the bit width of dot product does not exceed 32, two 64-bit dot products are interleaved into one 64-bit vector with instruction $v4int\_l$ for later parallel processing. For dot product of vectors with more elements, $v2dotp$ and cascaded $v2dotpa$ instruction are employed. The $v2dotpa$ instruction can add the dot product to the destination register. For example, if we need the dot product of two 8-word vectors, instruction v2dotp is employed to get the dot product of the first half part and instruction v2dotpa is employed to add it with the rest half part. In order to get the dot product of two two-word vectors, instruction $v2muls$ is used to parallel calculate two 32-bit products and then instruction $v4add$ to get two sums, as shown in Fig. 9, in which CEE is the coefficient for even-even intermediate variable.

At last, the 32-bit matrix multiplication result is rounded into 16-bit. The two 32-bit offset number derived from shift number is loaded into one 64-bit vector, then added to the dot product vector with $v4add$ instruction, and parallel right shifted with $v4shrs$ instruction. Finally, the 32-bit data are parallel clamped into 16-bit with $v4packsc$ instruction and stored into destination output memory with st instruction. The rounding process in (1) is given in Fig. 10.

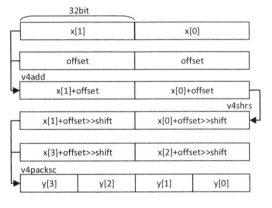

Figure 9. Process of dot product of two two-element vectors.

Figure 10. Parallel rounding process.

In SIMD implementation, the data need to be rearranged frequently. By appropriately utilizing interleave instructions ($v2int\_l$, $v2int\_h$, etc.) and $shuffle$-$bytes$ instruction, we can get any data permutation of vectors.

3.2 Acceleration of HEVC IDCT

IDCT is the inverse process of DCT. As the input data used for dot product are not adjacent in memory, they cannot be loaded into register directly. For example, in order to get the odd intermediate variables of 8×8

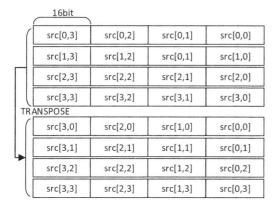

16bit

src[0,3]	src[0,2]	src[0,1]	src[0,0]
src[1,3]	src[1,2]	src[0,1]	src[1,0]
src[2,3]	src[2,2]	src[2,1]	src[2,0]
src[3,3]	src[3,2]	src[3,1]	src[3,0]

TRANSPOSE

src[3,0]	src[2,0]	src[1,0]	src[0,0]
src[3,1]	src[2,1]	src[1,1]	src[0,1]
src[3,2]	src[2,2]	src[1,2]	src[0,2]
src[3,3]	src[2,3]	src[1,3]	src[0,3]

Figure 11. Process of vector transposition.

IDCT, the input data in each odd row of same column needs to be loaded into one vector. While, there is memory address stride between each row. We load four four-word vectors first and use a transposition process composed of interleave instructions (*v2intl_l* and *v2intl_h*) to transpose them, as shown in Fig. 11. By this process, the non-adjacent data are loaded into one register. The output of IDCT should be in the range of 16-bit signed integer (from -32768 to 32767), instruction *v4packsc* is applied to saturate the results to the appropriate range.

Table 2. Instruction cycles of DCT functions.

DCT Size	Average Origin Cycles	Average Accelerated Cycles	Saving Rate
4×4	143	84	41.26%
8×8	562	298	46.98%
16×16	3544	1728	51.24%
32×32	32154	9125	71.62%

Table 3. Instruction cycles of IDCT functions.

IDCT Size	Average Origin Cycles	Average Accelerated Cycles	Saving Rate
4×4	130	74	43.08%
8×8	546	315	42.31%
16×16	3639	2201	39.52%
32×32	37046	15202	58.96%

Table 4. Compression performance loss by optimized DCT.

Sequence	BD Bit Rate	BD PSNR
BasketballDrive	0.238	-0.005
BQTerrace	0.030	-0.003
Cactus	0.063	-0.001
Kimonol	0.221	-0.003
ParkScene	0.126	-0.003

4 EXPERIMENTAL RESULTS

We use the DCT and IDCT modules of the HEVC C++ codes as the base for the acceleration and transplant them on Tilera multicore platform. The 9-bit signed random integers (range from -256 to 255) are the source input of DCT and 16-bit signed random integers (range from -32768 to 32767) for IDCT. We compare the output of the original function and the SIMD accelerated function to guarantee the correctness. In order to measure the acceleration performance, the function is executed for 200 times to get the average instruction cycles.

Table 2 gives the comparison of execution instruction cycles of DCT functions of four different sizes. The results indicate that the SIMD accelerated DCT functions can save 41.26%–71.62% cycles. Table 3 gives the comparison of execution instruction cycles of IDCT functions of four different sizes, which indicates that the accelerated IDCT functions can save 39.52%–58.96% cycles. The saving rate of IDCT is slightly less because of the transposition process. The saving rate in DCT and IDCT increases with larger size as more *v2dotp* instruction is applied, and instruction *v2dotp* can process more data than *v2muls*.

All the DCT and IDCT optimized functions are error-free compared with the original ones, except for the vertical one-dimensional DCT functions. In the design of the vertical one-dimensional DCT, the source input data are rounded into less bits to maintain parallel processing level, so there exists rounding error as shown in Table 1. We simulate the optimized DCT and IDCT modules in our HEVC code transplanted on Tilera platform to evaluate the compression performance loss. We use five 1920×1080 sequences and four QP (22, 27, 32 and 37) to test the PSNR performance [13]. The results are given in Table 4. The experiment results indicate that the BD PSNR [14] drop is no more than 0.005 and this compression performance loss is definitely negligible. In previous related work, intermediate variables are stored in 32-bit in DCT, so the parallel processing level of DCT is limited and IDCT has significant more speed-up [5]. In our DCT SIMD implementation, we can achieve similar parallel processing level to that of IDCT with negligible PSNR loss.

5 CONCLUSION

In this paper, we analyze the process of DCT and IDCT modules in HEVC and propose an SIMD acceleration method on full-fledged 64-bit Tilera multicore processor. In particular, rounding the source input data of vertical one-dimensional DCT into less bit width is employed, which can significantly improve parallel processing capabilities compared with lossless SIMD implementations. This provides a new approach to achieve higher parallel processing level for SIMD implementation of HEVC DCT and IDCT. According to the experiment results, the acceleration strategy can reduce 40%–70% execution instruction cycles with negligible compression performance loss.

ACKNOWLEDGMENT

This work was supported in part by National Natural Science Foundation of China (61221001, 61133009, 61301116), the 111 Project (B07022), the Shanghai Key Laboratory of Digital Media Processing and Transmissions (STCSM 12DZ2272600), National Key Technology R&D Program of China (2013BAH53F04).

REFERENCES

[1] G. J. Sullivan, et al., "Overview of the high efficiency video coding (HEVC) standard," Circuits and Systems for Video Technology, IEEE Transactions on, vol. 22, pp. 1649–1668, 2012.

[2] Il-Koo Kim, "High Efficiency Video Coding (HEVC) Test Model 10 (HM10) Encoder Description", JCTVC-L1002_v3, Geneva, CH, Jan. 2013

[3] T. Wiegand, et al., "Overview of the H. 264/AVC video coding standard," Circuits and Systems for Video Technology, IEEE Transactions on, vol. 13, pp. 560–576, 2003.

[4] M. Budagavi, et al., "Core Transform Design for the High Efficiency Video Coding (HEVC) Standard," 2013.

[5] H. Yong, et al., "Acceleration of HEVC transform and inverse transform on ARM NEON platform," in Intelligent Signal Processing and Communications Systems (ISPACS), 2013 International Symposium on, 2013, pp. 169–173.

[6] K. Chen, et al., "Efficient SIMD optimization of HEVC encoder over X86 processors," APSIPA ASC, pp. 1–4, 2012.

[7] C. C. Chi, et al., "Parallel HEVC Decoding on Multi-and Many-core Architectures," Journal of Signal Processing Systems, vol. 71, pp. 247–260, 2013.

[8] C. Yan, et al., "Highly parallel framework for hevc motion estimation on many-core platform," in Data Compression Conference (DCC), 2013, 2013, pp. 63–72.

[9] C. Yan, et al., "A Highly Parallel Framework for HEVC Coding Unit Partitioning Tree Decision on Many-core Processors," 2014.

[10] Intel Corp., Intel® 64 and IA-32 Architectures Software Developers Mannual.

[11] Tilera Corp., Tilera® TILE-Gx Instruction Set Architecture

[12] Tilera Corp., Tilera® Tile Processor Architecture Overview For The TILE-Gx Series

[13] F. Bossen, "Common test conditions and software reference configurations", JCTVC-F900, Torino, Italy, Jul. 2011

[14] Stephane Pateax, "An exel add-in for computing Bjontegaard metric and its evolution", VCEG-AE07, Marrakech, Ma, Jan. 2007

Multimedia Technology IV – Farag, Yang & Jiao (Eds)
© 2015 Taylor & Francis Group, London, ISBN: 978-1-138-02794-7

Early CU termination based on SKIP/Merge RD cost for B frames in HEVC

Jing Shen, Xiaoyun Zhang, Zhiyong Gao & Jia Wang
Institute of Image Communication & Information Processing, Shanghai Jiao Tong University, Shanghai, China

ABSTRACT: Compared to H.264/AVC, High Efficiency Video Coding (HEVC) aims to deliver the same video quality at half the bit rate. However, it imposes enormous computational complexity because of taking advantage of a more adaptive quad-tree structure, rate distortion optimization (RDO) and etc. In this paper, a fast decision method is proposed to reduce HEVC encoder complexity of B frames which avoids unnecessary mode decision and rate distortion optimization (RDO). It is found that there exist strong correlations between PU modes, depth distribution and SKIP/Merge RD cost. We statistically analyze the prediction mode distribution according to SKIP/Merge RD cost of current CU depth and depth distribution according to SKIP/Merge RD cost of 64 × 64 and 32 × 32 CUs. Based on the analysis results, the proposed algorithm includes an early detection of SKIP mode and a depth pruning to skip searching for 8 × 8 and 16 × 16 CUs. This algorithm enables us to skip unnecessary RDO by early termination of mode decisions in CUs. Experimental results show that the encoding complexity can be reduced by 50% on average with only 1.25% BD-rate increase compared to the HEVC test model (HM) 12.0 reference software.

Keywords: HEVC, Mode Decision, SKIP/Merge RD cost, RDO

1 INTRODUCTION

HEVC is the latest video coding standard developed by ITU-T Video Coding Experts Group and the ISO/IEC Moving Picture Experts Group. The main goal of the HEVC standardization effort is to enable significantly improved compression performance relative to existing standard – to reduce 50% bit rate on average for equal perceptual video quality [1]. To achieve this goal, several efficient coding algorithms were introduced to HEVC which also made HEVC encoders several times more complex than H.264/AVC encoders. In [2], the authors described several complexity-related aspects that were considered in the standardization process, including quad-tree-based block partitioning, motion estimation, RDO and so on.

HEVC adopts a more adaptive quad-tree structure based on a coding tree unit (CTU) instead of a macroblock in H.264/AVC. This allows HEVC to support coding unit (CU) size from 64 × 64 to 8 × 8. Kim *et al* [3] show that the benefits from the use of larger CU size become really significant when the test sequences are high-resolution video sequences. CU is a basic unit of region splitting used for intra/inter prediction, which allows recursive subdividing into four equally sized blocks. Additionally, in inter frames, each CU enables different prediction unit (PU) modes: SKIP mode, Merge mode, Inter 2N × 2N, Inter N × 2N, Inter 2N × N, Inter 2N × nU, Inter 2N × nD, Inter nL × 2N, Inter nR × 2N, Inter N × N (only available for the smallest CU), Intra 2N × 2N and Intra N × N

(only available for the smallest CU). To obtain the best CU block partitioning and coding modes, the HEVC encoder needs to test all the possible modes and select the one which provides the smallest RD cost by means of rate distortion optimization (RDO) process. This greatly increases computational complexity of the encoder. Tan *et al* [4] illustrates that using a fixed CU size of 16 × 16 involves 1584 times of RDO process, while using a CTU structure of 64 × 64 and a maximum quad-tree depth of 4 involves 8415 times of RDO process.

RD cost of coding modes is computed through the RDO process by a Lagrange cost function (J_{mode}) as follows:

$$J_{mode} = (SSE_{luma} + \omega_{chroma} \cdot SSE_{chroma}) + \lambda \cdot B_{mode} \tag{1}$$

where B_{mode} is the bitrate cost of corresponding coding mode, SSE is the sum of square error between original pixels and reconstructed pixels, ω_{chroma} is a weighting factor for chroma component and λ is the Lagrange multiplier. To obtain reconstructed pixels and bitrate, Motion Estimation (ME), Motion Compensation (MC), Transform, Quantization, Entropy Coding, Inverse Quantization, Inverse Transform are conducted at the HEVC encoder, which make RD cost computation really complex. However, RD cost computation of SKIP and Merge mode is simple because there is no residue information for SKIP mode and Merge mode doesn't need ME process. In addition, SKIP mode has a very high occurrence probability

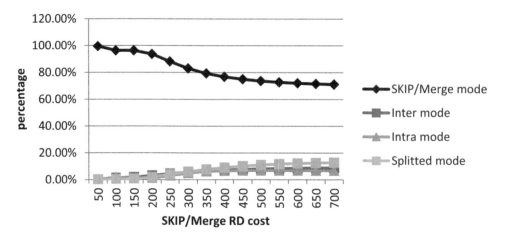

Figure 1.   Best mode distribution of 32 × 32 CUs in Kimono1 with SKIP/Merge RD cost.

in HEVC. So it is worthwhile to take advantage of SKIP/Merge RD cost to skip other complex RDO process. Our proposed algorithm is mainly based on this idea.

The rest of the paper is organized as follows. Section 2 briefly reviews some relevant fast algorithms. Section 3 introduces the proposed fast algorithm in details. Performance evaluations and analysis are presented in Section 4. At last, the conclusion is drawn in Section 5.

2   RELATED WORK AND BACKGROUND

Recently, a number of fast algorithms have been proposed to reduce the complexity of Inter picture prediction. And they mainly focus on early skip detection and depth decision. These two algorithms achieve good results by skipping unnecessary RDO and ME.

As SKIP mode is the dominant mode in HEVC, a fast algorithm of early SKIP detection is really desirable. The algorithm proposed in [5] checks the differential motion vector (DMV) and a coded block flag (CBF) after searching the best Inter 2N × 2N mode. In [6], the RD cost of Inter 2N × 2N and SKIP mode are compared to skip other AMVP modes in current CU. These two algorithms both check Inter 2N × 2N that introduces ME and complex RDO. Shen *et al* [6] proposed an algorithm to detect early SKIP mode by using prediction modes of spatially/temporally adjacent CUs and parent CU in the upper depth level of the current CU.

In addition, as mentioned in Section 1, quadtree blocking partition brings considerable complexity because of RDO processes. As a result, it is also necessary to decrease depth searching. Fan *et al* [8]–[9] illustrate the correlation of depth range between adjacent LCUs to determine the depth range of current LCU. By referring to depth situation of spatially and temporally adjacent CUs, the algorithm achieves a satisfying result. CU Depth Pruning algorithm proposed

in [4] prunes CU depth search by comparing the sum of the RD cost of 4 sub-CUs and the best current RD cost of their parent CU. However, in these algorithms, RD cost is not made full use of as RD cost is the only criterion in mode decision.

In this paper, we first analyze the relationship between RD cost of SKIP/Merge and PU modes to propose a novel early SKIP detection since RDO process of SKIP/Merge mode is relatively simple. Then we find that we can take advantage of RD cost of SKIP/Merge mode of 64 × 64 and 32 × 32 CU size to skip unnecessary RDO and ME for small size CUs. By fully exploiting these correlations, we propose two methods, novel early SKIP detection and CU depth pruning, based on SKIP/Merge RD cost to skip the unnecessary procedure of ME and RDO.

3   PROPOSED ALGORITHM

3.1   *Novel early skip detection*

We assume that other PU modes in current depth needn't to be checked and current CU needn't to be splitted if SKIP/Merge RD cost of current CU is small enough, because SKIP/Merge mode has a high probability to be the optimal mode for current CU in this case. To illustrate this assumption, we fully checked every 2N × 2N CUs by RDO process and classify the best mode into 4 types: SKIP/Merge mode, Inter mode, Intra mode and Splitted mode. SKIP/Merge mode includes SKIP mode and Merge 2N × 2N mode. Inter mode includes Inter 2N × 2N, Inter 2N × N, Inter N × 2N, Inter 2N × nU, Inter 2NxnD, Inter nLx2N, Inter nR × 2N, Inter N × N. Intra mode includes Intra 2N × 2N and Intra N × N while Splitted mode means that current CU should be splitted to achieve the smallest RD cost. Furthermore, in order to compare RD cost with CUs of different depth, the RD cost mentioned in this paper is normalized to 4 × 4 block. Figure 1 shows the relation between SKIP/Merge RD cost of 32 × 32

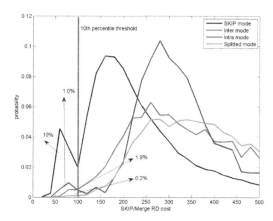

Figure 2. The probability density curve of all modes with SKIP/Merge RD cost.

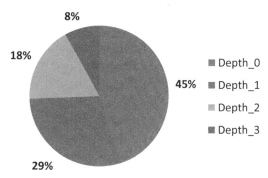

Figure 3.   Average percentage of all depths in sequences of Class B.

Table 1.   10th percentile threshold of different depths and different QPs in Kimono1.

QP Depth	22	27	32	37
0	40	50	70	138
1	51	66	98	146
2	54	70	101	157
3	54	74	115	201
average	49.75	65	96	160.5

CUs and percentage of 4 different modes which current CU finally adopts. This test was conducted on HM12.0 using the "Kimono1" test sequence with QP 32 in RA (randomaccess) profile. It can be easily seen that SKIP/Merge mode accounts for more than 95% of CU modes when SKIP/Merge RD cost is small enough. So we can terminate current CU search when SKIP/Merge RD cost is smaller than some threshold. In addition, when SKIP/Merge RD cost is bigger than 700, SKIP/Merge mode still accounts for more than 60%. It means SKIP/Merge mode is a dominant PU mode in this situation. Actually, this also happens when it comes to different video sequences and different QPs.

Based on statistical data, we set the threshold as 10th percentile of SKIP/Merge RD cost of SKIP/Merge mode in different CU depths. Here we adopt a very strict threshold to bring encoding performance loss as less as possible. Figure 2 shows the percentile of other modes that will be wrongly considered to be SKIP/Merge mode while we use this 10th threshold in 32x32 CU in Kimono1. For this threshold, only 1.0%, 1.9% and 0.2% of Inter mode, Intra mode and Splitted mode are mistaken for SKIP/Merge mode. To investigate the relationship between 10th percentile thresholds and different CU depths, we conduct the test on Kimono1 of all possible CU depths with QP 22, 27, 32, 37 and results are listed in Table 1. Here we define this threshold as *threshold_skip[i], i = 0, 1, 2, 3,*

for different CU depths. As there is no obvious relation among 10th percentile thresholds of different CU depths, *threshold_skip[i]* will share the same initial value.

3.2   CU depth pruning

Because of the more adaptive quad-tree structure of coding tree unit, great computation complexity has been introduced into the HEVC encoder. So it is also necessary to skip searching unnecessary CU depth and splitting. We find that low CU depths (Depth_0 and Depth_1) are much more likely to be selected than deep depths (Depth_2 and Depth_3) for high resolution video sequences. Depth_i, i = 0, 1, 2, 3, here means that current CU need to be splitted to depth i after full searching. For example, if a CU of depth 0 (64 × 64 CU) adopts Depth_2, it means the smallest CU size in this 64 × 64 CU is 16 × 16 of depth 2 after full searching. To obtain the percentages of different depths, tests are conducted on all 5 sequences of Class B with QP 22, 27, 32, 37 in RA profile. Average percentages of all 4 depths are listed in Figure 3. It shows that Depth_0 and Depth_1 account for about 74% while Depth_2 and Depth_3 only take 26%. So in some cases there is no need to check RD cost of Depth_2 and Depth_3.

According to this statistical result, we assume that Depth_0 or Depth_1 is the best depth for current LCU if their SKIP/Merge RD cost is small enough. According to this assumption, we can take advantage of SKIP/Merge RD cost of 64 × 64 and 32 × 32 CUs to skip searching Depth_2 and Depth_3. This strategy will prune unnecessary CU depth searching and reduce encode complexity to some extent. Figure 4 shows the probability density curve of depths with SKIP/Merge of 64 × 64 CUs in Kimono1 with QP 32. According to Figure 4, only 12%, 5.8% and 2.9% of Depth_1, Depth_2 and Depth_3 are mistaken for Depth_0 while adopting 50th percentile of SKIP/Merge RD cost of 64 × 64 CUs. In addition, 32%, 19% and 10% of Depth_1, Depth_2 and Depth_3 are mistaken for Depth_0 when adopting the 70th percentile of SKIP/Merge RD cost. So we use 50th percentile threshold to skip 16 × 16 and 8 × 8 CU

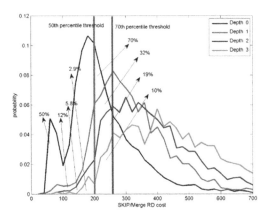

Figure 4. The probability density curve of depths with SKIP/Merge RD cost.

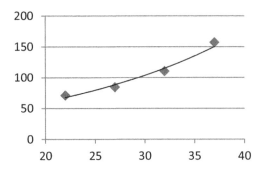

Figure 5. Exponential curving fitting of threshold_skip[i] with different.

searching and 70th to skip 8×8 CU searching. For 64×64 CUs, we define 50th percentile threshold and 70th percentile threshold as *threshold_depth_0_50* and *threshold_depth_0_70* to early skip unnecessary depth checking and early CU termination. Similar situation happens in 32×32 CUs. The 50th percentile threshold of SKIP/Merge RD cost of 32×32 CUs are defined as *threshold_depth_1_50*. Here we take advantage of *threshold_depth_1_50* to skip 8×8 CU searching for 32×32 CUs.

3.3 Adaptive threshold updating

Threshold setting has an important impact on the trade-off between coding quality and complexity reduction. The initialization of all the thresholds mentioned above is set according to tests of all 5 sequences in Class B. They are tested in RA profile when QP equals to 22, 27, 32 and 37 separately. The average values of *threshold_skip[i]* with different QPs are shown in Figure 5 and formula (2). Other thresholds are listed in formula (3), (4), (5).

$$threshold\_skip[i] = 21.179e^{0.053*QP} \quad (2)$$

$$threshold\_depth\_0\_50 = 7.0337e^{0.01124*QP} \quad (3)$$

$$threshold\_depth\_1\_50 = 8.6663e^{0.1084*QP} \quad (4)$$

$$threshold\_depth\_0\_70 = 5.2503e^{0.1323*QP} \quad (5)$$

In addition, thresholds are initialized for every frame according to the corresponding QP value and adaptively updated in formula (6) on corresponding conditions. For example, *threshold_skip[0]* will be updated if the best mode of the 64×64 CU is SKIP mode and *threshold_depth_0_50* will be updated if the best mode of the 64×64 CU is Splitted mode and the best depth is Depth_1. The value of λ is also a tradeoff of encoding efficiency.

$$threshold = \frac{\lambda*threshold+SKIP/Merge\ RDCost}{\lambda+1} \quad (6)$$

3.4 Flow of overall algorithm

Here we combine the two algorithms and propose our full algorithm. The flow is in Figure 6. All CUs in the same LCU share the same Depth[i], i = 0, 1, 2, 3, which are set False for every LCU.

4 EXPERIMENTAL RESULTS

4.1 Test condition

The experiments are implemented in HM 12.0 reference software [10] and simulation environment is set up as Table 2. The BD-rate (%) and BD-PSNR (dB) [11] are used to evaluate the performance of the proposed algorithm. The average time saving is used to measure the complexity reduction of the proposed algorithm, defined as *TS* by (7). And the value of λ in (6) is set to 7 according to our experimental tests.

$$TS = \frac{1}{4}\sum_{\substack{qp=22 \\ qp=+5}}^{37} \frac{EncTime(HM)-EncTime(Proposed)}{EncTime(HM)} \times 100\% \quad (7)$$

4.2 Experimental results

Table 3 shows the performance of proposed algorithm compared with HM12.0 for high resolution sequences of Class A, B and E. The algorithm can significantly reduce encoding time by 50% on average while less than 0.03dB video quality affection. But we also find that this proposed algorithm is more appropriate for videos with many regions of high stationarity and homogeneity, i.e. videos of Class E. PeopleOnStreet(A) achieves 33% time saving while increasing about 3% BD-BR. Because PeopleOnStreet(A) is full of details and has complex motion, which makes it tend to have more small CUs and less SKIP mode. But results of Class E are really attractive, which achieve about 58% time saving on average with bitrate only increasing about 0.4%. Videos of Class B have moderate motion and details. Our algorithm achieves a

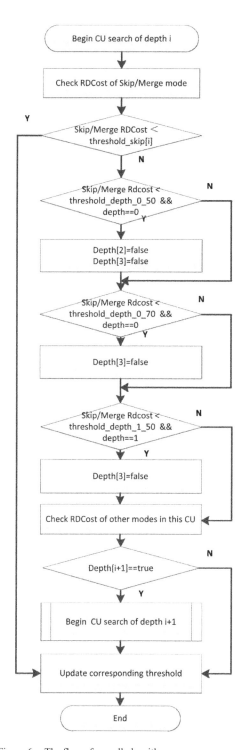

Figure 6.   The flow of overall algorithm.

Table 2.   Simulation environment.

Test Condition	Configuration
Hardware Platform	Intel (R) Core (TM) i7-2600 CPU @3.40 GHz RAM: 4.00 GB
Software Platform	Win 7 64-bit VS 2010 HM 12.0
Test Condition	Common Test Condition
Profile	Randomaccess & Lowdelay P main
Test Sequences	Class A, B, E for HM test sequences
QP	22, 27, 32, 37
Number of frames	100

Table 3.   Results of proposed algorithm for high resolution sequences with RA profile.

Sequence (class)	BD-BR (%)	BD-PSNR (dB)	TS (%)
PeopleOnStreet (A)	3.1978	−0.0922	32.91%
Traffic (A)	1.3580	−0.0327	50.87%
BasketballDrive (B)	2.2207	−0.0424	44.45%
BQTerrace (B)	0.4065	−0.0059	46.23%
Cactus (B)	1.9076	−0.0321	47.74%
Kimono1 (B)	1.6298	−0.0360	48.48%
ParkScene (B)	1.3102	−0.0307	47.08%
FourPeople (E)	0.4463	−0.0138	57.53%
Johnny (E)	0.4015	−0.0091	58.44%
KristenAndSara (E)	0.4903	−0.0128	58.34%
Vidyo1 (E)	0.3921	−0.0087	58.45%
Average	1.2510	−0.0288	50.05%

Table 4.   Results of proposed algorithm for Class B with lowdelay P profile.

Sequence (class)	BD-BR (%)	BD-PSNR (dB)	TS (%)
BasketballDrive (B)	3.8592	−0.0791	46.51%
BQTerrace (B)	2.0715	−0.0252	43.12%
Cactus (B)	2.8668	−0.0480	43.55%
Kimono1 (B)	2.4539	−0.0587	46.10%
ParkScene (B)	2.1715	−0.0471	41.12%
Average	2.6846	−0.0516	44.08%

satisfying result, about 45% time saving with bitrate increasing 1.5%.

Although tests and analysis above are conducted in RA profile, we also test our algorithm in HM12.0 with lowdelay P main profile and results are listed in Table 4. Compared with RA profile, results with lowdelay P profile are not so attractive but also bearable. This mainly results from the difference between B frame and P frame. For example, B frames tend to have more 64×64 and 32×32 CUs and have a higher hit rate of SKIP mode and skipping small CUs in our proposed algorithm because of bipredictive coding. In addition, initial thresholds are obtained from RA profile, which is also one reason of this result. Our future work should be focused on improving results of our algorithm in P frames.

5 CONCLUSION

In this paper, we fully investigate the relation between PU mode distribution, depth distribution and SKIP/Merge RD cost because computing process of SKIP/Merge RD cost is relatively simple. It is found that we can skip checking other PU modes and further split of current CU depth if SKIP/Merge RD cost is small enough. In addition, it is also doable to skip further split of 64×64 and 32x32 CU according to their SKIP/Merge RD cost. So, we base on SKIP/Merge RD cost to propose our algorithm including novel early SKIP detection and CU depth pruning, which can skip unnecessary mode decision and RDO process by early CU termination. Experimental results show that compared to HM12.0 in RA profile the proposed method can largely reduce computation complexity by 50% on average with marginal quality loss of video performance, less than 0.03dB BD-PSNR on average, for high resolution videos.

ACKNOWLEDGEMENTS

This work was supported in part by National Natural Science Foundation of China (61221001, 61133009, 61301116), the 111 Project (B07022), the Shanghai Key Laboratory of Digital Media Processing and Transmissions (STCSM 12DZ2272600), National Key Technology R&D Program of China (2013BAH53F04).

REFERENCES

[1] Sullivan, G. J., Ohm, J., Han, W. J., & Wiegand, T. (2012). Overview of the high efficiency video coding (HEVC) standard. *Circuits and Systems for Video Technology, IEEE Transactions on*, 22(12), 1649–1668.

[2] Bossen, F., Bross, B., Suhring, K., & Flynn, D. (2012). HEVC complexity and implementation analysis. *Circuits and Systems for Video Technology, IEEE Transactions on*, 22(12), 1685–1696.

[3] Kim, I. K., Min, J., Lee, T., Han, W. J., & Park, J. (2012). Block partitioning structure in the HEVC standard. *Circuits and Systems for Video Technology, IEEE Transactions on*, 22(12), 1697–1706.

[4] Tan, H. L., Liu, F., Tan, Y. H., & Yeo, C. (2012, March). On fast coding tree block and mode decision for high-efficiency video coding (HEVC). In *Acoustics, Speech and Signal Processing (ICASSP), 2012 IEEE International Conference on* (pp. 825–828). IEEE.

[5] Kim, J., Yang, J., Won, K., & Jeon, B. (2012, May). Early determination of mode decision for HEVC. In *Picture Coding Symposium (PCS), 2012* (pp. 449–452). IEEE.

[6] Yang, S., Lee, H., Shim, H. J., & Jeon, B. (2013, June). Fast inter mode decision process for HEVC encoder. In *IVMSP Workshop, 2013 IEEE 11th* (pp. 1–4). IEEE.

[7] Shen, L., Zhang, Z., & Liu, Z. (2014). Adaptive inter-mode decision for HEVC jointly utilizing inter-level and spatio-temporal correlations.

[8] Zhang, Y., Wang, H., & Li, Z. (2013, March). Fast coding unit depth decision algorithm for interframe coding in HEVC. In *Data Compression Conference (DCC), 2013* (pp. 53–62). IEEE.

[9] Fan, R., Zhang, Y., Li, Z., & Wang, N. (2014, January). An Improved Similarity-Based Fast Coding Unit Depth Decision Algorithm for Inter-frame Coding in HEVC. In *MultiMedia Modeling* (pp. 529–540). Springer International Publishing.

[10] https://hevc.hhi.fraunhofer.de/svn/svn_HEVCSoftware/tags/HM-12.0/

[11] G. Bjontegaard, "Calculation of Average PSNR Differences between RD-curves," Document VCEG-M33, Apr. 2001.

Multimedia Technology IV – Farag, Yang & Jiao (Eds)
© 2015 Taylor & Francis Group, London, ISBN: 978-1-138-02794-7

A multipurpose image watermarking algorithm based on DWT and Sudoku

Xilan Yan, Jingming Xie & Maohua Xiong
School of information Engineering, Guangzhou Panyu Polytechnic, Guangzhou, China

ABSTRACT: In this paper, a new multipurpose image watermarking algorithm is proposed based on DWT and 16×16 Sudoku. Original image is blocked with 8×8 and each block is transformed by DWT. By adopting HVS and changing low frequency coefficients, robust watermark can be embedded. For the process of image authentication, by adopting the concept of Sudoku, fragile watermark is embedded. Experimental results have shown that the proposed robust-fragile watermarking algorithm is indeed superb in terms of robustness and fragility and can achieve both the copyright protection and tamper detection of the original image.

Keywords: robust watermark; fragile watermark; DWT; Sudoku puzzle

1 INTRODUCTION

With the development of digital multimedia techniques and increased usage of Internet, digital watermarking[1]is gaining increasing popularity as a way to meet copyright protection and content authentication of multimedia data. Robust watermarking is generally used for copyright protection and ownership verification, while fragile watermarking is usually used for image integrity verification and tamper detection[2–3]. Conventional watermarking algorithms are mostly designed for either copyright protection or content authentication. However, in recent years, some multipurpose watermarking[4] algorithms have been proposed to achieve the goal of both copyright protection and content authentication.

In this paper, Original image is divided into 8×8 blocks and each block is transformed by DWT. A visual model is used to calculate JND threshold. Watermark can be embedded by changing the LL-coefficient of original image. Robust is guaranteed because watermark is embedded into low-frequency with JND model of DWT. In the fragile process, A reference matrix (M)(a 256×256 matrix) can be generated by using a Sudoku grid.

2 RELATED WORK

2.1 Just noticeable difference (JND) threshold in DWT domain

JND is related to characteristics of Human Visual System (HVS). It is defined as a measure referring to the capability of a human observer and adaptive to contents of visual signal under consideration. Original image of size M × N is decomposed by DWT[5].

The visibility threshold JND [6–7] of wavelet domain coefficient is derived by the formula:

$$JND_l^\theta(i,j) = S(l,\theta) \times L(l,i,j) \times T(l,i,j)^{0.034} \quad (1)$$

where $S(l,\theta)$ denotes the frequency sensitiveness in lth sub-band and θ direction, $L(l,i,j)$ denotes the luminance sensitiveness of (i,j) in lth sub-band and $T(l,i,j)$ denotes the texture sensitiveness of (i,j) in lth sub-band. Frequency sensitiveness can be calculated by the formula following:

$$S(l,\theta) = \begin{cases} \sqrt{2} & if \quad \theta = HH \\ 1 & otherwise \end{cases} * \begin{cases} 1.00 & if \quad l=0 \\ 0.32 & if \quad l=1 \\ 0.16 & if \quad l=2 \\ 0.10 & if \quad l=3 \end{cases} \quad (2)$$

Luminance sensitiveness can be calculated by:

$$L(l,i,j) = \frac{1}{256} I_3^3\left(l + \left\lfloor \frac{i}{2^{3-l}} \right\rfloor, l + \left\lfloor \frac{j}{2^{3-l}} \right\rfloor\right) \quad (3)$$

As for texture masking, the formula is:

$$T(l,i,j) = \sum_{k=0}^{3-l} \frac{1}{16^k} \sum_\theta \sum_{x=0}^{1} \sum_{y=0}^{1} \left[I_{k+l}^\theta\left(y + \frac{i}{2^k}, x + \frac{j}{2^k}\right) \right]^2$$
$$\times Var\left[I_3^3\left(l + y + \frac{i}{2^{3-l}}, l + x + \frac{j}{2^{3-l}}\right) \right] \quad (4)$$

2.2 Sudoku puzzle

Sudoku is a logic-based number placement puzzle whose objective is to fill a 9×9 grid using the digits from 1 to 9. By employing 9×9 Sudoku, Chang et

1	10	8	4	7	15	12	3	11	2	13	6	9	5	14	0	1	10	8	4
3	11	14	9	2	5	8	10	12	4	7	0	15	6	13	1	3	11	14	9
0	13	5	6	14	1	4	11	10	8	9	15	2	12	7	3	0	13	5	6
15	12	7	2	13	0	9	6	3	5	1	14	8	10	4	11	15	12	7	2
11	1	15	8	9	13	14	12	7	0	4	2	5	3	10	6	11	1	15	8
5	6	0	10	4	11	7	15	8	14	3	1	13	9	2	12	5	6	0	10
13	4	3	12	5	10	0	2	15	11	6	9	7	8	1	14	13	4	3	12
2	7	9	14	3	6	1	8	5	13	12	10	0	11	15	4	2	7	9	14
12	8	1	15	6	7	13	9	2	3	14	5	11	14	0	10	12	8	1	15
4	3	13	5	1	12	11	0	9	15	10	7	14	2	6	8	4	3	13	5
6	0	10	11	15	3	2	14	4	12	8	13	1	7	9	5	6	0	10	11
9	14	2	7	8	4	10	5	1	6	0	11	3	13	12	15	9	14	2	7
10	9	12	13	0	8	6	7	14	1	5	3	4	15	11	2	10	9	12	13
14	2	6	3	11	9	5	4	0	7	15	12	10	1	8	13	14	2	6	3
7	5	4	0	12	2	15	1	13	10	11	8	6	14	3	9	7	5	4	0
8	15	11	1	10	14	3	13	6	9	2	4	12	0	5	7	8	15	11	1
1	10	8	4	7	15	12	3	11	2	13	6	9	5	14	0	1	10	8	4
3	11	14	9	2	5	8	10	12	4	7	0	15	6	13	1	3	11	14	9
0	13	5	6	14	1	4	11	10	8	9	15	2	12	7	3	0	13	5	6
15	12	7	2	13	0	9	6	3	5	1	14	8	10	4	11	15	12	7	2

Figure 1. An example of reference matrix M.

al Proposed a data embedding method to design a low computation cost data embedding method[8]. In this paper, Sudoku's puzzle is to fill a 16×16 grid using the digits from 1 to 16, Every element in Sudoku puzzle is decreased by one. According to 16×16 Sudoku puzzle, The reference matrix is designed to be 256×256 size, as shown in Figure 1.

3 PROPOSED METHOD

3.1 Watermark embedding procedure

By altering LL coefficients of approximate sub-image blocks, robust watermark is embedded and by modifying the selected pixel pairs in cover image, fragile watermark is embedded. Watermark embedding is implemented through the following procedures.

Step 1: Generate robust watermark and fragile watermark

One binary image is used as original robust watermark W_1. It is transformed into W_1' by Arnold transform and scanned on-line and then transformed into one-dimensional sequence W_{m1}, $W_{m1} = \{w_j | w_j \in \{0, 1\}, j = 1, 2, \ldots, K\}$, Where K is the number of watermark sequence. Original fragile watermark W_2 is transformed into one-dimensional sequence and converted into n digits of 16-basenu-meralstream W_{m2}, $W_{m2} = \{d_1, d_2, \ldots d_n\}$, $d_i \in \{0, 1, \ldots, 15\}n$ is the total number of converted secret digits.

Step 2: Compute JND and Generate number sequence

Compute JND by using Eq.(1) and put a secure key X into a random number generator to produce random number sequence Q.

Step 3: Robust watermark embedding

Original image I of size $M \times N$ is divided into 8×8 blocks, Transform each block into DWT coefficient matrix block. Let $F(u, v)$ denotes LL sub-band coefficients of sub-blocks selected by number sequence Q. Coefficients $F(1, 2)$ and $F_k(4, 3)$ are selected to be embedded. Embedding is done as formula (5) and (6):

If $W_{m1} = 1$ and $\Delta > 0$

$$\begin{cases} F_k'(1,2) = F_k(1,2) + \Delta/2 + \Delta/4 \\ F_k'(4,3) = F_k(4,3) - \Delta/2 - \Delta/4 \end{cases} \quad (5)$$

Where $\Delta = JND_k - F_k(1,2) + F_k(4,3)$.

If $W_{m1} = 0$ and $\Delta > 0$

$$\begin{cases} F_k'(1,2) = F_k(1,2) - \Delta/2 - \Delta/4 \\ F_k'(4,3) = F_k(4,3) + \Delta/2 + \Delta/4 \end{cases} \quad (6)$$

where $\Delta = JND_k + F_k(1, 2) - F_k(4, 3) \cdot W_{m1}$ is Robust watermark signal. Through Inverse DWT, watermarked image I_1 can be obtained.

Step 4: Convert watermarked I_1 and Partition the pixels

Watermarked image I_1 should be scanned on-line and then transformed into one-dimensional sequence. The pixels in the watermarked I_1' are paired by a pairing technique and each pixel-pair (p_i, p_{i+1}) located onto the reference matrix M at the row p_i and the column p_{i+1}.

Step 5: Select the candidate elements

For the located element M (p_i, p_{i+1}) three sets of candidate elements CE_H, CE_V and CE_B are found by following rules:

If $p_{i+1} < 6$, then $CE_H = \{M(p_i, j) | 0 \le j < 16\}$;

Else $CE_H = \{M(p_i, j) | (p_{i+1} - 9) < j < (p_{i+1} + 8)\}$.

If $p_i < 6$, then $CE_V = \{M(j, p_{i+1}) | 0 \le j < 16\}$;

Else $CE_V = \{M(j, p_{i+1}) | (p_{i+1} - 9) < j < (p_{i+1} + 8)\}$.

If $p_i < 255$ and $p_{i+1} < 255$,

Else $CE_B = \langle EMPTY \rangle$.

Step 6: Fragile watermark embedding

Three candidates $M(x_H, y_H)$, $M(x_V, y_V)$ and $M(x_B, y_B)$ are selected respectively from CE_H, CE_V and CE_B such that $M(x_H, y_H) = M(x_V, y_V) = M(x_B, y_B) = d_i$, where d_i is 16-base numeral stream W_{m2}, $W_{m2} = \{d_1, d_2, \ldots, d_n\}$. The Watermarked I_1' pixel-pair (p_i, p_{i+1}) is modified as (p_i', p_{i+1}') to conceal fragile watermark W_{m2} with small distortion by minimum distortion candidate element $M(x_{min}, y_{min})$ which is selected by formula (7).

$$M(x_{min}, y_{min}) = \min_{j = H, V, B} \{ |p_i - x_j| + |p_{i+1} - y_j| \} \quad (7)$$

3.2 Watermark extraction procedure

(1) Extraction of robust watermark

Step 1: Extract Watermark

Watermarked image is divided into 8×8 sub-blocks, Each block is transformed by DWT to obtain decomposed sub-block $F'(u, v)$ Let $F'_k(u, v)$ denotes LL sub-band coefficients of sub-blocks selected by number sequence Q. Extract the one-dimensional sequence W'_{m1} as formula (8):

$$W'_{m1} = \begin{cases} 1 & if \quad F'_k(1,2) \geq F'_k(4,3) \\ 0 & if \quad F'_k(4,3) > F'_k(1,2) \end{cases} \tag{8}$$

Step 2: Obtain robust watermark

Transform W'_{m1} into two-dimensional watermark image, and robust watermark can be obtained after Arnold transform.

(2) Extraction of fragile watermark

Step 1: Convert watermarked image I_{12}

Watermarked image should be transformed into one-dimensional sequence. $I'_{12} = \{p'_1, p'_2, \ldots, p'_{H \times W}\}$. The pixels in the watermarked I'_{12} are partitioned by a pairing technique and each pixel-pair (p'_i, p'_{i+1}) located onto the reference matrix M at the row p'_i and the column p'_{i+1}.

Step 2: Point out the corresponding watermark digit

Each watermarked pixel-pair (p'_i, p'_{i+1}) is located onto the same reference matrix M at the position M

(p'_i, p'_{i+1}) to point out the corresponding watermark digit.

4 EXPERIMENTAL RESULTS

Experimental results are simulated by MATLAB. 512×512 of original Lena image are used as original image and two binary watermark images for the test. Original image and watermark images are shown in the Figure 2.

In this paper, Normative Correlation (NC) is employed to measure the similarity of extracted and original watermark[9−10]. Normative Correlation (NC) is given in equation (9):

$$NC(W, W') = \frac{\sum_{i=1}^{M} \sum_{j=1}^{N} W(i, j) W'(i, j)}{\sqrt{\sum_{i=1}^{M} \sum_{j=1}^{N} W^2(i, j)} \sqrt{\sum_{i=1}^{M} \sum_{j=1}^{N} W'^2(i, j)}} \tag{9}$$

where W is original watermark and W′ is extracted watermark with size M × N.

4.1 *Robustness of watermark*

Table 1 shows the Performance analysis results; From the Table 1 we can see that that the proposed method provides better results in painting, Gaussian noise, median filtering and cropping attack.

4.2 *Tamper location of fragile watermark*

Figure 3(a) and 3(c) performed modification attacks on watermarked images and Figure 3(b) and 3(d) performed watermark detection and tamper location on forged watermarked images. From the experimental results, the tampered location will be detected by proposed scheme.

5 CONCLUSIONS

In this paper, a new robust-fragile double image watermarking algorithm is presented. The proposed

(a)   **(b)**   **(c)**

Figure 2. (a) Original image, (b) Watermark W_1, (c) Watermark W_2.

Table 1. The performance results for the proposed method.

Attacks	JPEG (Q=40)	Painting	Median Filtering (3×3)	Gaussian Noise (0.3%)	Crop in the upper corner 1/4
Attacked Watermarked image					
Extracted Robust Watermark	多重	多重	多重	多重	多重
NC	0.935	0.902	0.871	0.887	0.883

| (a) | (b) | (c) | (d) |

Figure 3. (a) Cropping Watermarked, (b) Tamper location watermark, (c) Painting Watermarked, (d) Tamper location watermark.

multipurpose scheme not only can be used for copyright protection, but also be used in the fields of image content integrity verification. Watermark extraction procedure does not need to take into consideration extraction order of robust watermark and fragile watermark.

Simulation results demonstrate that this method can get a watermarked image with perceptual invisibility. High fragility of watermark and high robustness of watermark are obtained at the same time, which shows that the proposed watermarking method achieves the goal of multipurpose effectively.

ACKNOWLEDGMENT

This research was supported by The Key Research Project of Guangzhou Municipal Colleges and Universities "The Research and realization of 3D Game Engine based on Android" (No. 2012A164).

REFERENCES

[1] A. Salama, R. Atta, R.Rizk and F. Wanes. A Robust Digital Image Watermarking Technique Based on Wavelet Transform [C]. 2011 IEEE International Conference on System Engineering and Technology, Shah Alam, 27–28 June 2011, pp. 100–105.

[2] Nyeem H, Boles W, Boyd C. On the robustness and security of digital image watermarking [C]. Informatics, Electronics & Vision (ICIEV). Dhaka, 2012, pp. 1136–1141.

[3] H. J. He, C. Fan, Y. R. Huo. Self-Embedding Fragile Watermarking Scheme Combined Average with VQ Encoding. Digital Forensics and Watermarking Lecture Notes in Computer Science Volume 7809, 2013, pp. 120–134.

[4] Sushila Kamble,Vikas Maheshkar, DWT-based Multiple Watermarking for Privacy and Security of Digital Images in E-commerce. 2011 International Conference on Multimedia, Signal Processing and Communication Technologies, 2011, pp. 224–227.

[5] Sivavenkates R V, Shekhawat R S. A DWT-DCT-SVD based digital image watermarking scheme using particle swarm optimization[C], IEEE Advancing Technology for Humanity, 2012, pp. 1–4.

[6] S. Zhu, J. M. Liu, A Novel Adaptive Watermarking Scheme Based on Human Visual System and Particle Swarm Optimization Springer-Verlag, Berlin, 2009, pp. 136–146.

[7] Y. Zhang, Blind Watermark Algorithm Based on HVS and RBF Neural Network in DWT Domain WSEAS Transactions on Computers, Vol. 8, No. 1, 2009, pp. 174–183.

[8] C.C. Chang, Y.C. Chou, and T.D. Kieu. An Information Hiding Scheme Using Sudoku Proceedings of the Third International Conference on Innovative Computing, Information and Control, Dalian, China, 2008, pp. 171–175.

[9] Lee T.Y., Lin S.D. Dual Watermark for Image Tamper Detection and Recovery [J]. Pattern Recognition, 2008, 41(11), pp. 3497–3506.

[10] Run R S, Horng S J, Lai J L. An improved SVD-based watermarking technique for copyright protection[J]. Expert Systems with Applications, 2012, 39(1), pp. 673–689.

Author index

Printed and bound by CPI Group (UK) Ltd, Croydon, CR0 4YY

18/10/2024

01776219-0002